Spreadsheet Models for Urban and Regional Analysis

Spreadsheet Models for Urban and Regional Analysis

Edited by
RICHARD E. KLOSTERMAN,
RICHARD K. BRAIL, and
EARL G. BOSSARD

Published by the Center for Urban Policy Research
New Brunswick, New Jersey 08903

Printed in the United States of America

Library of Congress Cataloging-in-Publication Data

Spreadsheet models for urban and regional analysis / edited by
Richard E. Klosterman, Richard K. Brail, and Earl G. Bossard.
       p.   cm.
    Includes bibliographical references.
    ISBN 0-88285-142-X
    1. Regional planning—Mathematical models.   2. City planning—
Mathematical models.   3. Regional planning—Computer programs.
4. City planning—Computer programs.   5. Electronic spreadsheets.
I. Klosterman, Richard E.   II. Brail, Richard K.   III. Bossard, Earl G.
HT391.S658   1993
361.6'01'51—dc20   92-18834
                                               CIP

Contents

PART ONE
Spreadsheet Modeling

PART TWO
Demographic Analysis and Forecasting

PART THREE
Economic Analysis and Forecasting

PART FOUR
Environmental Analysis and Modeling

PART FIVE
Management and Decision Making

Part Six
Other Applications

Tables

Exhibits

Figures

Acknowledgments

The editors would first and foremost like to acknowledge the continued patience, support, and understanding of their wives and families during the three years it took to complete this "quick and easy" project. They also acknowledge the dedicated assistance of Melissa Lee and Becky Evans, who did an outstanding job of preparing several versions of the text. The book could not have been completed without their help.

Introduction

Electronic spreadsheets—software programs that store data in two-dimensional tables that instantly display the results of calculations performed with these data—are second only to word processors as the most widely used microcomputer software tool and have been called, with some justification, "God's gift to planners."[1] Electronic spreadsheets are, most importantly, user friendly: easy to learn, forgiving of errors, and immediately useful with only a minimal knowledge of computer fundamentals. Their simple format and logical structure provide a comfortable environment for examining quantitative problems that can be formulated as two-dimensional tables. In addition, their ability to instantly report the results of changing values stored in the spreadsheet allows analysts to quickly and easily conduct "what-if" analyses, examining the implications of alternative policy choices and different assumptions about the state of nature.

Modern spreadsheet programs also provide an extensive array of built-in functions for displaying, printing, and graphing the information stored in the spreadsheet, for conducting a wide variety of computational procedures, and for performing simple data base management functions. In addition, they provide a range of sophisticated "macro" commands that can be used to automate repetitive tasks and to develop spreadsheet "templates" or "models" that can provide easy-to-use tools for conducting a wide range of analytic procedures.

This book, *Spreadsheet Models for Urban and Regional Analysis,* and the accompanying disk use the capabilities of electronic spreadsheet programs to provide nineteen spreadsheet models that can be used for a wide range of urban and regional analysis and planning applications. The models have been developed for Lotus 1-2-3® for the IBM personal computer and compatible systems and can be adapted for use with other spreadsheet programs. The models incorporate a common set of procedures for entering data, conducting analyses, and displaying results. This makes it easy for users to become familiar with and use the different models provided in the collection. The models also provide extensive internal documentation allowing users to understand how the models operate and modify them to suit their needs, if desired.

The first chapter identifies the hardware and software required to use the models, describes the typographical conventions used in this book, provides detailed instructions for installing and using the models, and indicates how users can obtain assistance in using the models. The second chapter provides general guidelines for developing spreadsheet models that are understandable and easy to use. The third chapter uses examples drawn from the models in the collection to illustrate the use of advanced spreadsheet "macro" commands to produce sophisticated and easy-to-use analysis models in a spreadsheet environment.

The remaining chapters describe the nineteen spreadsheet models provided in the collection. Each chapter describes: (1) the model's intended application and conceptual basis; (2) the different components of the model, with a map showing the location of the components; (3) the specialized commands and options that are provided for using the model; (4) sources and procedures for entering required data; (5) guidelines for interpreting and using model outputs; (6) a sample model application that includes a complete set of input and output data; (7) an evaluation of the model and suggestions for possible extensions; and (8) references for further information.

NOTE

1. The quotation is from Professor Joseph Fereirra, Jr., of the Department of Urban Studies and Planning, Massachusetts Institute of Technology.

PART ONE

Spreadsheet Modeling

Chapter 1

Installing and Using the Models

Richard E. Klosterman

This chapter provides the information needed to install and use the spreadsheet models described in chapters 4 through 22. The discussion assumes that the reader is familiar with IBM-compatible personal computers and with electronic spreadsheets, such as Lotus 1-2-3°. Users who are not familiar with either of these are advised to consult introductory discussions, such as Brail (1987), Norton (1989), or Que Corporation (1989).

This chapter: (1) specifies the hardware and software required to use the models; (2) identifies the typographical conventions used in the remainder of this book; (3) outlines the required procedures for installing the models; (4) provides general guidance on using the models, including a description of the standard macros included in all of the models; and (5) indicates how users can obtain further assistance in using the models. Any additional guidance that becomes available after the printing of this book will be provided in the READ.ME file included on the disk with the spreadsheet models. The READ.ME file can be displayed on the screen by entering **TYPE READ.ME** at the DOS (disk operating system) prompt or copied to a printer by typing **COPY READ.ME PRN** at the DOS prompt.

BEFORE USING THE MODELS

System Requirements
The spreadsheet models that accompany this text require:

1. An IBM-compatible computer with at least 640 kilobytes (KB) of random access memory (RAM);
2. A hard disk with at least 3 megabytes (MB) of free disk space to install all nineteen of the models; the models can also be installed individually and are between 35 and 250 KB in size; and
3. Lotus 1-2-3° version 2.01 or above or a 100 percent compatible spreadsheet program.[1]

Conventions Used in This Book

A number of special typographical conventions are used in this book to identify particular keys on the standard IBM-compatible keyboard, information entered by the user, and messages displayed by the program. These conventions are described and illustrated below:

1. Information that the user should enter directly into the computer (e.g., the year **1992**) is printed in **bold**;
2. The first letters of commands that the user should enter into the keyboard (e.g., /**F**ile **S**ave **R**eplace) are printed in **bold**;
3. "Alt-key" macro commands (e.g., **Alt-M**) that require the user to press simultaneously the ALT key and a letter key are printed in **bold**;
4. Special keys on the standard IBM-compatible keyboard, such as the ENTER, ESC, and PGDN keys, are identified with SMALL CAPITAL LETTERS;
5. Function keys, such as the F9 (Calc) key, that are assigned particular functions by the Lotus 1-2-3° program are identified both by name and by their corresponding function;
6. Cell references (e.g., cells A1 to A20), macro commands (e.g., MENUBRANCH), range names (e.g., MAIN_MENU), spreadsheet modes and messages (e.g., READY and GRAPH), and file names (e.g., EXTRAP.WK1) are all printed in UPPERCASE LETTERS; and
7. Keystrokes within a macro command are printed in lowercase letters; for example, the /rncTEST macro command sequence is equivalent to the user typing /**R**ange **N**ame **C**reate **TEST** into the computer.

Installing the Programs

The spreadsheet models that accompany this text are distributed on a single three-and-a-half-inch 1.44 MB diskette. Copies of the programs on other disk formats are available from the senior editor at the address provided in the list of contributors. The models are stored in a compressed format and, with only a very few exceptions, are too large to be used on a floppy disk. As a result, they must be expanded and copied to a computer's hard disk before being used.

The following discussion assumes that the models are being installed from drive B to a subdirectory named "SMURA" on hard disk drive C. The instructions can easily be modified to install the models from drive A or to a different drive and/or directory by making the appropriate substitutions. For example, to install the programs from drive A, replace all of the references to drive B in the following discussion by drive A.

Three options are available for installing the models: (1) creating a new subdirectory for storing them; (2) installing all of the models on a hard disk; and (3) installing individual models on a hard disk. These options are described below.

Creating a New Subdirectory. It is advisable to create a new directory for storing the spreadsheet models in this collection to minimize the possibility of accidentally deleting or writing over them or other spreadsheet, program, or data files.

To create a new directory named "SMURA" on drive C:

1. Type C:\ and press ENTER to switch to the DOS system prompt on drive C (indicated by "C>" or "C:\>");
2. Type **MD \SMURA** and press the ENTER key to create the new directory.
3. Type **CD \SMURA** and press ENTER to switch to the new directory, ensuring that it has been created correctly; if an error message is encountered, repeat steps 1 and 2.

Installing All Models. The spreadsheet models have been compressed with LHA, version 2.11, a copyrighted file compression utility that can be freely distributed.[2] Further information on the program can be obtained by inserting the disk containing the programs into drive B and typing **B:LHA211** at the DOS prompt. This creates a working version of the LHA program along with complete program documentation.

Each of the spreadsheet models has been compressed with any auxiliary data files in a single file with the model's name and a ".EXE" file name extension. For example, the RETAIL.EXE file contains a compressed version of the RETAIL spreadsheet model. Auxiliary data files that are provided with some of the models, such as the INTRO-IO model, are compressed with the spreadsheet model in the model's ".EXE" file.

The following steps can be used to install all of the models and associated files in the newly created "SMURA" directory on drive C:

1. Insert the disk containing the compressed spreadsheet models into drive B;
2. Type **B:** at the DOS prompt and press ENTER to switch to drive B; and
3. Type **INSTALL C:\SMURA** and press ENTER to extract all of the compressed files from the diskette and copy them to the SMURA directory on drive C.[3]

Installing Individual Models. The complete set of spreadsheet models occupies nearly 3 megabytes of hard disk space. Users who wish to only use some of the models may not want to copy all of them to their hard disk. Instead, they may wish to use the following procedure to copy an individual file or set of files to the SMURA directory on drive C:

1. Insert the disk containing the compressed spreadsheet models in drive B;
2. Type **B:** at the DOS prompt and press ENTER to switch to drive B;
3. Type *model* **C:\SMURA** and press ENTER to extract the spreadsheet named *model* from the disk and copy it to the SMURA directory on drive C; for example, type **RETAIL C:\SMURA** and press ENTER to install the RETAIL model in the SMURA directory; and
4. Repeat step 3 to install any other desired models.

USING THE MODELS

The models in this collection are Lotus 1-2-3° spreadsheets that can be loaded and run like any other Lotus spreadsheet. If the models have been copied into a separate directory using the procedures outlined above, they can be accessed by starting Lotus, entering /File Directory **C:\SMURA**, and pressing ENTER to change the Lotus default directory to the SMURA directory on drive C. The user can then enter /File **R**etrieve, select the desired model from the list displayed on the screen, and press ENTER to load the model.

After loading the model, the user is shown a welcome screen similar to the one shown in Exhibit 1.1. The welcome screen provides the following information:

1. Identifies the model, in this case, the TRANSIT model;
2. Identifies the model's developer(s) and institutional affiliation(s);
3. Briefly describes the model's function and use;
4. Displays the model's copyright notice;
5. Indicates that the model is part of the collection that accompanies this book; and

Exhibit 1.1

Sample Welcome Screen

TRANSIT.WK1
===

Richard K. Brail
Department of Urban Planning and Policy Development
Rutgers University
New Brunswick, New Jersey 08903-5078

This model estimates capital and operating costs for a fixed guideway
system. The model was designed to estimate costs for an automated
guideway system but can be adapted to other fixed guideway
installations.

(C) 1992   Richard K. Brail
===
Richard E. Klosterman, Richard K. Brail, and Earl G. Bossard, eds.
SPREADSHEET MODELS FOR URBAN AND REGIONAL ANALYSIS
(New Brunswick, NJ: Center for Urban Policy Research, 1992)

PRESS ANY KEY TO CONTINUE

---

6. Highlights the prompt message at the bottom of the screen indicating that the user should press any key to continue.

Using the Spreadsheet Macros

After pressing any key, the user is shown a menu listing the "Alt" macros that are provided for use with the model. These macros are activated by pressing the ALT key and the designated letter key simultaneously. For example, the user can simultaneously press the ALT and **D** (uppercase or lowercase) to activate the **Alt-D** macro.[4]

The complete set of macros that are available for use with each model is listed in the chapter describing the model. Any specialized macros that are provided for a particular model (for instance, customized printing or graphing macros) are also described in detail in the model chapter.

All of the models include the seven standard macros identified in Table 1.1. These macros operate in the same way in all of the models, providing a uniform procedure for conducting basic functions that are required to use all of the models. The procedure for using each of these macros is described below:

Table 1.1

Standard Macros

Alt-D	Go to Documentation
Alt-L	Go to Location map
Alt-M	Go to Main menu
Alt-Q	Quit/save model
Alt-R	Go to Range descriptions
Alt-W	Go to Welcome screen
Alt-Z	Go to macros

Alt-D, Go to Documentation. This macro takes the user to the model's internal documentation that briefly describes the model and the procedures for using it.

Alt-L, Go to Location Map. This macro takes the user to the model's location map, which provides a "map" showing the location of the different sections of the model.

Alt-M, Go to Main Menu. This macro returns the user to the main menu listing the available "Alt" macros. This menu is also displayed after the user views the welcome screen.

Alt-Q, Quit/Save Model. This macro produces a Lotus-style command menu providing the following suboptions for exiting and/or saving the model:

1. Backup, save the model with the current name—*replacing the currently saved work sheet with this name*—and continue using the model;
2. New_name, save the model with a new name and continue using it;
3. Exit, save the model with the current name and exit the spreadsheet program;
4. Quit, exit the spreadsheet program without saving the current model;
5. Another, load another model without saving the current model; the new model is selected by moving the cursor to the desired choice and pressing the ENTER key; and
6. Main_menu, return to the main menu listing the available "Alt" macros.

Alt-R, Go to Range Descriptions. This macro takes the user to a list that identifies:

1. The names for all of the ranges used in the model;
2. The cell or cells to which each range corresponds; and
3. The contents of the range.

Alt-W, Go to Welcome Screen. This macro takes the user to the welcome screen displayed when the model is loaded. The user must press any key to continue to use the model, just as must be done when the model is loaded.

Alt-Z, Go to Macros. This macro takes the user to the section of the model containing the model's macros. The list includes the names of the macros, the macro commands, and a brief description of each command.

GETTING FURTHER ASSISTANCE

The spreadsheet models in this collection have been carefully developed and thoroughly tested to ensure that they work as easily, efficiently, and accurately as possible. The discussion in the text is similarly designed to provide as complete and accurate a description of the models as is possible within the available space. Nevertheless, it is inevitable that some users will have questions or experience difficulties in adapting these models to particular applications or in modifying them to suit their own needs.

A list of mailing addresses, telephone and fax numbers, and electronic mail addresses of the editors and the model developers is provided in the list of contributors. Any questions on installing the models or on the general procedures for using the models should be addressed to the editors. Questions concerning the use of particular models should be addressed to model developer(s) at the address or phone number provided in the list of contributors.

NOTES

1. Versions of the models for other spreadsheet programs may also be available. Contact the publisher for further information.

2. LHA, version 2.11, Copyright © Haruyasu Yoshizaki, 1989-91.

3. This procedure uses a simple batch file and the self-extracting feature of the LHA program to extract all of the files stored in each .EXE file and copy them to the directory specified after the INSTALL command.

4. More complete information on spreadsheet macros is provided in chapter 3.

REFERENCES

Brail, R. K. 1987. *Microcomputers in urban planning and management.* New Brunswick, NJ: Center for Urban Policy Research, Rutgers University.

Norton, P. 1989. *Peter Norton's DOS guide.* New York: Brady.

Que Corporation. 1989. *Using 1-2-3 Release 2.2, special edition.* Indianapolis: Que Corporation.

Chapter 2

Spreadsheet Design Guidelines

Earl G. Bossard

Impressive improvements in spreadsheet capabilities have led to the development of increasingly larger and more complex spreadsheet models. These models typically have been constructed in a "quick and dirty" mode by their self-taught user/developers who often pass their models along to others. These hand-me-down models, while usually understandable to their originators, are often confusing and misleading to other users, leading to unrecognized computational errors and inappropriate analysis conclusions (Ditlea 1987). These problems can be avoided only by carefully designing and creating work sheets so that they can be effectively used by others (Duffy 1987; Nevison 1989; Nguyen and Little 1987; Sawicki 1985).

This chapter presents a series of principles for effectively designing and organizing spreadsheet models and demonstrates how they can be utilized. These guidelines allow model developers to produce spreadsheet models that can easily and effectively be used by analysts who may be unfamiliar with electronic spreadsheet software.

EFFECTIVE SPREADSHEET MODELS

Types of Spreadsheet Model Applications

Spreadsheet models or templates are electronic work sheets designed to be used repetitively over time with different data and perhaps by different users for different purposes. Model developers can use spreadsheet templates to simplify repetitive computational tasks. Clerks can use spreadsheet models routinely to enter new information and update previous analyses without understanding the computational procedures built into the model. Instructors can use spreadsheet models to help teach computational procedures and analytic techniques that can readily be expressed in spreadsheet form. Perhaps most importantly, they can be used to provide a general analytic model that professionals can readily customize to meet their own analytic needs.

The guidelines presented in this chapter can be used to develop models that can by used as "black boxes" without understanding the model's internal workings. However, the principles are also helpful for developing models whose internal workings can be more readily understood and modified by users.

Hierarchy of Design Concepts
The spreadsheet design process should begin with a plan and a set of model development goals based on a definition of the problem to be addressed, the expected analytic results, and application of the model results (Alberte-Hallam et al. 1985; Schatt 1989). The design process should consider two levels of design concepts: (1) general principles for developing well-designed spreadsheet models and (2) specific design guidelines for the various sections of the model being designed.

GENERAL DESIGN GUIDELINES

General Principles
Electronic spreadsheet models, like all well-designed computer systems, should be: (1) easy to understand; (2) easy to learn; (3) easy to use; and (4) productive (Nguyen and Little 1987). These general principles suggest the following model design guidelines (Nguyen and Little 1987):

Prepare the User. The model developer must prepare the user to use the template by providing printed documentation identifying the intended model application, the required input data, the actions required from the user, and the expected model output. The internal documentation guidelines described later help satisfy this requirement.

Guide the User. Guidelines for running the model should be readily accessible, and first-time users should be shown the steps to be followed.

Present Informative Screen Displays. Screen displays should be understandable and provide clues regarding the next required action.

Provide Consistent Operations. All actions required to use the model should be consistent, with procedures that are predictable and easy to follow.

Use Understandable Commands. Model commands and menu choices should be expressed in the language of the intended users and should not require them to know the spreadsheet program's command language.

Anticipate Users' Needs. The system should anticipate the users' needs and guide them accordingly.

Provide Immediate and Positive Feedback. Model use should be organized into a series of stages that yield intermediate results that can be observed and confirmed by the operator. Timely support for these actions will increase the users' confidence as they complete each stage.

Minimize Required Actions. Menus should be organized so that frequently used operations are easier to reach than infrequently used ones.

Provide Speedy Execution. The program must seem to be fast for the user to perceive it to be productive.

These guidelines reflect a general belief that a well designed spreadsheet must be based on the requirements of the user. Operations should be logical, consistent, and organized in a way that foresees the users' needs and reinforces their actions, ideally in a speedy and efficient way.

SPECIFIC DESIGN GUIDELINES

One of the most important guidelines for developing understandable spreadsheet models is to organize the work sheet by functional area (Duffy 1987; Miller 1989; Nevison 1989). Clustering functional components in distinct locations allows the model user—and developer—to more easily understand the functional components of the model and the ways in which these components are related. Good model organization is especially helpful when one attempts to reuse old work sheets whose details may have been forgotten.

The following functional areas are a basis for organizing the specific design guidelines presented in the remainder of this chapter: (1) model introduction and welcome, (2) documentation, (3) data entry, (4) data processing, (5) output, and (6) macros and menu control.

Model Introduction Guidelines

A formal introduction section should be provided that identifies the model and its developer, describes the model's purpose, gives general directions for using the model, and provides references to background information. The introductory title section should be prominently located near the A1 "home" location or displayed by a macro, which automatically executes when the template is loaded (Duffy 1987).

The introductory section should identify: (1) the name of the model; (2) the name of the file, its latest revision date, and date printed; (3) the name of the author and person responsible for file maintenance; and (4) the phone number and/or address of a contact for further assistance (Grauer and Sugrue 1989; Weisskopf 1988). A brief description of the model's purpose should be provided so that potential users can quickly determine whether the model is able to meet their needs. General directions for using the model, such as brief guidelines for accessing the menus and activating the macros, should be provided in the introductory section. Detailed instructions on operating the model should be placed in the documentation section described below.

References for background information and a table of contents describing the model organization should be provided in the introductory section, generally as a schematic location map of functional areas (Brail 1987; Nevison 1989). It may also be desirable to include a directory list of range names and cell locations in the introductory documentation section; however, these documentation details frequently belong in the less prominent area where macro codes are located.

Sample Model Introduction. The EXTRAP model described in chapter 4 provides an example of the spreadsheet guideline applications described in this chapter. The EXTRAP model, like all of the models in this book, has an "Alt-0" autoexecuting macro that calls up a welcome screen with background documentation and instructions.[1] The welcome screen identifies the model developer and the use of the model. Instructions for proceeding from the welcome screen to the main menu are provided at the bottom of the screen.

A location map is helpful for all but the smallest of work sheets. See, for example, the location map for the EXTRAP model shown in Exhibit 4.1. Note that the Introductory Documentation screens are clustered around the welcome screen at the A1 or "home" location. The main menu and location map are located immediately below and alongside the welcome screen. The documentation is below the welcome screen.

The data entry section is at the edge of the data computation area, which contains six computation areas. The output area includes three tables. Note that having the output evaluation table above, rather than alongside, the other tables is a violation of the guidelines outlined in this chapter. The sensitive macro programming code area is placed out of the way in the far upper right-hand corner of the model.

Documentation Guidelines

The more complete and better organized the internal documentation is, the better the chance that the template can be successfully used by others (Bianchine 1989). Documentation should ideally be provided in an accompanying text, in a separate documentation section, and throughout the model. Documentation should also be prepared as an ongoing task, not as one of the last things to be done when completing the model.

The following general guidelines can be identified for preparing the internal documentation.

Frame Data Columns with Distinguishing Symbols. Users can more easily understand the roles of various components of the template if distinctive markings are used as row or column borders for areas with particular functions. For example, the row above and below input data areas can be filled with "!!!!!" symbols; output data areas can be framed by "======" symbols; model parameters by "+++++", consistency checks by "?????"; and directions or descriptions by "~ ~ ~ ~ ~" symbols.

Place Operating Instructions within the Template. Directions on using the model should be included within the model rather than on external pages that may become separated from the template. The directions should outline the data requirements of the model and the exact steps to be followed with a typical application (Schatt 1989).

Place Explanatory Text within the Template. Identify and label all assumptions used in the model, explicitly spelling them out in a distinctive area (Nevison 1989).

Document Formulas. Explain formulas, usually in plain English in adjoining cells, and provide access to textual descriptions of all formulas. A formula can be documented by using the F2 (edit key) to temporarily put a quotation mark in front of the formula in order to turn it into a label. The label can then be copied to an adjoining cell where the formula's components will be displayed on the screen (Weisskopf 1989). The original formula cell can then be restored to operating order by removing the quotation mark.

Sample Documentation Section. For example, five pages of internal documentation for the EXTRAP model are located directly below the welcome screen. Individual pages can be reached directly from the Lotus-style Documentation menu, which is activated by the **Alt-D** macro. The Documentation menu displays a full line describing the contents of the page being considered in the menu prompt area.

Data Entry Guidelines

The data entry guidelines presented below are designed to promote efficient data entry and reduce the quantity of incorrect data that are entered into the model.

Provide a Distinct Data Entry Area. With one distinct data entry area, the user knows exactly where to go to enter the data, check previously entered data, and/or revise these data (Nevison 1989; Schatt 1989).

Make the Data Input Area Resemble Existing Forms. If the template is being developed to replace existing paper forms, the transition to a computer-based system can be eased if the data entry area resembles familiar forms (Duffy 1987; Schatt 1989).

Enter Data Only into Columns or Rows. Data should be entered either into rows or columns but not both. This admonition applies to simple models for which the user must only press the down or right arrow to reach the next data entry cell (Duffy 1987; Schatt 1989).

Use Cell Protection. The spreadsheet's cell protection feature should be used to control access to areas where data should not be entered. (Duffy 1987; Miller 1989; Schatt 1989). It is generally advisable to protect all cells with labels, formulas, or output that the user is not expected to need to change. The data input area and areas reserved for the users' comments, notes, and personal documentation can then be unprotected to allow data and text entry.

Use Manual Recalculation. The spreadsheet's manual calculation feature should be used when entering data in large models so that the user must not wait for the model to recalculate after entering each data item. However, instructions must then be included for the user to press the F9 (Calc) key after the data entry is completed unless a macro is provided that automatically recalculates the work sheet after data entry is completed.

Incorporate Internal Checks on Input Data. A variety of means can be used to provide checks on the data entered by the user (Miller 1989; Nguyen and Little 1987; Weisskopf 1988). Program code can be provided that tests cell entries for upper and lower limits.[2] The column widths for data entry cells can also be formatted not to allow more digits than expected. The line graph of the input data range can be used to quickly identify inconsistent input data. Macros can also use string functions to ensure that the input data have the expected number of places and to display a table of standard data entry codes to promote uniformity of data base entries.

Sample Data Entry Section. For example, data entry in the EXTRAP model is handled entirely under the direction of macros activated from the **Alt-I** Input menu. The HEADING DOC macro queries the user to input five items of headings documentation information that are displayed in the output and computation tables and graph titles. Data are then entered into the first of six computation areas. The user is asked to type in the first and last observation years, the interval between observations, and the last year for which a projection is desired. These data are automatically transformed into a listing of all observed and desired projection periods. The computed year ranges are presented in the Data Entry table under a heading "Are values below as expected ???" so users can confirm that the year ranges have been properly entered.

Data Processing Section Guidelines

Unrecognized errors in work sheets may lead to inaccurate computational results (Berry 1989; Ditlea 1987; Sawicki 1985). The guidelines presented below suggest ways to organize a model's data processing section in order to reduce the number of errors. However, there can be no substitute for careful model construction and thorough model documentation (Ditlea 1987).

Set Aside a Separate Data Processing Section. The model's data processing commands should be isolated from the data entry and output sections to reduce the potential for accidently modifying or deleting the computational formulas (Nevison 1989).

Use Intermediate Computational Cells. Instead of using massive cell references to carry out large computations in a single cell, subcomponents of the calculation should be calculated independently in separate cells so that they can be easily inspected for the consistency and reasonableness of the intermediate data values.

Use Range Names. Range names should be used for important cells so that it is easier to understand formulas that refer to these cells. Range names also eliminate the need to modify computational equations if rows or columns are added to or deleted from the work sheet.[3]

Test Work Sheets Carefully. Testing should be an ongoing part of the model building process. All formulas should be hand-checked with simple data as they are developed. The calculation procedures should then be checked with actual data. Extreme data values can be used in the completed model to test its robustness under conditions that might cause the program to crash (Miller 1989; Nguyen and Little 1987; Sawicki 1985). Most large work sheets contain errors, often errors with serious consequences, that could be eliminated with more thorough testing (Ditlea 1987).

Incorporate Internal Error Checks. Triangulation techniques, redundancy, and cross-checks can all be used to verify critical work. These internal checks may be as simple as confirming that the sums of the rows equal the sums of the columns for a rectangular matrix of data or as complex as using duplicate equations to calculate desired results. @IF commands testing whether a predefined test condition is true or false can be used to print warning messages if internal checks are not satisfied (Grauer and Sugrue 1989; Miller 1989; Nevison 1989; Sawicki 1985).

Save Model Template Under a Different Name. New users often benefit by having a copy of a successful previous run or a copy of an empty model with data entry areas cleared and ready for new data. These can be provided by having the user save revised models under a different file name so the original file is preserved intact. This can be accomplished by: (1) providing an autoexecuting macro that prompts for a new file name whenever the template is loaded; (2) supplying menu commands that facilitate saving the model under a new name, including an on-screen prompt during the process of quitting the spreadsheet; or (3) including an appropriate suggestion in the documentation (Duffy 1987).

Output Section Guidelines

Well-organized output tables and graphs are essential for turning analysis results into useful information. The following guidelines can be used to achieve that end.

Set Aside a Separate Area for Output. Separate output areas can facilitate printing and give "black box" model users a place to direct their attention (Duffy 1987).

Do Not Stack Output Reports Above Each Other. Output reports should have no other sections above or below them in order to eliminate problems in setting the ideal column widths for each report. One way to do this is to locate all of the work sheet sections in a diamondback diagonal pattern in which each section is below and to the right of the one on its left.

Provide a Variety of Output Formats. Paying attention to details, such as clearly labeling rows and columns of output reports, helps to make them more functional and attractive. The analysis date and time can also be included in output reports by using the @NOW function. Graphic output should be prepared carefully with graphs laid out in a familiar and appealing style (Nevison 1989). Major conclusions should be included in the graph title. A separate work area for storing graph data and labels should be provided.

Report options should be selectable from menus and/or titles included in macros that automatically define the ranges to be displayed or printed. Add-in programs, such as Allways® and Impress®, as well as graphics-oriented spreadsheets, such as Excel® or Quattro Pro®, can also be used to refine output formats.

Use Range Names for Output Ranges. Range names should be provided for output areas so that output section values can be more easily identified and the user can more easily adjust the output ranges to accommodate particular data entries.

Use Macros for Print Routines. Macro print routines save time when generating output and maintain the default output printouts, reducing the potential for keyboarding errors (Weisskopf 1988).

Macro Design Guidelines

Simple spreadsheet models may be developed without menus. However, menus should always be provided in frequently used models or models developed for other users (Weisskopf 1988). Simple "go-to" menus can be created that allow a user to quickly and easily view various sections of the model (Bianchine 1989; Ewing 1986; Nguyen and Little 1987; and Weisskopf 1988). Suggestions for using more advanced macro commands to develop sophisticated and easy-to-use spreadsheet models are outlined in chapter 3.

The design guidelines presented below are not applicable for all types of spreadsheet models. For example, models designed to be used as "black boxes" should strictly follow the first three guidelines, which never release control of the work sheet to users. However, templates designed to teach the user about their structure and operation should allow the user to view the well-documented macro programming instructions and perhaps include suggestions for modifying those instructions.

Isolate Macros. The macro code should be located in a section of the model where users are not likely to interfere with them. This is especially important for models that will be used by people who are not familiar with the model's operation.

Always Use Menus. Menus should be used to offer analysis choices, add documentation, and allow users to easily go to different parts of the model.

Never Release Control of a Work Sheet. One way to keep a novice clerical user out of trouble is to have macros and menus control every aspect of data entry, data computation, and data output process (Bianchine 1989).

Advantages of Macro-Driven Models. Macro-driven spreadsheet models are useful for facilitating training and increasing the productivity of personnel, maintaining the integrity of data, keeping users away from these sections, and perhaps requiring less support from the model's developer (Bianchine 1989).

Disadvantages of Macro-Driven Models. Macro-driven models can possibly retard performance, particularly on older computers. Also, more planning, programming, and maintenance are required for macro-driven models (Bianchine 1989). In addition, as one author suggests, "Macros are hard to read; documentation is easy" (Nevison 1989, p. 82).

CONCLUSIONS

Just as using an excellent word processor does not make one a great writer, using an outstanding spreadsheet program does not necessarily mean that one will develop excellent work sheets. Spreadsheet model development is a craft in which skill and judgment must be thoughtfully applied within a logical framework. The guidelines presented in this chapter are designed to aid in the development of models that are soundly structured, well documented, and thus easier to run, interpret, and maintain.

NOTES

1. Work sheets normally load with the cursor at the location when the program was last saved. Using an autoexec macro to always present the welcome screen assures that a consistent opening procedure is provided whenever the model is loaded.

2. The use of conditional branching based on an IF-THEN-ELSE type of validation process is discussed in detail by Nguyen and Little (1987). They also discuss error-trapping techniques, which they define as ". . . the art of anticipating the things that can potentially go wrong, and preparing contingency plans to deal with the various complications" (Nguyen and Little 1987, p. 169).

3. Cell references expressed in the form of range names are automatically adjusted when rows or columns are deleted from the model. This does not occur if row and column notations are expressed in terms of standard row and column notation.

REFERENCES

Alberte-Hallam, T., Hallam, S. F., and Hallam, J. 1985. *Microcomputer use.* Orlando: Academic Press.

Berry, T. 1989. The trouble with spreadsheets. *Personal Computing* 13, 61–63.

Bianchine, J. J. 1989. Macro-driven templates: you and your template users will be happiest if your macros never release control of the work sheet. *Lotus* 5, 4, 40–42.

Brail, R. K. 1987. *Microcomputers in urban planning and management.* New Brunswick, NJ: Center for Urban Policy Research, Rutgers University.

Ditlea, S. 1987. Spreadsheets can be hazardous to your health. *Personal Computing* 11, 60–69.

Duffy, T. 1987. *Four software tools.* Belmont, CA: Wadsworth Publishing.

Ewing, D. P. 1986. *1-2-3 macro library.* Indianapolis: Que Corporation.

Grauer, R. T. and Sugrue, P. K. 1989. *Microcomputer applications*, 2d ed. New York: McGraw-Hill.

Miller, S. E. 1989. Eight ways to avoid worksheet errors. *Lotus* 5, 2, 50–53.

Nevison, J. M. 1989. *1-2-3 spreadsheet design.* New York: Simon and Schuster.

Nguyen, T. K. and Little J. R. 1987. *Applied 1-2-3: creating spreadsheet systems for others*. New York: Brady-Prentice Hall.
Sawicki, D. S. 1985. Microcomputer applications in planning. *Journal of the American Planning Association* 51, 209–215.
Schatt, S. 1989. *Spreadsheets, financial modeling, and statistical software: Microcomputers in business and society*. Columbus: Merrill Publishing.
Weisskopf, G. 1988. *Lotus 1-2-3 tips and tricks*. San Francisco: Sybex.

Chapter 3

Advanced Spreadsheet Modeling

Richard E. Klosterman

The spreadsheet models that accompany this book illustrate the application of the capabilities of modern electronic spreadsheet programs to provide a range of public sector applications. This chapter will use examples drawn from these models to illustrate ways in which the most powerful of these capabilities—spreadsheet macros—can be used to develop advanced spreadsheet models. The discussion briefly reviews the basic procedures for developing and using spreadsheet macros and illustrates the use of more advanced macro commands. While the examples consider only the particular commands provided in Lotus 1-2-3[*], the general principles can easily be transferred to other spreadsheet programs.

The discussion begins by introducing spreadsheet macros and the general procedures for developing and using them. The next section provides general guidelines for developing and documenting more easily understood macro programs. The final section illustrates the use of macros for moving to different parts of a model, accepting user input, and controlling the flow of the program.

SPREADSHEET MACRO BASICS

When 1-2-3 was first released in 1983, Lotus Corporation referred to macros as "typing alternatives." While this name was later dropped, it is still useful in highlighting the fact that a macro is similar to the scroll of music in a player piano. The music scroll contains a recorded series of keystrokes for playing the piano; a spreadsheet macro is a recorded series of keystrokes—commands, text, or numbers—for operating an electronic spreadsheet. When you turn on a player piano, it reads and plays the notes recorded on the scroll. When a spreadsheet user runs a macro, the spreadsheet program reads and executes the keystrokes and commands stored in the macro. In this way, spreadsheet macros provide an alternative to entering information from the keyboard—hence, the name "typing alternative."

In addition to stored keystrokes, spreadsheet macros can also contain special programming commands that allow the macro to do things that cannot be done easily by pressing keys. These commands can be used to create custom menus that look and operate like the menus that are provided by the spreadsheet program; to solicit input from the user; and to incorporate many of the functions of custom programming languages, such as BASIC, Fortran, or C, within a spreadsheet model. It is these capabilities that provide much of the power and convenience of the spreadsheet models that accompany this text.

Creating Spreadsheet Macros

Macros are nothing more than specially named text cells. They are created in exactly the same way as any other text cell: by typing a label prefix and the desired textual information into a spreadsheet cell. The only difference is that in this case, the characters that follow the label prefix are not normal text but keystrokes or macro commands that represent keystrokes. While any of the normal spreadsheet label prefixes (for example, ', ", |, or ^) may be used, the ' symbol is generally used so that the macro command is aligned at the left edge of the cell. All macros that begin with nontext characters (for instance, /, \, +, -, and .) or numbers must also be started with a label prefix so that the following characters are not interpreted as normal numbers or letters.

Like all other text cells, the cells that make up a macro are saved when the work sheet that contains them is saved. When the work sheet containing the macros is retrieved, the macros are automatically loaded as well. Unfortunately, for Lotus 1-2-3° versions 2.2 and below, macros can be stored only as part of a work sheet means and must be reentered or copied to a new work sheet before they can be used.

Consider, for example, a simple macro for erasing a spreadsheet range. Normally this is done by entering the following keystrokes /**R**ange **E**rase into the computer and then specifying the range to be erased. This three-key procedure can be replaced by the following macro:

'/re

The ' identifies the cell as a text cell; the remaining three characters are shorthand for the /**R**ange **E**rase keys one must enter to erase a range. As a result, when the '/re macro is played back by the spreadsheet program, it automatically executes the corresponding commands and waits for the user to specify the cell(s) to be erased. The characters in the macro can be either uppercase or lowercase; lowercase letters are used by convention in this book.

Spreadsheet macros can contain not only keystrokes but also characters that represent special keys and spreadsheet commands. One of the most widely used specialized keys is the tilde (~) key (located at the upper left-hand corner of most keyboards), which represents the ENTER key. Other symbols and words within the "{" and "}" braces are used to represent other special keys on the keyboard. For example, {RIGHT} represents the right arrow key; {END} represents the END key; and {CALC} represents the F9 function key, that is, the Lotus CALC key. The most widely used specialized macro keys for Lotus 1-2-3° (version 2.01 and below) are listed in Table 3.1.

Consider, for instance, the following slightly more advanced version of the macro described above:

'/re{END}{RIGHT}
{END}{DOWN} ~

The first three characters of the first line are identical to the previous macro, that is, equivalent to the user pressing /**R**ange **E**rase. The {END} is equivalent to pressing the END key and {RIGHT} is equivalent to pressing the right arrow. Together they specify the range to be erased using the END-right arrow key combination to move the cursor to the last nonempty cell on the right.

Table 3.1

Special Key Representations in Macros

Key	Action
Function Keys	
{EDIT}	Edits contents of current cell (same as F2)
{NAME}	Displays list of range names in the work sheet (same as F3)
{ABS}	Converts relative reference to absolute (same as F4)
{GOTO}	Jumps cell pointer to cell coordinates (same as F5)
{WINDOW}	Moves cell pointer to other side of split screen (same as F6)
{QUERY}	Repeats most recent query operation (same as F7)
{TABLE}	Repeats most recent table operation (same as F8)
{CALC}	Recalculates work sheet (same as F9)
{GRAPH}	Redraws current graph (same as F10)
Cell Pointer-Movement Keys	
{UP n}	Moves cell pointer up n rows
{DOWN n}	Moves cell pointer down n rows
{LEFT n}	Moves cell pointer left n columns
{RIGHT n}	Moves cell pointer right n columns
{PGUP}	Moves cell pointer up 20 rows
{PGDN}	Moves cell pointer down 20 rows
{HOME}	Moves cell pointer to cell A1
{END}	Used with {UP}, {DOWN}, {LEFT}, or {RIGHT} to move cell pointer to next boundary between blank and nonblank cells in the indicated direction
Editing Keys	
{DELETE} or {DEL}	Used with {EDIT} to delete character from a cell definition
{INSERT}	Toggles editor between INSERT and OVER-TYPE modes
{ESCAPE} or {ESC}	Indicates the Esc key
{BACKSPACE}, or {BS}	Indicates the BACKSPACE key

As this macro illustrates, macros can contain more than one line of commands; after executing the first row of commands, the macro executes the commands in any lines below it until it encounters a blank line, which terminates the macro. In this case, after executing the END right arrow key combination, the macro executes an END-down arrow key combination, moving the cursor to the last nonempty cell below the current cell. Together, the first and second lines indicate that the range to be erased should include all of the nonempty cells to the right and below the initial cell. The final tilde ($\sim$) is equivalent to pressing the ENTER key, specifying that the range to be erased has been specified. This completes the operation; the spreadsheet then erases the range and returns to the READY mode.

Naming Macros

Before a macro can be used, it must be assigned a unique name to differentiate it from the normal text cells and other macros stored in the work sheet. A macro that is invoked directly by the user is named by assigning a special range name, consisting of a backslash (\) and a single letter (for instance, \A or \a) to the first cell in the macro. The macro name can be either an uppercase or lowercase letter; uppercase letters are used by convention in this book. The name assigned to the macro allows the user to run the macro and tells the spreadsheet program where to find the keystrokes and commands it contains. To the extent possible, the macro names should be descriptive of the macro's function. For example, the models in this book use Alt-M to access the Main macro menu, Alt-D to go to the Model documentation, and so on.

Because the names of user-invoked macros must contain a letter and there are only twenty-six letters in the alphabet, a spreadsheet can contain only twenty-six invokable macros. There are two ways to get around this limitation, however. Every work sheet can have an Alt-0 (Alt-zero) macro that is invoked automatically when Lotus loads a work sheet; the macro cannot be run by pressing the Alt-0 key combination. This type of automatically executing macro is used in the accompanying models to display the welcome screen when the model is first loaded. An unlimited number of additional macros can also be created that are invoked by other macros and not directly by the user; these macros do not need to have Alt-letter names.

Assume, for instance, that the second macro described above is stored in cells AB1 and AB2 and named Alt-E (for erase). The macro can be named by moving the cursor to cell AB1 and issuing the /**R**ange Name Create command, entering \e (or \E) for the range name, and pressing ENTER twice. After this is done, the spreadsheet program will automatically execute the range deletion macro described above whenever the user presses the **Alt-E** key combination.

This simple naming procedure has a serious limitation, though, in not providing a visual indication that cells AB1 and AB2 contain a macro. It is therefore preferable to separate the macro name from the macro itself to provide direct documentation of the macro's location and name. This can be done by entering the '\e label in cell AA1, that is, the cell immediately to the left of the first cell in the macro. Keeping the cell pointer in cell AA1, enter the /**R**ange Name Labels **R**ight command and press the ENTER key twice. This assigns the range name \e to the cell immediately to the right of the current cell (AA1), that is, to cell AB1 containing the macro. This procedure does not affect the macro execution but does provide a useful reminder of the macro's name and location.

Running Macros

Macros are run by simultaneously pressing the ALT key and the letter name of the macro. For example, after entering and naming the Alt-E macro described above, the user must only press the ALT and e (or **E**) keys simultaneously to run the Alt-E erasing macro. As soon as the Alt-letter combination is invoked, 1-2-3 looks for a macro with the specified name in the current work sheet. If it is found, the program "plays back" the keys and commands stored in the macro. If 1-2-3 does not find the macro, it beeps and waits for the user to issue another command. If no errors are found, 1-2-3 automatically runs the macro from the top down until it encounters a blank cell or is instructed to stop by its internal commands.

Debugging Macros

Like all computer programs, spreadsheet macros are literal creatures that attempt to follow the commands they contain exactly—even when they are mistaken. For example, a user will recognize immediately that {GOTI} is a misspelling of {GOTO}. However, a macro cannot recognize this; it blindly tries to execute the misspelled word and issues an error message when it cannot.

Fortunately, 1-2-3 provides a rudimentary tool that facilitates the process of eliminating (or debugging) the inevitable errors in a macro program. This is the "step" function that is invoked by pressing the **ALT-F2** key combination before entering the Alt-letter command for running a macro. After the macro is started, the step function executes the macro, one step at a time, and waits for the user to press a key before continuing; the space bar is generally used for this purpose. This allows the user to follow the macro, step by step, until the error is found. **ALT-F2** can then be pressed to exit the STEP mode and ESC pressed one or more times until the READY mode indicator appears. The user can then correct the error and rerun the macro to ensure that all of the errors have been corrected.

PRINCIPLES OF GOOD PRACTICE

Like any technical activity, developing sophisticated and easy-to-use analysis models in a spreadsheet environment is greatly enhanced by following a number of fundamental principles of good practice. This section discusses three of the most important principles for using macros: (1) using range names instead of absolute cell references, (2) documenting the macro commands, and (3) isolating the macros from the rest of the spreadsheet model. These principles are generally reflected in the models that accompany this book and are highly recommended for anyone attempting to develop all but the simplest spreadsheet macros. Additional guidelines for developing easy-to-use and understandable spreadsheet models are outlined in chapter 2.

Use Range Names
The most important principle to follow in developing spreadsheet macros is to always use range names and not absolute cell references when referring to specific locations within a model. This is essential because macros, as simple text cells, do not change when the cells in a spreadsheet are added, deleted, or moved.

Consider, for example, the simple print macro listed below that prints the model output stored in cells I1 to P40:

```
'/pp
'rI1..P40~
'agq
```

The first line selects the **Print Printer** option. The second line specifies the print range—cells I1 through P40. The third line selects in the **Align** option, issues the **Go** command—telling 1-2-3 to print the range—and then selects **Quit** from the print menu, returning 1-2-3 to the READY mode.

This macro will work fine as long as no changes are made to the model that modify the print range. However, consider what would happen if an additional column is inserted to the left of the existing column I. The range to be printed now includes cells J1 to Q40. Unfortunately, the second row of the macro does not change accordingly, and when the macro is run, the incorrect portion of the model is printed. This problem can be corrected only by revising the macro's cell reference each time changes are made to the left of column I or above row 40—an extremely tedious and error-prone process.

This problem could easily be avoided by using range names. To do this, the initial output range (cells I1 to P40) could first be assigned a range name, say OUTPUT, and the second line of the macro changed to 'r**OUTPUT** ~ to specify that the OUTPUT range should be printed. Then if a column is added to the left of column I, the OUTPUT range is automatically adjusted to include cells J1 to Q40. Since the macro now uses the name OUTPUT to specify the desired print range, these changes are automatically incorporated into the macro and it always prints the correct part of the model. Putting this rule into practice avoids a great deal of time and aggravation for model developers and users alike.

Document Fully

As spreadsheet macros become more numerous, longer, and complex, it becomes increasingly more difficult to remember exactly what they do and how they work—particularly when the developer has not looked at them for weeks or months. It is even more difficult to understand complex macros that have been written by others. As a result, it is extremely useful to follow the lead of professional programmers and provide internal documentation that describes each step in the macro. Documenting the macros makes them easier to use and, even more importantly, easier to correct when something goes wrong.

The first step in writing easy-to-understand, fully documented macros is to break complex macro commands into smaller pieces that are listed on separate lines. For instance, the simple print macro described in the previous section could have been written on a single line, that is:

'/pprI1..P40 ~ agq.

The spreadsheet program can interpret the one-line version of the macro just as quickly and easily as the three-line version. It is even possible to specify more than one macro command on a single line. It is much easier for a person to understand the three-line version, though, particularly the portion of the macro that specifies the print range. The need for following this general principle becomes increasingly apparent as macro commands become longer, more complex, and increasingly more difficult to understand.

After breaking extensive macro commands into separate lines, it is advisable to include explanatory comments in documentation cells adjacent to each row of the macro. The models that accompany this book provide three columns of information for each macro, as shown in the documentation section for the standard Alt-Z, Go to macros, macro in Exhibit 3.1.

The Description column briefly describes the macro command (or commands) that are on the corresponding line of the macro. For example, the second line of the description indicates that the Alt-Z macro is used to go to the model's macro documentation section. The Name column contains the labels for the ranges lying to their right (in this case, the \Z macro name) assigned by using the /Range Name Labels Right procedure outlined above. The Instructions column contains the actual macro commands. For instance, the instructions in the second line of the macro move the user to the model's documentation section identified by the MACRO_DOCUMENT range name.

The first line of Exhibit 3.1 illustrates an additional documentation feature that is much more useful than it may appear to be. As the description suggests, the first line is a "null" command that does nothing more than mark the place of the cell reference in the middle column of the table. It is a "null" command because it does not affect the model operation in any way. All it does is instruct the program to insert a period in the current cell and then use the backspace key to erase the period, effectively doing nothing at all.

However, the null command does provide an easy way of identifying the cell to which the "\Z" cell label in the middle column refers. Identifying the cell reference is easy in a simple example such as this but can often be very difficult in more complex looping macros that refer to particular cells within a long string of macro commands. In these cases, keeping track of the exact place to which a cell reference is made can greatly reduce the potential for making hard-to-find—and to correct—macro errors.

Exhibit 3.1

Sample Macro Documentation

Description	Name	Instructions
Null command place holder	\Z	.{bs}
Go to macro documentation		{goto}MACRO_DOCUMENT~

Isolate Macros

Because macros are nothing more than text cells that have been assigned special range names, they can be placed anywhere in a work sheet. Nevertheless, it is highly recommended to locate all of the macros in a separate area outside of the main portion of the model. In particular, it is advisable to place macros in a part of the work sheet that is unlikely to be affected when rows or columns are inserted or deleted in developing or refining the model. Otherwise, one or more macro commands might be accidently deleted when rows are deleted and unwanted blank cells may be inserted into a macro when a row is added. Even worse, an entire macro may be erased when a column is deleted.

There are no universally accepted rules for placing macros in a spreadsheet model. Many authors recommend placing macros to the far right-hand side of the model; unfortunately, this may make macros more difficult to find and may cause problems if rows are added to or deleted from the main model. Others recommend placing macros below the main model; this may cause problems if adjusting columns in the main model affects the macros. Still others suggest that macros be placed below and to the right of the main model. Fortunately, more recent versions of 1-2-3 allow macros to be placed outside of the rectangle containing the main model without consuming large amounts of memory.

Wherever the macros are located, it is extremely useful to store them in a common part of the model and assign this area with an identifiable range name such as, MACROS. It is also advisable to provide a simple "go to" or "navigation" macro that takes the user to the macro storage area. The Alt-Z, Go to macros command provided in the models that accompany this book implements this strategy. Isolating the macros and providing a simple navigation macro allow the model user—and developer—quickly and easily to find and inspect all of a model's macros.

MACRO BUILDING BLOCKS

The most recent versions of Lotus 1-2-3° provide more than seventy macro commands, only some of which are listed in Table 3.1. The following discussion will not attempt to describe and illustrate the use of all of these commands. For that, readers can consult the documentation that comes with the program and books dedicated to the use of 1-2-3, such as Cobb (1986) and Que Corporation (1989). Instead, it will describe and illustrate the commands that have been widely used in the models that accompany this text. The macros will be grouped by the following major functions: (1) moving around the model; (2) accepting user input; and (3) controlling program flow.

Moving Around the Model
One of the simplest and most important functions that a spreadsheet macro can perform is to assist the user in moving around a model. This type of macro is essential for any model that occupies more than one or two screens of data and is used extensively in the models that accompany this text.

Cell Pointer Movement. As Table 3.1 illustrates, 1-2-3 provides a number of cell pointer movement commands that are equivalent to the user pressing one of the arrow keys. For example, the {UP *n*} command is equivalent to the user pressing the up arrow key *n* times; {UP} without an argument is equivalent to pressing the up arrow key one time. The other commands are self-explanatory, with the possible exception of the {END} command. This command is equivalent to the user pressing the END key and is used in conjunction with the other cursor movement keys to move the cursor in the direction indicated to the next intersection between an empty and nonempty cell. This command is particularly useful for specifying print ranges.

{GOTO} Command. Exhibit 3.1 illustrates the use of an even more powerful and useful macro command—the {GOTO} command. This com-

mand is equivalent to the user pressing **F5**, the Lotus GoTo key, and takes the user directly to the specified cell or range. For example, the command in the second line of Exhibit 3.1 takes the user to the "MACRO_DOCUMENT" range containing the model's internal documentation. Note that a tilde (~) must be included after the cell or range to represent the user pressing the ENTER key after specifying the location to which the cell pointer should be moved.

Accepting User Input

A second useful function that is used widely in the models allows the user to create a "user-friendly" interface for entering data into a model. This interface can include prompts that help the user enter data more easily and edit checks that evaluate the data before storing it in the work sheet.

{?} Command. The simplest macro for accepting user input is the {?} command. This command causes the program to wait until the user enters some information from the keyboard and presses the ENTER key before proceeding. No prompt is displayed on the screen and any type of information may be entered.

An illustration of the {?} command is provided by the "New_name" option within the Alt-Q, Quit/save, macro described in chapter 1. This option allows the user to specify a new name for saving the currently loaded work sheet and continue using it. The following commands are used to do this:

/FS{?}{quit}

The first three characters correspond to the user selecting the /File Save options for saving the current spreadsheet. The {?} command causes the program to pause until the user specifies the new name for saving the file and presses the ENTER key. The {QUIT} command ends the macro, returning control of the keyboard to the user.

GET Command. A slightly more sophisticated macro for accepting data from the user is provided by the {GET} command. The {GET} command has the following format:

{get *location*}

This command accepts a single keystroke from the user and places it into the designated work sheet cell specified by the *location* parameter. The model can then test the keystroke in a number of ways and use the test results to change the flow of the program.

For example, Exhibit 3.2 shows the Alt-W macro used in models that accompany that text. The macro uses the {GET} command and allows the user to press any key and exit the welcome screen when it is displayed. The first line of the macro is the null command placeholder described previously. The next two lines use the {GOTO} command to move the cell pointer to the range containing the welcome screen and then to the prompt line at the bottom of the screen. The fourth line waits until the user presses a key. The {GET} command then stores the key stroke in the RESPONSE range shown at the bottom of Exhibit 3.2 The final line of the macro uses the {BRANCH} command, to be described below, to transfer control of the program to the commands starting in the MAIN_MENU range.

Exhibit 3.2

Sample {GET} Command Application

Description	Name	Instructions
Null command place holder	\W	.{bs}
Go to Welcome screen		{goto}WELCOME_SCREEN~
Go to prompt line		{goto}WELCOME_PROMPT~
Get user response		{get RESPONSE}
Go to MAIN_MENU		{branch MAIN_MENU}
Stores \W response	RESPONSE	

GETLABEL and GETNUMBER Commands. Two other commands for accepting input from the user—the {GETLABEL} and {GETNUMB-ER} commands—are widely used in the models that accompany this book. The {GETLABEL} command has the following format:

{getlabel *prompt, location*}

The {GETLABEL} command displays the *prompt* message in the 1-2-3 control panel, waits for the user to enter any type of information from the keyboard, and then stores the response as a label in the work sheet cell specified by the *location* parameter.

Consider, for example, the following macro that asks the user to enter their name:

{getlabel "Enter your name: ",NAME} ~

This macro displays the "Enter your name: " prompt in the 1-2-3 control panel and waits for the user to enter his or her name and press the ENTER key. The user's response is then stored in the range labeled "NAME."

The format and function for the {GETNUMBER} command are identical to those for the {GETLABEL} command. The only difference is that this command accepts only numeric answers that are then stored—as numbers—in the cell specified by the location parameter. If anything other than a number is entered or the ENTER key is pressed without entering anything, the program enters ERR into the *location* cell.

Controlling Program Flow

A third important function that macro commands can perform is using information provided in the model or supplied by the user to determine the commands to be performed by the model and the order in which these commands are performed. These program control commands have been used with the user input command described above to provide many of the sophisticated computational procedures incorporated in the spreadsheet models described in the remainder of this book.

{BRANCH} Command. The {BRANCH} command provides the simplest way to change the program flow by unconditionally transferring the macro to a specified cell or range. Program control does not return to the originating cell unless it is transferred back by another {BRANCH} statement. For instance, the last line of the Alt-W macro shown in Exhibit 3.2 unconditionally transfers the program to the MAIN_MENU range after the user presses any key.

{MENUBRANCH} Command. A much more flexible method of transferring program command is provided by the {MENUBRANCH} command. This command allows the model developer to create a menu-selection structure from which the user can select from up to eight options, just as he or she would from the standard 1-2-3 option menus. This powerful command is used in the standard Alt-Q, Quit/save, macro,

in the Alt-S system menus provided in many models, and in nearly all of the models in the collection.

A typical {MENUBRANCH} application is the Alt-I, Input data macro from the ECONBASE model shown at the top of Exhibit 3.3. The Alt-I macro is a data entry macro that provides the user with three options: (1) entering local employment data, (2) entering national employment data, or (3) returning to the main macro menu.

The first line of the Alt-I macro is the null command placeholder described previously. The second line contains the {MENUBRANCH} command that directs the program to execute the menu structure stored at the INPUT_MENU location, that is, the cells to the right of the IN-PUT_MENU range label. A {MENUBRANCH} menu consists of one to eight consecutive columns in the work sheet; three are used in this example. Each column corresponds to one item in the menu and contains three or more rows.

The first row of each column specifies the option name as it is displayed in the Lotus control panel. Thus, for this example, the Alt-I menu displays the following three options: Local, National, and Main_Menu.

The second line shows the expanded description for each choice that is displayed below the list of options. For instance, "Enter local employment data" is displayed when the "Local" option is selected.

The third line in each menu option is the first instruction to be carried out when an option is selected from the menu. The macro will continue to execute any other commands that are found below this instruction until it encounters a blank cell or is instructed to transfer program control to another location. For example, the "Main_Menu" option in the Alt-I macro uses the {BRANCH} command to transfer program control to the MAIN_MENU range.

{MENUCALL} Command. The {MENUCALL} command is identical to the {MENUBRANCH} command except that 1-2-3 executes the menu program as a subroutine. That is, after the selected menu program has been executed, program control returns to the cell immediately below the cell that contains the {MENUCALL} statements.

The "Local" and "National" menu options of the Alt-I macro menu shown in Exhibit 3.3 illustrate the use of the {MENUCALL} command. After the user selects either one of these options, the {MENUCALL} command transfers program control to the INPUT_OPTIONS menu shown in the middle of Exhibit 3.3. This menu provides two options: (1) New_Data, for entering new data, or (2) Revise_Data, for revising

Exhibit 3.3

Sample Program Control Applications

Description	Name			
Null command place holder	\I	.{bs}		
User enters Input option		{menubranch INPUT_MENU}		
Input options menu	INPUT_MENU	Local	National	Main_Menu
Input options description		Enter local employment data	Enter national employment data	Return to Main Menu
Input option commands		{menucall INPUT_OPTIONS}	{menucall INPUT_OPTIONS}	{branch MAIN_MENU}
Input options commands		{branch ENTER_LOCAL}	{branch ENTER_NATIONAL}	
Input options menu	INPUT_OPTIONS	New_Data	Revise_Data	
Options description		Enter new data	Revise existing data	
Set INPUT_OPTION		{let INPUT_OPTION,1}	{let INPUT_OPTION,0}	
Return to Input menu		{return}	{return}	
	INPUT_OPTION	1		

previously entered data. In either case, the program uses the {LET} command described below to specify which option the user has selected.

{RETURN} Command. The {RETURN} command at the end of each of the INPUT_OPTIONS columns identifies the end of the subroutine. This command returns the macro to the line of the Alt-I menu directly below the {MENUCALL} command that transferred control to the INPUT_OPTIONS menu. Thus, for example, if the user had selected the "Local" input data option, program control would be returned to the line below the {MENUCALL} command in the first column. The {BRANCH} command would then transfer control to the commands in the ENTER_LOCAL range.

{LET} Command. The {LET} command places a specified value or string in a designated cell without moving the cell pointer to that location. The command has the following format

$$\{\text{let } location, expression\}$$

and places the value or string specified by the *expression* parameter in the location specified by the *location* parameter.

For instance, the {LET} command in the third line of the two INPUT_OPTIONS menu places a 1 in the INPUT_OPTION cell if the user selects the New_Data option and a 0 in the INPUT_OPTIONS cell if the Revise_Data option is selected. The value in the last line of Exhibit 3.3 indicates that the user selected the first option. This value can then be used with the {IF} command described below to determine the program's future flow, as will be shown below.

{IF }Command. The {IF} command uses the IF-THEN-ELSE logic provided by programs such as BASIC to control program flow on the basis of numeric or string values specified within the model. The command has the following general structure:

$$\{\text{if } condition\} \ \{true\}$$
$$\{false\}$$

The command executes the command specified by the *true* parameter if the logical *condition* is true; if the *condition* is false, it executes the command specified by the *{false}* command.

Two applications of the {IF} command are provided in the rather long and complex ENTER_LOCAL subroutine in the ECONBASE model shown in Exhibit 3.4. The subroutine is called by the main Alt-I, Input data, option, when the user enters the local employment data required by the model. The subroutine contains many advanced macro commands that will not be discussed here. It is also only one way to perform the desired functions; more efficient procedures may be available. Our only concern here will be considering the use of the {IF} command in the ninth line of the subroutine and in the LOCAL_LOOP section at the bottom of the subroutine.

The {IF} command in the ninth line of the subroutine uses the value of INPUT_OPTION cell specified with the INPUT_OPTIONS {MENU-CALL} procedure described above to determine the appropriate action to be taken in entering the local employment data. In this case, the logical condition to be tested is whether the value stored in the INPUT_OPTION cell is equal to zero or not. If the value is 0 the user has selected the "Revise_Data" option from the INPUT_MENU to revise previously entered data. In this case, the logical condition is true and the program executes the command on the line containing the {IF} command, that is, it executes the {BRANCH} command and transfers control to REVISE_LOCAL range.

If the value stored in the INPUT_OPTIONS cell is 1, that is, the user is entering new data, the logical condition will be false. In this case, the program executes the commands below the {IF} command. In this example, that means that the /Range Erase command sequence is used to erase the label currently stored in the REGION_NAME range. The {GETLABEL} command then enters a new region name, and so on.

Command Looping. The final program control function to be considered is the use of macro commands for providing program loops, that is, procedures for conducting repetitive functions until a predefined condition is satisfied. This application is illustrated by the last five lines of the ENTER_LOCAL subroutine shown in Exhibit 3.4.

The loop begins with the line labeled LOCAL_LOOP and ends at the last line with the {branch LOCAL_LOOP} that directs the macro to return to the line labeled LOCAL_LOOP. LOCAL_LOOP is a range name associated with the cell containing the null command placeholder. The next command within the loop, "/xlEnter Local Employment" is a version of the {GETNUMBER} command that prompts the user to enter a value and stores it in the cell containing the cell pointer.

The {IF} command in the next line provides a necessary component of all loops—a way of exiting the loop when the repetitive operation has

Exhibit 3.4

Sample {IF} Command and Loop Applications

Description	Label	Macro
Null command place holder	ENTER_LOCAL	.{bs}
Turn off windows		{windowsoff}
Go to data entry screen		{goto}ENTRY_UP_LEFT~
Set national column width		{right 3}/wcs12~
Turn on windows		{windowson}
Go to data entry screen		{goto}ENTRY_UP_LEFT~
Erase current date		{blank CURRENT_DATE}{goto}CURRENT_DATE~
User enters current date		{getlabel "Enter current date (MM/DD/YY): ",CURRENT_DATE}~
Branch if revising data		{if INPUT_OPTION=0}{branch REVISE_LOCAL}
Erase region name		{blank REGION_NAME}{goto}REGION_NAME~
User enters region name		{getlabel "Enter region name: ",REGION_NAME}~
Erase analysis year		{blank YEAR}{goto}YEAR~
User enters analysis year		{getnumber "Enter observation year: ",YEAR}~
Recalculate worksheet		{calc}
Erase previous local employ		{blank LOCAL_EMPLOY}
Go to local employ column		{goto}LOCAL_EMPLOY~
Null command place holder	LOCAL_LOOP	.{bs}
Enter employment value		/xnEnter Local Employment: ~ ~
Return if finished		{if @COUNT(LOCAL_EMPLOY)=90}{branch MAIN_MENU}
Move down one row		{down}
Branch to LOCAL_LOOP		{branch LOCAL_LOOP}

been conducted the proper number of times. In this case, the {IF} command uses the @COUNT function to determine whether the number of employment values entered in the LOCAL_EMPLOY range is equal to ninety. If it is equal to ninety, that is, the {IF} command's logical condition is true, the {BRANCH} command returns program control to the MAIN_MENU range. If it is not, the loop continues and (1) the {DOWN} command moves the cell pointer down one row and (2) the program returns to the LOCAL_LOOP cell, allowing the user to enter another local employment value. The loop continues until the number of local employment values is equal to ninety and the {BRANCH} command in the {IF} command exits the loop.

CONCLUSIONS

This chapter illustrates the use of spreadsheet macros by describing the structure and operation of these powerful tools in general and examining their use in some of the models that accompany this text. This discussion is intended to provide a useful beginning point for developing more complex structured spreadsheet models. However, we offer one caution: ***Do not attempt to be too fancy in your initial designs.*** This book contains some spreadsheets with very complex macro designs. While impressive, remember that these complex macros take a long time to develop and test. Begin small, and you may find that even a set of simple navigation macros will prove very useful.

REFERENCES

Cobb, D. 1986. *Douglas Cobb's 1-2-3 handbook*. New York: Bantam Books.
Que Corporation. 1989. *Using 1-2-3 Release 2.2, special edition*. Indianapolis: Que Corporation.

PART TWO

Demographic Analysis and Forecasting

Chapter 4

EXTRAP: Curve Fitting/Extrapolation

Earl G. Bossard

The EXTRAP model is designed to assist in the analysis and projection of time-series data. By helping identify the mathematical relationship that best describes past trends, the model can help an analyst understand these trends more clearly and identify their underlying causes better. If these trends are expected to continue without change and the historical data are reliable, then the trends can be extrapolated into the future to project future conditions. The reliability of the projection results depends on the continuity of underlying conditions and the goodness of fit between the estimates and the historic data.

The six extrapolation curves provided in the EXTRAP model have a rich applications history and can be used to analyze and project any variable for which observations are available at regular intervals over time. Possible applications include the analysis and projection of general population and employment trends, death rates, and other measures of activity for a variety of areas.

Users should be aware of the assumptions and requirements necessary for these extrapolation techniques to be useful if: (1) past trends continue without change, (2) the structure of relationships effecting the trends does not change, (3) the historical data are reliable, and (4) the chosen technique closely approximates the trend, *then* the technique can be very helpful. Thoughtless use of these models by simply entering the data and blindly accepting the extrapolation output as "computer-generated scientific projections" may be analogous to a situation where a fifteen-year-old youth steals the keys to a high-powered sports car to take a joyride. The only difference is that perhaps the joy rider may be more aware of the risks involved.

Seriously, these powerful models should be thoughtfully applied, and careful consideration should be given to both the nature of the data used and the statistical properties and requirements for effectively using these models. When given thoughtful attention by an analyst with a basic understanding of statistics, these models can facilitate data analysis and extrapolation. Users of the EXTRAP template who are not strongly grounded in statistics are encouraged to refer to a statistics text and to Klosterman (1990).[1]

CONCEPTUAL BASIS

All curve fitting/extrapolation models use a two-step process to describe past trends and extend them into the future. The first step, curve-fitting, attempts to identify the curve or mathematical relationship that most closely describes past trends[2]. The second step, curve extrapolation, continues this curve or mathematical relationship to project future values for the variable being studied. Shryock and Associates (1973; p. 681) have called extrapolation ". . . the art of inferring values that go beyond the given series of data by use of a mathematical formula or a graphic procedure."

The EXTRAP model fits six different mathematical curves to observation data provided by the user: linear, geometric, parabolic, modified exponential, Gompertz, and logistic.[3] The six curves incorporate different growth assumptions and are therefore appropriate for describing and projecting different types of historical trends.

The linear curve assumes that the dependent variable (for instance, a region's population) will always grow by equal amounts for equal time periods, for example, that a region's decennial population growth will be equal for all decades being studied.

The geometric curve assumes that growth will correspond to a constant growth rate, like the compounding of interest of a savings account. Thus, if the population growth rate of an area is a constant 2 percent per year, then a geometric curve would be most appropriate for it.

The parabolic curve assumes that growth increases or decreases by a constant amount. If the decennial population growth of an area was approximately 1,000 in the 1950s, 1,200 in the 1960s, 1,400 in the 1970s, and 1,600 in the 1980s, then the parabolic technique would be most appropriate for projecting its trend.

The modified exponential, Gompertz, and logistic curves assume that growth will move toward, or from, an asymptotic upper or lower growth limit. Of particular interest are cases in which the Gompertz and logistic curves take the form of an S-shaped curve in which growth begins slowly, increases rapidly for a while, and then slows to approach a fixed upper growth limit.

The EXTRAP model fits each of these curves to the observation data entered by the user and generates six sets of curve estimates and projections, one for each curve.[4]

Selecting the Best Curve

Three general types of decision criteria can be used to select the most appropriate projections for a given data set: input evaluation criteria, output evaluation criteria, and visual inspection. These criteria are described below.

Input Evaluation Criteria. The input evaluation criteria examine the observation (or input) data to identify the curve whose growth assumptions correspond most closely to the underlying trend in the input data.[5] For example, the linear curve assumes constant growth increments, that is, a constant change in the dependent variable for equal changes in the independent variable. The growth assumptions for each of the curves provided in the EXTRAP model are identified in Table 4.1. The test statistic that can be used to determine whether the observation data correspond to a curve's growth assumptions is also presented in Table 4.1. For instance, the first differences between consecutive observed data are examined for the linear curve to see if they are nearly equal.

The observed trends will rarely, if ever, correspond exactly to the growth assumptions of any of the six curves. As a result, the EXTRAP model computes a summary statistic, the coefficient of relative variation (CRV), to measure the relative dispersion of the six test statistics. The CRV is defined as one hundred times the standard deviation of the test statistic divided by its mean. The CRV values provide a relative measure of the extent to which the observation values correspond to a given curve. As a result, the curve with the smallest CRV value is the most appropriate curve by this criterion.

Table 4.1

Curve Assumptions and Test Statistics

Curve	Growth Assumptions	Test Statistic
Linear	Constant growth increments	First differences
Geometric	Constant growth rate	First difference of logarithms
Parabolic	Constant rate of change	Second differences
Modified Exponential	Constant ratio of growth increments	Ratio of successive first differences
Gompertz	Constant ratio of logarithms of growth increments	Ratio of first differences between logarithms
Logistic	Constant ratio of reciprocals of growth increments	Ratio of differences between reciprocals

Output Evaluation Criteria. The output evaluation criteria compare the estimated values for each observation period created by the six extrapolation techniques to the corresponding observation (or input) data to identify the curve whose estimates correspond most closely to the observed data. The output evaluation criteria assume that the extrapolation curve that best fits past growth trends will most accurately predict future values. While this assumption may be violated if the structure of relationships in the system changes, the stability of many relationships over time often make these output evaluation criteria useful.

The mean error (ME), mean absolute percentage error (MAPE), and sum of squared deviations (SSD) are three measures frequently used to evaluate the "goodness of fit" between the curve estimates and the observed values.[6] As a perfect fit would have no differences between observed and estimated values, the smaller the difference (or "error") between observed and estimated values, the better the fit. As a result, the smaller the ME, MAPE, or SSD value, the better the fit.

Another output evaluation measure evaluates the computed limits for the growth curves in comparison to the growth constraints for the area being studied. That is, the asymptotic values for the three growth curves —modified exponential, Gompertz, and logistic—should be compared to likely natural limits on the system when selecting the best extrapolation curve. A limited supply of developable land might also rule out long-term population projections for a city based on the three techniques without growth limits, that is, the linear, geometric, and parabolic.

Visual Inspection

Visual inspection of the observed and estimated values is often the quickest way to evaluate the alternative projections.[7] As all extrapolation forecasts are implicitly judgmental, visual inspection of the data should be used to look for anomalies or discontinuities in past trends and to determine whether an extrapolation curve adequately describes and extends observed growth patterns. Plots of the observed data for extended time periods may also be useful in identifying the historical period to which the extrapolation curves should be fitted.

COMPONENTS AND OPERATION

As the location map in Exhibit 4.1 indicates, the computational portion of the EXTRAP model is divided into nine sections (or tables). The computations sections for the six extrapolation curves are located across the model, starting with the linear curve (Table 1) and continuing through the logistic curve (Table 6). The top of each section provides documentary information such as the current date, analysis subject, and the region name.

The heart of each section includes the observation values supplied by the analyst, the computations data, and the computed estimates and projections. The bottom portion of each section (1) displays three measures of how well the curve estimates match the observed values, (2) documents the computational procedures, (3) shows intermediate computational steps, and (4) describes the calculations in text and numeric form. The computed growth limits are also displayed for the modified exponential, Gompertz, and logistic curves with a comment indicating whether they are upper limits of possible interest.

Exhibit 4.1

EXTRAP Location Map

Welcome A1..A20	Location Map D1..Z39								Macros	Tree GA1.GS18
Main Menu A21..A41	Range Names									
Instructions	D40..AD319							EY1..FN461		
	A42..A400						Freezable Code EO435..FD507	Graph Workarea		
						Table 8 Eval DB468..DL496	Table 9 Input Eval Tests DP500..EX614			
					Table 6 Logistic CN503..CZ594	Table 7 Summary Est DB507..DN536				
				Table 5 Gompertz CA503..CL581						
			Table 4 Mod Exp BP502..BY581							
		Table 3 Parabolic BB502..BN573								
	Table 2 Geometric AN504..AZ573									
Param AB468..AL488										
Table 1 Linear Regress AB504..AL573										

The input and output data for all six curves are displayed in Tables 7, 8, and 9. Table 7 reports the observed values entered by the analyst and the six sets of curve estimates and projections. Table 8 reports the ME, MAPE, and SSD output evaluation statistics for all six curves. Table 8 also includes the CRV input evaluation measures. Table 9 presents five input evaluation subtables. The first four tables show the derivation of the evaluation measures; the fifth table, Table 9E, presents the six CRV values, highlighting the lowest CRV with a "BEST CHOICE" label and distinctive "^^^^^^" markings above and below the data column.

Model Operation

As Table 4.2 indicates, fourteen macros are provided for use in conjunction with the EXTRAP model. The Alt-D, Alt-L, Alt-M, Alt-Q, Alt-R, Alt-W, and Alt-Z macros correspond to the standard macros described in chapter 1. The Appendix presents an outline of eight suggested steps for running the EXTRAP model.

General instructions for using these macros and the other spreadsheet macros are provided in chapter 1. The seven specialized macros provided for use with the EXTRAP model are described below.

Alt-C, Go to Computations Area Menu. This macro generates a menu that can be used to go to the upper left corner of the six extrapolation technique computation areas or return to the Main and System menus.

Alt-G, Go to Graph Menu. This option produces eleven bar or line graphs presenting information for the current model run. The following suboptions are provided:

1. Any_1 yields a menu that can be used to graph any one of the six extrapolation curves along with the observed values;
2. 1st_3 yields a graph comparing the observed values, estimates, and projections for the linear, geometric, and parabolic curves;
3. 2nd_3 produces a graph of the observed values and projections for the modified exponential, Gompertz, and logistic curves;
4. CRV_stat produces a graph of the coefficient of relative variation input evaluation measures, with a subtitle identifying the technique with the lowest CRV;
5. Error_stat produces a bar graph displaying the ME and MAPE statistics; and

6. SSD_stat produces a graph displaying the sum of squared deviations output evaluation measures for each of the six techniques. A subtitle identifies the technique with the best fit.
7. Main_menu accesses the main macro menu.

Table 4.2

EXTRAP Macros

Alt-C	Go to Computations area menu
Alt-D	Go to Documentation
Alt-G	Go to Graph menu
Alt-I	Go to Input menu
Alt-L	Go to Location map
Alt-M	Go to Main menu
Alt-O	Go to Output summary
Alt-P	Go to Print menu
Alt-Q	Quit/save model
Alt-R	Go to Range descriptions
Alt-S	Go to System menu
Alt-V	Go to View menu
Alt-W	Go to Welcome screen
Alt-Z	Go to macros

Alt-I, Go to Input Menu. The Input menu offers the following suboptions:

1. Data_entry initiates the macro-driven data entry process described in the "Required Data and Entry Procedures" section of this chapter;
2. Head_doc is used to enter five items of documentation that will be displayed as output headings;
3. In_eval generates a submenu for viewing the five Table 9 input evaluation tables;
4. System goes to the System menu;
5. Main_menu goes to the main macro menu; and
6. Y_help displays documentary text describing the Alt-I menu options.

Alt-O, Go to Output Summary. The menu accessed by this macro provides the following principal options:

1. Estimates presents Table 7 which shows the six sets of estimates and projections and the observed values;
2. Out_eval presents Table 8, which displays several goodness of fit measures; and
3. Graphs goes to the Graphs menu accessed with the **Alt-G** macro.

Alt-P, Go to Print Menu. This macro provides access to a menu that can be used to print out any of six output tables individually. All six tables can be printed by choosing the All option.

Alt-S, Go to System Menu. This option allows the user to access all of the other macro commands from a Lotus-like command menu. The following options are provided:

1. View goes to the View menu accessed with the **Alt-I** macro;
2. Input goes to the Input menu accessed with the **Alt-I** macro;
3. Output goes to the Output and evaluation menu accessed with the **Alt-O** macro;
4. Quit/save accesses the standard **Alt-Q**, Quit/save, menu;
5. Print goes to the Print menu accessed with the **Alt-P** macro;
6. Main_menu goes to the main macro menu; and
7. Help displays documentation on the **Alt-S** menu options.

Alt-V, Go to View Menu. The menu accessed by this macro provides the following options:

1. Comp goes to the Computation area menu;
2. Doc goes to the Documentation areas menu;
3. Loc_map goes to the location map;
4. Tree displays a tree diagram of the System menus;
5. Param is used to view the data entry parameters;
6. Range goes to the range name descriptions area; and
7. System goes to the System menu; and
8. Main_menu goes to the main macro menu.

Data Entry
The EXTRAP model requires observation values for between three and

twenty-one periods; the number of values should be an even multiple of three.[8] Values must be entered for each year or period; missing values can be estimated by averaging the preceding and following observations. Typical periods are four-digit years from the twentieth or twenty-first centuries, although any sequence of numbers with fixed intervals between observations can be used.[9]

Entering Output Labels. Choosing the **Alt-I** Head_doc option takes the user to the Headings Documentation entry area. Five headings, of up to 29 characters each, can be entered here with a DOWN ARROW. This information is included in the headings of the work sheet tables and macro generated graphs. The "subject name" entry identifies the type of data being analyzed. The "region name" identifies the geographic area. The "measurement units" label can be useful if thousands or millions of units are employed, such as "Thousands of Persons." The "date" entry should be the date on which the analysis is done. The analyst's name can also be entered. Exhibit 4.2 shows the portion of the model where the output headings and observation data are entered.

Entering Observation Data. The **Alt-I** Data_entry option must be used to prepare the model for data entry. There are two parts to the EXTRAP model data entry process: (1) entering the years or periods, and (2) entering the observed data values.

Year/period entry proceeds under macro control. Screen prompts direct the entry of four year or period values: (1) the starting year; (2) the interval between consecutive years; (3) the last observation year; and (4) the last projection year. These inputs are used to add or delete rows, sizing the template to include the range from the first observation year to the last projection period. Each value is entered with the ENTER key and is tested by error trapping macros. Do not use the DOWN ARROW here.

The error trapping macro menus guide the entry of the year/period values, catching troublesome entries and giving an explanation of problems and a menu of choices for solving them. Responses include: (1) reentering the problem year, (2) viewing an explanation of the problem, or (3) abandoning data entry. After all four year entries have been made, a menu can be used to confirm the entries and proceed to enter the observed data values or to revise the year entries. Selecting "Yes" from the "Confirm Year Input" menu activates macros that set the number of rows for calculations, insert or delete rows, and copy relevant formulae. Do not press any keys while this macro is operating.

Exhibit 4.2

EXTRAP Data Entry Area

##

Subject Name:	SMURA Tutorial	Time & Date Last..
Region Name:	SW England	ReCalc: 02:21 pm
Measurement Units:	Thousands of Persons	06-Jul-92
Date:	July 5, 1992	Saved: 06-Jul-92
Analyst's Name:	A User	12:48 pm

###----------
LINEAR REGRESSION COMPUTATIONS-TABLE 1A   Bot right = AL573
                (based on CAPT, Tables A.1, A.3)
###----------

Period	Year	Observ. Value (Y)	Index Value (X)	Index Squared (X^2)	Product of Obs.&Inde (XY)	..
		(1)	(2)	(3)	(4)	(5)
		!!!!!!!!!!!!!!!!!!				..
1	1978	4313	-5	25	(21,565)	..
2	1980	4361	-3	9	(13,083)	..
3	1982	4397	-1	1	(4,397)	..
4	1984	4462	1	1	4,462	..
5	1986	4543	3	9	13,629	..
6	1988	4634	5	25	23,170	..
7	1990	!Input above	7			..
8	1992		9			..
9	1994		11			..

Space below periods

9	SUM =	26,710	...	70	2,216

==

N =	6	= count of observed values
Index max =	3	= max index value for X
@MOD(N/2)	0	= 1 if odd # of observ., = 0 if even.

##
THE LINEAR REGRESSION EQUATION:
##

$$Yc = a \quad + \quad b \quad * X$$
$$Yc = 4451.7 \quad + \quad 31.65 \quad * X$$

The macro pauses after adjusting the rows to present a data entry information screen. The user should respond to the macro prompt and enter the observed values into cells next to their year or period labels. The macro will move the cursor to the next data entry cell. Observed data values of up to 9,999,999 can be entered without any commas. Decimal values can be entered. Reformatting with the \Range Format command may be required to display decimals or commas. After entering the last observed value, the user should pause while macros compute the curve extrapolations, calculate various statistics, and prepare the data and labels for graphs. Incorrect data entries can be replaced with correct entries after the macro is finished.

After all the observation values have been entered, the observed and estimated values can be viewed by choosing the **Alt-O** Estimates option. This can be used to confirm that the data have been properly entered and the model is operating satisfactorily. If incorrect year labels and/or an incorrect number of values are found in Table 7, then the data should be reentered using the **Alt-I Data_entry** option. If the only problems are incorrect observed data entries or heading labels, the user can correct these items in Table 1 and press the F9 (Calc) key to transfer the values.

The following subtables of input evaluation statistics[10] can be accessed from the **Alt-I In_eval** submenu: (1) **Lr_geo_para** shows the first and second differences between consecutive data entries and the first differences between the logarithms of these values that can be used to determine the suitability of the linear, parabolic, and geometric curves respectively and (2) **Mod_exp** and (3) **Gomp & log** show data for determining the suitability of the modified exponential, Gompertz, and logistic curves.

Selecting Appropriate Projections. Table 4.3 identifies the input and output evaluation statistics and summary data accessible from the **Alt-O** and **Alt-I** macros. The input evaluation statistics can be observed by selecting the **Alt-0 In-eval** option. These data should be carefully examined in order to identify the most appropriate extrapolation curve.

The output evaluation statistics can be viewed by selecting **Alt-O Out_eval**. Table 8 is displayed, showing the computed ME, MAPE, and SSD values and computed growth limit for the three asymptotic growth curves. The curve with the smallest value for each of the first three statistics is the preferred option for that criterion. The computed growth curve limit may be meaningful or not, depending on the computed values of the curve parameters as indicated by the "YES" or "NO" comments.[11]

Table 4.3

EXTRAP Input and Output Options

Menu and Selections	Table or Graph Viewed
Alt-G Graph menu	
1st_3	Linear, geometric, and parabolic output versus observed values
2nd_3	Modified exponential, Gompertz, and logistic output vs. observed values
CRV_stat	CRV statistics for six curves
Error_stat	ME and MAPE statistics for six curves
SSD_stat	SSD statistics for six curves
Alt-I Input eval menu	
LR_Geo_Para	Table 9A—Input evaluation statistics for first three curves
Mod_Exp	Table 9B—Input evaluation statistics for modified exponential curve
Gomp & Log	Table 9C and 9D—Input evaluation statistics for Gompertz and logistic curves
CRV	Table 9E—CRV for all six curves
Alt-O Output menu	
Estimates	Table 7—Summary of observed data and estimates/projections
Out_eval	Table 8—ME, MAPE, SSD, and CRV statistics

DATA SOURCES

Any data that are consistently defined and collected for regular intervals over time can be used in the EXTRAP model. Extrapolation techniques are frequently used to project the populations of cities, towns, and other areas for which desegregated population data required by the sophisticated cohort-component projection technique are not available (see, for example, the COHORT model in chapter 6).

Annual population estimates for local areas are prepared jointly by the U.S. Bureau of the Census and designated state agencies under the

Federal-State Cooperative Program (FSCP) for Local Population Estimates. Under this program, uniform data sets and standard estimation procedures are developed and annual population estimates are published for counties, metropolitan statistical areas (MSAs), and subcounty areas. Alternate estimation methods are tested using the decennial censuses. The most appropriate estimation procedure for each state is determined by the results of the tests. Additional details regarding the FSCP, the methods used to generate the local population estimates, and the results of the 1980 tests can be found in Klosterman (1989) and several U.S. Bureau of the Census publications.[12]

The EXTRAP template can also be used to project a wide variety of economic data for local areas, with the U.S. Bureau of the Census's *County Business Patterns* an excellent source for county data.

SAMPLE APPLICATION

The sample application will estimate the population of southwest England (the region containing the historic port city of Bristol) for 1990, 1992, and 1994 using the data in Table 4.4.

The first step is to use the **Alt-D** Steps option to review the eight steps for running the EXTRAP model. The user can then select the **Alt-I** Head_doc option to enter the following headings information: (1) subject name **SMURA Tutorial**; (2) region name, **SW England**; (3) measurement, units, **Thousands of Persons**; (4) date, the current date; and (5) Analyst's Name, your name. The DOWN ARROW key must be pressed after each response.

Next the user should select the **Alt-I** Data_entry option to erase all of the current data. The model then prompts the user to enter data for the required benchmark years and automatically adjusts the data matrices and labels. The user should then enter the following values: (1) start year, **1978**; (2) interval, **2**; (3) last observed value year, **1988**; and (4) last projection year, **1994**.

After confirming that the entries are correct, the user should choose "Yes" from the displayed menu. The model then displays the "Matrix Adjustment Processing Screen" while it adjusts the number of rows and copies the computational formulae. The "Data Entry Information Screen" is displayed when the model is ready to receive the observed data values. Pressing any key moves the cursor to the location for entering the first observed value. A value of **4313** should be entered for the year 1978 and the ENTER key should be pressed. The user should then enter the remaining values shown in Table 4.4 and wait while macros calculate the extrapolations and evaluation measures. The work sheet can then be saved under a new filename by using the **Alt-Q New_name** option.

Table 4.4

Resident Population of Southwest England
(Thousands of persons)

Year	Population
1978	4,313
1980	4,361
1982	4,397
1984	4,462
1986	4,543
1988	4,634

Source: U.K. Government Statistical Service, 1990 editions and earlier.

Next, the user can confirm that the data have been properly entered by selecting **Alt-C LR** to check the values for the observation years. If the values are not correct, select **Alt-V Param** to view the model parameters. This screen may indicate the source of possible problems. If an "Adjustment in # of Rows Needed!" message is displayed the **Alt-I Data_entry** option should be rerun.

The user should then confirm that the observed data are correct. Incorrect values can be replaced directly with the correct observed values. If any corrections are made to the observed values, press the F9 (Calc) key four times to recalculate all of the model's formulae and messages.

The user can then select the **Alt-G CRV_stat** option to display a bar graph of the CRV values for the six extrapolation techniques. The graph should be similar to Exhibit 4.3.

The graph implies that the geometric technique fits best; the linear regression, modified exponential, Gompertz, and logistic techniques also provide similar fits. However, the parabolic technique appears to be ruled out by this measure because it has a relatively high CRV value.

Exhibit 4.3

Sample EXTRAP Input Evaluation Output

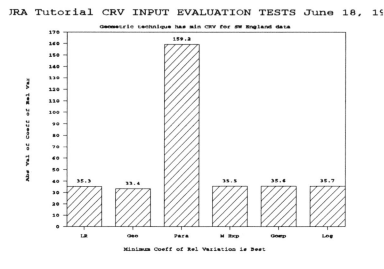

JRA Tutorial CRV INPUT EVALUATION TESTS June 18, 19

The graphs showing the observed and estimated values can be examined by selecting **Alt-G** 1st_3 to view the linear regression, geometric, and parabolic estimates. Values **Alt-G** 2nd_3 can be used to view the modified exponential, Gompertz, and logistic curves.

The summary data for all six extrapolations can be viewed by selecting the **Alt-O** Estimates option and scrolling around Table 7 to examine the projected values for each technique and the maximum, minimum, and mean of the projections for each period. Sample output are shown in Exhibit 4.4.

The output evaluation statistics can be reviewed by selecting **Alt-G** Err_stat to view the ME and MAPE output evaluation graph. **Alt-G** SSD_stat can be used to view the SSD output evaluation graph.

The **Alt-O** Out_eval option can be used to examine Table 8 that brings together the ME, MAPE, SSD, and CRV curve evaluation results, along with information on the suitability of the asymptotic growth curves, i.e., whether the asymptotic limit is a meaningful growth limit.

Exhibit 4.4

Sample EXTRAP Projection Output

```
#####################################################################
TABLE 7 - ALTERNATIVE ESTIMATES & PROJECTIONS SUMMARY
#####################################################################
```

Subject Name:	SMURA Tutorial			
Region Name:	SW England		--->	
Measurement Units:	Thousands of Persons		Date & Time Last..	
Date:	July 5, 1992		ReCalc: 06-Jul-92	02:21pm
Analyst's Name:	A User		Saved: 06-Jul-92	12:48pm

```
#####################################################################################
```

ALTERNATE ESTIMATES AND PROJECTIONS - TABLE 7

(based on CAPT, Table 3.1)

Period	Year	Observ. Value (Y)	Linear Regres- sion	Geo- metric	Para- bolic	Mod. Exp.	Gom- pertz	Logis- tic
		(1)	(2)	(3)	(4)	(5)	(6)	(7)	(8)
1	1978	4313	4293.4	4295.3	4316.9	4319.7	4319.6	4319.5
2	1980	4361	4356.7	4356.7	4352.0	4354.3	4354.4	4354.4
3	1982	4397	4420.0	4418.9	4401.2	4399.7	4399.8	4399.8
4	1984	4462	4483.3	4482.0	4464.5	4459.3	4459.2	4459.1
5	1986	4543	4546.6	4546.0	4541.9	4537.3	4537.2	4537.0
6	1988	4634	4610.0	4610.9	4633.5	4639.7	4640.0	4640.3
7	1990	NA	4673.3	4676.8	4739.1	4773.8	4776.3	4779.0
8	1992	NA	4736.6	4743.5	4858.8	4949.8	4958.6	4968.2
9	1994	NA	4799.9	4811.3	4992.7	5180.4	5204.5	5232.3

| OBSV. PER. MEAN = | 4,452 | 4,452 | 4,452 | 4,452 | 4,452 | 4,452 | 4,452 |
| ALL PROJ_PERIODS MEAN = | | 4,547 | 4,549 | 4,589 | 4,624 | 4,628 | 4,632 |

```
============================================================
```

| Note: | OBSV. PER. MEAN covers: | 1978 | to | 1988 |
| | ALL PROJ_PERIODS MEAN covers: | 1978 | to | 1994 |

```
============================================================
```

EVALUATION AND EXTENSIONS

The EXTRAP model allows users easily to generate and evaluate a range
of forecasts using different data and/or observation periods. The ease of

operation of this model makes it possible for data to be entered and output generated readily by users without detailed knowledge of spreadsheet commands or the extrapolation techniques. This may facilitate experimenting with different forecasts and/or observation periods. For example, the model can be used to display a long series of observations from which to select the most recent trend pattern for detailed analysis. The model can also be used for interpolation (that is, estimating cases lying between observed values).[13] For instance, the mid-decade population could be estimated for areas to which a trend line has been fit using decennial data.

The curve-fitting/extrapolation process, while cloaked in precise formulas, is a subjective art because a large number of computationally correct projections can easily be prepared for a region by selecting different observation periods, assuming different growth limits, and modifying or deleting questionable observation values. Subjective judgment is needed to choose the extrapolation curve that best describes the past. It is also necessary to identify the most relevant historical period to use when projecting the future of a region. The judgment process can be improved by becoming familiar with the factors and forces shaping the phenomena being examined.

The data analysis aspects of the judgment process can be improved by carefully reviewing graphs of the curves generated by the various techniques, along with the observed data they are being fit to. Also, the long-term implications of alternative projection curves can be considered by extending the curves beyond the projection date and by examining the computed growth curve limits. If the long-range projections or upper limits appear unreasonable based on past trends, then perhaps the short-term projections should be questioned.[14]

The curve-fitting/extrapolation technique assumes that past trends will continue into the future. If this assumption is incorrect, the best-fitting curve will not necessarily provide the best forecasts. Unfortunately, we cannot be sure that past trends will continue unabated. Close agreement with past data may result by coincidence or from the aggregate effect of underlying causal processes that may change in the future. Many regions experience long-term cyclical trends of growth and decline that cannot be predicted from short-term trends. More importantly, many extrapolation techniques cannot, by their very nature, predict turning points; those that can, such as the Gompertz and logistic curves, cannot easily fit observed turning points, let alone predict them.[15]

Recognizing that the equation that best fits the past may not necessarily predict the future, analysts should select the equation (or equations) that produce results consistent with their expectations of the most likely future considerations. A number of projections can also be prepared, reflecting a variety of assumptions about the future. For example, alternate forecasting scenarios, including a "baseline" extrapolation of past trends, a "high plausible," a "low plausible," and a "preferred" or "planning" series, can be prepared to inform public officials and the public of the range of futures they may face.[16]

While careful analysis of the data using sophisticated extrapolation and evaluation procedures may be helpful in gaining some understanding of the phenomena being modeled, quantitative analysis of the data cannot replace the need for an understanding of the causes of past trends and informed choices about the ways in which these trends will (or will not) continue in the future. The more analysts know about the past and present, the better they will be able to predict the future.

NOTES

1. This model was developed to accompany the extrapolation sections of Klosterman (1990). See that text for more detail regarding both the extrapolation techniques and their application.

2. See Shryock (1973) for a discussion of demographic curve fitting.

3. For a more complete description of these curves see Klosterman (1990) and Shryock (1973).

4. The computational procedures used to fit the curves and compute the estimated and projected values are described in detail in Klosterman (1990). "Estimates" are values generated by the techniques for periods that lie within the years used to fit the curves; "projections" are values for periods beyond the range of the observed values.

5. Croxton and Associates (1968) apply fourteen tests to a smoothed curve to select the most appropriate trend type.

6. Use of the mean error and mean absolute percentage error as output evaluation procedures is discussed in Klosterman (1990). Note that minimizing the sum of squared residuals is equivalent to picking the line that maximizes the coefficient of determination, which is often called R^2. See Willemain (1980).

7. This discussion draws heavily on Klosterman (1990).

8. If the number of observed values is not an exact multiple of three, the three asymptotic growth curves cannot be used.

9. Only the last two digits of the year or period values will be displayed on the graphs. For example, the year 1992 will be displayed as 92 and observation period 12 will be displayed as 12.

10. See Klosterman (1990) for a detailed discussion of the input evaluation procedures upon which these tables are based.

11. See Klosterman (1990) for a discussion of the asymptotic growth curves and their limits.

12. See, for example, Klosterman (1989) and the U.S. Bureau of the Census (1980, 1985).

13. Earl Babbie (1989) raises this application in his broad-ranging text.

14. Klosterman (1990).

15. Schroeder (1987) is even more pessimistic, claiming that time-trend analysis "will never predict a turning point."

16. These terms are from Klosterman (1990).

REFERENCES

Babbie, E. 1989. *The practice of social research*. Belmont, CA: Wadsworth Publishing.

Catanese, A. J. 1971. *Scientific methods of urban analysis*. Urbana: University of Illinois Press.

Croxton, F. E., Crowden, D. J., and Klein S. 1968. *Applied general statistics*. 3d ed. London: Sir Isaac Pitman and Sons.

Klosterman, R. E. 1990. *Community analysis and planning techniques*. Savage, MD: Rowman and Littlefield Publishers.

―――. 1989. *Community analysis and planning programs users guide*. Akron, OH: Center for Urban Studies, The University of Akron.

Schroeder, L. D. 1988. Forecasting government expenditures and revenues, *Management policies in local government finance*. 3d ed. Aronson, J. R., and Schwartz, E. eds. Washington, DC: International City Management Association.

Shryock, H. S., Siegel, J. S., and Associates. 1973. *The methods and materials of demography*. Washington, DC: U.S. Government Printing Office.

U.K. Government Statistical Service, Central Statistical Office. 1990. *Regional trends 25, 23, 21, 19, 17*. London: HMSO.

U.S. Bureau of the Census. 1980. Current Population Reports, Series P-25, No. 699. *Population and per capita money income estimates for local areas: detailed methodology and evaluation*. Washington, DC: U.S. Government Printing Office.

———. 1985. Current Population Reports, Series P-25, No. 963. *Evaluation of the 1980 subcounty population estimates*. Washington, DC: U.S. Government Printing Office.

Willemain, T. R. 1980. *Statistical methods for planners*. Cambridge, MA: MIT Press.

APPENDIX

EXTRAP Operating Steps

1. Enter documentation headings (**Alt-I** Headings doc)

   1-1   Enter subject name;
   1-2.   Enter region name;
   1-3.   Enter measurements units;
   1-4.   Enter analysis date;
   1-5.   Enter analyst's name;

2. Enter analysis year or period parameters and observed data (**Alt-I** Data entry)

   2-1.   Enter start year;
   2-2.   Enter interval;
   2-3.   Enter last observed value year;
   2-4.   Enter last projection year;
   2-5.   Pause while macros add and/or delete rows and copy formulas;
   2-6.   Enter data for start year;
   2-7.   Enter data for second year or period; continue until all observed values have been entered;
   2-8.   Wait for macros to calculate extrapolations and evaluation statistics

3. Save work sheet under new filename (**Alt-Q** New_name)

4. Confirm that data has been properly entered

   4-1.   View input data (**Alt-C LR**);
   4-2.   Confirm that years or periods in cells AC523..AC525+ are correct;
   4-3.   Confirm that observed data in cells AD523..AD525+ are correct;
   4-4.   Correct any incorrect observed data entries. If the number of years or periods is incorrect, view data entry parameter work area (**Alt-V Param**) then return to Step 2-1 and redo all data entries;

5. View input evaluation graph (**Alt-G CRV_stat**);

6. View extrapolation output

   6-1.   View graphs of regression, geometric, and parabolic extrapolations (**Alt-G 1st_3**);

6-2. View graphs of modified exponential, Gompertz, and logistic extrapolations (**Alt-G 2nd_3**);

6-3. View summary data for all six extrapolations (**Alt-O E**stimate);

7. View output evaluation statistics

7-1. View ME and MAPE output evaluation graph (**Alt-G ERR_**stat);

7-2. View SSD output evaluation statistics (**Alt-G SSD_**stat);

7-3. View output and input evaluation statistics (**Alt-O O**ut_eval);

8. Print selected output

8-1. Print summary output table (**Alt-P E**st);

8-2. Print output evaluation table (**Alt-P O**ut_eval).

Chapter 5

SPOP: Small-Area Population Projection

Iskandar Gabbour

The SPOP model can be used to prepare population projections for municipalities or other small areas that lie within a larger region or county. It can also be used to project other small-area characteristics, such as the number of households, local employment, or consumer retail expenditures.

CONCEPTUAL BASIS

An area's future population provides an important basis for planning and public policy-making. It is the main input necessary to assess the area's future needs for housing, community facilities, transportation, and other population-related facilities. It can also be used to forecast the area's future expenditures, revenues, and tax receipts. The fact that this information can be quickly and easily provided is thus of particular importance to urban and regional planning and management.

Several projection methods, such as the COHORT model in chapter 6, can be used to prepare these projections. However, these models are often unsatisfactory for small areas that are "open" systems, subject to substantial migration flows. As a result, these methods are generally more applicable to larger regions whose populations tend to be much more stable.

The SPOP model prepares small-area population projections by relating them to projections prepared at the regional level. The model does this by projecting the small area's percentage share of the regional population and the region's total population. The projected small-area shares are then converted into population projections by applying them to the projected regional population.

The model uses six mathematical functions to project the subarea shares and the total regional population and selects the best function for each projection. The six functions are the linear, power or multiplicative, exponential, and three asymptotic functions: modified exponential, Gompertz, and logistic.

The regional and subarea projections are prepared by applying a seven-step procedure. First, the observed subarea values are converted into percentage shares of the regional total. Second, the best-fitting parameters for all six functions are computed for each set of subarea shares and for the total population. Third, the six functions are used to compute estimates for the subarea shares and the regional population. Fourth, the six sets of estimates for each subarea share and for the regional total are compared to the observed values to identify the function that provides the best fit. Fifth, the best-fitting function is used to project the percentage shares for each subarea and for the regional total. Sixth, the projected subarea percentage shares are adjusted so that their sum equals one hundred. Finally, the projected regional population is multiplied by the projected regional shares to project the small-area population values.

This procedure will be illustrated by applying it to the observed population values for four fictitious municipalities—Abbott, Barrow, Clarke, and Dorion—that comprise the total population of Meritt County. The example will project the observed subarea and county population values for the six equally spaced years shown in Table 5.1 to the year 1996.

1. Computing Percentage Shares. The first step is converting the observed population values in Table 5.1 into the percentage shares shown in Table 5.2. For example, Abbott's percentage share for 1961 is equal to 646 divided by 2,527 times 100 or 25.56.

2. Identifying Parameters. The best-fitting parameters for the six functions are then identified for each municipality's observed percentage shares and for the county's total population. The best-fitting parameters for each function are identified by applying the following computational procedures (adapted from Catanese 1972; Croxton, et al. 1967).

Table 5.1

Observed Population, 1961–1986

Year	Abbott	Barrow	Clarke	Dorion	County Meritt
1961	646	530	1,133	218	2,527
1966	665	743	1,258	267	2,933
1971	690	971	1,410	360	3,431
1976	750	1,077	1,506	456	3,789
1981	864	1,363	1,834	537	4,598
1986	1,118	2,088	2,309	723	6,238

Municipality columns: Abbott, Barrow, Clarke, Dorion

Table 5.2

Percentage Shares, 1961–1986

Year	Abbott	Barrow	Clarke	Dorion	County Meritt
1961	25.56	20.97	44.84	8.63	100.00
1966	22.67	25.33	42.89	9.11	100.00
1971	20.11	28.30	41.10	10.49	100.00
1976	19.79	28.42	39.75	12.04	100.00
1981	18.79	29.64	39.89	11.68	100.00
1986	17.92	33.47	37.02	11.59	100.00

Municipality columns: Abbott, Barrow, Clarke, Dorion

Linear function: $y = a + bx$

$$a = \frac{\Sigma x \, \Sigma xy - \Sigma y \, \Sigma x^2}{(\Sigma x)^2 - n \, \Sigma x^2}$$

$$b = \frac{\Sigma xy - (\Sigma x \Sigma y/n)}{\Sigma x^2 - [(\Sigma x)^2/n]}$$

where:

x = year
y = subarea share
n = number of observations

Power function: $y = ax^b$
This function is first converted to the linear form by applying logarithms to yield the following:

$$\log y = \log a + b(\log x)$$

Using capital letters to represent logarithmic values, the preceding equation can be expressed as:

$$Y = A + b\,X$$

which is identical to the linear curve equation except that y, a, and x have been replaced by Y (log y), A (log a), and X (log x). Therefore, the best-fitting power function parameters can be computed as follows:

$$A = \frac{\Sigma X\ \Sigma XY - \Sigma Y\ \Sigma X^2}{(\Sigma X)^2 - n\ \Sigma X^2}$$

$$b = \frac{\Sigma XY - (\Sigma X\ \Sigma Y/n)}{\Sigma X^2 - [(\Sigma X)^2/n]}$$

where:

X = logarithm of year
Y = logarithm of subarea share
n = number of observations

The a parameter for the power function can then be computed by raising the base 10 to the power A, that is, $a = 10^A$.

Exponential function: $y = a\,b^x$
The exponential function can also be converted to the linear form by applying logarithms. That is,

$$\log y = \log a + (\log b)x.$$

Substituting Y for log y, A for log a, and B for log b yields,

$$Y = A + Bx$$

The A and B parameters can then be computed as follows:

$$A = \frac{\Sigma x\ \Sigma xY - \Sigma Y\ \Sigma x^2}{(\Sigma x)^2 - n\ \Sigma x^2}$$

$$B = \frac{\Sigma xY - (\Sigma x\ \Sigma Y/n)}{\Sigma x^2 - [(\Sigma x)^2/n]}$$

where:

x =   year
Y =   logarithm of subarea share
n =   number of observations

The a and b parameters for the exponential function can then be computed by raising the base 10 to the A and B powers, that is, $a = 10^A$ and $b = 10^B$

Modified exponential function: $y = k + a\ b^x$
The a, b, and k (asymptote) parameter values for the three asymptotic functions are obtained by dividing the observations into three subgroups that contain the same number of observations (two in this example). For the modified exponential curve:

$$b = n\sqrt{\frac{\Sigma_3 y - \Sigma_2 y}{\Sigma_2 y - \Sigma_1 y}}$$

$$a = (\Sigma_2 y - \Sigma_1 y)\ \frac{b-1}{b\ (b^n - 1)^2}$$

$$k = \frac{1}{n} \left[\frac{\Sigma_1 y \, \Sigma_3 y - (\Sigma_2 y)^2}{\Sigma_1 y + \Sigma_3 y - 2 \, \Sigma_2 y} \right]$$

where:

$\Sigma_i y$ = sum of values in ith subgroup

n = number of values in each subgroup

Gompertz function: $y = ka \exp (b^x)$

$$b = n \sqrt{\frac{\Sigma_3 Y - \Sigma_2 Y}{\Sigma_2 Y - \Sigma_1 Y}}$$

$$A = (\Sigma_2 Y - \Sigma_1 Y) \frac{b-1}{b \, (b^n - 1)^2}$$

$$K = \frac{1}{n} \left[\frac{\Sigma_1 Y \, \Sigma_3 Y - (\Sigma_2 Y)^2}{\Sigma_1 Y + \Sigma_3 Y - 2 \, \Sigma_2 Y} \right]$$

where:

$\Sigma_i Y$ = sum of logarithms of values in ith subgroup

n = number of values in each subgroup

The a and k parameters for the Gompertz function can be obtained by raising the base 10 to the A and K powers, that is, $a = 10^A$ and $k = 10^K$.

Logistic function: $y^{-1} = k^{-1} + a \, b^x$

$$b = n \sqrt{\frac{\Sigma_3 y^{-1} - \Sigma_2 y^{-1}}{\Sigma_2 y^{-1} - \Sigma_1 y^{-1}}}$$

$$a = (\Sigma_2 y^{-1} - \Sigma_1 y^{-1}) \frac{b-1}{b \, (b_n - 1)^2}$$

$$\frac{1}{k} = \frac{1}{n} \left[\frac{\Sigma_1 y^{-1} \, \Sigma_3 y^{-1} - [\Sigma_2 y^{-1}]^2}{\Sigma_1 y^{-1} + \Sigma_3 y^{-1} - 2\Sigma_2 y^{-1}} \right]$$

where:

$\Sigma_i y^{-1}$ = sum of inverses of values in ith subgroup

n = number of values in each subgroup

3. Computing Estimates. The parameter values for each function can then be used to compute six sets of estimates for each subarea share and for the total regional population. These estimates are obtained by substituting the parameter values and the x value for each year into each curve equation to derive the calculated estimate, y_c, for each small-area share and for the region's population. Since the years are equally spaced, the years values (1961, 1966, and so on) can be replaced by simple index values (1, 2, and so on) as long as the projection year is also represented by an index value (8 in this example).

4. Identifying Best-fitting Function. The function that provides the best fit for each set of subarea shares and for the regional population is identified by computing a coefficient, R^2, that is identical to the coefficient of determination. For the subareas, the coefficient is calculated after converting the percentage shares to absolute values. The R^2 coefficient is computed as follows:

$$R^2 = \frac{TV - UV}{TV}$$

TV is the total variation for the observed values, that is, the sum of the squares of the differences between the observed values, y_i, and their mean, y. UV is the unexplained variation, for instance, the sum of the squares of the differences between the observed values, y_i, and the calculated estimates, y_{ci}.

The computed values of the R^2 coefficient for this example are shown in Table 5.3. The last column of the table identifies the highest coefficient in each case, which is the best-fitting function for each case because it explains the largest proportion of the total variance between

Table 5.3

R^2 for Different Functions

	Linear	Power	Expon.	Mod.Exp.	Gomp.	Logis.	Maximum
Abbott	0.8988	0.9877	0.9219	0.9868	0.9868	0.9864	0.9877
Barrow	0.9179	0.9450	0.9021	0.9354	0.9320	0.9281	0.9450
Clarke	0.9462	0.9193	0.9485	0.9368	0.9379	0.9390	0.9485
Dorion	0.8009	0.8617	0.7670	0.7416	0.7910	0.8241	0.8617
Meritt	0.9069	0.8143	0.9555	0.9875	0.9878	0.9877	0.9878

5. Projecting Shares and Regional Population. The best-fitting functions for each subarea share and the total regional population are then used to project the regional shares and total population in the projection year. For example, the power function has been identified as the best-fitting function for the municipality of Abbott. The power function equation for this municipality is the following:

$$y = 25.6187 \, x^{-0.1963}.$$

Substituting a value of 8 for the x variable yields the following:

$$y = 25.6187 \, (8^{-0.1963}) = 17.03.$$

That is, the municipality of Abbott is projected to have 17.03 percent of the region's total population in the year 1996. Similar procedures can be used to compute the power function shares projection for Barrow and Dorion and the exponential function projection for the municipality of Clarke. The computed values for each municipality's projected percentage share are recorded in Table 5.4.

The Gompertz function has been found to provide the best-fitting equation for the total regional population. As a result, the region's total population can be projected with the following equation:

$$y = 1308.16 \, X \, 1.6994 \, \exp \, (1.1867^x)$$

where the second term is equal to 1.6994 raised to an exponent of 1.1867, raised to the power x. Substituting a value of 8 for the x variable yields the following:

$$y = 1308.16 \text{ X } 1.6994 \exp (1.1867^8) = 11,017$$

Table 5.4

Projected Shares, 1996

Shares	Municipality				Total
	Abbott	Barrow	Clarke	Dorion	
Computed	17.03	34.52	34.95	12.77	99.27
Adjusted	17.16	34.77	35.21	12.86	100.00

6. Adjusting Shares. Table 5.4 indicates that the projected percentage shares do not total one hundred. As a result, the projected percentage share for each municipality must be adjusted by applying an adjustment factor equal to one hundred divided by the total of the projected shares. For example, for the municipality of Abbott, the adjusted value shown in Table 5.4, 17.16, is equal to the computed value, 17.03, multiplied by the adjustment factor, 100 divided by 99.27. The adjusted percentage shares total one hundred, as they should.

7. Projecting Subarea Populations. The subarea population values can then be projected by multiplying the projected regional population by the projected subarea shares converted to proportions. For example, for the municipality of Abbott, the projected population in 1996 is equal to 11,017 times 17.16 divided by 100, or 1,890.

The projected populations for the subareas and the region for 1996 are reported in Table 5.5.

Table 5.5

Projected Population 1996

Year	Municipality				County
	Abbott	Barrow	Clarke	Dorion	Meritt
8	1,890	3,831	3,879	1,417	11,017

Exhibit 5.1

SPOP Location Map

Data Entry	Parameter Computations	Percentage Computations	Welcome BG1..BG20	Macros
A1..L40			Main Menu BG21..BG40	
Data in % A41..L60				
R-Squared A61..L80				
Output A81..L100				BH1..BQ126
Documentation A101..L120				
	M1..AV140	AW1..BF140		
Best Function A141..AP160		Projections AS141..BF160		
		Location Map AW161..BF189		
		Range Descriptions		
		AX193..BE223		

COMPONENTS AND OPERATION

As the location map in Exhibit 5.1 illustrates, the computational portion of the SPOP model occupies an area consisting of nine vertical screens and five horizontal screens defined by cells A1 to BF214. The core of the spreadsheet is used to compute the parameters for the six functions and up to six subareas and the entire region; as a result, the core occupies seven vertical screens. Each horizontal screen is used to compute the parameters for two functions, thus, three horizontal screens are required for each spatial unit.

To the left of this central area are two data entry screens and a screen for transforming the data into percentage shares. The shares data are taken from this screen to compute the parameters in the core area of the spreadsheet. The R^2 coefficients, tabulated in the Table of Coefficients, are compared to identify the highest coefficient for each small area and for the region. The projection results are displayed in the Output screen. A brief Documentation screen is provided just below the Output screen.

Another vertical band, located to the right of the core area, is used to compute the values required to graph the "best" function for each area. The functions are also displayed in full detail below the core area of the spreadsheet. The macros are stored at the bottom of the spreadsheet and a menu of available macros is provided in the Macro menu area. A location map is provided to the right of the macros area.

Model Operation

As Table 5.6 indicates, eleven macros are provided for use in conjunction with the SPOP model. The Alt-D, Alt-L, Alt-M, Alt-Q, Alt-W, and Alt-Z macros correspond to the standard macros described in chapter 1. General instructions for using these macros and other spreadsheet macros are provided in chapter 1. The specialized macros provided in the SPOP model are described below.

Alt-C, Compute Estimates/Projections. This macro is used to compute the six sets of curve estimates and projections. After these values are computed the macro display screen shows the observation data, the coefficients for the "best" functions, and the projection results for the projection year.

Alt-G Graph Output. This macro is used to view graphs of the "best" function for the percentage share of up to six subregions and the total population of the region. This option evokes a Lotus command menu that can be used to select the area to be graphed. The options are identified by the name of the small areas and the region. Thus, a maximum of seven options, six small areas and the region, are available. An eighth option, Main_menu, can be used to return to the main menu.

Alt-I, Input Data. This macro is used to display the data entry screens used to enter the data needed to run the SPOP model. The procedures for using this option are described in the Sample Applications section below.

Alt-P, Print Output. This macro can be used to send a table showing the observed and projected population values to the printer.

Table 5.6

SPOP Macros

Alt-C	Compute estimates/projections
Alt-D	Go to Documentation
Alt-G	Graph output
Alt-I	Input data
Alt-L	Go to Location map
Alt-M	Go to Main menu
Alt-P	Print output
Alt-Q	Quit/save model
Alt-R	Go to Range descriptions
Alt-W	Go to Welcome screen
Alt-Z	Go to macros

DATA SOURCES

The population, household, and employment data that can be used with the SPOP model can be obtained from the national censuses of population and employment or from any other municipal or county source. In the United States, the main data source is the *Census of Population and Housing* conducted by the U.S. Bureau of the Census. In Canada, the corresponding source is Statistics Canada and its publications on population and housing characteristics by census tract. The American and Canadian censuses are undertaken on a decennial basis with a one-year shift, that is, the American census is conducted in years ending in "0" and the Canadian census is conducted in years ending in "1." In both countries, other sources of data are available at other spatial levels, such as counties, metropolitan areas, or urban communities.

SAMPLE APPLICATION

The numerical example presented earlier can be used to illustrate the procedure for using the SPOP model. The data entry procedure starts by pressing **Alt-I**, Input data, to go to the first data entry screen. The names for the four subareas and the county are entered first; a maximum of six letters can be used for each label. Next, the observation years are entered. Six equally spaced time periods (for example, 1961, 1966, 1971, and so on) are required. The year for which the projections are desired is then entered.

The completed entry screen for the sample data is illustrated in Exhibit 5.2. Information is entered for: (1) the name of the county, **Meritt**; (2) the number of municipalities, **4**; (3) the names of the four municipalities, **Abbott, Barrow, Clarke**, and **Dorion**; (4) the years of observation, **1961, 1966, 1971, 1976, 1981**, and **1986**; and (5) the projection year, **1996**.

The PGDN key can then be pressed to move to the second entry screen into which the observation years and municipality and county names are automatically copied from the previous data entry screen. The population figures for each municipality in each of the observation years are entered in this table. The county populations appear to the right of the table and are automatically calculated as the sum of the municipal populations in each observation years.

At the bottom of the table, one is asked to invoke **Alt-C**, Compute estimates/projections, the macro that triggers the whole projection operation. The macro displays the model results screen illustrated in Exhibit 5.3. This screen reports the population values entered previously, the projection year, and the projected population values for each municipality and for the county. In addition, the table shows the R^2 value for each municipality and for the county.

Three options are then available to the user: (1) using the **Alt-G** macro to examine the graphs; (2) using the **Alt-P** macro to print the projection results, as shown in Exhibit 5.3; and (3) using the **Alt-Q** macro to end the session. The **Alt-G** macro displays a list of options for specifying the area for which a graph is desired. In this example, the options refer to the names of the municipalities and of the county.

Finally, one can invoke **Alt-I** to return to the data entry section of the model to change the data, the projection year, or both, and rerun the projection. One can also invoke **Alt-Q** to end the session.

Exhibit 5.2

SPOP Data Entry Form

SMALL-AREA POPULATION PROJECTION MODEL`DATA ENTRY

Please enter the following data:

A. Name of County: Meritt
B. Number of municipalities (between 2 & 6):   4
C. Name of municipalities (6 letters maximum):

1. Abbott	4. Dorion
2. Barrow	5.
3. Clarke	6.

D. Years of observations, equally spaced (exactly 6):

1. 1961	4. 1976
2. 1966	5. 1981
3. 1971	6. 1986

E. Projection year: 1996   PRESS PG-DN

F. Population by municipality and year:

Year	Municipality				County
	Abbott	Barrow	Clarke	Dorion	Meritt
1961	646	530	1,133	218	2,527
1966	665	743	1,258	267	2,933
1971	690	971	1,410	360	3,431
1976	750	1,077	1,506	456	3,789
1981	864	1,363	1,834	537	4,598
1986	1,118	2,088	2,309	723	6,238

Exhibit 5.3

Sample SPOP Output

DATA AND PROJECTION TO YEAR 1996

Year	Municipality				County
	Abbott	Barrow	Clarke	Dorion	Merritt
1961	646	530	1,133	218	2,527
1966	665	743	1,258	267	2,933
1971	690	971	1,410	360	3,431
1976	750	1,077	1,506	456	3,789
1981	864	1,363	1,834	537	4,598
1986	1,118	2,088	2,309	723	6,238
1996	1,890	3,831	3,879	1,417	11,017
R2	0.9877	0.9450	0.9485	0.8617	0.9878

EVALUATION AND EXTENSIONS

The SPOP model can be used to prepare small-area projections for the population, number of households, employment, or any variable subject to fluctuations within a larger region. The model assumes that it is better to project the subarea shares of the regional total rather than subarea values directly. The projected shares are then applied to the regional total to yield projected values for the subareas.

Small-area projections are especially important for evaluating the physical and social needs of the population residing in a region. These needs range from housing and community facilities to social programs for particular segments of the population. This information also assists planners in projecting other variables of interest, such as future school enrollments, consumer expenditures, trip generations, and tax revenues. The model outputs can thus serve as input to any number of other models for applications ranging from urban activity location to urban transportation planning.

The model currently projects the characteristics of up to six subareas and the region that comprises them for six equally spaced time periods. A minimum of six time periods is required to divide the values evenly into three subgroups for computing the asymptotic curve parameters. Equally spaced time periods are also required to compute all six sets of parameters.

The model could be revised to consider data for more than six time periods as long as the total number of periods is evenly divisible by three, that is, 9, 12, 15, and so on. However, this would require modifying the data entry, computational, and output components of the model to accommodate the larger number of observations and computed estimates. The model can also be expanded to prepare projections for regions with more than six subareas. In these cases, the model can be used to prepare projections for five subareas in one model run, with the remaining areas aggregated into a sixth dummy region. The model can then be rerun as needed to generate projections for new sets of five subareas (and corresponding dummy areas) until projections have been prepared for all subareas.

The model could also be extended to incorporate error and consistency checks on the data entered by the user. For example, the model uses logarithms to compute some of the function parameters. Logarithms can be computed only for positive numbers, so error checks could be provided to check for negative values, indicating that inappropriate data values may have been entered.

REFERENCES

Catanese, A. J. 1972. *Scientific methods of urban analysis.* Urbana, IL: University of Illinois Press.

Croxton, F. E., Cowden, D. J., and Klein, S. 1967. *Applied general statistics,* 3d ed. Englewood Cliffs, NJ: Prentice Hall.

Chapter 6

COHORT: Cohort Component Population Projection

Ned Levine

COHORT is a simplified cohort component model that generates population projections for a twenty-year period. The cohorts are five-year age groups from 0 to 4 through 80 to 84; the oldest age group is 85 and over. The accounting is done separately for females and males. The user enters data for a base year population (by age-sex groups), the population ten years earlier (by age-sex groups), and survival rates (that is, the probability that a cohort will survive to the next age group).

The program then estimates existing fertility and net-migration levels. Fertility is calculated by taking the ratio of children to women of childbearing age (child-women ratios). These are done for two age groups: 1) children 0 to 4 relative to women ages 10 to 49, and 2) children 5 to 9 relative to women ages 10 to 49. Migration is inferred from the data. The program calculates net migration ratios between the two time periods and will calculate how many additional net-migrants will arrive in the next ten years assuming no change. The user can then adjust future estimates of mortality, fertility, and migration for each of the two ten-year periods, yielding projections for five, ten, fifteen, and twenty years after the base year.

CONCEPTUAL BASIS

The cohort component technique is one of the oldest and most widely used procedures for projecting populations. The technique has a long and

85

illustrious history. It was developed by Edwin Cannon in 1895 as a simple method of accounting for population growth (Cannon 1895). It is based on the so-called balancing equation where population growth is the result of added births, deducted deaths, added in-migrants, and deducted out-migrants. It is usually written as:

$$P_1 = P_0 + (B - D) + (IM - OM)$$

where P_0 is the initial population at time, t_0, P_1 is the population at a later time, t_1, B is the number of births occurring between times t_0 and t_1, D is the number of deaths occurring in the time period, IM is the number of in-migrants to the area in the time period, and OM is the number of out-migrants from the area in the time period. The difference between births and deaths is called natural increase while the difference between in-migrants and out-migrants is called net migration.

This model is true by definition. There is no other way that population can change except through births, deaths, in-migration, and out-migration. It is an "accounting" equation; one simply adds and subtracts changes to the existing population base. Cannon applied this equation to individual age cohorts. He diminished the population of each age group by assuming a constant mortality probability and added births by taking the ratio of births to women between the ages of twenty and forty. He did not consider net migration in his equation nor did he consider that both mortality and fertility probabilities might change. Consequently, his predictions for twenty and thirty years in the future were considerably off by the time they arrived.

The modern use of cohort components comes from Whelpton (1936), who considered separately each of the three components of population growth in cohorts—deaths, births, and migration. The balancing equation is applied to individual age groups. Thus, the general equation for the population older than ages t_0-t_1 becomes

$$p_{1i} = p_{0i} - d_i + (im_i - om_i)$$

because there are no more "births" into these age groups; p, d, b, im, and om have the same meaning as before except that they are applied to individual age groups, i. For those younger than ages t_0-t_1, the equation becomes

$$p_{1i} = p_{0i} + (b_i - d_i) + (im_i - om_i)$$

For the youngest age group, p_{oi} is obviously zero.

The accounting is done within each age group. For all those age groups who were alive at the beginning time period, t_0, change is enumerated by subtracting those persons who die, adding those persons who migrate into the analysis region and subtracting those persons who leave the region. Usually this is done in three steps. First, mortality is subtracted from the earlier population by applying a survival ratio; this is the probability that a member of the cohort will survive until the next age group.

Second, for all age groups that were born since the beginning time period, t_0, births must be added to the equation. Fertility is calculated using a variety of techniques. For example, a simple ratio of the number of children ages zero to four to women in the reproductive years (for instance, 10 to 49) can be applied to project the expected number of surviving children. More elaborate techniques can be used based on extrapolations of age-specific birthrates.[1]

Third, migration is either inferred from the model or estimated independently. It can be inferred by applying the balancing equation in reverse. If one knows the population for two census years and a correct enumeration of births and deaths, then net migration (the difference between in-migrants and out-migrants) can be calculated for each age group. If one is willing to assume that the ratio of calculated net-migration for an age group to the population of the age group will remain constant over the next time period, then a projection of future net migration can be made.

This accounting is done for each age group and the end result is a model of the population at time, t_1. If we are willing to assume that t_1 is some time in the future and to make assumptions about future mortality, fertility, and migration, then the model becomes a forecast of the population at this future time.

A distinction should be made in using the model for estimation compared to using it for projection. In *estimation*, one is using the analysis to interpolate population values for intermediate years between two enumerations. Thus, if a census is carried out at one period of time, say 1980, and another census is carried out ten years later, 1990, then one can use the cohort component method to estimate the population for intermediate years (for example, 1985). In this case, P_0 and P_1 are known exactly for individual age groups and births and deaths are known fairly accurately for individual age groups; as a result, one can usually interpolate intermediate years fairly accurately. Further, because the population sizes, births, and deaths are known, it is possible to estimate the net effect of migration by manipulating the balancing equation.

Using the method to forecast a population into the future, however, is a different matter altogether. *Projection* requires the extrapolation of past population values into the future. There is no guarantee that the extrapolation will be correct. In the case of the cohort component method, each component—births, deaths, and net migration—is extrapolated into the future, say ten or twenty years. The extent to that past trends will hold in the future is, of course, a leap of faith.

The advantage of the cohort component technique as a projection tool is that it accounts for each individual age group, thereby minimizing enumeration errors. For all those age groups which were alive at the time of the latest census, one has to estimate future mortality and net migration. For all those cohorts who are to be born after the latest census, one must estimate expected fertility levels. As we shall see, these can be formidable tasks.

COMPONENTS AND OPERATION

As Exhibit 6.1 shows, the COHORT model is divided into four general sections: (1) a data entry section; (2) a section containing the projections for the first ten years; (3) a section containing the projections for the second ten years; and (4) a section for entering adjustment values for future survival rates, net migration ratios, and child-women ratios.

In the *data entry* section, the user enters population values (by age-sex groups) for the base year, the population ten years earlier, and a survival table. Sources for these data are described in the data sources section.

The program then calculates for each age group: (1) the proportion of the population in the age group for the base year and ten years earlier; (2) the expected number of survivors from ten years earlier; and (3) differences between the number of persons enumerated in the base year (the "observed" population) and the expected population; this difference is taken as "net migrants." Net migrants are then calculated as a proportion of the earlier population (net migration ratios) and projected ten years into the future, assuming constant net migration ratios hold. Child-women ratios are also calculated for the base year. These are done for two age groups: (1) children under five as a proportion of women ages

Exhibit 6.1

COHORT Location Map

BASEYEAR DATA	LAST TEN YEAR	NEXT TEN YEARS	CHILD WOMEN RATIOS	AGE GROUP PROPORTIONS	SECOND TEN YEARS	WELCOME SCREEN	MACROS	LOCATION MAP	RANGE DESCRIPT
B2..K31	L2..R32	S2..AT32	AJ2..AL30	AM2..BD32	BF2..DC32	DG1..DI20		DZ1..ER15	ET1..EW45
						MAIN MENU DG21..DI40			
						MODEL DOCUMENT DG41..DI71			
							DK1.DT141		

10 to 49, and (2) children between five and ten (5 to 9) as a proportion of women ages 10 to 49.

Model Operation

As Table 6.1 indicates, thirteen macros are provided for use in conjunction with the COHORT model. The Alt-D, Alt-L, Alt-M, Alt-Q, Alt-R, Alt-W, and Alt-Z macros correspond to the standard macros described in chapter 1. General instructions for using these macros are provided in chapter 1. The eight specialized macros provided for the COHORT model are described below:

Table 6.1

COHORT Macros

Alt-A	Enter identification labels
Alt-C	Compute projections
Alt-D	Go to Documentation
Alt-G	Graph output
Alt-I	Input data
Alt-L	Go to Location map
Alt-M	Go to Main menu
Alt-O	Show Output
Alt-P	Print output
Alt-Q	Quit/Save model
Alt-R	Go to Range descriptions
Alt-W	Go to Welcome screen
Alt-Z	Go to macros

Alt-A, Enter Identification Labels. This macro provides two options for entering identification labels that are transferred to the template at several locations.

1. Place, that is used to enter the region name; and
2. Base_year, that is used to enter the year for which the observed population data are provided.

Alt-C, Compute projections. This option computes the projected population ten and twenty years into the future. This option should be used after the data have been initially entered, and whenever a model's assumptions have been changed.

Alt-G, Graph output. This option is used to generate graphical displays of the model output. The following options are provided:

1. Migration, graph net migration ratios for the ten years prior to the base year;
2. Future, graph future and current age distributions. The following suboptions are provided: (1) 5_Years, graph population five years in the future; (2) 10_Years, graph population ten years in the future; (3) 15_Years, graph population fifteen years in the future; (d) 20_Years, graph population twenty years in the future. Each of these options allows the user to then graph either the male or female population; and
3. Main_menu, return to the Main menu.

Alt-I, Input Data. This macro is used to enter the required population data. It generates a Lotus-style menu that provides the following options:

1. Population, for entering the population by age group; three suboptions are provided: (1) Base_Year, enter the base year population; and (2) Previous, enter the population ten years previously; and (3) Main_menu; return to the main menu;
2. Births, for entering child-women rations for ages 0 to 4 and 5 to 9. Two suboptions are provided: (1) First, enter child-women ratios for the first ten years; and (2) Second, enter child-women ratios for the second ten years;
3. Adjustments, for adjusting the survival rates and migration ratios; the following suboptions are provided: (1) Survival, adjust the survival rates; (2) Migration, adjust the migration rates; and (3) Add/Subtract, add or subtract net migrants. The following alternatives are provided for each alternative: (1) First, make adjustments for the first ten-year period; and (2) Second, make adjustments for the second ten-year period; and
4. Main_menu, for returning to the Main menu.

Alt-O, Show Output. This option displays the projection generated by the COHORT model. The following options are provided:

1. Population, for showing the projected population. The following suboptions are provided: (1) **5_Years**, show the population five years in the future; (2) **10_Years**, show the population ten years in the future; (3) **15_Years**, show the population fifteen years in the future; (4) **20_Years**, show the population twenty years in the future;

2. Age, for showing the projected age distribution. The following suboptions are provided: (1) **5_Years**, show the age distribution five years in the future; (2) **10_Years**, show the age distribution ten years in the future; (3) **15_Years**, show the age distribution fifteen years in the future; (4) **20_Years**, show the age distribution twenty years in the future;

3. Migration, show net-migration ratios for the previous ten years; the following suboptions are provided: (1) Initial, show ratios for ten years prior to base year; (2) Estimated, show estimated ratios for ten years after the base year; and

4. Main_menu, return to Main menu.

Alt-P, Print Output. This option prints the entire spreadsheet.

Preparing Ten-Year Projections

To prepare a projection for the first ten years, the user must make assumptions about future survival rates, net-migration ratios, and child-women ratios. Assumptions about future survival rates are made by modifying the existing survival tables separately for each age group. This is done by varying a survival multiplier value for each age-sex group that is preset to 1.0000. To indicate that a survival rate will improve, one changes the multiplier to a number greater than 1.0000 (for example, 1.0050); to indicate that the survival rate will decrease, one changes the multiplier to a number less than 1.0000 (for instance, 0.9995).

It is highly recommended that a user *not* make any adjustments to the survival rates unless there is an overriding reason for doing so. Survival rates are already very high in the United States and other developed countries; changes for the future are liable to be very slight (that is, changing only in the third or fourth decimal place, for example, 1.0004). If a user chooses too high a multiplier, the number of persons surviving could be greater than the original population cohort!

Next, the user must make assumptions about changes in net-migration ratios. The multipliers to be applied to each age-sex group are initially preset to 1.0000. To indicate that migration will increase by more than what is expected, the user enters a number greater than 1.0000; to indicate that migration will decrease, the user enters a multiplier less than 1.0000. The program will then calculate the expected number of net migrants in each age-sex group *after* this adjustment. The user can then add (or subtract) more net migrants to each age group, depending on independent information.[2]

Finally, the user must make assumptions about changes in future child-women ratios for the two age groups (that is, children 0 to 4 and 5 to 9 as proportions of women 10 to 49). The program will inform the user what the expected child-women ratio would be *if* current trends continue; this is done for information only. The user must choose appropriate child-women ratios and enter them into the model.

It should be noted, though, that child-women ratios rarely continue in a linear fashion. Since at least the last century, there have been cyclical swings in child-women ratios that are by-products of swings in fertility (Easterlin 1968). Intuitively, the user must balance changes in the number of children who are born over the next ten years with changes in the number of women between the ages of 10 and 49.[3] If the birthrate of the population is declining (which has historically happened in the United States since the late 1950s), then the number of children born in any one year will tend to be smaller than in the previous year. However, this can be partly compensated for by an increase in the number of women in childbearing ages. If the number of women in these ages (10-49) increases, then more children will be born even though the birthrate is declining.

To estimate future child-women ratios, therefore, the user will have to estimate how rapidly the child-women ratios are changing. Usually during a period of birth rate decline, these ratios will also decline. After a period, though, the number of women in childbearing age will also decline, thereby lowering the denominator of the ratio as well as the numerator. It is then possible that the child-women ratios could increase or oscillate over a period of years. As a result, the user should be careful in selecting child-women ratios and try different ones to see how sensitive the final results are to different assumptions.

After the user specifies assumptions for future mortality, net migration, and fertility, the model projects the population for ten years in the future. It calculates the number of females and males in each age group in ten years, the total population in ten years, and the proportion of males and females in each age group. An intermediate projection for each of these characteristics is also prepared for five years in the future.

Preparing Twenty-Year Projections

To prepare a projection for the second ten years, the user repeats the previously cited steps for a second ten-year period. In this case, the projected population ten years in the future becomes the baseline for the second ten-year period. Thus, net-migration ratios are calculated from the first ten-year period, as are child-women ratios. The user can adjust the survival table used in the first ten-year period and the net-migration ratios. Finally, the user must enter appropriate child-women ratios for the second ten years. The program then calculates a population for each age-sex group twenty years in the future as well as the proportional age distribution.

The user must be aware that the second ten-year period is based on the projected population over the first ten-year period, which is itself a projection. Therefore, any error introduced in the first ten-year period will become amplified during the second ten-year period. That is, the population predicted for ten years after the base year becomes the baseline population for the second ten years. From this predicted population, net-migration ratios and child-women ratios will be calculated. The user can assume these ratios will remain constant or can adjust them. In addition, the survival table used for the first ten-year projection will be carried forward for the second ten-year period; again, the user can accept these values or adjust them. Therefore, any errors developed during the projection for the first ten years are incorporated into the second ten-year period as inputs.

DATA SOURCES

To run the model, the user needs accurate population data by age groups for females and males separately for seventeen age-sex groups. The data must be in five-year age groups until age 85 and must be separately enumerated for females and males. Most likely, these data will come from the Census of Population. In the United States, the census is enumerated every ten years in years ending in "0." In Canada and the United Kingdom, the census is enumerated every ten years in years ending in "1." Many other countries also enumerate the census every ten years. It should be possible to obtain population data for each of two consecutive censuses.

Census data are increasingly being released on magnetic tape (for mainframe computers) and compact discs (for microcomputers). For example, in the United States, the entire 1990 census is being released on magnetic tape and compact disc. Summary Tape File 1 (STF-1) has the basic age-sex breakdowns for census tracts and block groups; STF-2 provides age-sex data for zip codes. Other summary tape files provide more detailed information (for instance, population by ethnicity).[4]

Several sources of age-sex population data are available in printed form. In the United States, age-sex data are printed after each census.[5] In addition, the *Statistical Abstract of the United States* (U.S. Bureau of the Census, annual volume) and state statistical abstracts provide these data. Between censuses, there are periodic surveys conducted by the census bureau (for example, the *Current Population Survey* in the United States) and state or metropolitan estimates by an official demographic agency. For countries other than the United States, data can usually be obtained from national statistical abstracts or from the *Demographic Yearbook* published by the United Nations (annual volume).

In addition to population data by age-sex groups, the user needs a base year ten-year survival table showing the probability of a cohort surviving for the next ten years. It is derived directly from a life expectancy table. If one has the data, the user can calculate these rates using programs such as HALLEY (Levine 1985). Alternatively, one can use published survival tables. The National Center for Health Statistics publishes survival tables for the United States as a whole and for each of the fifty states, usually computed from decennial population information and mortality data for the three-year period surrounding the census year.[6] If a state survival table cannot be obtained, then one can use the national table, though some error will be introduced by doing this.

In the United States and most developed countries, high life expectancies are the rule and survival probabilities change very slowly. Therefore, whether one uses a local, state, or national survival table will probably make little difference to the final forecast. However, in a developing country, where mortality conditions are improving rapidly and there are major regional differentials, the use of a national survival table may introduce significant error if the population has mortality conditions considerably different from the national average.[7]

Data Reliability

Obtaining the data required to use the COHORT model should not be difficult. Problems may occur though because the data are inadequate. First, there are errors in the data, which will vary from population to population. Age distortion is one common type of error, especially in developing countries and among poor populations (Shryock, et al. 1976). There are also errors in correctly enumerating mortality data. It has been noted for a long time that urban areas in the United States have higher mortality for all age groups than adjacent rural areas. The reason for this, apparently, is the high concentration of hospitals in cities; some persons who die in the hospital are listed as having their residence in that city when they in fact lived somewhere else.

Second, errors are introduced by using five-year age groups rather than one-year age groups. This introduces errors in estimation, as there will be subtle differences in survival, migration, and fertility rates within an age group. Third, data are rarely available on in- and out-migration, at least in the United States and other countries that do not have a population register. Consequently, it is difficult to know whether the estimated net-migration ratios over the ten years between two censuses will apply for the following twenty years. It will be necessary to monitor changes in net migration either by following ongoing national surveys (for example, the *Current Population Survey*) or by obtaining data from local surveys, utility companies, newspaper companies, and so forth.

Fourth, it is often difficult to get age data for subgroups more finely divided than geographical area, sex, or ethnicity. Therefore, it may not be possible to conduct a cohort component analysis for all subpopulations. Fifth, and finally, errors are introduced by using wrong child-women ratios. While the model calculates base year child-women ratios and presents the observed ratios for ten years earlier and projected ratios for ten years in the future, it is often difficult to know what future child-women ratios will hold.

SAMPLE APPLICATION

Exhibit 6.2 presents sample age-sex data from the COHORT model. The data are for Los Angeles County; the base year is 1980. Age-sex data for the base year are entered into columns D and E. Exhibit 6.3 shows the five- and ten-year survival rates entered into columns H, I, J, and K.

Age-sex data for ten years prior to the base year (1970) are entered into columns M and N. These are the base data. Adjustments are then made for the two projection periods.

Exhibit 6.2

Sample COHORT Input Data

PLACE = LOS ANGELES COUNTY			1980 = BASEYEAR	
EXACT AGE INTERVALS (T) X TO X+N	NUMBER OF FEMALES IN EACH AGE GROUP	NUMBER OF MALES IN EACH AGE GROUP	PROPORTION OF FEMALE POPULATION IN EACH AGE GROUP	PROPORTION OF MALE POPULATION IN EACH AGE GROUP
-1	59,735	62,327	0.0156	0.0171
1-4	212,073	220,660	0.0554	0.0605
5-9	259,149	270,137	0.0677	0.0740
10-14	278,076	285,878	0.0726	0.0784
15-19	324,135	332,962	0.0846	0.0913
20-24	370,807	376,748	0.0968	0.1033
25-29	354,980	360,464	0.0927	0.0988
30-34	313,001	308,935	0.0817	0.0847
35-39	244,452	242,134	0.0638	0.0664
40-44	201,384	198,995	0.0526	0.0545
45-49	188,414	183,775	0.0492	0.0504
50-54	200,400	188,234	0.0523	0.0516
55-59	201,383	183,057	0.0526	0.0502
60-64	166,307	145,896	0.0434	0.0400
65-69	143,581	113,110	0.0375	0.0310
70-74	112,462	77,110	0.0294	0.0211
75-79	87,997	50,725	0.0230	0.0139
80-84	59,579	27,985	0.0156	0.0077
85+	51,227	19,229	0.0134	0.0053
	3,829,142	3,648,361	1.0000	1.0000

For the first ten-year projection, adjustments to survival rates are made in columns T and U; in the example, no changes are made to the existing survival rates. Adjustments to the migration ratios are made in columns AB and AC; again, no changes to the calculated migration ratios are made for the sample projection. Additional net migrants can be introduced in columns AF and AG; in the example, none are added or subtracted to the estimated numbers. Finally, child-women ratios are entered into cells AK29 and AL29.

Exhibit 6.3

Sample COHORT Survival Rate Data

FEMALE 5-YEAR SURVIVAL RATE BY AGE GROUP sF 5 x	MALE 5-YEAR SURVIVAL RATE BY AGE GROUP sM 5 x	FEMALE 10-YEAR SURVIVAL RATE BY AGE GROUP sF 10 x	MALE 10-YEAR SURVIVAL RATE BY AGE GROUP sM 10 x
ages 0-4	ages 0-4	ages 0-4	ages 0-4
0.9981	0.9974	0.9969	0.9958
0.9988	0.9984	0.9969	0.9934
0.9981	0.9951	0.9950	0.9852
0.9969	0.9901	0.9932	0.9790
0.9963	0.9888	0.9917	0.9778
0.9955	0.9889	0.9896	0.9763
0.9942	0.9873	0.9855	0.9710
0.9913	0.9835	0.9780	0.9596
0.9866	0.9757	0.9658	0.9398
0.9789	0.9632	0.9480	0.9106
0.9684	0.9454	0.9219	0.8682
0.9520	0.9184	0.8843	0.8056
0.9288	0.8772	0.8271	0.7144
0.8904	0.8143	0.7436	0.5982
0.8351	0.7345	0.6199	0.4585
0.7422	0.6242	0.5509	0.3894
0.6832	0.5611	indeterminate	indeterminate
indeterminate	indeterminate	indeterminate	indeterminate

For the second ten-year projection, adjustments can be made to the survival rates (columns BS and BT), net-migration ratios (columns CA and CB), and additional net migrants (columns CE and CF). Child-women ratios for the second ten-year period are entered in cells CJ29 and CK29.

The remaining columns contain the model output, including: (1) net-migration ratios for the ten years prior to the base year (columns X and Y); (2) net-migration ratios for the ten years after the base year (columns BW and BX); (3) the projected population in five years (columns AN through AS); (4) the projected population in ten years (columns AU through AZ); (5) the fifteen-year population projection (columns CM through CR); and (6) the twenty-year population projection (columns CT through CY) after the base year. For all projections, the model produces separate projections for females and males and shows both the total projected number and the proportion of the population in each age group.[8] Sample output showing the projected population ten years after the base year are shown in Exhibit 6.4.

Exhibit 6.4

Sample COHORT Printed Output

EXACT AGE INTERVALS IN 10 YEARS X TO X+N	EXPECTED TOTAL POPULATION IN 10 YEARS	EXPECTED NUMBER OF FEMALES IN 10 YEARS	EXPECTED NUMBER OF MALES IN 10 YEARS	PROPORTION OF TOTAL POPULATION IN EACH AGE GROUP IN 10 YEARS	PROPORTION OF FEMALE POPULATION IN EACH AGE GROUP IN 10 YEARS	PROPORTION OF MALE POPULATION IN EACH AGE GROUP IN 10 YEARS
0-4	595,914	288,655	307,259	0.0752	0.0718	0.0786
5-9	568,514	281,415	287,100	0.0717	0.0700	0.0734
10-14	535,592	263,146	272,446	0.0676	0.0655	0.0697
15-19	535,590	262,372	273,218	0.0676	0.0653	0.0699
20-24	641,753	318,479	323,274	0.0809	0.0793	0.0827
25-29	774,461	377,948	396,513	0.0977	0.0941	0.1014
30-34	807,189	376,173	431,016	0.1018	0.0936	0.1102
35-39	663,693	329,512	334,182	0.0837	0.0820	0.0855
40-44	572,270	291,553	280,717	0.0722	0.0726	0.0718
45-49	443,049	224,697	218,352	0.0559	0.0559	0.0558
50-54	353,578	181,556	172,022	0.0446	0.0452	0.0440
55-59	314,702	161,834	152,868	0.0397	0.0403	0.0391
60-64	299,200	158,903	140,296	0.0377	0.0395	0.0359
65-69	279,562	156,339	123,223	0.0353	0.0389	0.0315
70-74	207,573	122,659	84,914	0.0262	0.0305	0.0217
75-79	158,820	98,512	60,307	0.0200	0.0245	0.0154
80-84	95,069	63,230	31,839	0.0120	0.0157	0.0081
85+	81,923	60,808	21,115	0.0103	0.0151	0.0054
	7,928,452	4,017,791	3,910,661	1.0000	1.0000	1.0000

Macros have been written to output the net-migration ratios calculated for the ten years prior to the base year and for the projected age distribution for males and females, five, ten, fifteen and twenty years after the base year. For example, Exhibit 6.5 shows the age distribution of females for twenty years after the base year; the graph compares the projected age distribution to the age distribution of the base year.

Exhibit 6.5

Sample COHORT Graphical Output

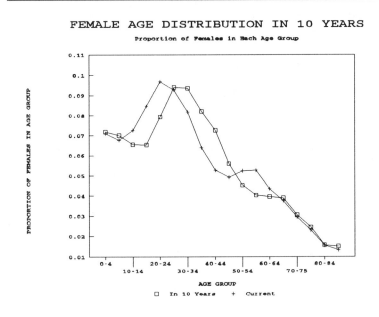

FEMALE AGE DISTRIBUTION IN 10 YEARS
Proportion of Females in Each Age Group

EVALUATION AND EXTENSIONS

The mechanics of COHORT are easy. Whether the projections generated make any sense, though, will depend on many things. Typically, projections work best for large populations and for stable demographic conditions. Problems arise when these assumptions do not hold.

Since the 1940s, the U.S. Bureau of the Census has been examining errors in forecasting both current and future years (see, for instance, U.S. Bureau of the Census 1980, 1981, 1985). Errors are examined, typically, by comparing the forecasts made for geographical areas with the population actually enumerated at the next census. There are several sources of error in forecasting. First, errors tend to accumulate by forecasting for a period and then using the forecast as the basis for the next forecast period. This means that the twenty-year projection is liable to be less accurate than the ten-year projection. Second, populations that are growing much faster or slower than average show the greatest error (Smith 1984). Third, smaller geographical areas tend to have larger errors. For example, the errors in projecting county populations over the 1970-1980 period averaged a little less than 4 percent compared to subcounty populations which averaged around 15 percent errors over the decade (U.S. Bureau of the Census 1985, 1986).

However, forecasting has its problems, even for large populations.[9] Errors for small populations, in which most planners are primarily interested, can be quite significant. The Census Bureau studies mentioned above have shown that typical forecasting errors for small populations over a ten-year period can be as large as the projections themselves! For instance, if a user forecasts a population of, say, four thousand for a particular census tract, the "true" value could be anywhere between zero persons and eight thousand persons. With such a range of uncertainty, small-area projections are very unreliable and should be viewed with extreme caution.

With small populations, slight deviations can upset the model. For example, if a user is projecting the population for a very small area, such as a census tract, a slight shift in the number of persons having babies in any one year can upset the calculated child-women ratios. A slight shift in factors affecting migration, such as the construction of one large apartment complex or the demolition of a large, single-room-occupancy hotel, can distort net-migration ratios. Projections for areas undergoing major change in the residential building stock are liable to be way off, even within a very short time.

To cite one case, projections at the census tract level for downtown Los Angeles yielded *negative* populations in two tracts and one whose projected population for twenty years in the future *exceeded* that of the entire downtown area in the base year of 1980! These absurd projections resulted from dramatic changes in the stock of residential buildings. In the two tracts that showed "negative populations," a large number of demolitions had occurred between 1970 and 1980; projecting these trends led to a negative population estimate. Conversely, in the one tract that showed an unrealistic increase, a large amount of building had occurred between 1970 and 1980; the demolitions had occurred earlier.

Another problem concerns institutional populations, for example communities with a large university campus or a large military population. With these populations, there is a rapid and predictable turnover in population (that is, students come and stay for four or five years then leave). The age distribution of institutional populations tends to remain stable. Including these institutional populations in the cohort component model is liable to distort any projected results; one cannot realistically assume that the cohorts are aging in the same way that populations do. It is better to model the institutional population separately from the "normal" community and then add them together in the end. The institutional population should be modeled with a different logic than the cohort component technique, for instance with a projection of the number of students that the university will enroll over a number of years.

Even with large populations, accurate population forecasting can occur only when demographic conditions are stable. In many developing countries, these assumptions are not true. Mortality conditions are improving rapidly; as a result, the use of current survival rates will typically underestimate the surviving population. If fertility rates are declining systematically, then the child-women ratios are liable to decline at a predictable rate. However, if the fertility rates oscillate—which they frequently do—then the child-women ratios are also liable to oscillate but in unpredictable ways. With a rapidly growing population, net-migration ratios will often vacillate and may overestimate the amount of in-migration because these ratios are calculated with respect to the base population; the opposite is true for very slowly growing populations.

There is no simple way to correct for these violations except to be aware of them and use common sense in interpreting the results. If fertility plummets, the user should be cautious in assuming that these trends will continue for the next ten or twenty years. If the migration rates are changing rapidly, the user should be careful in assuming a continuation of any trend. It is best to examine the consistency of a projection with other projections, for example, with regional projections made by the national Census Bureau. Also, the user should conduct a sensitivity analysis by varying the assumptions and seeing whether these affect the end results meaningfully. For instance, changes in the child-women ratios will affect the number of young persons projected but will not affect the population over twenty years of age. Similarly, changes in net-migration ratios will affect the young-to-middle-age population but will typically not affect the very young and very old. Depending on which age groups one is interested in, the accuracy of the projection results will vary depending on the assumptions.

Finally, caution should be used in making projections for many subpopulations, such as geographical areas or ethnic groups. Typically, subpopulation projections tend to be more unstable than total population projections. For example, if a user makes a projection for an entire population and then makes separate projections for each of several subpopulations, then the sum of the subpopulation projections will usually be greater than the projection for the total population by itself. The reason for this is that subpopulation estimates tend to "blow up" because of sensitivity to slight shifts in demographic conditions. Most analysts usually repeat the subpopulation projections, scaling them down so that they sum to the projection for the total population; the scaling is typically a linear multiplier.[10]

In conclusion, the cohort component population projection method is one of the most important projection techniques available to planners, partly because it relates to the basic question of population growth and partly because it fits existing data sources reasonably well. The technique also has its limitations. It is an unconstrained model of population growth, which may be unrealistic for many situations. It is also subject to errors in data sources, as are all models. Finally, two of the components—fertility and migration—are difficult to forecast with any reliability, thereby making the projected population subject to considerable uncertainty. Nevertheless, the cohort component method is invaluable as a tool for thinking about changes in population size and age distribution. The user must be aware of its limitations and must exercise judgment before accepting a particular result.

NOTES

1. See, for example, Shryock and Associates (1976), chapters 16 and 17.

2. It should be obvious that there is no such thing as a "net migrant." The concept is a derivative of the balancing equation–the difference between the number of in-migrants and out-migrants. Adding "net migrants" to each age group is an analytical adjustment that allows the accounting to be more accurate.

3. Historically, child-women ratios have been calculated relative to the number of women between fifteen and forty-five. However, in the United States over the last twenty years, fertility has increased enormously among

teenagers as well as among women over the age of thirty-five. Therefore, ten through forty-nine seemed a more realistic range for the childbearing ages.

4. For information on tapes and compact discs, contact the U.S. Bureau of the Census, Data User Services Division, Customer Services, Washington, DC 20233 (301) 763-4100.

5. The appropriate volumes and tables for the 1970 and 1980 censuses are: (1) 1970 *Census of Population* (U.S. Bureau of the Census 1973): Table 20—States; Table 24—MSAs, places of 50,000 or more, urbanized areas, and the urban balance of MSAs; Table 28—places of 10,000 to 50,000; and Table 35—counties; and (2) 1980 *Census of Population* (U.S. Bureau of the Census 1982): Table 19—States; Table 25—SCSAs, SMSAs, urbanized areas, places of 50,000 or more, and the central cities of SMSAs; Table 32—places of 10,000 to 50,000; and Table 45—counties.

6. The appropriate volumes for the 1970 and 1980 survival tables are: (1) U.S. National Center for Health Statistics (1975); and (2) U.S. National Center for Health Statistics (1985a and 1985b).

7. Methods of handling errors in age data and various graduation and interpolation techniques are discussed in Cox (1976) and Shryock and associates (1976).

8. For the proportion of the population in each age group (age distribution), separate calculations are made for the total population, all females, and all males.

9. A number of studies over many years have shown problems in forecasting even for relatively large populations and for short periods of time. See, for example, Ascher (1978), Hajnal (1955), Isserman (1977), Smith and Sincich (1988), and Stoto (1983).

10. For example, if the sum of the projected population for the individual subpopulations is 5 percent greater than that projected for the entire population, then each of the subpopulation projections is scaled down by 5%. This is usually done uniformly to all age-sex groups.

REFERENCES

Ascher, W. 1978. *Forecasting: appraisal for policy makers and planners*. Baltimore: Johns Hopkins University Press.

Cannon, E. 1895. The probability of cessation of the growth of population in England and Wales during the next century. *The Economic Journal* 5 (1895). Reprinted in *Population and Development Review* 4 (1978), 695–704.

Cox, P. 1976. *Demography, 5th ed*. Cambridge, MA: Cambridge University Press.

Easterlin, R. 1968. *Population, labor force and long swings in economic growth.* New York: National Bureau of Economic Research.

Hajnal, J. 1955. The prospects for population forecasts. *Journal of the American Statistical Association* 50, 309–322.

Isserman, A. M. 1977. The accuracy of population projections for subcounty areas. *Journal of the American Institute of Planners* 43, 247–259.

Levine, N. 1985. The construction of a population analysis program using a microcomputer spreadsheet. *Journal of the American Planning Association* 51, 496–511.

Shryock, H. S., Siegel, J. S., and associates. 1976. *The methods and materials of demography.* Condensed ed. by Stockwell, E. G. New York: Academic Press.

Smith, S. K. 1984. *Population projections: What do we really know?* Gainesville: University of Florida.

Smith, S. K., and Sincich, T. 1988. Stability over time in the distribution of population forecast errors. *Demography* 25, 461–474.

Stoto, M. A. 1983. The accuracy of population projections. *Journal of the American Statistical Association* 78, 13–30.

United Nations. Annual volume. *Demographic yearbook.* New York: United Nations.

U.S. Bureau of the Census. Annual volume. *Statistical abstract of the United States.* Washington, DC: U.S. Government Printing Office.

———. 1973. *1970 census of population* Vol. I: *Characteristics of the population,* Chapter B: *General population characteristics.* Washington, DC: U.S. Government Printing Office.

———. 1980. Population and per capita money income estimates for local areas: detailed methodology and evaluation. *Current Population Reports,* Series P-25, No. 699.

———. 1981. Small-area population estimates—methods and their accuracy and new metropolitan area definitions and their impact on the private and public sector. Report GE-41, No. 7. Washington, DC: U.S. Department of Commerce, Bureau of the Census.

———. 1982. *1980 census of population* Vol. I: *Characteristics of the population.* Chapter B: *General population characteristics.* Washington, DC: U.S. Government Printing Office.

———. 1985. Evaluation of 1980 subcounty population estimates. *Current Population Reports,* Series P-25, No. 963 (February).

———. 1986. Evaluation of population estimation procedures for counties: 1980. *Current Population Reports,* Series P-25, 1986, No. 984 (September).

U.S. National Center for Health Statistics. 1975. *U.S. decennial life tables for 1969-71.* Vol. II: *State life tables, 1969-71.* Rockville, MD: U.S.

Department of Health, Education and Welfare.

———. 1985a. *Vital statistics of the United States.* Vol. 2: *Mortality Part A.* Hyattsville, MD: U.S. Department of Health and Human Services, Public Health Service, National Center for Health Statistics.

———. 1985b. *Vital statistics of the United States.* Vol. 2: *Mortality Part B—Geographic detail.* Hyattsville, MD: U.S. Department of Health and Human Services, Public Health Service, National Center for Health Statistics.

Whelpton, P. K. 1936. An empirical method of calculating future population. *Journal of the American Statistical Association* 31, 457–473.

Chapter 7

COMPARE: Comparative Analysis Techniques

David L. Phillips

The first descriptive urban and regional studies often examine the spatial distribution of populations, housing types, employment groups, or other social and economic activities. The comparative analysis techniques in the COMPARE model provide a simple framework for analyzing the wealth of spatially related data provided by the U.S. Bureau of the Census and many local studies. By allowing analysts to quickly identify and analyze patterns in their local data, the model should be increasingly useful as information becomes available from the 1990 *Census of Population and Housing* and local geographic information systems (GIS).

The COMPARE model uses a series of matrices to transform data for subareas (such as census tracts) and subgroups with a common attribute (for example, family income, age of resident, housing type, and so on) into a series of conditional probabilities. These conditional probabilities are used to identify similarities and differences between the subareas or subgroups and the study region (for instance, city or county). The model also can be used to prepare graphs illustrating these relationships.

The analysis framework presented in the COMPARE model is particularly useful for examining demographic and economic data from the U.S. Bureau of the Census for the subareas of a region. Cities, counties, metropolitan areas, or planning districts are all appropriate study regions, and census tracts, minor civil divisions, ZIP code districts, or other spatial subdivisions may be subareas. Any demographic, social, economic, land use, or housing characteristics for these subareas that can be subdivided into mutually exclusive and exhaustive categories can serve as attribute classes. For example, the model can be used to examine the age distribution of the population, the income distribution of families, the value of owner-occupied housing, or the status of the labor force. Other state, regional, or local data also can be easily analyzed as long as the attribute classes are mutually exclusive and exhaustive.

CONCEPTUAL BASIS

The COMPARE model is based on general principles for exploratory data analysis and on the notion of conditional probabilities. As Tukey and Wilk (1970) suggest, data analysis should generally begin by examining basic information to obtain insight into the data rather than with an "objective" and exact analysis. This analysis starts with a tentative hypothesis or expected pattern and a set of techniques for revealing deviations from the expected patterns. The concept of conditional probabilities is extremely useful in this regard by providing a simple technique for analyzing data for any variable (for instance, income level, employment category, race, age of structure, and so on) that is reported by geographic subarea.[1]

The data matrices generated by the COMPARE model and the general procedures for deriving these matrices are illustrated in Figure 7.1. The detailed procedures for deriving these matrices are illustrated with a simplified numerical example that contains data for four thousand households that live in four subareas of a community (1, 2, 3, and 4) and are divided into three income subgroups (LOW, MID, and HI). The complete computational example is provided in Figure 7.2.

Basic Data Matrix

The analysis begins with a simple *Basic Data Matrix* that displays the observed data for each geographic subdivision or subarea (such as census tracts) and each attribute class or subgroup (such as income categories) in a cross-classification table or matrix. Data for the subdivisions are displayed as rows of the matrix; data for the attribute classes are displayed as columns of the matrix.

For example, the Basic Data Matrix at the top of Figure 7.2 shows the basic data for the number of households that are in each of the four

Figure 7.1

Conditional Probability Matrices Framework

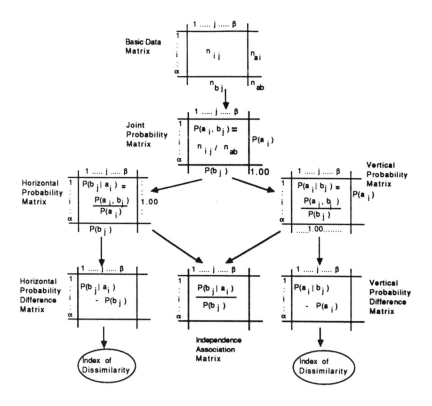

Figure 7.2

Conditional Probability Matrices Example

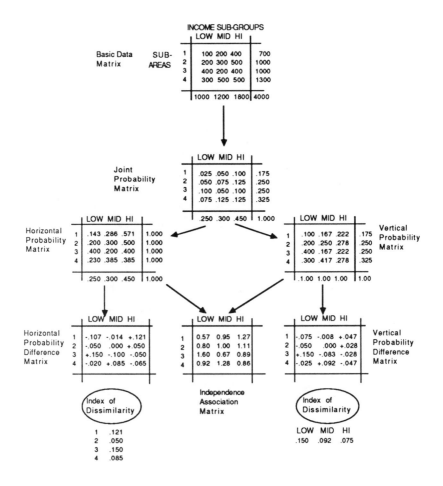

geographic subareas (rows) and each income subgroup (column). The number of households in a particular income category that reside in each subarea can be determined by reading the value for the appropriate row and column. For example, Area 1 (row 1) contains one hundred LOW-income households (column 1), two hundred MID-income households (column 2), and four hundred HI-income households (column 3). The marginal row and column contain the respective totals for each geographic subarea and attribute subcategory. For instance, a total of seven hundred households reside in subarea 1 (row 1) and eighteen hundred households are in the HI-income category (column 3).

Joint Probability Matrix

The joint probability of observing an entity with a given attribute in a particular subarea is computed by dividing the value in each cell of the Basic Data Matrix by the total number of entities in the matrix. That is,

$$P(a_i, b_j) = n_{ij} / n_{ab}; \quad i = 1, \ldots, \alpha; \quad j = 1, \ldots, \beta$$

where:

n_{ij} = observed value for subarea i and attribute class j
α = number of subareas
β = number of attribute classes
n_{ab} = total number of entities in the matrix

The results are displayed in the *Joint Probability Matrix* shown in the second row of Figure 7.2. For example, the joint probability that a household is located in area 2 and has MID income, $P(a_2, b_2)$, is equal to the value of the Basic Data Matrix for area 2 and the MID-income category (300) divided by the total number of entries in the matrix (4,000). The resulting value, 0.075, is shown in row 2, column 2 of the Joint Probability Matrix.

The row and column totals can also be divided by the total number of entries, n_{ab}, to yield the "simple" or marginal probabilities, $P(a_i)$ and $P(b_j)$. That is,

$$P(a_i) = n_{ai} / n_{ab}; \quad i = 1, \ldots, \alpha; \text{ and}$$

$$P(b_j) = n_{bj} / n_{ab}; \quad j = 1, \ldots, \beta$$

where:

n_{ai} =   marginal total for row i
n_{bj} =   marginal total for column j

For instance, the probability that a household is located in area 4, $P(a_4)$, is equal to the total number of households in area 4 (1,300) divided by the total number of households (4,000), or 0.325. Similarly, the probability that a household is in the LOW-income category is equal to the total number of LOW-income households (1,000) divided by the total number of households (4,000), or 0.250.[2]

Horizontal Probability Matrix

Analysts are often interested in studying specific subareas (such as, the characteristics of neighborhoods in the northeastern part of the city) or subgroups (such as, measuring the concentration of low-income families). The first type of equation examines the information for a given subarea reflected in rows of the Basic Data and Joint Probability matrices. The conditional probabilities for considering these questions are computed by dividing the probabilities in each row of the Joint Probability Matrix, $P(a_i,b_j)$, by the corresponding marginal column probabilities, $P(a_i)$. That is,

$$P(b_j \mid a_i) = P(a_i,b_j) / P(a_i); \quad j = 1,...,\beta$$

$P(b_j \mid a_i)$ is the probability that an element in the matrix is in category j, given that it is located in subarea i.

These values are expressed in percentage terms in the *Horizontal Probability Matrix* on the third row of Figure 7.2. For example, the conditional probability that a household will be in the MID-income category, *given that it is located in area 2*, is equal to the value from the Joint Probability Matrix for area 2 and the MID-income category (.075) divided by the row total for area 2 (0.250), or 0.300, as shown in row 2, column 2 of the Horizontal Probability Matrix.

Vertical Probability Matrix

Similarly, the elements of the Joint Probability Matrix, $P(a_i,b_j)$, can be divided by the marginal row probabilities, $P(b_j)$, to determine the conditional probability of being located in a particular subarea, given that one is the member of a given attribute category. That is,

$$P(a_i \mid b_j) = P(a_i, b_j) / P(b_j); \quad i = 1, \ldots, \alpha$$

$P(a_i \mid b_j)$ is the probability that an element in the matrix is located in subarea i, given that it is a member of category j.

The columns of this matrix profile the spatial distribution of the attribute associated with that column and are expressed in percentage terms in the *Vertical Probability Matrix*. For example, in Figure 7.2, the probability that a household is located in area 2, *given that it is in the MID-income category*, is equal to the value from the Joint Probability Matrix for Area 2 and the MID income category (0.075) divided by the column total for the MID-income category (0.300), or 0.250, as shown in column 2, row 2 of the Vertical Probability Matrix.

The Joint Probability, Horizontal Probability, and Vertical Probability matrices provide basic descriptive information on a geographic subarea or population subgroup. Each row of the Horizontal Probability Matrix and each column of the Vertical Probability Matrix can be summarized with descriptive measures, such as the mode or median, and displayed graphically in a pie diagram or histogram. For example, a pie diagram for area 1 of the sample income data set is displayed in Figure 7.3 and a histogram comparing the Horizontal Probability distribution of area 1 with the total area histogram is displayed in Figure 7.4.

These simple measures and diagrams provide useful summary information but do not reveal the additional information that can be obtained by comparing two distributions. The two marginal probability distributions for the study area provide the basis for the most useful comparisons because they address questions that are generally familiar to the analyst. For instance, they can be used to study the distribution of households among the tracts or the distribution of households among income classes. Here they are used as the initial hypotheses for making comparisons between different subareas or attribute categories. The distributions are also the weighted sum of the individual probability distributions and thus represent a mathematical expectation as well as an intuitive expectation. In addition, many social science analytic techniques can be shown to be based on comparisons between conditional and marginal probability distributions (Phillips 1976).

Figure 7.3

Percentage Composition of Area 1

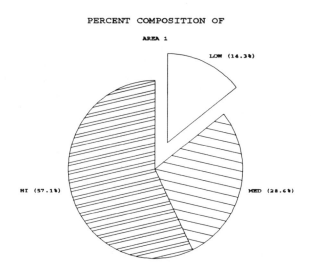

PERCENT COMPOSITION OF

AREA 1

LOW (14.3%)

HI (57.1%)

MED (28.6%)

Difference Matrices

One comparison approach examines the differences between the conditional probability distribution, $P(b_j \mid a_i)$ or $P(a_i \mid b_j)$ and the corresponding marginal probability distribution $P(b_j)$ or $P(a_i)$. The values in the *Horizontal Probability Difference Matrix* are calculated by subtracting the marginal probability values in the *Horizontal Conditional Probability Matrix* from the conditional values in the Horizontal Conditional Probability Matrix. That is,

$$P(b_j \mid a_i) - P(b_j); \quad j = 1,\ldots,\beta.$$

The values in each row of the Horizontal Probability Difference Matrix represent the difference between the distribution for a particular subarea and the distribution for the entire study area.

Figure 7.4

Comparison of Area 1 with Total Area

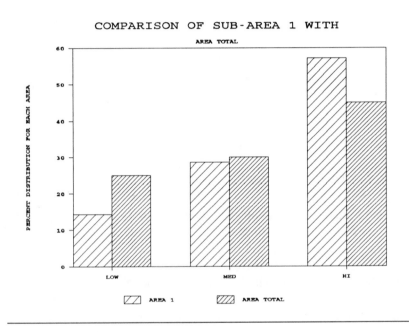

For example, in Figure 7.2, the values in the second row of the Horizontal Probability Difference Matrix compare the distribution of households among the three different income categories for area 2 to the distribution for the entire study area. The value for the first element in this row (-0.050) is computed by subtracting the marginal probability for the LOW-income category of the Horizontal Probability Matrix (0.250) from the value of the Horizontal Probability Matrix for area 2 and the LOW-income category (0.200). The negative indicates that the proportion of households in area 2 that is in the LOW-income category is smaller than the proportion of the total area's households that are in this category.

The *Index of Dissimilarity* values shown in the last row of Figure 7.2 can be computed by summing all of the positive or negative values in each row of the Horizontal Probability Matrix. For example, the index value for area 1, 0.121, is equal to the sum of the positive or negative values for row 1 of the Horizontal Probability Matrix. The index value of 0.150 for area 3 indicates that the income distribution of households in this area differs the most from the distribution for the whole study area. Area 2 is most similar, with an index value of only 0.050. The Index of Dissimilarity represents the proportion of entries in a row that would have to change places with other entities to get identical distributions in a subarea and in the total study area (Florence et al 1943).

Similarly, the *Vertical Probability Difference Matrix* is computed by subtracting the marginal column values of the Vertical Probability Matrix from the corresponding elements within the *Vertical Conditional Probability Matrix*. That is,

$$P(a_i \mid b_j) - P(a_i); \quad i = 1,...,\alpha$$

The Index of Dissimilarity for different attribute categories can also be computed from the values in each column of the Vertical Probability Difference Matrix. For example, the Index of Dissimilarity values in the bottom row of Figure 7.2 indicates that LOW-income households are the most segregated, with an Index of 0.150; HI-income households are the least segregated, with an index value of 0.075.

The Index of Dissimilarity is a traditional measure of relative spatial concentration or segregation and shows the proportion of the members of a subgroup who would have to exchange locations with those in other subareas to achieve a uniform distribution among all of the categories (Duncan and Duncan 1955).

Independence/Association Matrix
The conditional probability distribution and the marginal row and column distributions can also be compared by computing the ratio of their elements. For instance, each element in the Horizontal Probability Matrix can be divided by the corresponding marginal (row) probability:

$$P(b_j \mid a_i) / P(b_j); \quad j = 1,...,\beta$$

Similarly, each element of the Vertical Probability Matrix can be divided by the corresponding marginal (column) probability:

$$P(a_i \mid b_j) / P(a_i); \quad i = 1,...,\alpha$$

The result of either operation is the *Independence/Association Matrix*. The elements of this matrix are Independence/Association Indices, sometimes called Location Quotients, that measure relative specialization of each location with respect to the attribute in question. Index values greater than 1.00 indicate that an area has more than its proportional share of the attribute in question, that is, a positive association between the subarea and the subgroup. Values less than 1.00 indicate that the area has less than its share, that is, a disassociation. Values equal to 1.00 indicate the area has exactly its proportional share, that is, complete independence between the two attribute classes.

For example, the Independence/Association Index for area 3 and LOW-income is equal to the value of the Horizontal Probability Matrix for area 3 and LOW-income (0.400) divided by the marginal value for the LOW-income category (0.250), or 1.60. This indicates that area 3 is "specialized" in LOW-income households, i.e., it has 1.6 times the number of LOW income households that one would expect if LOW income households were distributed among the four subareas that is, in the same proportion as total households. The index values can also be interpreted directly in probability terms and graphed to show the pattern of association.[3]

Measures of the absolute and relative concentration of the attribute subgroups among the geographic subareas can also be derived from the Vertical Probability Matrix. The absolute concentration of these subgroups can be used to answer a number of simple descriptive questions such as "How many of the largest subareas are needed to account for 50 percent of a subgroup?" or "What proportion of the subgroup is located in the five largest subareas?" These questions can be easily generated by sorting and adding the values in the appropriate columns of the Vertical Probability Matrix. For example, in the sample income data shown in Figure 7.2, area 3 accounts for 40 percent of the low-income households and areas 3 and 4 together account for 70 percent of the low-income households; for middle-income households, 41.7 percent are in area 4 and 58.4 percent are in areas 3 and 4.

Graphic representations of the relative concentration, such as the Lorenz Curve (Lorenz 1894), and measures of the extent of concentration, such as the Gini Concentration Ratio, can also be derived from the Vertical Probability Matrix. As shown in Figure 7.5, the Lorenz Curve plots two cumulative probability distributions. The marginal probabilities for subarea i, $P(a_i)$, from the Joint Probability Matrix are plotted on the x-axis. The conditional probability that a data element is located in area i, given that it has attribute j, $P(a_i \mid b_j)$ (that is, information obtained from the Vertical Probability Matrix), is plotted on the y-axis. Values for the subareas are accumulated starting with the subarea with the lowest Independence/Association value and progressing to the largest before being plotted. Thus, the subareas are ordered by their relative intensity.

Figure 7.5

Sample Lorenz Curve

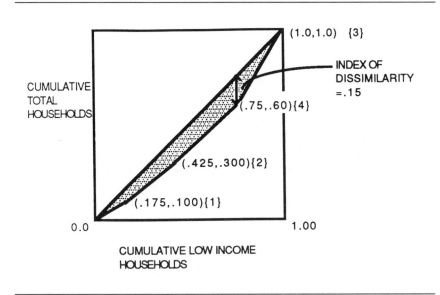

The Index of Dissimilarity is the maximum vertical distance of the curve's deviation from the diagonal in the Lorenz Curve. The Gini Concentration Ratio is the ratio of the shaded area in Figure 7.5 to the total area under the diagonal, or 0.190 for this example.[4]

COMPONENTS AND OPERATION

As the location map in Exhibit 7.1 indicates, the COMPARE model is divided into eight sections. The standard sections are the welcome and main menu windows, documentation windows, location map, macro list-

Exhibit 7.1

COMPARE Location Map

WELCOME A1..A20	DATA ENTRY B1..C26	MACROS				RANGE DESCRIPT	LOCATION MAP BO1..CG27
MAIN MENU A21..A40	ENTRY MACROS						
DOCUMENT							
	B30..C79						
A41..A138						BI1..BM150	
		E1..M207	BASIC DATA	JOINT PROB	INDEPEND ASSOC	SUB-AREA DISSIM INDEX	
			HORIZ PROB	HORIZ PROB DIFF	ABS VALUE HORIZ DIFF	CONCENTRAT COMPUTE	
			VERT PROB	VERT PROB DIFF	ABS VALUE VERT DIFF		
					CLASS DISSIM INDEX		

Note: Cell references not given when locations are dependent on the number of groups and attributes being analyzed.

ing, and range name descriptions. The computational portion of the
model consists of nine matrices and three computational arrays. The
dimensions of the matrices are initially set to eight columns (for eight
subgroups) and fifteen rows (for fifteen subareas). The matrix dimensions
are adjustable to accommodate the number of subgroups and subareas in
a particular study. This adjustment is accomplished using the **Alt-I**, Input
data, macro described below. Therefore, the exact spreadsheet locations
for these matrices shift from application to application and only the upper
left-hand corner (N150) is shown on the location map. Navigation among
the matrices regardless of their dimensions is done with the **Alt-N**,
Navigation, macro described below. The remaining sections are the data
entry window and the data entry macros.

Model Operation
As Table 7.1 indicates, fourteen macros are provided for use in conjunction with the COMPARE model. The Alt-D, Alt-L, Alt-M, Alt-Q, Alt-R,
Alt-W, and Alt-Z macros correspond to the standard macros described
in chapter 1. General instructions for using these macros and other
spreadsheet macros are provided in chapter 1. The seven specialized
macros provided for the COMPARE model are described below.

Table 7.1

COMPARE Macros

Alt-C	Compute concentration ratios
Alt-D	Go to Documentation
Alt-E	Extract matrix
Alt-G	Go to Graph menu
Alt-I	Go to Input data
Alt-L	Go to Location map
Alt-M	Go to Main menu
Alt-N	Go to Navigation menu
Alt-P	Go to Print output
Alt-Q	Quit/save model
Alt-R	Go to Range descriptions
Alt-W	Go to Welcome screen
Alt-X	Re-eXecute data entry
Alt-Z	Go to macros

Alt-C, Compute Concentration Ratios. The **Alt-C** macro is used to compute, display, and graph the absolute and relative spatial concentration values. These operations can be performed only after the data have been entered and the spreadsheet values have been calculated. The following options are provided on the command menu line:

1. Information lists available options and user responses;
2. Selection is a required command that is used to specify the subgroup to be used in computing the absolute and relative concentrations. The default is the first class. The analyst may select a different class by pressing Esc three times and using the pointing keys to highlight the entire contents of the desired column, including the column heading.
3. Absolute_conc lists the Vertical Conditional Probabilities in descending order and computes the location quotient values and cumulative totals. Two suboptions are provided: (1) **Print**, to print the results; and (2) **Return**, to return to the Alt-C menu;
4. Relative_conc compares the subgroup and study area probabilities and computes the Gini concentration ratio. Three suboptions are provided: (1) **Print**, to print the results and the Gini Concentration Ratio; (2) **Lorenz**, to graph a Lorenz curve; and (3) **Return**, to return to the Alt-C menu; and
5. Main_menu returns to the main menu.

Alt-E, Extract Matrix. The **Alt-E** macro is used to save data matrices on files as smaller work sheets that can be used to combine rows or columns for further study (Witzling and Greenstreet 1989), produce a cumulative probability distribution matrix, design graphs, or use as a data base. The following options are provided:

1. **Basic** saves the Basic Data Matrix;
2. **Joint** saves the Joint Probability Matrix;
3. **Horizontal** saves the Horizontal Probability Matrix;
4. **Vertical** saves the Vertical Probability Matrix;
5. **Indep/assoc** saves the Independence/Association Matrix; and
6. **Main_menu** returns to the main menu.

Alt-G, Go to Graph Menu. The **Alt-G** macro is used to display on-screen graphics. The following options are provided:

1. Pie_of_subarea displays the first subarea's probability profile;
2. Compare_area_% displays histograms comparing subarea percentages;
3. Sub-pop_compare displays histograms comparing the sub-group percentages;
4. Indep/assoc displays the Independence/Association vector as a line graph with the 1.00 reference line; and
5. Main_menu returns to the main menu.

After displaying the default graph, the user can press the Esc key and use the regular /Graph command menu to customize the graph, select another row or column to be displayed, or save the graph images to disk as a .PIC file.

Alt-I, Input Data. The **Alt-I** macro is used to enter the analysis data. The spreadsheet initially contains space for eight attribute subgroups and fifteen subareas. The input macro requests the name of the data set, the number of subgroups, and the number of subareas. The spreadsheet dimensions are then automatically adjusted. The Basic Data Matrix is then displayed for data entry, as described below.

Alt-N, Go to Navigation Menu. The **Alt-N** macro is used to move among the major data matrices. The following options are provided:

1. Basic goes to the Basic Data Matrix;
2. Joint goes to the Joint Probability Matrix;
3. Horizontal provides three suboptions described below;
4. Vertical provides three suboptions described below;
5. Indep/assoc goes to the Independence/Association Matrix; and
6. Main_menu returns to the main menu.

The Horizontal and Vertical options provide submenus that have the following options: (1) **Probabilities** that goes to the Horizontal Probability Matrix; (2) **Differences** that goes to the Horizontal Probability Difference Matrix; (3) **Index-of-Diss** that goes to the Index of Dissimilarity; and (4) **Return** that returns the user to the **Alt-N**, Navigation menu.

Alt-P, Print Output. The **Alt-P** macro is used to print the various matrices in compressed print mode. The following options are provided:

1. All prints all of the matrices;
2. Basic prints the Basic Data Matrix;

3. Joint prints the Joint Probability Matrix;
4. Horizontal prints the Horizontal Probability Matrix;
5. Vertical prints the Vertical Probability Matrix;
6. Ind/assoc prints the Independence/Association Matrix;
7. Dissim_index prints the Indices of Dissimilarity; and
8. Main_menu returns to the main menu.

The printer setup can be modified by amending the macro titled MPRINTSETUP. The user can substitute different margins, page length, and setup codes.

Alt-X, Re-eXecute Data Entry. The Alt-X macro is used to adjust the size of the matrices used in the COMPARE model. It is used when a mistake is made in entering data or when matrix size adjustments are desired to test alternate matrix allocations. When this option is selected, the user must specify the data set name and the desired matrix dimensions using procedures identical to those for the **Alt-I** Input Data macro.

Data Entry

The COMPARE model can be used with any data that can be classified into mutually exclusive and exhaustive attribute classes. Generally, one of the categories corresponds to geographic subareas of the study region that become the rows of the analyses matrices. The second dimension, the columns of the matrices, are generally attribute subgroups, such as age cohorts, income classes, or housing value categories. Short names or abbreviations with eight characters or less must be defined for the elements in both classes; these labels become the row and column headings in the matrices.

Data are entered by invoking the **Alt-I** macro to enter the data set name and the number of classes (columns) and areas (rows) in the data to be analyzed. A sample input window is displayed in Exhibit 7.2. Once these three items are entered, the COMPARE model prompts the user before adjusting the dimensions of the Basic Data Matrix. The subarea labels, column headings, and reference areas can then be entered in the Basic Data Matrix followed by the data for the subgroups and subareas. The spreadsheet can store data for up to three reference areas in addition to the total area. A completed Basic Data Matrix containing sample income data corresponding to the example described in the "Conceptual Basis" section is displayed in Exhibit 7.3.

Since data entry can take some time, it is desirable to extract the Basic Data Matrix portion of the spreadsheet occasionally during data entry using the **Alt-E**, Extract matrix, command and storing it in another work sheet file. If mistakes are made in entering the data, an earlier version of the extracted Basic Data Matrix can be combined with a COMPARE of the same dimensions by: (1) setting the matrix dimensions appropriately; (2) using the **Alt-N** Navigation macro to go to Basic Data Matrix; and (3) using the /File Combine Copy /Named-Range **BASIC.MTX** command to import the previously extracted data set.

Exhibit 7.2

Sample COMPARE Data Entry Screen

****

DATA ENTRY WINDOW:
Enter Name of Data Set and Dimensions..Matrix Size will then be adjusted.
If you make an error, reexecute ALT-X.
****

WHAT IS THE NAME OF YOUR DATA SET?:
Data Set Name

HOW MANY CLASSES IN YOUR DATA SET?	3
HOW MANY AREAS IN YOUR DATA SET?	4

Execute ADJUST MATRIX by ALT-A !!! To go to BASIC ALT-N Basic.
****

COMPUTATION RESULTS:

The number of COLUMNS now in matrix:	8
The number of ROWS now in matrix:	15
Adjustment needed by columns:	-5
Adjustment needed by rows:	-11

The values in all of the matrices are calculated by manually pressing the F9 (Calc) key. The results can be viewed by navigating among the matrices using the **Alt-N** macro. Graph images can be generated using the **Alt-G** macro. A pie diagram and bar diagram generated by the COMPARE model for the sample data are illustrated in Figures 7.3 and

7.4. Printed results can be obtained of any or all of the matrices using the **Alt-P** macro. An example of the output provided for the sample income data set is displayed in Exhibit 7.4.

Exhibit 7.3

Sample COMPARE Basic Data Matrix

Sample Income Data Set
BASIC DATA MATRIX

CLASSES:	LOW	MED	HI	TOTAL:
AREAS:				
AREA 1	100	200	400	700
AREA 2	200	300	500	1000
AREA 3	400	200	400	1000
AREA 4	300	500	500	1300
COMPUTED				
AREA TOTAL:	1000	1200	1800	4000
REF. AREA 1	78988	89400	130000	298388
REF. AREA 2	98765	38292	138537	275594
REF. AREA 3	177753	127692	259446	564891

The COMPARE model can be used to examine the subareas and subgroups of an analysis region in order to identify similarities and differences between them and the study area as a whole. This is described below in the "Sample Applications" section.

DATA SOURCES

The most readily available data for use with the COMPARE model are the data for small geographic areas provided in the decennial *Census of Population and Housing*. Detailed population data for major urban areas, including social and labor force characteristics and detailed housing data, are found in the PHC80-2 series of the 1980 Census (U.S. Bureau of the Census, 1983). This information is published by census tracts for the metropolitan statistical areas in each state. For regional studies, county and place data on population characteristics are found in parts A to D of the PC80-1 report series. Similar housing data are found in parts A and B of the PH80-1 report series. Similar data are available from the 1990 *Census of Population and Housing*.

Exhibit 7.4

Horizontal Probability Matrix Output

Sample Income Data Set

HORIZONTAL PROBABILITY MATRIX

(EXPRESSED AS PERCENTAGE OF EACH AREA TOTAL)

CLASSES:	LOW	MED	HI	TOTAL:
AREAS:				
AREA 1	14.29	28.57	57.14	100.00
AREA 2	20.00	30.00	50.00	100.00
AREA 3	40.00	20.00	40.00	100.00
AREA 4	23.08	38.46	38.46	100.00
AREA TOTAL:	25.00	30.00	45.00	100.00

The COMPARE model can also be used to analyze regional economic data, such as the information provided in the annual *County Business Patterns* report series (e.g., U.S. Bureau of the Census 1990). For example, the COMPARE framework can be used to analyze the number of employees or number of establishments at the one- or two-digit Standard Industrial Classification (SIC) code level reported for each county in the United States. Care must be taken, however, to ensure the same level of SIC aggregation is used for each county in a comparative study. Other employment and economic data for small geographic areas provided by a number of state and federal sources can also be analyzed with the COMPARE model.

SAMPLE APPLICATION

The sample data set considered in this chapter can be used to illustrate the procedure for using the COMPARE model. Use of the model begins by using the **Alt-I**, Input data, macro to enter the data set dimensions in the input data window. In this example, the data set name is entered as **Sample Income Data Set**; the number of classes is entered as **3**; and the number of areas entered as **4**. The dimensions of the various matrices are then adjusted and the user is placed in the Basic Data Matrix. The three class names, "LOW," "MID," and "HI," and area names, "Area 1," "Area 2," and so on, can be entered. The basic data values can then be entered into the matrix. The result is shown in Exhibit 7.3.

For a large data set, the user may wish to save the Basic Data Matrix periodically to avoid having to reenter data. This is accomplished using the **Alt-E**, Extract data, macro to copy the Basic Data Matrix to a named file on the disc. After all of the data have been entered, the F9 key is pressed to compute the model results.

The results of the computations are now available for analysis. Typically, one would start by examining the Indices of Dissimilarity to identify areas that are particularly different from the study area and attribute categories that are more spatially concentrated. In this example, one may wish to determine why areas 1 and 3 are substantially different from the total study area and note that the LOW-income population is more concentrated than other classes. This early screening is especially helpful when there may be as many as sixteen attribute classes and forty or fifty subareas.

Examination of the Independence/Association Matrix is often quite useful to identify areas that are specialized in specific attributes. For instance, area 3 is specialized in LOW-income households because it has 1.6 times as many of these households as one would expect if the income groups were distributed uniformly across the entire study area. Similarly, area 1 is specialized in HI-income households. The magnitudes of these distributions can then be explored by examining the Horizontal and Vertical Conditional Probability matrices. These results can be reviewed on the screen or printed out. For example, the **Alt-P** macro prints all of the comparative analysis matrices described above, one of which is displayed in Exhibit 7.4.

Simple pie diagrams and bar charts can be graphed, as shown in Figures 7.3 and 7.4. Line plots of the Independence/Association values can be plotted, as illustrated in Exhibit 7.5. These are initially generated using the **Alt-G**, Graph output, macro, which automatically displays the graph for the first area or class. Other graphs can be displayed by using the /Graph command and the respective named graph to select appropriate data ranges and rename the graph titles, legends, and axes appropriately.

The relative and absolute Concentration of a subgroup (such as the low-income households) can be calculated by using the **Alt-C** macro. Sample results are shown in Exhibit 7.6; the corresponding Lorenz Curve is shown in Exhibit 7.5. Other subgroups can also be selected by using the Selection option within the **Alt-C** macro.

Exhibit 7.5

Sample COMPARE Independence/Association Index Plot

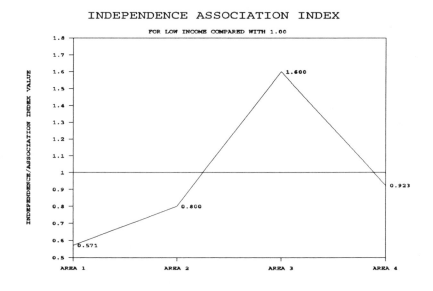

EVALUATION AND EXTENSIONS

The comparative framework embodied in the COMPARE model provides a wealth of descriptive information that often offers considerable insight into the nature and structure of a region. The framework embodied in this model is also very general and can be used to examine spatially related data from a number of viewpoints. For example, the information provided by the model has been used by demographers, economists, and regional scientists to develop a range of segregation, specialization, and concentration indices for evaluating spatial distributions and concentrations (Phillips 1976).

Exhibit 7.6

Sample COMPARE Relative Concentration Computations Output

CONCENTRATION COMPUTATION AREA:

CLASSES: AREAS:	SUB CLASS	TOTAL: TOTAL:	LOCATION QUOTIENT:	CUMULATE SUBAREA:	CUMULATE TOTAL:	GINI COMPUTE:
	-----------------------------------			0	0	
AREA 1	10. 00	17.50	0.571	10.00	17.50	0.009
AREA 2	20.00	25.00	0.800	30.00	42.50	0.050
AREA 3	30.00	32.50	0.923	60.00	75.00	0.146
AREA 4	40.00	25.00	1.600	100.00	100.00	0.200

GINI CONCENTRATION RATIO: 0.190

Model outputs range from simple percentage distributions to complex representations of relative concentration. This information provides a range of useful descriptive information that often can serve as the basis for the planning or policy study for a region. For instance, comprehensive plans usually examine a wide range of demographic, economic, housing, and land use measures to understand the basic condition of a community. They often go beyond a description of the entire community to identify special areas or populations within the community that deserve special attention or consideration. Many policy analyses also begin by determining whether a perceived problem has been correctly identified. This analysis often identifies the extent to which a particular situation differs from the general pattern or from a set of expectations. The framework embodied in the COMPARE model provides a useful tool that uses easily obtainable data to conduct these types of analyses.

The COMPARE model focuses on probability distributions and thus can be used to examine only one type of attribute data at a time.

However, many types of regional information consider the correlation between different types of attributes. For example, are older populations located in the same places as wealthier families? Are the less-educated populations isolated from employment opportunities?

These types of questions can be explored outside of the COMPARE model by exporting selected portions of the probability matrices to personal computer-based mapping and statistical analysis programs. For instance, elements of the Horizontal Probability Matrix provide information on selected characteristics of subareas and on the nature of the study area as a whole. Elements of the Vertical Probability Matrix provide information on the relative size of the subareas and on the concentration of characteristics among the subareas. Examination of the full probability distributions also aids in selecting important and discriminating data for subsequent analysis. Multidimensional analysis of the clustering of similar subareas can also be extended through the use of compositional data analysis (Aitchison 1986).

The analysis can also be extended to compare information for a single study area at two points in time. That is, the general framework of comparing conditional probabilities could be used to examine the equivalence between attribute classes and subareas in each analysis period. This can be done by comparing current conditions in the study area with a second reference region that contains information for the same region for a different time period. This would allow each subarea's current pattern to be compared with the study area's current and past patterns. Matrices for analyses conducted with data for two time periods could also be stored on disk and later combined to produce matrices containing selected information for both periods.

The COMPARE model has also been configured to use marginal distributions for the total study area as the default option. That is, the model provides space for three additional marginal row distributions that can be used to store information for other comparison regions, such as larger regions containing the study area. These values can be copied into the total study area row to make comparisons with other regions.

NOTES

1. The conceptual and computational framework that underlies the COMPARE model, has been developed over the past several years, first at Cornell University by Barclay Jones, Jon Lang, and the author and subsequently by Don Manson. More recent modifications and adaptation to the

microcomputer, undertaken at the University of Virginia by the author (Phillips 1976), demonstrate that many of the traditional descriptive tools of urban and regional spatial analysis can be related directly to this framework, eliminating many ambiguities and much confusion.

2. In the COMPARE model all probabilities are expressed as percentages, that is, one hundred times the probability.

3. If an index value is 2.0, the probability of observing a randomly selected entity within a particular subgroup, *given the knowledge it belongs in the particular subarea,* is twice the probability without that knowledge. The symmetric argument also holds.

4. The various Indices of Dissimilarity and Segregation used in sociology were thoroughly reviewed by Duncan and Duncan (1955). Similar measures have been used in economics and geography. These are also reviewed in Phillips (1976). A contemporary but less comprehensive review of segregation measures is provided in White (1983).

The Gini Concentration Ratio for subgroup $P(a_i \mid b_j)$ ($i = 1,\ldots,\alpha$) compared with the distribution of all entities $P(a_i)$ can be derived by first ordering the α pairs of values $P(a_i \mid b_j)$ and $P(a_i)$ according to the quotient $P(a_i \mid b_j)/P(a_i)$, the Independence/Association value. The values are ordered in ascending rank order k ($k = 1,\ldots,\alpha$). The corresponding elements of each of the ordered distributions are then summed such that E_k is the kth element of the summation of the conditional probability distribution and F_k the summation of the marginal probability. That is:

$$E_k = \sum_{n=1}^{k} P(a_i \mid b_j)$$

for $k = 1 \ldots \alpha$

$$F_k = \sum_{n=1}^{k} P(a_i)$$

The E_k and F_k values are the plotted values for the X$=/$ and Y$=$axis of the Lorenz Curve (Lorenz 1894), respectively. The Gini Coefficient, G, is then computed with the following equation:

$$G = \sum_{k=1}^{\alpha} E_k \, F_{k-1} - \sum_{k=1}^{\alpha} E_{k-1} \, F_k$$

where: $E_0 = F_0 = 0$ and $E_\alpha = F_\alpha = 1.00$.

REFERENCES

Aitchison, J. 1986. *The statistical analysis of compositional data.* New York: Chapman and Hall.

Duncan, O. D., and Duncan B. 1955. Residential distribution and occupational stratification. *American Journal of Sociology* 60, 493–503.

Florence, P. S., Fritz, W. G., and Gilles, R. C. 1943. Measures of industrial distribution. In U.S. National Resources Planning Board, *Industrial location and national resources.* Washington, DC: U.S. Government Printing Office.

Lorenz, M. O. 1894. Methods of measuring the concentration of wealth. *Publication of the American Statistical Association,* New Series 9, 209–219.

Phillips, D. L. 1976. *Comparative analysis techniques: a framework for regional analysis based on conditional probability.* Cornell Dissertation Series in Planning. Ithaca, NY: Graduate Field of City and Regional Planning, Cornell University.

Tukey, J. W., and Wilk, M. B. 1970. Data analysis and statistics: techniques and approaches. In Tufte, E. ed. *The quantitative analysis of social problems.* Reading, MA: Addison-Wesley.

U.S. Bureau of the Census. 1983. *1980 census of population and housing, census tracts.* Washington, DC: U.S. Government Printing Office.

————. 1990. *County business patterns, 1987.* Washington, DC: U.S. Government Printing Office.

White, M. J. 1983. The measure of spatial segregation. *American Journal of Sociology* 88, 1008 – 1010.

Witzling, L. and Greenstreet, R. 1989. *Presenting statistics: a manager's guide to the persuasive use of statistics.* New York: John Wiley and Sons.

Chapter 8

GTEXTRAP: Multiple Region Population Extrapolation

David S. Sawicki and William J. Drummond

Most population forecasts are made by using independent forecasts for the three components of population change: birth, death, and migration. Noncomponent extrapolation techniques focus only on the total population—of persons, households, or employees—without specifying any age, sex, or racial detail. It can be argued that since the population is not disaggregated in using these techniques, little is learned about the underlying demographic processes.

Nevertheless, noncomponent projection techniques continue to be important and widely used despite their theoretical limitations. First, they are central to component projection methods. Second, noncomponent methods are quickly done, not very demanding of data, and provide back-of-the-envelope checks for even the most sophisticated forecasts. Third, detailed age-sex data on birth, death, and migration are often unavailable for small geographic units. Finally, noncomponent techniques are often part of a more comprehensive modeling/forecasting effort or are used when an agency must make forecasts for hundreds of small areas and cannot use more sophisticated techniques for so many areas. For all these reasons, the local population analyst must have a firm grasp of noncomponent methods.

The GTEXTRAP model can be used as a teaching tool to learn and practice applying extrapolation methods. It can also be used to project population totals for different geographic units using ten different extrapolation techniques. The following discussion presents the concepts

133

of noncomponent methods at an intermediate level of detail; enough detail will be provided so that the reader can understand the concepts but not be overwhelmed by the mathematics. Citations are given to sources that present this material in greater detail.

CONCEPTUAL BASIS

The idea behind extrapolation is simple: if a total population (of humans, pigs, households, automobiles, and so on) has been changing over time in some discernible pattern, then we can reliably predict the future of that population by presuming that it will continue to change in the same way. In fact, persistence prediction is a powerful form of prediction.

Judgmental extrapolation is the simplest version of extrapolation. First, data are gathered on past population totals. An explicit decision is then made about the time period of the analysis. Finally, a curve is fit visually through the existing data and extended to future time periods. Figure 8.1 demonstrates the method for the total population of Richmond County, Georgia. In this and future examples, data for 1930 to 1970 will be used to predict the 1980 population and that prediction will be compared to the actual 1980 population. Note that the convention is to plot time on the abscissa and population total on the ordinate (Pittenger 1976).

Figure 8.1 plots the total population against time. However, this is only one way to look for a pattern in past population changes. We might also look at rates of change, the rate at which an area is filling up with housing, or compare the area's rate of change to some larger area's. Three types of extrapolation methods are described below: trend extrapolation, share extrapolation, and differential extrapolation.

Trend Extrapolation
In Figure 8.2, the 1980 population total for Camden County is predicted by adding the average number of people gained in each decade from 1930 to 1970 to the total population in 1970. This procedure seems to work reasonably well, mainly because the total change has been relatively consistent throughout the period. The same method is used in Figure 8.3 to predict Gwinnett County's population change between 1970 and 1980. Because Gwinnett grew rapidly from 1970 to 1980, the

average change for each decade between 1930 and 1970 did not predict
the 1970 to 1980 population change well.

Figure 8.1

Judgmental Extrapolation for Richmond County

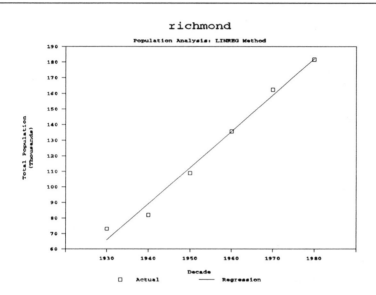

A regression line can also be drawn through the total population
values and extended into the future to project the future population. This
line seeks to minimize the squared deviations between the data points and
the line, achieving the best fit possible. Readers unfamiliar with
regression techniques should consult a textbook on the topic, preferably
one that explains it in a demographic context, such as Klosterman (1990)
or Krueckeberg and Silvers (1974).

This technique can be employed for Richmond and Gwinnett
counties which were considered earlier. Figure 8.1 shows that the
regression equation predicts the 1980 Richmond County population total
almost perfectly; however, a bit of luck was involved. Figure 8.4 shows
that regression analysis is inappropriate for Gwinnett County because
there has not been a consistent pattern of equal growth in each decade.

As a result, the 1980 projected population for Gwinnett County is a large underprediction.

Figure 8.2

Trend Extrapolation for Camden County

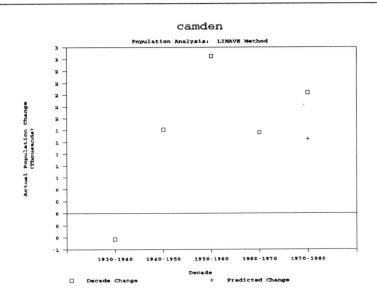

Projecting future populations by assuming an equal number of persons will be added or subtracted in each time period seems rather artificial. An alternative approach looks for patterns in an area's rates of change. Geometric curves are often preferred for these situations because population growth is usually reported in discrete time periods (annually or decennially) rather than continuously. Logarithms can be used to transfer the geometric curve into the linear form. Linear regression can then be used to project the logarithms of future population totals, which can then be converted into the projected population totals. Readers unfamiliar with logarithms should consult a standard reference, such as Klosterman (1990), Krueckeberg and Silvers (1974), or Pittenger (1976).

Figure 8.3

Trend Extrapolation for Gwinnett County

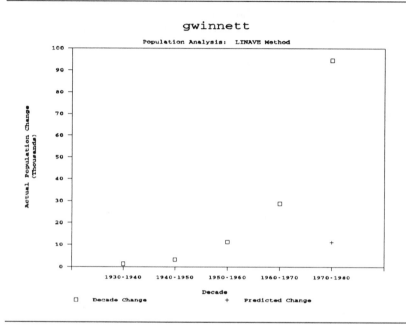

Figure 8.5 shows the results of drawing a regression line through the logarithms of Camden County's population totals. The fit is not bad but the projection for 1980 is off by a bit because the changes in the county's rate of population change were not consistent over time.

Use of the geometric growth model assumes that the population will continue to grow at the growth rate it has experienced in the time period used to fit the geometric curve. This is not a bad assumption in the short run, as many growing populations have done just that. However, geometric growth rates cannot be sustained in the long run. At some point, constraints to growth, such as the availability of developable land, the availability of sewer and water, or the resistance of current residents, will emerge.

For example, between 1970 and 1980, Gwinnett County, Georgia, grew at a phenomenal 131 percent rate. If this rate were continued to the year 2050, a relatively rural county that had a total population of 276,800 and a density of 636 persons per square mile in 1960 would have a total population of more than 58 million and a population density of 91,195 persons per square mile which exceeds the borough of Manhattan in New York City. That scenario is unlikely to be realized in a suburban Atlanta county.

Another possible method, not shown here, computes the average rate of change for the past and extends that average rate into the future. Numerous other possible curves can also be fit to the historical data points. The parabolic, Gompertz, and the logistic curves are three that have been used in the past to describe some type of growth phenomenon, but they add some complexity without adding any additional insight into why populations grow the way they do. As a result, many population analysts do not employ these more complex curves. Readers interested in pursuing them may want to use the EXTRAP and SPOP models described in chapters 4 and 5, respectively, or consult Klosterman (1990), Isard (1960), or Pittenger (1976).

Figure 8.4

Regression Projection for Gwinnett County

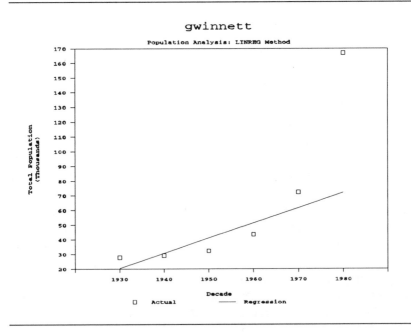

Figure 8.5

Projected Logarithms for Camden County

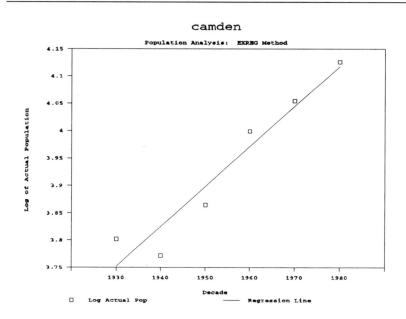

camden

Share Extrapolation

Share extrapolation techniques take advantage of the fact that the populations of larger areas are more easily predicted than the populations of smaller areas. Larger areas are likely to experience an averaging effect by containing areas that have both high and low growth rates. Smaller areas are more likely to experience more extreme short-term growth rates. Change can happen more quickly in a significant proportion of the base population of a small area. For example, half the population of women in their childbearing years could be replaced within a decade by a group with rather different fertility rates. As a result, great care must be taken when forecasting population for areas smaller than counties.

The share extrapolation methods are based on formal projections that are usually available for larger areas, such as metropolitan regions. Past shares of the study area to the larger area can be computed and used to project the study area's share of the projected population of the larger area. To do this, a pattern must first be established for the study area's past shares.

For example, Table 8.1 shows the population totals and growth rates for the state of Georgia and for two fictitious Georgia counties, Hypo III and Hypo IV, from 1930 through 1990. Hypo III has maintained exactly the same share (2.3 percent) of Georgia's total population in the 1930 to 1980 time period. That makes it easy to predict its 1990 total population because the pattern is obvious.

Hypo IV also has a clear pattern: its share over time has grown by 0.1 percent in each decade from 1930 to 1980. We can thus predict that Hypo IV's 1990 share will be 1.6 percent. If Georgia's population in 1990 is projected to be 6,462,313, then Hypo IV's projected population will be 103,397, that is, 1.6 percent of Georgia's projected population.

Table 8.1

Sample Population Data for Share Extrapolation

Area	1930	1940	1950	1960	1970	1980	1990*
Georgia	2,891,803	3,132,723	3,444,578	3,943,026	4,587,930	5,463,377	6,462,313
Hypo III	66,511	72,053	79,225	90,690	105,522	125,658	148,633
III/Georgia Share	2.3%	2.3%	2.3%	2.3%	2.3%	2.3%	2.3%
Hypo IV	28,918	34,460	41,335	51,259	64,231	81,951	103,397
IV/Georgia Share	1.0%	1.1%	1.2%	1.3%	1.4%	1.5%	1.6%

*1990 totals are predicted

Differential Extrapolation

The differential extrapolation technique is closely associated with the share techniques. The historic data in this case are the differential growth rates for the smaller and larger areas. Again, we are looking for a pattern in these two rates. One method presumes that any differences have remained stable over time. The other assumes that the differences have been changing at a constant rate.

For example, Table 8.2 shows the population totals and growth rates for a fictitious metropolitan area called Hypometro and two of its constituent counties, Hypo V and Hypo VI. Hypometro has been growing steadily at 10 percent a decade since 1930. Hypo V has grown steadily also, but by 20 percent a decade. Hypo VI, on the other hand, has rates that have grown by 5 percent in each decade. Figure 8.6 shows a plot of these differences between the county and metropolitan growth rates over time and extends them to the year 2000.

Choosing an Appropriate Noncomponent Model

In choosing the most appropriate projection model, the pragmatic criterion holds: choose the method that works best. Since these techniques do not attempt to explain why a population is growing or declining, theory cannot be used to choose one technique over the other. In addition, very little research has attempted to measure the performance of alternative extrapolation techniques; the exceptions include Beaumont and Isserman (1987), Isserman (1977), and Smith (1987).

Andrew Isserman (1977) used ten different extrapolation methods to project the populations of Illinois and Indiana townships. Historical data were used to project the population in years for which actual population totals were available. Two measures of forecast accuracy were used. The first, the mean absolute percentage error, divided the difference between each set of projected and actual values by the actual value, removed any negative signs, and then averaged the absolute percentage errors for all areas. The second measure, the percentage distribution of errors, categorized each type of township by the degree to which a particular method overprojected or underprojected the actual population. This allowed Isserman to determine the distribution of errors for one or more extrapolation methods for a particular type of township.

Table 8.2

Population Totals and Rates by Year and Decade

Area	1930	1940	1950	1960	1970	1980	1990*
Hypo V	40,000	48,000	57,600	69,120	82,944	99,533	119,439
V Decade Rate	---	20%	20%	20%	20%	20%	20%
Hypo VI	40,000	42,000	46,200	53,130	63,756	79,695	103,604
VI Decade Rate	---	5%	10%	15%	20%	25%	30%
Hypometro	100,000	110,000	121,000	133,100	146,410	161,051	177,156
Metro Rate	---	10%	10%	10%	10%	10%	10%

*1990 totals are predicted

Figure 8.6

Observed and Projected Growth Rates

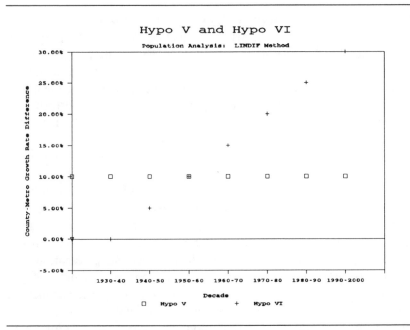

Hypo V and Hypo VI

For example, Isserman found that linear (arithmetic) extrapolation methods were most accurate for modestly growing townships. Geometric methods worked best for rapidly growing townships. Trend extrapolation methods worked better than the differential methods and most share methods. All of the methods worked least well for areas that changed the most.

Isserman's findings are interesting but cannot be generalized easily because they pertain only to a particular time period, to relatively slow-growing populations, and to subcounty units in Illinois and Indiana. Most analysts do not have the benefit of using historical studies on the accuracy of extrapolation techniques for their area. As a result, they can judge only how well each model fit the historical data up to the present. Detailed statistical tests are available for determining how well a particular mathematical model fits the historical data.

Other methods use statistical tests to measure the extent to which the historical data fit the assumptions of any model. For example, the arithmetic change model assumes that an area will grow by equal amounts in each reporting period. The statistical test in this case determines how far each time period's change deviates from the average of all changes. The R^2 statistic serves as the measure of goodness of fit when regression analysis is used. For detailed discussions of different measures of goodness of fit, see Klosterman (1990) and Armstrong (1978).

The easiest and by far the most important method is also the simplest: plot the observation data and the model results on the same graph. Many examples of this approach are provided above. Not only can the appropriateness of a model for fitting the data be judged immediately, it is also possible to judge whether the time period chosen for the historical data is the best. Historical data points that appear to be anomalous for whatever reason can also be discarded.

All of these methods are ultimately less important than asking several key questions: Is this area likely to continue experiencing this pattern of change in the future? If so, for how long? How long has this pattern existed (that is, what time frame should be used for this historical data), and how long can it be expected to persist? Finally, are the projection results reasonable when they are plotted? The answers to these questions provide the final and most acceptable criteria for evaluating alternate extrapolation projections.

GTEXTRAP Projection Techniques

As previously mentioned, Isserman (1977) tested the accuracy of ten different extrapolation methods using data from 1930 to 1950 to prepare projections for 1960 and data from 1930 to 1960 to prepare projections for 1970. These ex-post facto projections were then compared to the actual 1960 and 1970 population totals to assess each method's accuracy. Projections were prepared for 1,579 townships in Illinois and 198 townships in Indiana. Isserman used a mainframe computer to make his projections and assess their accuracy. The GTEXTRAP model allows users to do comparable studies with a personal computer.

The extrapolation methods adopted from Isserman can be divided into three types. For purposes of discussion, the unit of analysis is assumed to be the county (other possible units are discussed below). The first general method, population extrapolation, extends past trends of the counties' growth. This is done five ways: (1) extending the average of population change in previous decades (LINAVE); (2) extending a least-squares regression line through past population totals (LINREG); (3) extending the average rate of population change (EXAVE); (4) extending a least-squares regression line through the logarithms of past population totals (EXREG); and (5) extending a regression line through the logarithm of population against the logarithm of time (DLOG). The first two techniques are linear, the second two are exponential, and the last is double logarithmic.

The second general technique, share extrapolation, extends past trends of the county's share of a larger area's total population. Other possibilities include projecting the county's shares of the region's population or group of counties selected by type, for example, metropolitan or nonmetropolitan counties. Three techniques comprise this set: (1) using the last observed share to project the next share (CONSH); (2) extending a regression line through the historic shares (LINSH); and (3) extending a regression line through the logarithm of a county's share of the larger area over time (EXPSH). The techniques are, in order: constant, linear, and exponential share.

The third general type of technique, differential extrapolation, extends past trends in the difference between a county's growth rate and the rate for a larger area. Two techniques are employed: (1) using the last observed difference in growth rates as the predicted rate (CONDIF); and (2) extending a regression line through the historical differences between county and larger area growth rates (LINDIF). The techniques are, in order, the constant and linear differential. Table 8.3 provides a summary of the ten projection methods.

COMPONENTS AND OPERATION

The GTEXTRAP model is rather complex because it requires the calculation of ten different models for each subarea, five of which require bivariate regression. In addition, the models can utilize input data for three different periods (for instance, 1930 to 1970, 1930 to 1980, or 1930 to 1990) and must calculate predicted values for four years (for example, 1980, 1990, 2000, and 2010). The model results can be displayed as graphs for individual subareas, output tables for all subareas, and an overall error distribution table.

Exhibit 8.1 shows the location of the major components of the GTEXTRAP model, which is constructed in five layers or tiers. The top tier contains the ten models' control structure, including the global variables, macro subroutines, display screens, macro menus, and the macros.

Table 8.3

GTEXTRAP Projection Methods

Method Type	Method	Acronym	Description
Population Extrapolation	Linear	LINAVE	Average population change in previous decades
		LINREG	Regression of population against time
	Exponential	EXAVE	Average rate of population change in previous decades
		EXREG	Regression of logarithm of population against time
	Double Logarithmic	DLOG	Regression of logarithm of population against logarithm of time
Share Extrapolation	Constant Share	CONSH	Share of county population's last observed share
	Linear Share	LINSH	Regression of share of county population against time
	Exponential Share	EXPSH	Regression of logarithm of share of county population against time
Differential Extrapolation	Constant Differential	CONDIF	Difference between county and state growth rates' last observed difference
	Linear Differential	LINDIF	Regression of difference against time

Source: Isserman (1977).

Calculations that are shared by the ten models are collected in the second tier, the precalculation area, so they do not need to be duplicated for each model. The third tier contains the model input data and calculations for the first through fifth models. The fourth tier calculates models six through ten. To save memory, each model is first calculated, the results are moved to the output table area, and the model calculations are erased (unless they are required by a later model). After each model is calculated, the results are generated for three different input data periods: 1930 to 1970, 1930 to 1980, and 1930 to 1990.

The third and fourth tiers each contain a line above the main calculations that calculates values for a single subarea. This line serves as the original version of the model calculation formulas that is copied below for all subareas; it also allows the subarea calculations to be quickly carried out prior to the graphing. The fifth tier contains the four output tables that collect the predicted values for the ten models.

The error distribution calculations utilize the Lotus @DCOUNT function to scan the error tables and count the number of severe underprojection errors (actual value 25 percent or more above predicted value), severe overprojection errors (actual value 25 percent or more below predicted), and middle-range errors (actual value between minus 25 percent and plus 25 percent).

Model Operation

As Table 8.4 indicates, fourteen macros are provided for use with the GTEXTRAP model. The Alt-D, Alt-L, Alt-M, Alt-Q, Alt-R, Alt-W, and Alt-Z macros correspond to the standard macros described in chapter 1. General instuctions for using these macros and other spreadsheet macros are provided in chapter 1. Descriptions of the remaining macros are provided below.

Alt-A, Alter Input Data. This macro allows the user to make minor alterations to the input data. After invoking this macro, the user will see a screen with the input values highlighted in green. Individual values may then be changed; no areas may be added or deleted. After each change the user must press RETURN. After making the last alteration, the user must press RETURN twice to exit.

Alt-C, Compute Projections. This macro is used to compute the projections. The following options are provided:

1. Datayear provides a submenu for selecting the final year's data to be analyzed;
2. Calcyear provides a submenu for selecting the year for which output are to be displayed;
3. Go calculates the projected values; and
4. Return returns to the previous menu.

Exhibit 8.1

GTEXTRAP Location Map

Global Variables F1..G14	Macro Subroutines	Screens	Macros	Location Map BJ1..BO21	Range Descript
	L1..Y74	AD1..AE60 Welcome			
Pre-calc		AE61..AJ80 Main Menu			
E90..M125		AE100..AJ119 Document			
		AE144..AJ163	AK1..AT163		CA1.CG150
	Model 1	Model 2		Model 3	Model 4	Model 5
	D172..AD227 Model 6	AF172..AX227 Model 7		AZ172..CK227	CM172..EH227	EK172..GC227 Model 10
	E241..X296	Z241..BT296			Model 8	Model 9
				BV241..DP296	DR241..EK296	EM241..GN296
				Error Distrib AT336..BE351	
Output Table 1 D325..I364	Output Table 2 J325..P364	Output Table 3 Q325..W364	Output Table 4 Y325..AD364		

Table 8.4

GTEXTRAP Macros

Alt-A	Alter input data
Alt-C	Compute projections
Alt-D	Go to Documentation
Alt-G	Graph output
Alt-I	Input data
Alt-L	Go to Location map
Alt-M	Go to Main menu
Alt-O	Go to Output tables
Alt-P	Print output
Alt-Q	Quit/save menu
Alt-R	Go to Range descriptions
Alt-S	Go to System menu
Alt-W	Go to Welcome screen
Alt-Z	Go to macros

Alt-G, Graph Output. This macro is used to prepare graphs showing the model results. It displays a menu that provides the following options:

1. County provides a submenu for selecting the county to graph;
2. Datayear provides a submenu for selecting the data year to graph;
3. Model provides submenus for selecting which of the ten models to graph;
4. Save saves the most recently created graph as a Lotus.PIC file; and
5. Return returns to the previous menu or macro.

Alt-I, Input Data. This macro is used to enter the data. It produces a menu with the following options:

1. List lists the work sheet files in a user-specified directory;
2. File selects a particular work sheet file to load;
3. Go loads the selected file; and
4. Return returns to the previous menu or macro.

Alt-O, Go to Output Tables. This macro allows the user to choose among five output tables for on-screen viewing. The following options are provided:

1. Lin/Dlog-Pred views the four linear and double log predicted values;
2. Lin/Dlog-Err views the four linear and double log errors;
3. Other-Pred views the other model predicted values;
4. Other-Err views the other model errors;
5. Error-Dist views the distribution of the error terms;
6. Down pages down through a long table;
7. Up pages up through a long table; and
8. Return returns to the previous menu or macro.

Alt-P, Print Output. This macro is used to print the output. It shows a menu that contains the following options:

1. Calculate calculates the output tables (if they have not been calculated), using the menus invoked with the Alt-C macro;
2. Go prints the five output tables described in the Alt-O, Go to Output tables, macro; and
3. Return returns to the previous menu.

Alt-S, Go to System Menu. This option provides a Lotus-compatible menu system for performing all of the operations that are provided by the standard macro menu. The following options are provided:

1. Help displays the model documentation screen and returns the user to the system menu;
2. Input enters a work sheet or a work sheet range into the GTEXTRAP model; the available options correspond to those provided by the **Alt-I** macro;
3. Alter modifies one or more data values; the available options correspond to those of the **Alt-A** macro;
4. Graph graphs the model results; the available options correspond to the **Alt-G** macro;
5. Calculate calculates the model output; the available options correspond to the **Alt-C** macro;

6. View views output tables; the available options correspond to the **Alt-O** macro;
7. Print prints the predicted or error terms; the available options correspond to the **Alt-P** macro; and
8. Main returns to main menu

PROCEDURAL STEPS

Three general operations are involved in using the GTEXTRAP model. First, the basic population data must be entered into the model and adjusted, if necessary. Second, graphs can be prepared showing the output for any of the models and any of the subareas. Third, the user can view or print a series of five tables showing the predicted values, the percentage errors, and the distribution of those errors for all subareas and for all ten models. These three operations will be discussed in turn.

Data Entry and Modification

The first step is the preparation of a separate work sheet that contains the input data. The GADATA.WK1 work sheet supplied with the model can be consulted for an example of how such a work sheet should be created. The input data spreadsheet consists of a rectangular data area that is ten columns wide and has one row for each subarea to be studied. The number of subareas the model can accommodate is dependent on the amount of free memory available in the microcomputer. Most microcomputers can handle fifty subareas. A computer with 640 kilobytes of memory and no memory resident programs can usually handle about twenty-five subareas.

The first row of the data area holds the data for the reference area, in this case the state. The other rows hold the data for each subarea, for instance, county. The first column of the data area contains a label specifying the name of the area in that row. The second through eighth columns hold the populations for 1930, 1940, 1950, 1960, 1970, 1980, and 1990 (if available). For the first row only (the reference area), the ninth and tenth columns hold the population projections for the years 2000 and 2010.

Once the data work sheet is prepared and saved, you may load in the model spreadsheet. The model can take several minutes to load. The model can be run by two basic methods: the main system menu and keyboard macros. The following discussion will describe the use of the keyboard macros.

The first step in using the model is loading the data file. Press **Alt-I** to summon the input menu. Select the List option if you need to see a list of files, then choose the File option and enter the name of the data file (the drive and path may be included). Then choose **Go** and your data will load.

If you need to make small alterations to your data, press **Alt-A**. You cannot add new areas but you can change the population values for existing areas or add reference area projections for 2000 and 2010, if necessary. Simply move the cursor to each cell you wish to change and enter a new number (without commas). When you have altered your final value, press RETURN twice.

Graphing Results

You may now view a graph of the projected-versus-actual results for any of the ten models, applied to any subarea, utilizing a data range that includes 1930 to 1970, 1930 to 1980, or 1930 to 1990. Press **Alt-G** to begin graphing. First, select the county you wish to view with the County option. On the right of the screen, a list of counties will appear, and the top county will be highlighted by the cursor. Choose **Down** to move the cursor down to the name of the county you wish to graph. You may also select **Up** to move the cursor upward. Once the cursor is highlighting the correct county, use Select to choose that county. You will return to the graph menu.

Now select the **Datayear** option from the graph menu. Decide whether you wish the range of base data years to end in 1970, 1980, or 1990. Typically one would use 1930 through 1970 to predict 1980 and 1930 through 1980 to predict 1990 and compare the predicted and actual values. Data for 1930 through 1990 would typically be used to predict the values for 2000 or 2010. Select your option from the Datayear menu and you will return to the graph menu.

Last, you must choose the model you wish to view. Select the Model option from the Graph menu and you will see a menu with two main selections: one for the Linear/Dlog models and the second for the Other (share and rate difference) models. Choose one of these two options.

Either option will present you with an additional menu showing five models labeled with the letters A, B, C, D, and E. Choose the letter of the model you wish to view and the model results will appear on the screen. Press any key to continue when you are finished viewing the results. You may now select any of the other four models or you can jump directly to another menu to select from the five remaining models. You can also move to the County menu to select a new county for viewing. When you are finished viewing graphs, continue selecting Return to return to each previous menu level until you see the list of keyboard macros.

Calculation, Viewing, and Printing

The third major operation involves the production of comprehensive tables showing the projection-versus-actual results for all ten models and all subareas. Applying ten models to fifty areas means that the model must calculate the results from five hundred different equations, which may take five to ten minutes on a slow computer with no math co-processor.

Press **Alt-C** and you will see the Calculate menu. Select the **Da**tayear option and specify whether you wish to use data from 1930 to 1970, 1930 to 1980, or 1930 to 1990. Now select the **Ca**lcyear option to determine whether you will calculate predicted values for 1980, 1990, 2000, or 2010 or error terms for 1980 or 1990. Now press **Go**. Be prepared for a wait while your computer carries out the many calculations you have just specified.

Press **Alt-O** to review the output tables. The View menu gives you the choice of selecting five tables: (1) the predicted values for the linear and dlog models, (2) the error terms for the linear and dlog models, (3) the predicted values for the other (share and rate difference) models, (4) the error terms for the other (share and rate difference) models, and (5) the error distribution tables. Again, if you selected the Calcyear as 2000 or 2010 (or if you selected 1990 and there are no actual 1990 population values), there will be no valid error terms or distribution of error terms since there were no actual population values to calculate the error terms. The predicted values will be valid, however.

For tables with a substantial number of subareas, press **D** to move downward through the table or **U** to move upward. Once you have completed viewing, press **R** to return to entering keyboard macros. If you want a printed copy of the tables, first make sure your printer is on and loaded with paper then press **Alt-P**.

Model Output

The GTEXTRAP model produces future projections for all of the subareas that are fed into it. Sample projection output is shown in Exhibit 8.2. Users can prepare projections for up to two time periods beyond the last date of their historic data. The model can also be used to analyze the accuracy of each of the ten extrapolation methods for each subarea category employed by the user. This is done by comparing the actual population value to the projected value. The model reports the percentage errors (shown in Exhibit 8.3) and the distribution of errors, projected/actual (shown in Exhibit 8.4) for each method and each group of areas. Most importantly, the model allows the user to automatically generate graphs of the historical population totals for each of the extrapolation methods.

Exhibit 8.2

Sample GTEXTRAP Projection Output

Predicted Values for 1990 Last Year Data Utilized: 1980	Average Absolute Change	Linear Regression	Share Linear Regression	Area/ Subarea Difference Linear Regression	Loglog Regression
	LINAGE	LINREG	LINSH	LINDIF	DLOG
NAME	LINAVEP	LINREGP	LINSHP	LINDIFP	DLOGP
Georgia DeKalb	566,359	563,925	653,355	633,943	696,698
Chattahoochee	25,491	28,439	31,378	27,982	29,433
Columbia	49,101	49,030	53,415	71,321	50,073
Madison	20,471	19,697	21,621	27,102	20,244
Cobb	362,170	360,971	407,519	482,111	438,083
Gwinnett	211,900	216,300	233,642	347,588	213,622
Clayton	180,257	171,062	195,426	244,858	229,082
Rockdale	44,174	41,683	45,526	65,380	42,618
Douglas	65,437	61,731	68,131	93,720	65,988
Houston	91,337	90,457	104,380	107,119	112,091
Cherokee	62,158	63,026	66,411	81,959	60,021

DATA SOURCES

Two issues are important in using the GTEXTRAP model. First, the larger the area, the more appropriate is the extrapolation tool. Ideally, it should be used on well-defined economic systems (or labor markets), such as metropolitan areas. However, extrapolation tools are also appropriate for counties in the United States, even though they vary considerably in size from state to state. Isserman (1977) used them

Exhibit 8.3

Sample GTEXTRAP Projection Errors Output

Errors Terms for the Year 1990 Last Year Data Utilized: 1980 NAME	Average Absolute Change LINAVE LINAVEE	Linear Regression LINREG LINREGE	Share Linear Regression LINSH LINSHE	Area/ Subarea Difference Linear Regression LINDIF LINDIFE	Loglog Regression DLOG DLOGE
Georgia DeKalb	-0.7	-1.1	14.6	11.2	22.2
Chattahoochee	-18.9	-9.6	-0.2	-11.0	-6.4
Columbia	-21.7	-21.8	-14.8	13.8	-20.1
Madison	-7.4	-10.9	-2.2	22.6	-8.4
Cobb	-14.2	-14.5	-3.5	-14.2	3.8
Gwinnett	-28.9	-27.4	-21.6	16.7	-28.3
Clayton	-5.0	-9.8	3.0	29.1	20.8
Rockdale	-14.7	-19.5	-12.1	26.2	-17.7
Douglas	-12.3	-17.3	-8.7	25.6	-11.6
Houston	-2.5	-3.4	11.4	14.4	19.7
Cherokee	-24.9	-23.8	-19.8	-1.0	-27.5

quite successfully for townships. Many analysts may want to use minor civil divisions (MCDs) as their analytical unit. While this is fine, MCDs often change their boundaries over time; dealing with this issue in some states can be extremely difficult. Clearly, historic data cannot be used if the analytical units have not maintained consistent boundaries over time.

The second issue is the time frame of the analysis. The GTEXTRAP model has been written for time frames of five (for instance, 1930 to 1970) to seven (for example, 1930 to 1990) reporting periods. The optional number of time periods to use is not easy to determine. Two points stand out to making this decision, though. Most importantly, the data for the past should have a consistent pattern over time. If the data after a certain date seem to exhibit a completely different pattern from the data before it, the older data probably should not be employed. However, all other things being equal, more time periods will yield better projections.

Data availability is also an issue. County population totals for 1970, 1980, 1986, and 1990 are available in printed and electronic version in the *City and County Data Book*. County population totals from before 1970 must be gathered from printed reports. Data on metropolitan areas or on MCDs are more difficult to assemble and may not be consistent over time.

Exhibit 8.4

Sample GTEXTRAP Errors Distribution Output

Errors Terms for the Year 1990					
Last Year Data Utilized: 1980	LINAVEE	LINREGE	LINSHE	LINDIFE	DLOGE
Under -25%	1	1	0	0	2
-25% to +25%	10	10	11	8	9
Over +25%	0	0	0	3	0
Total	11	11	11	11	11
	EXAVEE	EXREGE	EXPSHE	CONSHE	CONDIFE
Under -25%	0	2	0	1	1
-25% to +25%	10	9	8	10	7
Over +25%	1	0	3	0	3
Total	11	11	11	11	11

SAMPLE APPLICATION

GTEXTRAP comes with data that can be used to learn about extrapolation methods. The 159 counties of the state of Georgia have been categorized by their 1960 to 1970 and 1970 to 1980 growth rates. These data can be used to project the 1980 and 1990 county totals using either the 1930 to 1970 or the 1930 to 1980 data. A file containing these data (called GADATA.WK1) has been provided that allows the user to extract a subset of counties for use in the model. A first run might employ these data to test the accuracy of the ten methods at using 1930 to 1970 data to project 1980 totals. The model can also use the data for 1930 to 1980 to predict the 1990, 2000, and 2010 populations or the 1930 to 1990 data to predict the 2000 or 2010 populations for these counties. Once familiar with the model, the user may want to use his or her own population data.

EVALUATION AND EXTENSIONS

Noncomponent projection techniques are quite valuable. They can be used quickly, need little data, and are readily understood. They provide an easy check on other, more sophisticated methods. There is even some evidence that in certain situations they are as accurate as more sophisticated projection methods (Beaumont and Isserman 1987; and Smith 1987a, b).

Extrapolation techniques are used ubiquitously in demographic analysis, making knowledge of them essential for local demographic analysts. GTEXTRAP can be used by those who teach population analysis and forecasting. The most obvious application is to use data on geographic areas in which the students are located. Numerous other exercises can be created using GTEXTRAP that reinforce assigned readings on population forecasting. A sample set of exercises is provided in the Appendix to this chapter.

GTEXTRAP can also be used by professionals who want to produce a set of noncomponent forecasts for a number of small geographic areas in a minimum amount of time. The model could be improved by adding artificial intelligence-like techniques to determine which extrapolation methods worked best on which types of geographic areas and then assigning a single most likely best technique to each area. Clearly, counties would first have to be categorized by some sensible criterion, such as the previous decade's growth rate. Once that task is complete, users could duplicate Isserman's (1977) procedure and evaluate hybrid techniques that worked best, again, employing artificial intelligence rules to choose the most appropriate technique for each area.

REFERENCES

Armstrong, J. S. 1978. *Long-range forecasting: from crystal ball to computer*. New York: John Wiley and Sons.

Beaumont, P. M., and Isserman, A. 1987. Comment. *Journal of the American Statistical Association* 82, 1004–1009.

Isard, W., et al. 1960. *Methods of regional analysis: an introduction to regional science.* Cambridge, MA: MIT Press.

Isserman, A. M. 1977. The accuracy of population projections for subcounty areas. *Journal of the American Institute of Planners* 43, 247–259.

Klosterman, R. E. 1990. *Community analysis and planning techniques.* Savage, MD: Rowman and Littlefield Publishers, Inc.

Krueckeberg, D. A., and Silvers, A. L. 1974. *Urban planning analysis: methods and models.* New York: John Wiley and Sons.

Pittenger, D. B. 1976. *Projecting state and local populations.* Cambridge, MA: Ballinger Publishers.

Smith, S. K. 1987a. Tests of forecast accuracy and bias for county population projections. *Journal of the American Statistical Association* 82, 991–1003.

———. 1987b. Rejoinder. *Journal of the American Statistical Association* 82, 1009–1012.

United States Department of Commerce, Bureau of the Census. 1983, 1988. *County and city data book.* Washington DC: U.S. Government Printing Office (printed reports), The Bureau (machine-readable data files).

Appendix

Sample GTEXTRAP Questions

Before using the model to develop your own population projections, you should either be an experienced user of extrapolation methods or give yourself a quick review by employing the Georgia county data that have been provided. Using the template, you should be prepared to answer the following types of questions:

1. Describe why a certain method works best for predicting the population totals for a specific (growth) class of counties. Do this for each of the five growth classes. Use graphs to document the points you make in prose. Dig into the assumptions behind each of the ten extrapolation models to explain its performance.

2. Do exactly the same task as (1) above but explain why a particular method is the worst for a specific class of counties.

3. In (1) and (2) above, you will have employed a definition of "works best" and "works worst." Discuss the concept of accuracy in a demographic context and explain your definition for the purposes here.

4. Compare the results you discussed above with those achieved by Isserman and reported in his 1977 article. Reread especially the eleven points he made on page 251.

5. Presuming you were asked to use noncomponent techniques to project the populations of Georgia's 159 counties, how might you alter one of the ten models to make the projections for 2000 and 2010 likely to be more accurate?

6. Describe one or two alternatives to dividing up the counties by their previous decade's growth rate to classify Georgia's 159 counties so that they can be grouped and projected by the ten methods. Explain your rationale for choosing these methods.

7. As a prelude to learning more sophisticated analytical and projection techniques, suggest different projection concepts that address the shortcomings of noncomponent methods for projecting county population totals. What are the likely pros and cons of your suggested approaches?

PART THREE

Economic Analysis and Forecasting

Chapter 9

ECONBASE: Economic Base Analysis

Richard E. Klosterman and Yichun Xie

The ECONBASE model can be used to prepare economic base analyses for counties, states, and small nations. The results of these analyses can be used to identify the sectors of the local economy that serve nonlocal demand that are often the prime stimulants of local economic growth and development. Economic base studies can be used to identify an overdependence on a single industry or group of industries and to estimate the total impact of short-term changes in the industries serving nonlocal demand. They can also be used in conjunction with projection techniques, such as the ones provided in the SHFT-SHR model in chapter 10 to project long-term changes in a region's economy.

The economic base technique is the oldest, simplest, and most widely used technique for regional economic analysis and projection.[1] The economic base technique assumes that local firms that serve external demand (the "basic sector") are the prime cause of local economic growth—the "economic base" of the local economy. This assumption is expressed in terms of a "base multiplier," *BM*, which equals the ratio of the total local employment, e_T^t, to the total basic employment, b_T^t. That is,

$$BM = \frac{e_T^t}{b_T^t}$$

where:

e_T^t = total local employment in year t
b_T^t = total basic employment in year t

The base multiplier is assumed to be invariant over time, which implies that changes in the basic sector will be accompanied by corresponding changes in the total economy. For example, if a region's basic sector employment increases by 10 percent, the total local employment is also assumed to grow by 10 percent. Given this assumption, the base multiplier can be computed from historical data and used to project future changes in the total economy.

The economic base technique is used to analyze a local economy, estimate the impact of local employment changes, and project future states of the local economy. Procedures for using the economic base technique in these situations are described in the "Sample Application" section.

CONCEPTUAL BASIS

The economic base technique assumes that the local economy can be divided into two sectors: (1) a "basic" or "nonlocal" sector and (2) a "nonbasic" or "local" sector. The basic sector consists of firms and parts of firms whose economic activity is dependent on factors external to the local economy. The basic sector includes exporting firms, federal and state government, and local firms that sell to tourists and temporary community residents, such as university students. The nonbasic sector consists of firms and parts of firms whose economic activity is dependent largely on local economic conditions. The nonbasic sector includes local firms and organizations that provide goods and services to local residents and local government.

The economic base technique assumes that all local economic activities can be assigned to either the basic or the nonbasic sector. Firms that sell to both the local and the export market are divided between the basic and nonbasic sectors using the estimation techniques described in the following section.[2]

Field surveys and interviews provide the most accurate measure of a region's basic and nonbasic sectors but are rarely used because they are extremely expensive and time consuming.[3] As a result, most economic base studies use secondary data sources and the indirect measurement techniques provided in the ECONBASE model to identify the basic and nonbasic sectors.

Assumption Approach

The assumption approach assigns activities entirely to the basic and nonbasic sectors on the basis of assumed sales patterns for different types of industries. Local economic activity in manufacturing, mining, forestry, fishing, agriculture, and federal and state government is assumed to be determined largely by external conditions and is assigned entirely to the basic sector. The remaining activities, such as retail, wholesale, transportation, and services, are assumed to serve local markets and are assigned to the nonbasic sector.

The assumption approach is easily applied and widely used. However, it fails to account for bakeries and brick plants (manufacturing) and truck farms and dairies (farming) that serve largely local markets. It is also inaccurate for service industries, such as the home offices of insurance companies and regional financial institutions, that serve primarily nonlocal markets. Assigning an industry's local employment entirely to the basic or nonbasic sectors also fails to recognize that most firms serve both a local (nonbasic) and a nonlocal (basic) market. The assumption technique, though, is appropriate for activities that are basic (such as federal and state government and tourism) or nonbasic (for instance, local government and contract construction) by definition.

Location Quotient Approach

The location quotient approach gets its name from the ratio or "location quotient" that equals the industry's share of the local economy divided by its share of the national economy. That is,

$$LQ_i = \frac{e_i^t/e_T^t}{E_i^t/E_T^t}$$

where:

e_i^t = regional employment in industry i in year t
e_T^t = total regional employment in year t
E_i^t = national employment in industry i in year t
E_T^t = total national employment in year t.

Industries with location quotients greater than one have local economic shares (e_i^t/e_T^t) that are larger than their national shares (E_i^t/E_T^t), indicating that the local economy is specialized, relative to the nation, in these industries. Local production in these industries is therefore assumed to exceed local demand, allowing the excess to be exported. Industries with location quotients less than or equal to one are assumed to serve only local demand and are thus assumed to have no basic sector employment.

The basic sector employment in industries with location quotients greater than one is computed with the following equation (Isserman 1977):

$$b_i^t = \left(\frac{e_t^i}{E_i^t} - \frac{e_T^t}{E_T^t} \right) E_i^t$$

Nonbasic activity in these industries can be determined by subtracting the estimated basic sector employment from the total employment. Attempts to apply the equation to industries with location quotients less than one yield negative basic employment estimates, indicating that an error has been made.[4]

Caution must be used, however, in using the location quotient technique to identify industries that do, or do not, contain basic sector activity. Local industries such as "Hotels and Lodging" (Standard Industrial Classification [SIC] 70) and federal and state government are dependent largely on nonlocal factors and can be assumed to be entirely basic, regardless of the location quotient value. Local government is similarly nonbasic, by definition, even though the location quotient may be greater than one.

Similarly, location quotients larger than one for general construction and real estate in rapidly growing areas do not indicate that the construction serves nonlocal demand or that property is being exported. It only means that the region's rapid growth—caused by factors such as a booming economy or an influx of retirees—has been reflected in an unusually high level of activity in growth-related activities, such as construction and real estate. As a result, activities clearly associated with local demand should be assigned to the nonbasic sector regardless of the location quotient value. In all of these cases, the location quotient values cannot be interpreted blindly without a familiarity with the study region and a careful assessment of the resulting assignments.[5]

Minimum Requirements Approach

The minimum requirements approach compares an industry's local employment share to its share in a sample of similarly sized regions. It estimates an industry's basic employment by applying the following equation:

$$b_i^t = \left(\frac{e_i^t}{e_T^t} - \frac{e_{im}^t}{e_m^t} \right) e_T^i$$

The e_m^t and e_{im}^t terms refer to the total employment and the local employment in industry i in the minimum shares region, m, a comparable region with the smallest employment share in industry i (that is, the smallest value for the ratio e_i^t/e_T^t). The minimum requirements approach assumes that local production in the minimum shares region is just sufficient to satisfy local requirements, that is, there are no exports. The export share for all other regions in the size category is assumed to equal the difference between the industry's local employment share (e_i^t/e_T^t) and the industry's employment share in the minimum shares region (e_{im}^t/e_m^t).

The minimum requirements basic employment estimates can be computed by using the minimum shares estimation parameters developed by Moore and Jacobsen (1984). Given these parameters, the minimum employment share, s_i^t, for employment category i in year t for a region with population p_t can be estimated by applying the following equation,

$$s_i^t = a_i + b_i(logP^t)$$

where a_i and b_i are the minimum shares estimation parameters identified by Moore and Jacobsen (1984).

The minimum employment share estimate, s_i^t, is equivalent to the second term in the minimum requirements estimation equation, expressed as a percentage. As a result, the basic employment in employment category i in year t, b_i^t, can be estimated by using the preceding equation to estimate s_i^t and then applying the following equation:

$$b_i^t = \left(\frac{e_i^t}{e_T^t} - \frac{s_i^t}{100} \right) e_T^t$$

The assumption technique must be used for employment categories, such as agriculture and construction, for which minimum shares estimation parameters are not provided.[6]

Economic Base Applications

The basic and nonbasic employment estimates prepared by the ECONBASE model identify local industries that serve nonlocal demand and, by hypothesis, are the prime causes of local economic growth or decline. This information can help local officials reveal weaknesses in the local economy such as an overdependence on a single industrial sector, and assess the region's ability to attract or retain basic industries that stimulate future economic growth (Tiebout 1962).

The basic employment estimates prepared with this model can also be used with projection techniques in the SHFT-SHR model to project the total basic sector employment in the future. The total future employment can then be derived by multiplying the projected basic employment by the base multiplier. That is,

$$e_T^{t'} = b_T^{t'} \times BM$$

where:

$$BM = \frac{e_T^{t'}}{b_T^{t'}}$$

$e_T^{t'}$ = projected total local employment in year t'
$b_T^{t'}$ = projected basic employment in year t'
e_T^t = observed total local employment in analysis year t
b_T^t = estimated basic employment in analysis year t

The ECONBASE output can also be used to predict the impact of short-term economic changes, such as proposed plant expansions or closings. The total effect, Δe_i^t, of a projected local employment change is equal to the projected nonbasic employment change, Δn_i^t, plus the induced effect caused by the change in the basic employment. That is,

$$\Delta e_i^t = \Delta n_i^t + (\Delta b_i^t \times BM)$$

where:

Δe_i^t = total impact of a projected employment change in industry i;

Δn_i^t = projected nonbasic employment change in industry i;

Δb_i^t = projected basic employment change in industry i.

The projected basic employment change, Δb_i^t, can be computed by multiplying the projected employment change, Δe_i^t, by the proportion of basic employment, p_i^t:

$$\Delta b_i^t = \Delta e_i^t \times p_i^t$$

The proportion basic is estimated by dividing an industry's estimated basic employment in the analysis year by its total employment in the same year. The projected nonbasic employment change can be computed by subtracting the projected basic employment change from the projected total employment change.

Consider, for example, an industry with 2,000 local employees in the analysis year, an estimated basic employment of 1,600, and a regional base multiplier of 2.0. The proportion basic is 1,600 divided by 2,000 or 0.80. If the industry plans to add an additional 1,000 employees in the next year (that is, Δe_i^t is 1,000), the projected basic employment change (Δb_i^t) is 1,000 times 0.80, or 800, and the projected nonbasic employment (Δn_i^t) is 1,000 minus 800, or 200. Therefore, the total projected employment change (Δe_i^t) is equal to 200 plus (800 times 2.0), or 1,800.

COMPONENTS AND OPERATION

As the location map in Exhibit 9.1 indicates, the computational portion of the ECONBASE model is divided into eight sections. The Data Entry section is used to enter the output labels and employment values for the

Exhibit 9.1

ECONBASE Location Map

Welcome A1..A20			
Main Menu A21..A40	Location Map B1..P20	Macro Document	
Model Document A41..A113	Range Descript B22..M128	S1..Z420	
Data Entry	AG1..AJ119 Assume Assign	AG120..AN239	
Compute Residuals	AP1..AS119 Assume Output	AP120..AT239	
LQ Output	AV1..AZ119 LQ Compute and Assign	AV120..BG239	
Min Req Compute	BI1..BQ39	Min Req Output BI120..BM152	

analysis year. The Compute Residuals section then computes the residual employment in each SIC Division that is not included in the data provided by the user. For example, if the total local employment in SIC Division A is one thousand and the total reported employment for the five two-digit Major Groups in Division A is eight hundred, the model computes the residual employment of two hundred in "Other Division A" in the Compute Residuals section. The employment values in this section are used to prepare all three sets of basic and nonbasic estimates.

The Assume Assignment section is used in conjunction with the assumption technique to assign the observed local employment to the basic or nonbasic sector. The local employment values and labels for all industries with local employment are copied from the Compute Residuals section to this section. After the user specifies the sector assignment for each industry, the assumption technique output is copied to the Assume Output section for printing or graphing.

The Location Quotient Computations and Assignment section is used to compute the location quotients and location quotient basic/nonbasic employment estimates and to assign the industries to the basic or nonbasic sectors. The local employment and national employment values and labels for all industries with local employment are first copied from the Compute Residuals section to this section. The location quotient values and location quotient basic employment estimates are then computed, allowing the user to specify the sector assignment for each industry. The location quotient output is then copied to the Location Quotient Output section for printing or graphing.

The Minimum Requirements Computations section is used to compute the minimum requirements basic and nonbasic estimates for each local industry. The local employment values are first copied from the Compute Residuals section into the appropriate minimum require-ments employment categories in this section. The minimum requirements basic and nonbasic employment estimates are then computed for all industries for which estimation parameters are provided; the remaining industries are automatically assigned to the basic and nonbasic sectors. The minimum requirements output is then copied to the Minimum Requirements Output section for printing or graphing.

The noncomputational portions of the ECONBASE model include the model documentation, location map, range descriptions, and macro documentation sections provided with all of the models in this book.

These sections can be accessed by using the Alt-D, Alt-L, Alt-R, and Alt-Z macros described in chapter 1.

Model Operation

As Table 9.1 indicates, twelve macro commands are provided for use in conjunction with the ECONBASE model. The Alt-D, Alt-L, Alt-M, Alt-Q, Alt-R, Alt-W, and Alt-Z macros correspond to the standard macros described in chapter 1. General instructions for using these macros and other spreadsheet macros are provided in chapter 1.

Table 9.1

ECONBASE Macros

Alt-C	Compute basic/nonbasic estimates
Alt-D	Go to Documentation
Alt-G	Graph output
Alt-I	Input employment data
Alt-L	Go to Location map
Alt-M	Go to Main menu
Alt-O	Go to Output
Alt-P	Print output
Alt-Q	Quit/save model
Alt-R	Go to Range descriptions
Alt-W	Go to Welcome Screen
Alt-Z	Go to macros

The five specialized macros provided for the ECONBASE model are described below.

Alt-C, Compute Basic/Nonbasic Estimates. This macro is used to compute the estimated basic and nonbasic employment in each local industry. The following suboptions are provided:

1. Assumption, compute assumption estimates;
2. LQ, compute location quotient estimates;
3. Requirements, compute minimum requirements estimates; and
4. Main_menu, return to the main menu.

This option should be used after the required employment data have been entered and requires the user to specify the basic and nonbasic assignments for the assumption and location quotient approaches. The procedures for making these assignments are described in the next section.

Alt-G, Graph Output. This macro displays bar graphs showing the estimated basic and nonbasic employment in each local industry. The following suboptions are provided:

1. Assumption, graph assumption estimates;
2. LQ, graph location quotient estimates;
3. Requirements, graph minimum requirements estimates; and
4. Main_menu, return to the main menu.

This option should be used only after the required employment data have been entered and the basic/nonbasic estimates have been computed with the Alt-C macro.

Alt-I, Input Employment Data. This macro is used to enter the employment data required to compute the basic and nonbasic employment estimates. The following suboptions are provided:

1. Local, enter local data and output labels;
2. National, enter national data; and
3. Main_menu, return to main menu.

The first two options provide two suboptions: (1) New_data that is used to enter new employment data; and (2) Revised_data that can be used to revise previously entered employment data. Procedures for entering these data are described in the next section.

Alt-O, Go To Output. This macro displays the basic and nonbasic employment estimates on the screen. The following options are provided:

1. Assumption, display assumption output;
2. LQ, display location quotient output;
3. Requirements, display minimum requirements output; and
4. Main_menu, return to main menu.

Alt-P, Print Output. This macro prints out the estimated basic and nonbasic employment in each local industry. The following options are provided:

1. Assumption, print assumption output;
2. LQ, print location quotient output;
3. Requirements, print minimum requirements output; and
4. Main_menu, return to main menu.

Data Entry

Four sets of data are required by the ECONBASE model: a set of output labels; the local employment in the analysis year; the national employment in the analysis year, and the local population in the analysis year. The user must also specify the basic or nonbasic sector assignments for the assumption and location quotient approaches. Procedures for entering these data and making the sector assignments are described below. The "Sample Application" section provides additional guidance on entering these data using the sample data set provided with the ECONBASE model.

Entering Output Labels. The ECONBASE model provides three labels that are included in the program output: the current date; the name of the analysis region; and the year for which the analysis is being made. This information is entered by selecting **Alt-I** Local New_data.[7]

The current date is normally entered in the standard North American format, **MM/DD/YY** (that is, month, day, and year as two-digit numbers), although it can be entered in any format as long as the total number of characters is no larger than eight. The name of the analysis region is entered as a label that cannot exceed thirty characters in length. The year for which employment data are being provided is entered as a four-digit number.

Entering Local Employment Data. The local employment data are entered after the output labels described in the preceding section. A list of all of the one- and two-digit SIC Divisions and Major Groups is provided, allowing the user to enter the local employment in each industry. Employment values can be entered with the numeric keypad; pressing the ENTER key automatically moves the cursor down one row, allowing the next value to be entered. The system automatically returns to the main menu after all of the local employment data have been entered.

The **Alt-I** Local Revise_data command sequence can be used to revise local employment data that have been previously entered. These commands allow the user to enter the current date and then move the cursor to the top of the column containing the local employment data values. The local employment values can then be modified. The Alt-M command should then be used to return to the main menu after the data have been modified.

Entering National Employment Data. The national employment data used to compute the location quotient estimates are entered by selecting **Alt-I** National New_Data. The user can then enter the national employment at the one- and two-digit SIC levels using the procedures for entering the local employment data. The system automatically returns to the main menu after all of the data have been entered. The **Alt-I** National Revise command sequence can also be used to revise national employment data that have been entered previously.

Entering Total Population Data. The total regional population in the analysis year is used to compute the minimum requirements basic employment estimates. It is entered in the control panel after selecting the **Alt-C** Requirements option.

Specifying Basic and Nonbasic Sector Assignments

The assumption and location quotient techniques require the user to assign each local industry to the basic or nonbasic sector. This avoids the use of general assignment procedures, such as assigning all manufacturing employment to the basic sector or all service employment to the nonbasic sector, that may be inappropriate for a particular region.

The assumption approach requires that the user enter the local employment data and then select the **Alt-C** Assumption option. The model then displays the local employment in each industry and allows the user to specify whether this employment should be assigned to the basic or nonbasic sector. If an uppercase or lowercase **B** is entered, the industry's local employment is assigned entirely to the basic sector. If an uppercase or lowercase **N** is entered, the employment is assigned entirely to the nonbasic sector. The system automatically moves to the next row after an assignment has been made. The assumption approach output is displayed on the screen after all of the sector assignments have been made.

The location quotient approach requires that the user enter the local and national employment data and then select **Alt-C LQ**. The model then computes the location quotient value for each local industry and displays it on the screen, allowing the user to specify the assignment for each industry. If an uppercase or lowercase **N** is entered, the employment is assigned entirely to the nonbasic sector. If an uppercase or lowercase **A** (for all basic) is entered, the employment is assigned entirely to the basic sector. If an uppercase or lowercase **B** is entered, the location quotient basic employment estimate is used if the location quotient value is greater than one; if the location quotient is one or less, the basic employment is set to zero. The location quotient output is displayed on the screen after all of the sector assignments have been made.

DATA SOURCES

The *County Business Patterns* (*CBP*) reports prepared annually by the U.S. Bureau of the Census (for example, U.S. Bureau of the Census 1990) present employment information at the two-, three-, and four-digit SIC levels for counties, states, the District of Columbia, Puerto Rico, and the United States. The *CBP* data include all wage and salary employment of private nonfarm employers and nonprofit organizations covered by the Federal Insurance Contributions Act (FICA)—commonly known as Social Security—and all employment of religious organizations covered under the elective provisions of FICA. Data for the following types of establishments exempt from FICA are excluded: agricultural production, government, railroads, foreign ships at sea, and self-employed and domestic service workers.

County, state, and national employment data are also available from the U.S. Department of Labor's Bureau of Labor Statistics employment and wages program, commonly called the ES-202 program. The ES-202 data are published in the annual *Employment and Wages* reports (for example, United States Bureau of Labor Statistics 1990), which record the average annual employment for counties, states, and the U.S. at the two-, three-, and four-digit SIC levels. The ES-202 data cover approximately 98 percent of total hourly wage and salaried civilian employment, almost 40 percent of agricultural workers, and more than 90 percent of state and local government workers. The principal exclusions are members of the armed forces, railroad employees, most domestic workers and agricultural employees, the self-employed, and unpaid family members.[8]

SAMPLE APPLICATION

The procedures for using the ECONBASE model and the types of information produced by the model will be illustrated with the 1985 employment data for Wayne County, Ohio, used in chapters 10 and 11 of *Community Analysis and Planning Techniques* (Klosterman 1990). The sample employment data are provided in the ECONBASE model and can be viewed by selecting **Alt-I** Local Revise. The example reviews the three major steps required to use the ECONBASE model: (1) entering labels and employment data; (2) specifying basic and nonbasic assignments; and (3) viewing model output.

Entering Labels and Employment Data
Exhibit 9.2 contains a portion of the sample data entry worksheet used to enter the output labels and employment data required by the ECONBASE model. As the figure illustrates, the following labels are entered

Exhibit 9.2

ECONBASE Data Entry Form

Current Date: 1/1/92
Analysis Region: Wayne County
Observation Year: 1985

SIC		1985 Employment	
Code	Industry	Local	National
A	AGRICULTURE, FOREST & FISHING	5,360	7,666,007
01	Agricultural production-crops	5,240	7,096,533
02	Agricultural production-livestock	0	0
07	Agriculture services	120	569,474
08	Forestry	0	0
09	Fishing, hunting and trapping	0	0
B	MINING	913	923,143
10	Metal mining	0	0
11	Anthracite mining	0	0
12	Bituminous coal mining	0	0
13	Oil and gas extraction	0	0
14	Nonmetallic mining & quarrying	0	0
C	CONSTRUCTION	1,378	4,642,735
15	General Construction	0	0
16	Heavy Construction	0	0

---

at the top of the data entry screen: (1) the date on which the analysis is being conducted, in this case 1/1/92, (2) the name of the region for which the analysis is being conducted, **Wayne County**, and (3) the year for which the employment data are being provided, **1985**. These data are entered by using the **Alt-I** Local New_Data command sequence.

The employment in each local industry can then be entered to the right of the appropriate SIC code and industry label. Zero values should be entered for industries reporting no local employment in the analysis year (1985 in this example). The national employment in each industry reporting local employment in the analysis year can then be entered by using the **Alt-I** National New_Data command sequence.

Specifying Basic and Nonbasic Assignments

Exhibit 9.3 shows a portion of the location quotient sector assignments table used to assign the local employment in each industry to the basic or basic sectors. The first four columns list the following information for each industry reporting local employment in the analysis year: (1) SIC code; (2) industry label; (3) local employment; and (4) computed location quotient value.

The last column is used to specify the procedure to be used in estimating the basic and nonbasic employment in each industry. For industries such as the first one for which the user specifies **B** (for "Basic"), the basic and nonbasic employment are estimated using the standard location quotient estimation equation. For industries such as the second one for which the user specifies **N** (for "Nonbasic"), the local employment is assigned entirely to the nonbasic sector—regardless of the computed location quotient value. For industries such as the third one for which the user specifies **A** (for "All basic"), the local employment is assigned entirely to the basic sector—regardless of the computed location quotient value. The last two options are provided for use with sectors such as "Hotels and other lodging places," "State government," and "Local government" that are assumed to always be basic (in the first two cases) or nonbasic (in the third case).

A similar assignment table is provided for the assumption estimation technique. The only differences are that the location quotient values are not displayed and only two assignment options are provided: (1) **B** to assign the local employment entirely to the basic sector and (2) **N** to assign the local employment entirely to the nonbasic sector.

Exhibit 9.3

Location Quotient Sector Assignments Table

Basic and Nonbasic Assignments for Wayne County
Location Quotient Approach

SIC Code	Industry	Employ Local	Location Quotient	Sector Assignment
01	Agricultural production-crops	5,240	1.7479	b
07	Agriculture services	120	0.4988	n
B	MINING	913	2.3412	a
C	CONSTRUCTION	1,378	0.7026	n
20	Food and kindred products	1,687	2.4936	b
24	Lumber and wood products	639	2.1732	b
25	Furniture and fixtures	140	0.6705	n
26	Paper and allied products	1,091	3.8102	b
27	Printing and allied industries	213	0.3538	n
28	Chemicals and allied products	385	0.8728	n
30	Rubber and plastic products	2,198	6.6066	b
32	Stone, clay, and glass products	426	1.7153	b
33	Primary metal industries	882	2.5757	b
34	Fabricated metal products	2,398	3.8583	b
35	Machinery, except electrical	1,035	1.1198	b
36	Electrical equipment and supplies	189	3.2033	n
37	Transportation equipment	1,022	1.2225	b
DD	Other Division D	972	0.8452	n
47	Transportation	612	5.3200	b

Viewing Model Output

As the sample output in Exhibit 9.4 indicates, the header for the ECON-BASE output identifies: (1) the date on which the analysis was conducted, **January 1, 1992**; (2) the name of the analysis region, **Wayne County**; (3) the approach used to prepare the basic and nonbasic estimates, the location quotient technique in this example; and (4) the year for which the basic and nonbasic estimates are prepared, **1985**. The body of the output provides the following information for all the industries identified in the input data: (1) the SIC code and industry name, (2) the total local employment in the industry, and (3) the estimated basic and nonbasic employment in the industry. In addition, the output provides the calculated value for the Base Multiplier, that is, the total employment divided by the total estimated basic employment.

Exhibit 9.4

Sample ECONBASE Printed Output

Basic and Nonbasic Employment for Wayne County
Location Quotient Approach

SIC Code	Industry	Local	1985 Employment Basic	Nonbasic
01	Agricultural production—crops	5,240	224	2,998
07	Agriculture services	120	0	120
B	MINING	913	913	0
C	CONSTRUCTION	1,378	0	1,678
20	Food and kindred products	1,687	1,010	677
24	Lumber and wood products	639	345	294
25	Furniture and fixtures	140	0	140
26	Paper and allied products	1,091	805	286
27	Printing and allied industries	213	0	213
28	Chemicals and allied products	385	0	385
30	Rubber and plastic products	2,198	1,865	333
32	Stone, clay, and glass products	426	178	248
33	Primary metal industries	882	540	342
34	Fabricated metal products	2,398	1,776	622
35	Machinery, except electrical	1,035	111	924
36	Electrical equipment and supplies	189	0	189

Exhibit 9.5 illustrates the graphical output generated by selecting one of the **Alt-G** Graph output options. The graph contains a series of bar graphs showing the estimated basic and nonbasic employment in each industry. The industries are listed across the bottom of the graph and SIC code and the estimation technique is identified in the graph subheading.

EVALUATION AND EXTENSIONS

The economic base model is the most widely used—and criticized—technique for local economic analysis.[9] Most economists prefer the input-output technique that improves on the economic base model by dividing the local economy into fifty or more sectors and reporting how the inputs and outputs of each sector are distributed among the remaining sectors of the economy. This allows analysts to determine the direct, indirect, and induced effects of projected changes in one or more sectors for each sector of the economy. Interregional input-output models can also be prepared to study regional balance of payments and interregional trade flows—questions that cannot be examined within the economic base framework.

Exhibit 9.5

Sample ECONBASE Graphical Output

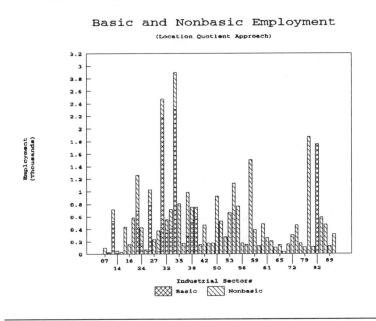

Nevertheless, the economic base continues to be used—and will be used for quite some time—because theoretically more appealing approaches such as the input-output techniques are expensive, hard to understand and implement, and often do not yield significantly better results. The critiques of the economic base technique also suggest that it is more appropriate for small, isolated regions and short-term impact analyses than it is for diversified metropolitan regions and long-term projections. As a result, the technique is particularly useful for short-term analyses of small regional economies for which the resources and data required by more sophisticated models are generally unavailable.

A number of practical adjustments can also be incorporated into the ECONBASE models to help account for factors that can seriously distort the location quotient and minimum requirements basic employment estimates. Local and national value-added data can be used to help account for regional productivity differences. Local and national personal income data can be used to help adjust for regional consumption differences. Information on national exports-related employment can be used to reduce the effect of national exports. The model can also be expanded to allow for analyses at the three-digit SIC level data to minimize the effects of cross hauling and product mix. An alternate set of estimation parameters could also be used to compute the minimum requirements employment estimates (Isserman 1977, 1980; Klosterman 1990).

The economic base technique is especially attractive when compared to other simple projection techniques, such as the curve-fitting/extrapolation procedure provided in the EXTRAP model in chapter 4. It uses readily available information to examine past trends and determine the implications of alternative assumptions about the future. It also incorporates a model of local economic change that is admittedly simple but perfectly appropriate for many applications. As a result, if applied cautiously and appropriately in specific contexts, the economic base technique can provide a highly useful tool for understanding current economic conditions and projecting the future.

ACKNOWLEDGMENTS

The authors would like to acknowledge the assistance of Professor David L. Phillips and the students in the "Analysis of the Urban System" course at the University of Virginia in testing and improving the ECONBASE model, during the summer of 1991.

NOTES

1. The early development of the economic base technique by Homer Hoyt and others is described by Isard (1960); Lane (1966); and Pfouts (1960); for a review of more recent articles see Richardson (1985).

2. See Klosterman (1990) for a more complete discussion of the economic base technique including issues of identifying the study area, selecting

measurement units, and a description of the Standard Industrial Code (SIC) classification system.

3. See Gibson and Worden (1981) and Tiebout (1962) for more complete discussions of direct measurement approaches.

4. However, a "negative basic employment" estimate can be interpreted as an indirect measure of the additional regional employment required to make the region self-sufficient in an industry. This deficit represents an opportunity for expanding local production to satisfy a demand that is currently being satisfied by imported goods and services.

5. For a more complete discussion of the location quotient technique see Klosterman (1990).

6. The minimum requirements estimation approach may yield negative basic employment estimates in some cases. In these cases, the negative basic employment value should be ignored and the industry's local employment assigned to the nonbasic sector.

7. The current date is also entered in conjunction with the **Alt-C** Compute estimates option.

8. For further information on these and other employment data sources, including information on the hard-to-obtain agricultural and government sectors, see Klosterman (1989).

9. See, for example, Blumenfeld (1955) and Richardson (1978).

REFERENCES

Blumenfeld, H. 1955. The economic base of a community. *Journal of the American Institute of Planners* 21, 114–132.

Gibson, L. J., and Worden, M. A. 1981. Estimating the economic base multiplier, a test of alternative procedures. *Economic Geography* 57, 146–159.

Isard, W. 1960. *Methods of regional analysis: an introduction to regional science*. Cambridge, MA: MIT Press.

Isserman, A. M. 1977. The location quotient approach to estimating regional economic impacts. *Journal of the American Institute of Planners* 43, 33–41.

———. 1980. Estimating export activity in a regional economy: a theoretical and empirical analysis of alternative models. *International Regional Science Review* 5, 155–184.

Klosterman, R. E. 1989. *Community analysis and planning programs users guide*. Akron, OH: Center for Urban Studies, University of Akron.

————. 1990. *Community analysis and planning techniques*. Savage, MD: Rowman and Littlefield.

Lane, T. 1966. The urban base multiplier: an evaluation of the state of the art. *Land Economics* 42, 339–347.

————, and Jacobsen, M. 1984. Minimum requirements and regional economics, 1980. *Economic Geography* 60, 217–224.

Pfouts, R. W., ed. 1960. *The techniques of urban economic analysis*. West Trenton, NJ: Chandler-Davis.

Richardson, H. W. 1978. The state of regional economics: a survey. *International Regional Science Review* 3, 1–48.

————. 1985. Input-output and economic base multipliers: looking backward and forward. *Journal of Regional Science* 25, 607–662.

Tiebout, C. M.   1962.   *The community economic base study*. Committee for Economic Development Supplementary Paper No. 16. New York: Committee for Economic Development.

U.S. Bureau of the Census. 1990. *County business patterns, 1989*. Washington, D.C: U.S. Government Printing Office.

U.S. Bureau of Labor Statistics. 1990. *Employment and wages: annual averages, 1989*. Washington, D.C: U.S. Government Printing Office.

Chapter 10

SHFT-SHR: Local Employment Projection

Richard E. Klosterman and Yichun Xie

The SHFT-SHR model provides two techniques for projecting the employment and other characteristics of a region from national- or state-level projections and historical data relating past growth trends in the two regions. These techniques—the constant-share and the shift-share techniques—take advantage of the fact that large-area projections are generally more detailed and more reliable than small-area forecasts. As a result, these techniques are particularly useful when large-area projections are available and small-area projections are not.

CONCEPTUAL BASIS

Constant-Share Technique
The constant-share projection technique assumes that the study area's share of a larger "reference" region's activity will remain constant over time.[1] When used to project local employment, the technique assumes the local area's share of the state or national employment in an industry is constant over time.[2] That is,

$$\frac{e_i^t}{E_i^t} = \text{constant for all } t$$

where:

e_i^t = local employment in industry i at time t

E_i^t = reference region employment in industry i at time t

The local employment share can remain constant only if the industry's employment in the study area and the reference region grow at the same rate. That is, for the preceding equation to be true, it must also be true that

$$e_i^{t'} = (1 + R_i^{t\text{-}t'}) \, e_i^t$$

where:

e_i^t = local employment in industry i in year t

$e_i^{t'}$ = projected local employment in industry i in year t'

$R_i^{t\text{-}t'}$ = projected reference region growth rate in industry i for time period t to t'

The constant-share technique can also be used in an identical fashion to project the basic employment estimates prepared with the ECONBASE model described in chapter 9. That is,

$$b_i^{t'} = (1 + R_i^{t\text{-}t'}) \, b_i^t$$

where:

b_i^t = basic employment in industry i in year t

$b_i^{t'}$ = projected basic employment in industry i in year t'

The reference region growth rate, $R_i^{t\text{-}t'}$, is defined as the change in the reference region's employment in industry i over the time period t to t' divided by the reference region's employment in year t. That is,

$$R_i^{t\text{-}t'} = \frac{E_i^{t'} - E_i^t}{E_i^t}$$

The local growth rate, $r_i^{t\text{-}t'}$, is similarly defined as the local employment change in industry i over the time period t to t' divided by the local employment in year t. That is,

$$r_i^{t\text{-}t'} = \frac{e_i^{t'} - e_i^t}{e_i^t}$$

Constant-share employment projections are prepared by applying the following three-step procedure: (1) computing the projected growth rates for the reference region; (2) adjusting these rates to account for different time periods; and (3) using the adjusted growth rates to project the local employment.

These steps will be illustrated with the following sample data to project the local employment in Standard Industrial Classification (SIC) Code 24, "Lumber and wood products," to the year 2010: (1) the local employment in SIC 24 in 1990, that is, e_{24}^{1990}, is 600; (2) the state employment in SIC 24 in the year 1983, that is, E_{24}^{1983}, is 15,000; and (3) the projected state employment in this sector for the year 2000, that is, E_{24}^{2000}, is 20,000. These data correspond to the types of information that are available from the data sources described in the "Data Sources" section.

Computing Projected Growth Rate. Given these data, the projected state growth rate for SIC 24, $R_{24}^{1983-2000}$, can be computed as follows:

$$R_{24}^{1983-2000} = \frac{E_{24}^{2000} - E_{24}^{1983}}{E_{24}^{1983}}$$
$$= \frac{20,000 - 15,000}{15,000}$$
$$= 0.3333.$$

Adjusting Growth Rate. This growth rate cannot be used directly to project the local employment in 1990 to the year 2010 because the projection periods are different. That is, a twenty-year period is required to project the local employment from 1990 to 2010. However, the projected state growth rate is computed from data for 1983 and 2000, that is, for a seventeen-year period. The computed state growth rate is therefore smaller than the projected local growth rate because it is based on a shorter time period.

As a result, the seventeen-year growth rate must be converted into an equivalent twenty-year growth rate before projecting the local employment. Growth rates can be converted from one time period to equivalent rates for a different time period by using the following equation:

$$R_i^m = (1 + R_i^n)^{m/n} - 1$$

where:

R_i^m = growth rate for time period of m years

R_i^n = growth rate for time period of n years[3]

For example, the projected seventeen-year growth rate for SIC 24 can be converted into an equivalent twenty-year rate as follows:

$$
\begin{aligned}
R_{24}^{20} &= (1 + R_{24}^{17})^{20/17} - 1 \\
&= (1 + 0.3333)^{20/17} - 1 \\
&= (1.3333)^{1.1765} - 1 \\
&= 0.4027
\end{aligned}
$$

That is, a growth rate of 0.3333 for the seventeen-year period, 1983 to 2000, is equivalent to a growth rate of 0.4027 for the twenty-year period, 1990 to 2010.

Projecting Local Employment. The projected local employment in the year 2010 can then be computed by applying the projected twenty-year growth rate to the observed local employment in the year 1990. That is,

$$
\begin{aligned}
e_{24}^{2010} &= (1 + R_{24}^{1990-2010}) \; e_{24}^{1990} \\
&= (1 + 0.4027) \; 600 \\
&= 842
\end{aligned}
$$

This procedure can be applied to the employment in each local industry to project the future local employment in all industries. It can also be applied to the estimated basic employment in each industry to project the basic employment in the future.

Shift-Share Technique

The constant-share projection technique assumes that the local economy will maintain a constant share of the reference region's employment in all industries. The shift-share projection technique introduced in 1960 by Edgar S. Dunn, Jr. and others (Dunn 1960; Perloff et al. 1960) recognizes that this assumption is rarely correct.[4] In some cases, an industry's local employment will grow more rapidly than the national or state employment, causing the region's share to increase. In other cases, the local employment will grow more slowly, causing the region's share to decline. Rarely will the two areas grow by exactly the same rate, as the constant-share projection technique assumes.

The shift-share projection technique modifies the constant-share projection formula by adding a "shift" term that accounts for differences between local and reference region growth rates, which cause an industry's employment to shift into or out of a region. That is,

$$e_i^{t'} = (1 + R_i^{t \cdot t'} + s_i^{t \cdot t'}) \, e_i^t$$

where:

e_i^t = local employment in industry i in year t

$e_i^{t'}$ = projected local employment in industry i in year t'

$R_i^{t \cdot t'}$ = projected reference region growth rate for industry i for the period t to t'

$s_i^{t \cdot t'}$ = projected employment shift for industry i for the period t to t'

The shift term, $s_i^{t \cdot t'}$, is equal to the difference between an industry's local growth rate, $r_i^{t \cdot t'}$, and its growth rate in the reference region, $R_i^{t \cdot t'}$ for the period t to t'. That is,

$$s_i^{t \cdot t'} = r_i^{t \cdot t'} - R_i^{t \cdot t'}$$

The first term in the shift-share projection equation, $1 + R_i^{t \cdot t'}$, is identical to the constant-share formula and projects the local employment change that would occur if the local industry grew by the projected rate for the reference region. The shift term, $s_i^{t \cdot t'}$, adjusts the constant-share growth rate by the projected difference between the local and reference region growth rates. If the local employment is projected to grow faster than the reference region employment, the shift term will be positive, inflating the combined growth rate and the projected employment. If the local employment is projected to grow more slowly than the reference region employment, the shift term will be negative, reducing the combined growth rate and the projected employment.

The projected employment shift, $s_i^{t \cdot t'}$, is unknown because the projected local employment, $e_i^{t'}$, and thus the projected local growth rate, $r_i^{t \cdot t'}$, are unknown. As a result, the projected employment shift must be assumed to equal the observed employment shift for a past period for which local and reference region employment data are available. The shift term is therefore commonly referred to as the "constant shift" term to reflect the assumption that observed differences between the local and reference region growth rates are constant over time.

Shift-share employment projections are prepared by adding the following steps to the procedures for applying the constant-share technique: (1) computing local and state growth rates for the past; (2) computing the corresponding past and projected employment shifts; and (3) using these rates and the constant-share growth rates to project the local employment. This procedure will be illustrated with the sample data considered above.

Computing Past Growth Rates. Two additional pieces of information are required to compute the past local and state growth rates—the local and state employment in each industry at one additional point in time. In this example, the local and state employment in 1978 will be used to compare the observed local growth between 1978 and 1990 to the state employment growth between 1978 and 1983. The year 1978 is used because the state- and metropolitan-level data described in the "Data Sources" section are available for that year.

Assume, for example, that the local employment in SIC 24 in 1978, that is, e_{24}^{1978}, is 400 and the state employment in this industry, E_{24}^{1978}, is 13,000. Given the local employment for 1990 provided earlier, the observed local growth rate between 1978 and 1990, $r_{24}^{1978-1990}$, can therefore be computed as follows:

$$r_{24}^{1978-1990} = \frac{e_{24}^{1990} - e_{24}^{1978}}{e_{24}^{1978}}$$

$$= \frac{600 - 400}{400}$$

$$= 0.5000$$

Similarly, the observed state growth rate between 1978 and 1983 can be computed as follows:

$$R_{24}^{1978-1983} = \frac{E_{24}^{1983} - E_{24}^{1978}}{E_{24}^{1978}}$$

$$= \frac{15,000 - 13,000}{13,000}$$

$$= 0.1538$$

Computing Past and Projected Shifts. The observed local growth rate is for a twelve-year period from 1978 to 1990; the observed state growth rate is for a five-year period, 1978 to 1983. Therefore, the state growth rate must be converted into an equivalent twelve-year rate to compute the observed shift for the 1978 to 1990 period. That is,

$$
\begin{aligned}
R_{24}^{1978-1990} &= (1 + R_{24}^{1978-83})^{12/5} - 1 \\
&= [1 + 0.1538]^{12/5} - 1 \\
&= (1.1538)^{2.4} - 1 \\
&= 0.4097
\end{aligned}
$$

The observed employment shift for 1978 to 1990 can then be computed by subtracting the equivalent twelve-year state growth rate from the observed twelve-year local growth rate. That is,

$$
\begin{aligned}
s_{24}^{1978-1990} &= r_{24}^{1978-1990} - R_{24}^{1978-1990} \\
&= 0.5000 - 0.4097 \\
&= 0.0903
\end{aligned}
$$

The twelve-year observed employment shifts are then converted into equivalent twenty-year projected shift, $s_{24}^{1990-2010}$ to be consistent with the twenty-year constant-share projection term. That is,

$$
\begin{aligned}
s_{24}^{1990-2010} &= (1 + s_{24}^{.978-1990})^{20/12} - 1 \\
&= (1 + (0.0903)^{20/12} - 1 \\
&= 0.1550
\end{aligned}
$$

Projecting Local Employment. The shift-share employment projection for the year 2010 can then by computed by adding the projected shift to the constant-share projection term computed earlier and multiplying the sum by the local employment in 1990. That is,

$$
\begin{aligned}
e_{24}^{2010} &= [(1 + R_{24}^{1990-2010}) + s_{24}^{1990-2010}] \, e_{24}^{1990} \\
&= [(1 + 0.4027) + 0.1550] \, 600 \\
&= 935
\end{aligned}
$$

In this case, the local employment in SIC 24 grew faster than the state employment, causing the projected employment shift to be positive. As a result, the shift-share employment projection is larger than the equivalent constant-share projection. This is the result one would expect if the local employment continued to grow faster than the state rate that is the basis for the constant-share projection.

COMPONENTS AND OPERATION

As the location map in Exhibit 10.1 indicates, the left-hand side of the SHFT-SHR model contains the welcome screen, main menu, location map, and model documentation that are common to all of the models in this book. Five additional sections are provided to store the required input data, the intermediate computational values, and the model output.

The Parameter Entry section is used to enter and store the parameter values needed to use the SHFT-SHR model. The Imported Basic section is used to store basic employment estimates that are imported from the ECONBASE; these values are then copied into the Local Entry and Computations sections. The user can also enter the past and present employment in each local industry directly into the Local Entry section. The OBERS Entry and Compute section is used to enter the observed and projected OBERS employment data for the reference region (for example, state or nation) and compute the observed and projected reference region growth rates (see "Data Sources" section below for an explanation of the term OBERS).

The SHFT-SHR employment projections are prepared in the Computations section. This section computes the past and projected local and reference region growth rates using data that have been copied from other parts of the model. These rates are applied to the observed local employment values to compute the constant-share and shift-share employment projections. The desired projections are extracted from this section to the Projection Output section for displaying with the various SHFT-SHR output display options.

Model Operation
As Table 10.1 indicates, eleven macro commands are provided for use in conjunction with the SHFT-SHR model. The Alt-D, Alt-L, Alt-M, Alt-Q, Alt-R, Alt-W, and Alt-Z macros correspond to the standard macros described in chapter 1. General instructions for using these macros and other spreadsheet macros are provided in chapter 1. The four specialized macros provided for use with the SHFT-SHR model are described below.

Exhibit 10.1

SHFT-SHR Location Map

Welcome A1..A20	Location Map B1..P20	Macro Document	Param Entry AG1..AJ20			Imported Basic	OBERS Entry and Compute
Main Menu A21..A40	Range Descript						
Document A41..A60						BA1..BH80	BI1..BO80
					Computations	Project Output	
			Local Entry	Computations			
	B21..M160		AG81..AJ169	AL81..AY169	BA81..BE169		
		T1..AA331					

Table 10.1

SHFT-SHR Macros

Alt-C	Compute employment projections
Alt-D	Go to Documentation
Alt-G	Graph output
Alt-I	Input employment data
Alt-L	Go to Location map
Alt-M	Go to Main menu
Alt-P	Print output
Alt-Q	Quit/save model
Alt-R	Go to Range descriptions
Alt-W	Go to Welcome screen
Alt-Z	Go to macros

Alt-C, Compute Employment Projections. This macro is used to compute the constant-share or shift-share projections for the desired employment data. This option can be used only after the **Alt-I** option has been used to enter the required local and reference region employment data. The following suboptions are provided:

1. Total, project total employment;
2. Basic, project basic employment; and
3. Main_menu, return to main menu.

After one of the first three options is selected, a second menu is provided with three suboptions:

1. Constant, prepare a constant-share projection for the specified employment data;
2. Shift, prepare a shift-share projection for these data; and
3. Main_menu, return to the main menu.

The observed and projected employment values and the projected growth are then computed and displayed on the screen. After viewing the output, the user can use the **Alt-M** macro to return to the main menu.

Alt-G, Graph output. This option is used to prepare bar graphs showing the observed and projected employment in each local industry. Four suboptions are provided:

1. Total, graph the projected total employment;
2. Basic, project basic employment; and
3. Main_menu, return to main menu.

A second menu can then be used to choose among the following options:

1. Constant, prepare a constant-share projection;
2. Shift, prepare a shift-share projection; and
3. Main_menu, return to the main menu.

After viewing the bar graph, the user can press any key to return to the main menu.

Alt-I, Input Employment Data. This option is used to enter the parameter values, local employment, and reference region employment data required by the SHFT-SHR model. Seven suboptions are provided:

1. Param, this option is used to specify the model parameters;
2. 1st_local, this option is used to enter the local employment data for the first year for which employment data are required, that is, 1978 for the sample data considered in the preceding discussion;
3. Obs_local, this option is used to enter local employment data for the most recent observation year, that is, 1990 for the data considered above;
4. First_OBERS, this option is used to enter OBERS employment data for the first year for which these data are required, that is, 1978 for the data considered above;
5. Second_OBERS, this option is used to enter OBERS employment data for the second year for which these data are required, that is, 1983 for the data considered above;
6. Third_OBERS, this option is used to enter OBERS employment data for the third year for which these data are required, that is, 2000 for the data considered above; and
7. Main_menu, this option is used to return to the main menu.

The first six options provide a second menu, providing two suboptions: (1) New_data, enter new data, and (2) Revise_data, revise existing data. The Obs_local option provides a third option, Import, that can be used to import total employment values and basic employment estimates from another work sheet; these options are described in the "Data Entry" section.

Alt-P, Print Output. This option is used to send the output table showing the observed and projected employment in each local industry and the projected growth rate to the printer. Four suboptions are provided:

1. Total, print the observed and projected total employment;
2. Basic, print the observed and projected basic employment; and
3. Main_menu, return to the main menu.

A second menu can then be used to select among the following options:

1. Constant, prepare a constant-share projection for the specified employment data;
2. Shift, prepare a shift-share projection for these data; and
3. Main_menu, return to the main menu.

The user is automatically returned to the main menu after the output have been printed.

Data Entry
Three types of data are required to use the SHFT-SHR model: (1) the model parameters and output labels, (2) current and past employment data for the analysis region, and (3) three sets of OBERS employment data for the reference region. The three types of required information and the procedures for entering them into the model are described below.

Parameters. As Exhibit 10.2 illustrates, the following parameters must be specified to use the SHFT-SHR model:

1. The Analysis Region parameter identifies the area (for example, county) for which the analysis is being conducted; the name is entered as a label and cannot exceed 30 characters in length;
2. The OBERS Region parameter identifies the reference region (for instance, the state) for which the OBERS employment data

are to be entered; the name is entered as a label and cannot exceed thirty characters in length;

3. The First OBERS Year parameter specifies the first year for which OBERS employment data are to be entered, in this case 1978. It also defines the first year for which local employment data are to be provided and the beginning of the observation period used to compute the constant-shift growth rates;

4. The Second OBERS Year parameter specifies the second year for which OBERS data are to be entered. This value also defines the end of the constant-shift observation period and the beginning of the constant-share projection period. For instance, Exhibit 10.2 indicates that data for 1978 and 1983 will be used to compute the observed constant-shift growth rates;

5. The Third OBERS Year parameter specifies the last year for which OBERS data are to be provided and defines the end of the period used to compute the constant-share growth rates. For example, Exhibit 10.2 indicates that OBERS data for 1983 and 2000 will be used to compute the constant-share growth rates;

6. The Observation Year parameter identifies the year for which the observed employment data are to be entered. As a result, it is normally the most recent year for which local employment data are available (in this case, however, it is 1985); and

7. The Projection Year parameter identifies the year for which employment projections are desired, here, the year 2010.

Local Employment Data. Local employment data by two-digit SIC category are required for: (1) the first OBERS year, 1978 for the sample data in Exhibit 10.2; and (2) the observation year, 1990 for the sample data in Exhibit 10.2. The data can be entered in either order. Local employment data for the first OBERS year are entered by selecting the **Alt-I** and 1st_Local New_data options. The cursor is then moved to the Local Data Entry section of the model and the appropriate employment data column. A complete list of all the one-digit SIC Divisions and two-digit SIC Major Groups is provided, allowing the user to enter the required local employment data in the first OBERS year. Employment values can be entered with the numeric keypad; pressing the ENTER key automatically moves the cursor down one row to allow the next value to be entered. The system automatically returns to the main menu after all of the data have been entered.

Exhibit 10.2

SHFT-SHR Parameters

Analysis region:	Tutor County
OBERS region:	Tutor State
First OBERS year:	1978
Second OBERS year:	1983
Third OBERS year:	2000
Observation year:	1985
Projection year:	2010

Local employment data for the observation year are entered by selecting the **Alt-I** and Obs_local options. The user is then provided with three data entry options. The New_data option can be used to enter the data from the keyboard using procedures identical to those for entering employment data for the first OBERS year. The Revise_data option can be used to revise data that have been previously entered. The third option, Import, can be used to import employment data from a copy of the ECONBASE model into the SHFT-SHR model.

The **Alt-I** Obs_local Import option provides three options for selecting the basic data to be imported; (1) Total, import the total employment values; (2) Assume, import the assumption technique basic employment estimates; (3) LQ, import the location quotient basic employment estimates; and (4) Main_menu, return to the main menu. The user can then select the file from which the data can be imported from a list presented on the screen. Users should be aware that it may take several minutes to import the data from the ECONBASE model.

OBERS Employment Data. OBERS employment data are required for the first, second, and third OBERS years specified in the model parameters. The data are entered by selecting the **Alt-I** option and the First_OBERS, Second_OBERS, or Third_OBERS option as appropriate. All three options take the user to the OBERS Data Entry and Compute section of the model and place the cursor in the proper column of the data entry screen. The OBERS employment can be entered as decimal numbers using the numeric keypad, if desired. Pressing the ENTER key after each value is entered automatically moves the cursor down one row to allow the next value to be entered. The user is automatically returned to the main menu after all of the data for a given year have been entered.

DATA SOURCES

National and regional population, employment, and personal income projections are available from the OBERS report series prepared approximately every five years by the U.S. Department of Commerce, Bureau of Economic Analysis (BEA; U.S. Bureau of Economic Analysis 1985). The projections are called the "OBERS" projections because they were previously produced jointly by the U.S. Bureau of the Census, Office of Business Economics ("OBE," now the BEA), and the U.S. Department of Agriculture, Economic Research Service ("ERS"). The OBERS name has been retained for continuity even though the projections are now produced solely by the BEA.

The OBERS projections provide economic and demographic projections for the nation, states, BEA economic areas, metropolitan statistical areas (MSAs), and other substate areas.[5] The 1985 projections for the United States and the states include: (1) population aged 0 to 14, 15 to 64, and 65 and above; (2) personal income by major income component; and (3) employment and earnings (such as wages and salaries, other labor income, and proprietors' income) for fifty-seven industrial groups. Projections provided for MSAs and other substate areas include: (1) total population; (2) total personal income; and (3) earnings and employment for fourteen major industrial groups. The state-level projections are generally used because they provide disaggregated employment data at the lowest geographic level.

The 1985 OBERS reports include projections for 1990, 1995, 2000, 2005, 2015, and 2035 and historical data for 1969, 1973, 1978, and 1983. Because these state- or national-level employment data are used to compute the observed and projected growth rates for the reference region, projections can be prepared only for the years 2000, 2005, 2015, and 2035. Similarly, the state and local data used to compute the past employment shift must be for the years 1969, 1973, 1978, and 1983.

SAMPLE APPLICATION

The procedures for using the SHFT-SHR model and the types of information produced by the model will be illustrated with the 1985 employment data for Wayne County, Ohio, used in chapter 12 of *Community Analysis and Planning Techniques* (Klosterman 1990). The sample data are provided in the distribution copy of the SHFT-SHR model. The

Exhibit 10.3

Sample SHFT-SHR Local Employment Data

Local Employment Data Entry Sheet

SIC Code	Industry	--Local Employment-- Current	Past
A	AGRICULTURE, FOREST & FISHING	127	63
01	Agricultural production—crops	0	0
02	Agricultural production—livestock	0	0
07	Agriculture services	100	63
08	Forestry	0	0
09	Fishing, hunting, and trapping	0	0
B	MINING	804	521
10	Metal mining	0	0
11	Anthracite mining	0	0
12	Bituminous coal mining	0	0
13	Oil and gas extraction	720	433
14	Nonmetallic mining & quarrying	50	66
C	CONSTRUCTION	1,175	1,257
15	Building construction	439	478
16	Nonbuilding construction	151	0
17	Special trade contractors	585	735
D	MANUFACTURING	13,654	13,905
20	Food and kindred products	1,259	1,366
21	Tobacco manufactures	0	0
22	Textile mill products	0	0
23	Apparel and finished products	0	0
24	Lumber and wood products	426	459
25	Furniture and fixtures	65	0
26	Paper and allied products	1,028	1,469
27	Printing and allied industries	233	295
28	Chemicals and allied products	377	375

example reviews the four major steps required to use the model: (1) entering parameters; (2) entering local and state employment data; (3) entering OBERS employment data; and (4) viewing the model output.

Procedural Steps

Entering Parameters. The first step in using the model is using the **Alt-I P**aram option to enter the model parameters and output labels. As Exhibit 10.2 illustrates, seven parameters are required; these were described in detail in the "Data Entry" section above. The values shown in Exhibit 10.2 can be viewed by selecting the **Alt-I Param Revise_data** options; the user can then use the **Alt-M** macro to return to the main menu. New values are entered with the **Alt-I Param New_data** options; the Input employment data options menu is displayed after all of the values are entered to allow the user to enter another type of data.

Entering Local Employment Data. The user can then use the **Alt-I 1st_Local Revise_data** option to view the sample local employment data for the first OBERS year, that is, 1978. A portion of these data are shown in Exhibit 10.3. As the exhibit illustrates, a complete list of two-digit SIC employment categories is provided, allowing the user to enter the local employment in each industry in the first OBERS year. New employment values can be added by using the **Alt-I 1st_Local New_data** option.

The **Alt-I Obs_local Revise_data** option can be used to review the local employment for the observation year, here, 1985. The **Alt-I Obs_-local Import LQ** option can also be used to import the location quotient basic employment estimates for Wayne County that are distributed with the ECONBASE model. The Import Assume option can also be used to import the assumption technique basic employment estimates from the ECONBASE model.

Entering OBERS Data. The **Alt-I First_OBERS Revise_data** option can be used to review the OBERS employment data for the state of Ohio that are provided with the SHFT-SHR model. As Exhibit 10.4 indicates, a complete list of categories for OBERS national- and state-level employment data is provided, allowing the user to enter the required OBERS data directly from readily available published data sources.

Reviewing Model Output. Exhibit 10.5 displays a portion of the output provided by the SHFT-SHR model. The output header displays the current date, the name of the analysis region, the type of projection (that is, constant-share or shift-share) and the type of data (such as total employment, assumption basic estimates, or location quotient basic employment estimates). The body of the table lists: (1) the SIC number and industry name for each local industry; (2) the current and projected employment in each industry; and (3) the projected growth rate. The bar graph showing the observed and projected employment in each industry can be viewed by selecting the **Alt-G** option.

Exhibit 10.4

Sample SHFT-SHR OBERS Employment Data

OBERS Employment Data Entry Screen

Industry	--------OBERS Employment--------		
	1978	1983	2000
TOTAL EMPLOYMENT	4,880.1	4,605.2	5,483.9
FARM	143.5	133.4	125.4
NONFARM	4,746.7	4,471.8	5,358.6
PRIVATE	4,059.8	3,785.0	4,684.9
Agr. serv., forest & fishing	16.8	19.7	30.9
MINING	29.7	27.5	37.2
Coal mining	15.3	11.3	15.1
Oil and gas extraction	8.2	11.9	17.2
Metal mining	0.5	0.1	0.2
Nonmetallic minerals	5.7	4.3	4.8
CONSTRUCTION	227.2	179.2	239.4
MANUFACTURING	1,386.2	1,076.1	1,172.5
Nondurable goods	407.4	346.4	386.7
Food and kindred products	75.7	64.2	59.5
Tobacco manufactures	0.3	0.1	0.1
Textile mill products	5.9	4.6	3.6
Apparel and finished textiles	19.1	16.3	15.7
Paper and allied products	39.9	35.0	33.2
Printing and publishing	68.4	65.6	75.6
Chemicals and allied products	69.4	63.7	67.3

EVALUATION AND EXTENSIONS

The constant-share and shift-share projection techniques have been shrouded in controversy almost since their introduction.[6] However, they continue to be widely used because they are conceptually and computationally straightforward, require readily accessible data, and provide fast and reasonably accurate projections given their costs. Theoretically more appealing techniques, such as regional input-output and econometric forecasting models, are difficult to understand, much harder to implement, and generally require data that are difficult or even impossible to obtain.

Exhibit 10.5

Sample SHFT-SHR Output

15-Jan-92

Tutor County Constant-Share Total Employment Projections

SIC Code	Industry	--Employment--		Growth Rate
		1985	2010	
07	Agriculture services	100	194	0.9386
AA	Other Division A	27	25	-0.0869
13	Oil and gas extraction	720	1,238	0.7190
14	Nonmetallic mining & quarrying	50	59	0.1756
BB	Other Division B	34	53	0.5594
15	Building construction	439	672	0.5310
16	Nonbuilding construction	151	231	0.5310
17	Special trade contractors	585	896	0.5310
20	Food and kindred products	1,259	1,126	-0.1058
24	Lumber and wood products	426	669	0.5700
25	Furniture and fixtures	65	57	-0.1270
26	Paper and allied products	1,028	951	-0.0747
27	Printing and allied industries	233	287	0.2320
28	Chemicals and allied products	377	409	0.0842

Several studies have evaluated the relative accuracy of alternative constant-share/shift-share projection models.[7] The results of these comparative tests are inconclusive because they examine different projection models, data sets, geographic areas, and levels of industrial aggregation. They generally support the constant-share model, though, particularly for county-level projections with small industrial sectors and limited data that preclude more systematic modeling techniques.

Theoretical considerations provide little support for using either of these projection models. Nevertheless, the computational simplicity of these projection models, relative to more sophisticated techniques, provides a pragmatic justification for using them to prepare quick and reasonably accurate short-run projections. They are also appropriate for preparing long-term "baseline" forecasts examining the implications of continuing past employment trends into the future. Their use in both cases is justified largely by the lack of other readily accessible small-area employment projection techniques (Stevens and Moore 1980).

ACKNOWLEDGMENTS

The authors would like to acknowledge the assistance of Professor David L. Phillips and the students in the "Analysis of the Urban System" course at the University of Virginia in improving the SHFT-SHR model during the summer of 1991.

NOTES

1. The discussion of the conceptual basis of the SHFT-SHR model draws heavily on a similar discussion in Klosterman (1990).

2. For discussions examining the use of the constant-share and shift-share techniques to prepare small-area population projections see Isserman (1977) and Pittenger (1976).

3. For a more complete discussion of this procedure for computing equivalent growth rates see Klosterman (1990).

4. The shift-share (or "mix and share") technique can also be used as a descriptive device to analyze historical trends. For an introduction to this use of the technique see Bendavid-Val (1983); applications of shift-share as an analysis tool include Dunn (1960) and Perloff, et al. (1960).

5. For a more complete discussion of the OBERS projections and the methodology used to prepare the projections see Klosterman (1990). A complete list of the fifty-seven industrial groups for which OBERS projections are available at the national and state levels and the fourteen industrial groups for which projections are available at the substate level and corresponding SIC codes is provided in Klosterman (1990).

6. Particularly strong objections to the technique have been raised by Richardson, who concludes that shift-share is "a harmless pastime for small

boys with calculators" (1978a p. 202), that "can be far from harmless if used for policy (mis)guidance" (1978b p. 18). For a more complete evaluation of the constant-share and shift-share techniques see Klosterman (1990).

7. See, for example, Brown (1969), Greenberg (1972), and Hewings (1976). Stevens and Moore (1980) provide a useful review and assessment of these and other studies.

REFERENCES

Bendavid-Val, A. 1983. *Regional and local economic analysis for practitioners*. New York: Praeger.

Brown, H. J. 1969. Shift and share projections of regional economic growth: an empirical test. *Journal of Regional Science* 9, 1–17.

Dunn, E. S., Jr. 1960. A statistical and analytical technique for regional science. *Papers, Regional Science Association* 6, 15–23.

Greenberg, M. R. 1972. A test of alternative models for projecting county industrial production at the 2, 3, and 4 digit SIC levels. *Regional and Urban Economics* 1, 397–418.

Hewings, G. J. D. 1976. On the accuracy of alternative models for stepping down multi-county employment projections to counties. *Economic Geography* 52, 206–217.

Isserman, A. M. 1977. The accuracy of population projections for sub-county areas. *Journal of the American Institute of Planners* 43, 247–259.

Klosterman, R. E. 1990. *Community analysis and planning techniques*. Savage, MD: Rowman and Littlefield Publishers.

Perloff, H. S., et al. 1960. *Regions, resources and economic growth*. Lincoln: University of Nebraska Press.

Pittenger, D. B. 1976. *Projecting state and local populations*. Cambridge, MA: Ballinger.

Richardson, H. W. 1978a. The state of regional economics: a survey. *International Regional Science Review* 3, 1–48.

———. 1978b. *Regional and urban economics*. Harmondsworth: Penguin.

Stevens, B. H., and Moore, C. L. 1980. A critical review of the literature on shift-share as a forecasting technique. *Journal of Regional Science* 20, 419–435.

U.S. Bureau of Economic Analysis. 1985. *1985 OBERS, BEA regional projections*. Vol. 1: *State projections to 2035*. Washington, DC: U.S. Government Printing Office.

Chapter 11

INTRO-IO: Introduction to Input-Output Accounting and Modeling

Karen R. Polenske and Stephen F. Fournier

An input-output table provides a detailed statistical account of the flow of goods and services among the producing and purchasing sectors of an economy. In addition to showing complete details of the income and product accounts, input-output tables also show all intermediate transactions among producers and purchasers within a consistent accounting framework.

Table 11.1 shows the 1987 transactions for a seven-sector U.S. input-output table. Each row in the table shows the amount of an industry's output that was sold to intermediate and final consumers in 1987. To illustrate, the first row shows that of the $196.5 billion gross domestic output (GDO) produced by the Agriculture sector, $160.8 billion (about 80 percent) was sold to intermediate sectors, including sales of $51.9 billion to itself, $91.2 billion to the Manufacturing sector, plus some smaller sales to other sectors. Of the total GDO, the remaining $35.7 billion was purchased by the final demand sectors of the economy, which included purchases by private consumers, local, state, and national government purchasers, buyers of capital goods, and foreign traders (sales to exporters minus purchases from importers).

Each column of the input-output table provides complete details on the industry's purchases of goods and services, as well as the amounts paid for labor (wages and salaries), capital (profits, retained earnings, dividends, and interest), land (rent), and indirect taxes. In Table 11.1, all these payments to factors of production are combined and called value added.

Table 11.1

Seven-Sector Industry Transactions Matrix, U.S. 1987
($ 1982 millions)

Producing Sector	Purchasing Sector							Int.* Demand	Final Demand	Total Output
	1	2	3	4	5	6	7			
Agriculture	51949	80	1415	91220	4619	11187	348	160818	35684	196502
Mining	369	18346	4969	170920	1008	51499	3646	250757	-27477	223280
Construction	1534	470	826	20018	12473	66388	11115	112824	381933	494756
Manufacturing	36752	15700	176203	865110	79418	211830	8678	1393692	1016471	2410163
Trade/Trans**	10360	4342	56747	150767	66123	71618	5260	365217	693175	1058392
Services	14936	20698	47070	180771	172066	468030	15100	918671	1347464	2266136
Other	451	1035	1645	25133	16832	30492	2062	77650	398453	476103
Value Added	80150	162611	205881	906224	705852	1355091	429895	3845702	0***	3845702
Total Outlays	196502	223280	494756	2410163	1058392	2266136	476103	7125330	3845702	10971032

* Int. Demand = sum of elements in intermediate demand columns 1 to 7.
** Trans = Transportation.
*** No Data Provided.
   Sources Generated using data from the 228-sector historical input-output computer tape provided by the U.S. Bureau of Labor Statistics (BLS) Office of Employment Projections, January 25, 1991.

To produce its total output, the Agriculture sector (column 1) purchased $51.9 billion from itself, $36.8 billion from the Manufacturing sector, $14.9 billion from the Services sector, plus some smaller-value amounts of other intermediate products. In addition, the Agriculture sector paid out more than $80.1 billion in the form of wages, profits, rent, and other factor payments. The total outlay of $196.5 billion (sum of column 1) is exactly equal to the total output of the sector (sum of row 1).

Input-output accounts have several distinguishing characteristics. First, the intermediate portion of the U.S. input-output accounts is square; that is, the same number of sectors are listed as producing (rows) and consuming (columns) sectors. This is the case in most of the world, but a few countries, such as Canada, have constructed rectangular accounts (Gigantes and Matuszewski 1968).

Second, the total value of output sold to all intermediate and final users must be exactly the same as the total value of the payments made to all factors of production and intermediate producers. In other words, the total costs of production must be imputed to the value of the good sold. Thus, the sum of a row and the sum of the corresponding column in the accounting table will be identical if all transactions are recorded accurately.

Third, in an "open" input-output table, the total of the value added row represents the total national income valued as payments to the factors of production (capital, labor, land, and so on) and will be referred to hereafter as gross national income (GNI). It is comprised of profits, wages, rent, interest, dividends, and other income receipts. In this "open" input-output table, the total of the final demand column represents the total purchases made by final users and will be referred to hereafter as gross national product (GNP). The basic components of the GNP are private consumption expenditures, gross private fixed capital formation, net inventory change, net foreign exports (gross exports minus gross imports), and federal, state, and local government expenditures.

Within the input-output accounting framework, the total payments to the factors of production (GNI) exactly equal the total expenditures by final users (GNP). Additional details on this accounting consistency are provided in Chenery and Clark (1959). Thus, the elements of the value added row and final demand column in this open model represent the traditional national income and product accounts (NIPA) of an economy. An input-output account is therefore far more complete than the NIPA in that it includes sales and purchases to both intermediate and final producers and purchasers and assures consistency in the accounts.

Fourth, a comparison of the intermediate and final demand columns in Table 11.1 indicates that much of the total production in the U.S. economy is transformed before being sold to a final user. Of the seven sectors, three sell less than 50 percent of their total output directly to final users. As sectors are disaggregated, more and more fall into this category.

Fifth, each transaction in Table 11.1 is shown in producer prices; that is, the dollar flow shows the amount that the industry or final user must pay for the good before the transportation, wholesale and retail trade, and insurance costs of transferring it from the producer to the consumer are incurred. In this "producer-price table," the Trade and

Transportation sector row (row 5 in the present example) gives the cost of transferring goods from the producer to the purchasing sector or final user.[1]

In other words, each element in the row includes the costs of transferring all inputs to the respective purchasing sector (final user) represented by that column. They represent the costs associated with the inputs into the sector, not with the output of the sector. The costs include wholesale and retail trade, insurance, and transportation costs in the present example. Accountants call the difference between the producer and purchaser price the "markup" or "margin." In the United States, the different margins are constructed as separate tables so that users can relatively easily transfer from producer to purchaser prices or vice versa.

Sixth, almost all entries in the input-output accounting table are positive or zero. Negatives will occur: (l) if gross imports are larger than gross exports; (2) if inventory depletions (use of output from a previous year) are larger than inventory additions; (3) in the profit row for any sector for which profits are negative; and (4) for all entries in a subsidy row. Whenever a negative entry occurs, the user should check to be certain it makes sense.

An input-output table is a valuable accounting tool partially because of all the consistency checks that can be made to be certain data taken from different sources are appropriately recorded. The user can then transform the accounting data for use in modeling and forecasting.

ALTERNATE INPUT-OUTPUT FORMULATIONS

Input-Output Model

We can transform these accounts for use in static (a given year), i.e., comparative static (a snapshot of two or more given years), and dynamic (changes occurring over a period of years) modeling. An open input-output model is one in which the GNP (and corresponding GNI) components are treated exogenously; that is, the data for these components are determined outside the model. For a partially closed input-output model, one or more component of GNP (GNI) is treated endogenously.

The most frequently employed partially closed model, for example, is one in which the personal consumption expenditures portion of GNP and the corresponding wage and salary portion of GNI are included as an extra column and row, respectively, in the model. The static, open input-output model is based upon the following three assumptions:

1. Constant returns to scale, that is, no external economies or diseconomies of scale;
2. Homogeneous products with no joint production, that is, each sector produces only one type of product and each product is produced by only one sector;
3. Constant direct input (technology) coefficient, implying that the technology of a sector will not change significantly during the period of study.

Each of these assumptions can be relaxed if sufficient data are available.

Direct-Input Coefficients

By employing the third assumption, Leontief (1936, 1966) was able to transform the general equilibrium system of equations (explained later) into an elegant tool of analysis. An analyst can then examine the different input requirements of the sectors very systematically in terms of purchases required per unit of output. Because the U.S. accounts are constructed in dollars, we will use that as the unit of analysis.

When each element in a column of the transactions table (see Table 11.1) is divided by the total output for that particular industry (Total Output), a column of coefficients is obtained. Each coefficient, a_{ij}, shows the amount that a sector purchases directly from another sector per dollar's worth of output. The coefficient 0.187 in row 4, column 1 of Table 11.2, for example, indicates that the Agriculture sector purchases about 19 cents' worth of output from the Manufacturing sector per dollar of Agriculture output (divide the amount the Agriculture sector bought from the Manufacturing sector, $36,752 million, by the GDO of the Agriculture sector, $196,502 million). These coefficients are referred to as input coefficients, direct-input coefficients, or technical-input coefficients; Leontief (1936) refers to them frequently as "cooking recipes." We will use the names interchangeably in this discussion.

Each column of Table 11.2 indicates the technology required to produce a particular sector's product. The input requirements based upon monetary values may change over time because of three factors: (1) prices may change per unit of physical output; (2) the product mix of the sector may change and different subcomponents of output may have different input requirements; and (3) the technology of producing the physical product may change (Carter 1967, 1970).

Analysts who study technological change are trying to look at just the changes in technology, but unless data in physical units and in sufficient detail are available, they may be examining instead the first two changes. Changes in pricing is a straightforward concept. Changes in product mix occur when subcomponents of a sector change in relative importance. The Agriculture sector, for example, includes grains, livestock, fruits, vegetables, and so on, each of which requires different inputs (technologies) to produce. Any significant change in the relative amount of output of the four or more subcomponents produced will therefore create changes in the direct input coefficient even if the technology for each of the subcomponents remains constant.

Table 11.2

Direct-Input Coefficients
(Direct Input per unit of output)

	1	2	3	4	5	6	7
1 Agriculture	0.264	0.000	0.003	0.038	0.004	0.005	0.001
2 Mining	0.002	0.082	0.010	0.071	0.001	0.023	0.008
3 Construction	0.008	0.002	0.002	0.008	0.012	0.029	0.023
4 Manufacturing	0.187	0.070	0.356	0.359	0.075	0.093	0.018
5 Trade and Transportation	0.053	0.019	0.115	0.063	0.062	0.032	0.011
6 Services	0.076	0.093	0.095	0.075	0.163	0.207	0.032
7 Other	0.002	0.005	0.003	0.010	0.016	0.013	0.004
Value Added	0.408	0.728	0.416	0.376	0.667	0.598	0.903
Total	1.000	1.000	1.000	1.000	1.000	1.000	1.000

Source: Calculated from Table 11.1 as the direct input from a given industry divided by the total output of the industry that is purchasing the input.

The direct-input coefficient table also has some basic characteristics that an analyst should check prior to using the coefficients for analysis:

1. When all rows from the accounts are included in the division process, each column sum should be 1.0. (that is, $\Sigma a_{ij} \geq 1.0$).
2. Each coefficient should be equal to or larger than 0.0 (unless any of the negative entries fall in the intermediate portion of the table) and equal to or less than 1.0 (that is, $0 \geq a_{ij} \geq 1.0$).

3. Generally, the diagonal elements are the largest elements in the table.
4. The coefficients are multiplied by total output of a sector and therefore differ significantly from the direct and indirect coefficients, which we discuss next.

In order to use the direct-input coefficients for modeling, the table needs to be square, so we will drop the last two rows of Table 11.2.

Direct and Indirect Coefficients

The coefficients in Table 11.3, which are derived from the table of direct-input coefficients (see Table 11.2), represent the direct and indirect requirements per unit of final demand. Analysts refer to this table as the inverse, Leontief's inverse, or as the table of direct and indirect requirements. The calculation of these coefficients is explained in Miller and Blair (1985). Each element in the table describes the total amount that the sector listed at the left of the table must produce to fulfill the direct and indirect requirements generated by one unit of final demand for the product of the sector listed at the top of the table.

Table 11.3

Direct and Indirect Input Coefficients
(Direct and indirect input per unit of final demand)

	1	2	3	4	5	6	7
1 Agriculture	1.386	0.010	0.039	0.088	0.018	0.021	0.005
2 Mining	0.045	1.106	0.067	0.134	0.022	0.051	0.014
3 Construction	0.023	0.009	1.017	0.023	0.022	0.042	0.026
4 Manufacturing	0.467	0.157	0.639	1.660	0.185	0.235	0.056
5 Trade and Transportation	0.120	0.040	0.179	0.129	1.092	0.067	0.021
6 Services	0.210	0.155	0.231	0.211	0.249	1.310	0.055
7 Other	0.013	0.010	0.016	0.023	0.023	0.022	1.006

Source: Calculated from Table 11.2 using only the seven-sector direct-input coefficients by inverting the (I-A) matrix.

In the second column, for example, the second cell shows that if the final demand for Mining were to increase by \$1, the output of Mining products must increase by \$1.11 to fulfill the intermediate direct and indirect as well as final demand requirements. One dollar of the output is required by final consumers, 8.2 cents is a direct purchase by the Metal Mining sector of its own product (see Table 11.2), leaving a total of 2.4 cents as an indirect purchase. To obtain the total output that a sector must produce to satisfy a given set of final demands, multiply each element in the inverse coefficient row for that sector by the corresponding element in the set of final demands and sum the resulting figures.

The coefficients in the inverse table reflect the interdependence that exists within an economy. The direct coefficient in row 4, column 1 of Table 11.2, for example, shows that for every dollar of output, the Agriculture sector buys about 19 cents' worth of manufactured goods, but the coefficient in the same row and column of the inverse, Table 11.3, indicates that the 19 cents represents only the direct purchase of manufactured goods by the Agriculture sector. Indirectly, a dollar's worth of final demand for Agriculture requires that an additional 28 cents' worth of manufactured goods be produced.

This may result, for example, if an increase in the consumer demand for Agriculture causes the Agriculture sector to increase its purchase of Services. The Services sector then must produce and must buy additional inputs in the form of Manufactured goods to use in the production process. Thus, the increased demand for Agriculture in the example indirectly generates production of Manufactured goods in excess of the direct-input requirements of the Agriculture sector. Repercussions of the increased purchases by the final demand units are accounted for by the coefficients in Table 11.3.

Again, we note a few characteristics of the inverse table:

1. Each element, d_{ij}, in Table 11.3 is the same as or larger than the corresponding element in Table 11.2 (that is, $d_{ij} \geq a_{ij}$).
2. Each element on the main diagonal is equal to or larger than 1.0 (that is, $d_{ii} \geq 1.0$) because one unit of output must always be sold to final demand.
3. The sum of each column of the inverse will be equal to or larger than 1.0 (that is, $\Sigma d_{ij} \geq 1.0$).
4. The coefficients are multiplied by the total final demand of the corresponding sector. Note that for the direct coefficients, we

multiplied by the total output of the purchasing sector while here we multiply by the total final demand of the sector.

If each sector produced only for final users, all off-diagonal elements of the table would be zero. Economies become increasingly interdependent as they develop. Thus, countries with little industrialization will generally have very small or zero off-diagonal elements in their inverse tables. The off-diagonal coefficients for highly industrialized countries will be much larger and more of the coefficients will be nonzero.

Most square input-output tables can be inverted, but the user should always check to be certain the result is an inverse. This is done by multiplying the inverse (**D**) by (**I** - **A**). The result of this multiplication should give a matrix with ones along the main diagonal, that is, the identity matrix. If it does not, check the computer program and the input data to determine where the error is.

Secondary Production: USE and MAKE Tables

We have presented so far a single input-output table. Because the second assumption of no joint production usually does not hold, analysts must deal with what are referred to as primary and secondary products for each sector. Accounting officials construct two tables, one for primary products and one for secondary products of the sector. In the early input-output literature, the two tables were referred to as the primary and secondary tables. By the 1970s, U.S. input-output officials started to follow the U.N. System of National Accounts policy and referred to the two tables as the USE and MAKE tables. Because most countries follow this latter practice, we explain the USE and MAKE tables in detail here.

According to Bulmer-Thomas (1982), there are five types of secondary products: commodity-technology, industry-technology, by-products, joint products, and secondary production of nontraded commodities. All five types of secondary products are represented in the accounts for the United States. For simplicity, we will explain the USE and MAKE Tables, shown in Tables 11.4 and 11.5, respectively, by assuming that all secondary production is of the industry-technology type.

The USE table is a rectangular table with each row of the table representing the commodity being produced and each column of the table indicating the industry purchasing the commodity. Thus, the sums of the corresponding rows and the columns of this table are not equal. From Table 11.4, we see that in 1987, the Agriculture sector (column 1) purchased $51.9 billion of agricultural commodities (row 1) and $36.9 billion of manufacturing commodities (row 4), plus lesser amounts from other sectors in order to produce all of its output for a total of $196,502 billion, but it produced only $187,351 billion of agricultural products. We will see in the MAKE table (Table 11.5) that it also produced other commodities.[2]

Table 11.4

USE of Commodities by Industry, U.S. 1987
($ 1982 millions)

Commodity/ Industry	1	2	3	4	5	6	7	Int. Demand	Final Demand	Total Output
Agriculture	51861	10	939	89002	4154	9932	303	156201	31151	187351
Mining	200	18357	4234	168353	335	49994	3604	245077	-34446	210631
Construction	1534	470	826	20018	12473	66388	11115	112824	381932	494756
Manufacturing	36953	15398	177656	872252	77084	205183	8473	1392999	1002699	2395699
Trade/Transportation	9790	3705	54859	141286	61571	57920	4841	333973	656805	990778
Services	15890	22060	49966	191996	183361	499130	16091	978494	1435057	2413552
Other	123	669	396	21032	13561	22497	1782	60060	372503	432563
Value Added	80150	162611	205881	906224	705852	1355091	429895			
Total	196502	223280	494756	2410163	1058392	2266136	476103	3279628	3845702	7125330

Source: Generated from BLS computer tape (see Table 11.1). Numbers may not sum to total due to rounding.

Each commodity may be produced by one or more industry, and each industry purchases inputs not only for the production of its primary product but also for the production of any secondary products. Therefore, if direct coefficients are calculated for this table, the coefficients represent the technology for the industry but not for the commodity that represents the primary output of the industry. The table typically includes the final demand and value-added sectors.

The MAKE table is usually a square table with elements in each row of the table representing the various types of products the industry produces and the elements in each column indicating which industry produced a specific product. From Table 11.5, we can see that the Agriculture sector produced not only $187.3 billion of agricultural commodities (column 1) but also generated more than $5 billion worth of manufacturing commodities and provided more than $3.8 billion worth of services. Again, the sums of the corresponding rows and the columns of this table will not be equal; however, the sum of the rows of the MAKE table must be equal to the sum of the corresponding columns of the USE table, and the sum of the columns of the MAKE table must be equal to the sum of the corresponding rows of the USE table.

Table 11.5

MAKE Matrix, US 1987
($ 1982 millions)

Industry/ Commodity	1	2	3	4	5	6	7	Total
Agriculture	187279	0	0	5338	11	3875	0	196502
Mining	0	209308	0	8832	0	5139	0	223280
Construction	0	0	494756	0	0	0	0	494756
Manufacturing	20	1238	0	2363584	0	43578	1743	2410163
Trade and Transportation	53	0	0	17040	978651	62578	71	2410163
Services	0	85	0	831	3311	2261748	160	1058392
Other	0	0	0	74	8806	36634	430590	2266136
Total	187351	210631	494756	2395699	990778	2413552	432563	476103

Source: Generated from BLS computer tape (see Table 11.1). Numbers may not sum to total due to rounding.

CONSTRUCTING INPUT-OUTPUT MODEL

Technical Coefficients. An input-output table contains the complete set of transactions that occur in the economy during a given time period. The exact transactions, however, are often not known or may not be important for general discussion. In such cases, the information contained in Tables 11.1, 11.2, and 11.3 can be written using general mathematical notations. The variables will be defined as follows (small letters refer to single elements and capital letters specify an entire matrix):

x_{ij} =   the amount of output produced by industry i and purchased by industry j;

x_i =   the total output of industry i;

y_i =   the total consumption of the products of industry i by final users in the economy;

a_{ij} =   the amount of output produced by industry i and purchased by industry j per unit of output in industry j, referred to as the technical-input coefficient and calculated as: $x_{ij}/x_j = a_{ij}$; and

m =   the number of industries in the economy.

Table 11.1 can be written as a set of linear simultaneous equations, which in matrix notation is represented as follows.

$$\begin{array}{ccccc} \mathbf{A} & \mathbf{X} & + & \mathbf{Y} & = & \mathbf{X} \\ (m \times m) & (m \times 1) & & (m \times 1) & & (m \times 1) \end{array} \qquad (1)$$

The number of industries will be referred to as m, rather than 7, to represent the set of equations in its most general form.

Given a transactions table for an economy for a particular year, a set of technical coefficients can be calculated. Then, if technical coefficients, the a_{ij}'s, are calculated and if the outputs of each industry, the x_j's, for a future year are known, all of the interindustry transactions can be calculated, assuming that the technology in the economy has remained constant between the base year and the future year. Generally, the assumption is made that the technology of an economy does remain constant over a period of five to ten years. This assumption, of course, is less realistic for rapidly developing economies.

If the technology can be assumed to remain constant and if a set of final demands is available for a future year, the above set of equations can be solved for the unknown outputs. The variables in the set of Equation (1) can be rearranged so that all of the unknown outputs (**X**) are on the left-hand side of the set of equations and all the known final demands (**Y**) are on the right-hand side. That is,

$$\begin{array}{ccccc} \mathbf{X} & - & \mathbf{A} & \mathbf{X} & = & \mathbf{Y} \\ (m \times 1) & & (m \times m) & (m \times 1) & & (m \times 1) \end{array} \qquad (2)$$

$$\begin{array}{ccccccc} \mathbf{I} & \mathbf{X} & - & \mathbf{A} & \mathbf{X} & = & \mathbf{Y} \\ (m \times m) & (m \times 1) & & (m \times m) & (m \times 1) & & (m \times 1) \end{array} \qquad (3)$$

$$(I \quad — \quad A) \quad X \quad = \quad Y \qquad (4)$$
$$\text{(mxm)} \qquad \text{(mxm)} \text{ (mx1)} \qquad \text{(mx1)}$$

$$X \quad = \quad (I \quad — \quad A)^{-1} \quad Y \qquad (5)$$
$$\text{(mx1)} \qquad \text{(mxm)} \qquad \text{(mxm) (mx1)}$$

The inverse is obtained either by inverting the $(I - A)$ matrix or by approximating the inverse through the iterative series: $I + A + A^2 \ldots + A^n$. For a partially closed model, one or more rows and corresponding columns are added to the A, Y, and X matrices shown above.

Commodity-by-Industry Procedures

We have discussed the creation of a technical-input coefficient, a_{ij}, as the amount of output produced by industry i and purchased by industry j per unit of output in industry j. Using the assumption of industry-based technology, in the commodity-by-industry detail that is contained in the USE and MAKE matrices, we generate two sets of coefficients. We will refer to the column-standardized USE matrix as the B matrix, where each element, b_{ij}, is the amount of commodity i purchased by industry j per unit of output in industry j, to the column-standardized MAKE matrix as the E matrix, where each element, e_{ij}, is the fraction of total production of commodity j produced by industry i.

If we postmultiply the B matrix (commodity-by-industry) by the E matrix (industry-by-commodity), we generate a commodity-by-commodity matrix. The matrix $(I-BE)^{-1}$ is the commodity-by-commodity total requirements matrix. Premultiplying B by E results in an industry-by-industry matrix. The matrix $(I-EB)^{-1}$ is the industry-by-industry total requirements matrix, which is analogous to the $(I-A)^{-1}$ matrix.

Having generated the total requirements matrix, we can postmultiply it by a vector of final demands to generate a vector of total outputs. In the commodity-by-commodity formulation, the final demand vector would need to be in terms of commodities whereas in the industry-by-industry formulation we would work in terms of industries.[3]

COMPONENTS AND OPERATION

The INTRO-IO model facilitates the generation of both direct and total coefficient matrices from a supplied set of USE and MAKE matrices.

Moreover, this model also allows the user to generate estimated outputs from these data and supplied information on final demand.

As the location map in Exhibit 11.1 indicates, the INTRO-IO model can be divided into three major areas. The left-most portion of the work sheet contains supplied data for a seven and twenty-three sector set of USE and MAKE matrices, along with baseline information on final demands and outputs. The twenty-three-sector version is being included for those users who wish to test a larger data set. An identity matrix is also kept as part of this structure. The next areas are used for storing any user-supplied data, namely, a space for USE and MAKE matrices. The remainder of this area contains preassigned work spaces for generating the final set of matrices. The other areas of the model contain the actual macros and other presentation detail, such as welcome screens and menus, the location map, and range descriptions.

Model Operation

As Table 11.6 indicates, thirteen macros are provided for use in conjunction with the INTRO-IO model. The Alt-D, Alt-L, Alt-M, Alt-Q, Alt-R, Alt-W, and Alt-Z macros correspond to the standard macros described in chapter 1. Instructions for using these macros are described in that chapter. The specialized macros provided for use with the INTRO-IO model are described below:

Table 11.6

INTRO-IO Macros

Alt-C	Calculate outputs
Alt-D	Go to Documentation
Alt-G	Generate matrices
Alt-I	Input data
Alt-L	Go to Location map
Alt-M	Go to Main menu
Alt-P	Print output
Alt-Q	Quit/save model
Alt-R	Go to Range descriptions
Alt-S	Go to System menu
Alt-V	Save data matrices
Alt-W	Go to Welcome screen
Alt-Z	Go to macros

Exhibit 11.1

INTRO-IO Location Map

7-Sector Data A1..L14	Macros	Welcome AQ1..AQ20
23-Sector Data		Main Menu AQ21..AQ41
		Location Map
A24..AB80		AQ41..AQ83
Identity Matrix		Documentation
A83..Z107		
User's USE A108..Z133		AQ91..AQ127
User's MAKE		
A134..Z160		
Current USE	AE1..AM175	
	Range Names	
A161..Z187		
Current MAKE A188..Z212		
Standardized USE		
A213..Z238		
Standardized MAKE A239..Z264	AE176..AH266	
Direct Coefficient		
A265..Z290		
Matrix (I-A) A291..Z316		
Total Coefficients		
A317..Z344		
Final Demand and Output A345..Z370		

The INTRO-IO model is designed to be used primarily with a Lotus-style macro menu that is accessed from the **Alt-S**, Go to System menu, option. The procedures for using this option are described in detail below. The options included in the System menu are also provided in the following macros:

Alt-C, Calculate Outputs. This option is used to generate a set of outputs, given a set of final demands and the total multiplier matrix. It is equivalent to the Calculate option in the System menu.

Alt-I, Input Data. This option is used to select or enter the data to be used in the model. It is equivalent to the Input option in the System menu.

Alt-G, Generate Matrices. This option generates a number of data matrices after the appropriate USE and MAKE matrices data have been selected or supplied. It is equivalent to the Generate option in the System menu.

Alt-P, Print Output. This option is used to print one or more of the data matrices provided to a user-specified worksheet file. It is equivalent to the Print option in the System menu.

Alt-V, Save Data Matrices. This option is used to save portions of the work sheet that contain the information required for creating the various matrices generated by the model. It is equivalent to the Save option in the System menu.

Alt-S, Go to System Menu. This is the major System menu that provides the following options in a Lotus-like command menu:

1. Input. This option is used to identify the set of USE and MAKE matrices to be used in the model. Three suboptions are provided: (1) 1987_US_Data, for selecting the 1987 U.S. national data; (2) User_supplied_data, for entering a different set of USE and MAKE matrices; and (3) **Return**, for returning to the previous menu. The first option allows the user to choose either: (i) the seven-sector model (Small) or (ii) the twenty-three-sector model (Large). The second option is used to specify: (i) the number of industries (Industries); (ii) the number of commodities (Commodities); (iii) labeling information (Labels); (iv) the USE matrix elements (USE); and (v) the MAKE matrix elements (MAKE). The **Return** option returns the user to the System menu.

2. Generate. This option generates a number of data matrices after the appropriate USE and MAKE matrices data have been selected or

supplied. Copies of the appropriate USE and MAKE matrices are created. These copies are then column standardized. At this point, the user must determine whether these matrices should be combined into a commodity-by-commodity (COMxCOM) or an industry-by-industry (INDxIND) table. The resulting table of direct coefficients is kept. The total coefficients table is then generated by subtracting the direct coefficients table from the identity matrix and inverting the result.

3. Calculate. This option is used to generate a set of outputs, given a set of final demands and the total multiplier matrix.[4] Baseline final demands have been provided on a commodity basis for the two tables provided with the model. A vector of 1s has been provided for user-specified tables. To generate the desired output, the user must: (a) select the Modify/Create option to modify the provided set of final demands, then (b) select Generate_outputs to place the final demand and generated output matrices in the appropriate portions of the model. Return can be used to return to the previous menu.

4. Print. This option allows the user to print several of the matrices that are used and created by the model. The following suboptions are provided: (1) USE, to print the USE matrix; (2) MAKE, to print the MAKE matrix; (3) Direct, to print the direct coefficients matrix; (4) Total, to print the total coefficients matrix; (5) Final, to print the vector of final demands; (6) Outputs, to print the vector of estimated outputs; and (7) Return, to return to the previous menu.

5. Save. This option allows the user to specify the name of the work sheet file that is used to store a copy of all the matrices created during a particular run: the USE, MAKE, direct coefficients, total coefficients, final demand and output matrices.[5]

6. Main_menu. This option returns the user to the Main menu.

The System options may be invoked many times during a session. Only the Input and Generate options are absolutely necessary. The Generate step is used to generate a set of outputs, given a set of final demands and the total multiplier matrix. The Print and Save commands are used after a model is generated to print and/or save model results. Until the model is run again, the direct and total multiplier matrices are still resident. Thus, the user may choose a data set, run the model, and quit the System menu. In the same session, the user is then free to use the Generate and Print/Save routines repeatedly, for example, to generate different scenarios using alternative sets of final demands. Using the Input command *erases all of the work area* (B108-Z316), thus deleting any user-entered information and the results of any prior model generation. Be certain to save results before using this step for a second time in a single session.

Alternative Data Entry

The user may want to bring in USE and MAKE matrices from another Lotus work sheet file or files. To do so, use the /File Combine Copy command to bring: (1) the USE matrix to the location called CUSE (Copy of the USE); and (2) the MAKE matrix to the location called CMAKE (Copy of the MAKE). The USE matrix should have a row for value added.

A column vector of industry labels should also be brought (or entered) into the location called INDLAB. A column vector of commodity labels should also be brought into the location called COMLAB (do not include a label for value added). When the USE and MAKE matrices and labels are in these locations, the user may invoke the program with the **Alt-S** macro, *skipping the Input data step*. The program may then be run from the Generate step forward.

DATA SOURCES

The data used for the seven and twenty-three-sector models provided in this model are based on the historical input-output data developed for the U.S. Bureau of Labor Statistics, Office of Employment Projections. The data are based upon the 1977 U.S. national input-output tables provided by the U.S. Department of Commerce, Bureau of Economic Analysis (BEA), but have been revised for a variety of purposes.[6] The 1987 data were updated from the 1977 information in conjunction with other data. The figures are in 1982 constant dollars and are aggregated from a 228-sector version of the data (U.S. Bureau of Labor Statistics 1991).

The choice of industry detail was made to approximate the tables presented in Miller and Blair (1985). The latest data used in that text are for 1977. It is hoped that this model and these data can be used with that text to allow interested users to generate comparisons and examine issues related to national changes in technology and industrial structure. Moreover, this model and the 1972 and 1977 data on USE and MAKE matrices from Miller and Blair should allow users to work through the presentations in that text by generating many of the matrices presented there.

SAMPLE APPLICATION

Once we have constructed the input-output model (that is, generated the Leontief inverse), we can calculate a variety of estimated outputs by altering the vector of final demands. For example, if we were interested in the myriad relationships that exist between the Manufacturing sector and the other sectors, we could supply a vector of final demands that has an entry for the Manufacturing sector and zeros elsewhere. If we calculated these results using the seven-sector model, we would find that a demand for Manufacturing creates outputs not only from the Manufacturing sector but from every sector in the economy. An examination of the relative size of these outputs is the very essence of input-output modeling.

Re-Creating Baseline Values
To ensure that we have created the model properly, we can test the model by using the original set of final demands. Postmultiplying the inverse by the base-year vector of final demands should generate the base-year vector of outputs.

In order to generate the baseline values, the user should first bring up the INTRO-IO program and select **Alt-S** to invoke the System menu. The user should then choose the Input, 1987_U.S._Data, and Small options to examine the seven-sector 1987 U.S. data set provided with the model. The user will be returned to the main System menu.

Now that the data are available, the user should choose Generate to choose the type of model to be created and COMxCOM for a commodity-by-commodity formulation that is consistent with the data provided in the model.[7] At this point, the program will perform a variety of calculations that create several matrices, including the Leontief inverse. This step will also return the user to the main System menu.

The user is now ready to choose Calculate to assemble a set of final demands and calculate a set of outputs. The user should then select the Modify/Create option and press ENTER to use the data as they are and return to the System menu.[8] The user can then choose Generate_outputs to run the model and return to the System menu. Finally, the user can choose Main_menu to quit the System menu and examine the model results and the rest of the data in the model.

The vector of outputs that is generated (beginning in cell F347) should be compared to the supplied vector of total outputs (beginning in cell L6). The user should note that the results are almost identical; the minor differences result from rounding in the matrix-inversion process.

Re-Creating Industry-by-Industry Tables

The industry-by-industry direct- and total-coefficients tables shown in Tables 11.2 and 11.3 can also be re-created by running the seven-sector model with the industry-by-industry (INDxIND) option. To do this, the user should use **Alt-S** to invoke the System menu and choose Input, 1987_U. S._data, and Small to use the seven-sector version of the 1987 US data. The user will be returned to the System menu.

The user must then choose Generate and INDxIND to specify an industry-by-industry formulation. At this point, the model performs a variety of calculations and create several matrices, including the Leontief inverse. This step also returns the user to the main System menu.

The results of these computational steps can then be saved as a Lotus work sheet. To do this, the user should select the Save option from the System menu. The user will be prompted for a file name in which to store the model results. After entering the file name, the user can press ENTER to return to the System menu and Main_menu to return to the main menu.

The work sheet that is created will contain a copy of: (1) the USE matrix that starts at cell A1; (2) the MAKE matrix that starts at cell A28; (3) the column-standardized USE that starts at cell A53; (4) the column-standardized MAKE that starts at cell A79; (5) the direct-coefficients matrix that starts at cell A105; (6) an (I-A) matrix that starts at cell A131; and (7) the total-coefficients matrix that starts at cell A157. A copy of the current set of final demands that starts at cell A185 and the labels for the commodities and industries that starts at cell K87 are also retained. A copy of a file created in this way is provided in the SMALL.WK1 work sheet.

EVALUATION AND EXTENSIONS

Once these operations are learned, the analyst can quickly apply them to any set of input-output accounts for use in economic impact, forecasting, and other analyses. We have shown how to work with a static, open input-output model. Analysts interested in income distribution or fiscal policies will want to work with partially closed tables in order to pick up the induced effects of the respective personal or public consumption activities. Others will be interested in investigating technological change and working with dynamic models.

For some studies, analysts will refer to the version of the input-output model presented here as the primal model in which a set of fixed technologies and alternative sets of final demand are used to determine different levels and composition of output. Jun Han, Yu Hung Hong, and Karen R. Polenske, in chapter 12 of this book, explain the way in which the dual model can be used to calculate shadow prices. This is an especially useful technique for countries or regions where prices are severely distorted (Dorfman et al. 1958).

The reader is also referred to the references (Bruno 1962; Ciaschini 1988; Czamanski 1973; Miernyk 1965; Miller and Blair 1985; Miller et al. 1989; Polenske and Xikang 1991; Polenske and Skolka 1976; United Nations 1984) for some of the many ways in which the input-output technique can be used by national, regional, and corporation analysts for many different policy analyses in the United States and other countries.

NOTES

1. Sector 5 also includes utilities, but for the sake of discussion, we will assume it includes only "margin" items.

2. Notice that some of the numbers in Column 1 of Table 11.4 are larger than and others are smaller than the corresponding number in the transaction matrix (see Table 11.1)

3. We can also generate models that present industry-by-commodity or commodity-by-industry detail. The commodity-by-industry total requirements matrix is formulated as $(I - BE)^{-1}E^{-1}$. The industry-by-commodity formulation is $(I - EB)^{-1}E$.

4. At this point the user can enter original final demand information for the USE and MAKE matrices.

5. Using the Save command allows the user greater control over printing. When a file is saved, all of the matrices and labels are kept as part of the file. A user familiar with Lotus will be able to generate a variety of well-formatted results from this material.

6. The two most important reasons were to ensure consistency with the updated figures for the National Income and Product Accounts and to redefine

certain Standard Industrial Classification changes and redefinitions performed by the BEA.

7. After becoming more familiar with the program, the user is advised to choose the industry-by-industry formulation and enter the set of industry final demands from Table 11.1 to re-create the industry outputs presented there.

8. The Modify/Create command *must* be chosen in order to generate a vector of final demands to use either directly or after modification. The user is then free to alter any or all values of this vector. The program will resume when the user presses the ENTER key.

REFERENCES

Bruno, M. 1962. *Interdependence, resource use, and structural change in Israel.* Bank of Israel, Research Department, Special Studies No. 2. Jerusalem: Jerusalem Post Press.

Bulmer-Thomas, V. 1982. *Input-output analysis in developing countries.* New York: John Wiley and Sons.

Carter, A. P. 1967. Changes in the structure of the American economy 1947, 1958, 1962. *The Review of Economics and Statistics* 49, 209–224.

———. 1970. *Structural change in the American economy.* Cambridge, MA: Harvard University Press.

Chenery, H. B., and Clark, P. G. 1959. *Interindustry economics.* New York: John Wiley and Sons.

Ciaschini, M., ed. 1988. *Input-output analysis: current developments.* London: Chapman and Hall.

Czamanski, S. 1973. *Regional and interregional social accounting.* Lexington, MA: Lexington Books.

Dorfman, R., Samuelson, P. A. and Solow, R. 1958. *Linear programming and economic analysis.* New York: McGraw-Hill.

Gigantes, T., and Matuszewski, T. I. 1968. Rectangular input-output systems, taxonomy, and analysis. Paper presented at the Fourth International Conference on Input-output Techniques, Geneva.

Leontief, W. W. 1936. Quantitative input and output relations in the economic system of the United States. *The Review of Economic Statistics* 18, 105–125.

———. 1966. *Input-output economics.* New York: Oxford University Press.

Miernyk, W. H. 1965. *The elements of input-output analysis.* New York: Random House.

Miller, R. E., and Blair, P. D. 1985. *Input-output analysis: foundations and extensions.* Englewood Cliffs, NJ: Prentice Hall.

Miller, R. E., Polenske K. R., and Rose, A. Z. eds. 1989. *Frontiers of input-output analysis*. New York: Oxford University Press.

Polenske, K. R., and Skolka J., eds. 1976. *Advances in input-output analysis*. Cambridge, MA: Ballinger Publishing.

Polenske, K. R., and Xikang C., eds. 1991. *Chinese economic planning and input-output analysis*. Hong Kong: Oxford University Press. United Nations. 1984. *Proceedings of the seventh international conference on input-output techniques*. New York: United Nations.

U.S. Department of Commerce, Bureau of Economic Analysis. 1974. The input-output structure of the U.S. economy: 1967. *Survey of Current Business* 54, 24–56.

U.S. Department of Commerce, Office of Business Economics. 1965. The transactions table of the 1958 input-output study and revised direct and total requirements data. *Survey of Current Business*. 45, 33–49.

———. 1969. Input-output structure of the U.S. economy: 1963. *Survey of Current Business*. 49, 16–47.

———. 1970. The input-output structure of the U. S. economy: 1947.

U.S. Department of Labor, Bureau of Labor Statistics. 1966. *Projections 1970: interindustry relationships, potential demand, employment*. BLS Bulletin No. 1536. Washington, DC: U.S. Government Printing Office.

———. 1970. *Patterns of U.S. economic growth*. BLS Bulletin No. 1672. Washington, DC: U.S. Government Printing Office.

———. 1972. *Projections of the post-Vietnam economy, 1975*. BLS Bulletin No. 1733. Washington, DC: U.S. Government Printing Office.

———. 1987. Historical input-output magnetic tape documentation. Washington, DC: U.S. Bureau of Labor Statistics, Office of Employment Projections.

———. 1991. Computer Tape Provided by the BLS (January 25, 1991).

Chapter 12

APRAM: Accounting Price Ratio Analysis

Jun Han, Yu Hung Hong, and Karen R. Polenske

The accounting price ratio (APR) analysis model (APRAM) allows users to compute APRs for project appraisals. An APR for a good i, APR_i, is defined as the accounting price for the good divided by its domestic price. Accounting prices (or shadow prices) are prices measuring the real price to an economy of a good or service in terms of certain objectives, such as maximizing economic growth, improving the balance of payments, and promoting employment opportunities, consistent with a country's or region's development policies and resource endowments. When market prices are very distorted, accounting prices are used to reflect true market values. Planners use APRs instead of just the accounting prices because, in periods of inflation, the ratios are more stable over time than prices.

Accounting-price, benefit-cost, rate-of-return, and opportunity-cost concepts are widely used for project appraisals in the United States and abroad to assess the economic viability of investment projects.[1] The present discussion is limited to economic appraisals and to determining accounting prices, which are sometimes called shadow prices.

Many analysts conduct project evaluations. Much of the work done by international organizations, such as the World Bank, is not published but is done as part of the operational work of field staff, with reports written only for internal use. Analysts who have written general descriptions about project evaluations include Adler (1988), Harberger (1972), Jenkins and Harberger (n.d.), Little and Mirrlees (1974), Ray (1984), and Schwartz and Berney (1977). In addition, Bell and Associates (1982) discuss the use of project evaluation for regions.

Analysts use two different approaches for economic project appraisals. One is called the UNIDO approach because it is based upon the *Guide to Practical Project Appraisal*, written by the staff at the United Nations Industrial Development Organization (UNIDO 1972). The other is called the Little-Mirrlees/Squire-Van der Tak approach (Squire and van der Tak 1975). The objectives of the two approaches are very different. Analysts who use the UNIDO approach are interested in determining the contribution that an investment project makes to the stream of consumption expenditures, that is to the general welfare of the region or country. Those who use the Little-Mirrlees approach are interested in determining its contribution to free uncommitted foreign exchange. In the People's Republic of China (China) and many other developing countries, project-appraisal analysts are mainly interested in the second objective while in the United States and other industrialized countries they usually pursue the first objective.

Regardless of which approach is used, the analyst obtains data on the costs and benefits accruing from a given project for a given number of years, say, twenty. The costs and benefits are converted into income streams that are discounted by the opportunity cost of capital as determined by the returns on alternative uses of the capital. Analysts can then make either of two calculations: Net Present Value (NPV) or the Internal Rate of Return (IRR). The planner may select the project that has the highest NPV; if sufficient funds are available, the planner may select a number of projects that exceed a given cutoff NPV value, for instance, zero. As an alternative, the planner can accept a project if its IRR is greater than the opportunity cost of capital.

To determine the correct benefits and costs, the analyst must make a crucial decision as to the appropriate price to use. Market prices often do not represent accurately the true economic prices because of subsidies, administered prices, external economies, or other market distortions. Analysts therefore estimate accounting prices. Wood (1984) has written an especially helpful summary depicting the major issues in determining accounting prices in China. Here, we discuss the way in which these accounting prices can be determined with the use of a general equilibrium approach, namely, the dual (price) version of the input-output model. Only three previous analysts have provided detailed information on the use of the dual version of the input-output model for calculating shadow prices: Powers (1981) for Latin American countries, Lal (1980) for India, and Schohl (1979) for Colombia.

Shadow prices can be calculated for factors of production (land, labor, or capital), intermediate goods, and/or final goods (Roemer and Stern 1975). To date, most project analysts have calculated APRs by using a partial equilibrium approach; that is, they determine the accounting price for only one factor or commodity at a time, or, at least, they make little or no effort to ensure that different accounting prices are internally consistent. The benefit and cost measures thus generally represent only the direct, rather than the direct and indirect, effects unless the analyst makes special efforts to determine the second- and higher-round effects. Because in the past many input-output tables were not published on a timely basis, only a few analysts have used them to determine shadow prices or to estimate direct and indirect benefits and costs. However, analysts can now determine internally consistent accounting prices with the use of up-to-date input-output tables and microcomputers. We therefore anticipate that the general equilibrium input-output technique will quickly replace the partial equilibrium analyses.

CONCEPTUAL BASIS

The use of the input-output technique improves the quality of accounting price estimates significantly because an input-output table can account for the sectoral interdependencies present in an economy. With an input-output table, an analyst uses the following six-step procedure to calculate the APRs and accounting prices for nontraded goods and services (Powers 1981).

Step 1. Divide project outputs and inputs into two broad categories: traded goods and nontraded goods. A traded good is one whose production or use will affect foreign exports or imports of the good being considered. An obvious example is one in which part of the output of the project is directly exported.[2] A nontraded good is defined as a product that is either: (1) protected from international competition by trade quotas or prohibitive tariffs or (2) a naturally nontradable good, such as transportation services. An input-output technical coefficient (A) matrix and a factor coefficient (F) matrix are then constructed. For column vector j in the A and F matrices:

$$a_{ij} = x_{ij} / X_{oj} \tag{1}$$

and

$$f_{ij} = VA_{ij} / X_{oj} \tag{2}$$

where:

a_{ij} = technical coefficient, that is, purchases from sector i per unit of output in sector j

x_{ij} = intermediate input requirement of sector j from sector i

X_{oj} = total output in sector j

f_{ij} = factor coefficient, that is, factor payments to factor of production i per unit of output in sector j

VA_{ij} = value added, that is, factor input requirement from factor of production i per unit of output in sector j

Note: The coefficients in column j must sum to 1.0. That is,

$$\sum_{I=1}^{n} a_{ij} + \sum_{i=1}^{k} f_{ij} = 1 \tag{3}$$

Both the **A** and **F** matrices are rearranged so that the nontraded sectors appear first followed by the traded sectors. As a result, the **A** matrix has four major components and the **F** matrix has two. In Table 12.1 the new input-output structure is as follows:

Table 12.1

Input-Output Structure

Components	Nontraded	Traded
Nontraded	A_{11}	A_{12}
Traded	A_{21}	A_{22}
Factor Inputs	F_{11}	F_{12}

Step 2. Determine whether the goods in each of the traded sectors are imported or exported at the margin (or both), and calculate the corresponding APR using the following formulas, assuming all prices are producers' prices:

1. If the goods are imported:

$$APR_i = [1/(1 + t_{i,m} + v_{i,m})] \tag{4}$$

where:

APR_i = APR for good i

$t_{i,m}$ = import tariff for good i expressed as proportion of CIF (cost, insurance, and freight) value

$v_{i,m}$ = indirect taxes levied on good i at the point of entry

2. If the goods are exported[3]:

$$APR_i = [1 - d_{x,p} (APR_{d,p})]/(1 - t_{i,x} - d_{x,p}) \qquad (5)$$

where:

$d_{x,p}$ = total domestic transport and handling costs (including indirect taxes levied at producer level) associated with exporting the good, expressed as a proportion of FOB (free on board) values

$APR_{d,p}$ = APR for domestic transport and handling costs of exported good at producers' prices

$t_{i,x}$ = export tax on good i expressed as a proportion of FOB value

Step 3. Calculate the APRs for the nontraded sectors. The usual assumption is that additional quantities of these goods can be produced domestically. Thus, their APRs are based on the supply cost in which all inputs and factor services are valued at their accounting prices. Based on the new input-output structure, the demand for nontraded inputs per unit of nontraded output is given by the A_{11} matrix while the demand for traded inputs per unit of nontraded output is provided by the A_{21} matrix. The F_{11} matrix describes the demand for factor inputs per unit of nontraded output.

The APRs for nontraded goods are therefore the weighted average of the APRs for the intermediate and factor inputs into the production of nontraded goods. The weights are the A_{11}, A_{21}, and F_{11} matrices. In other words, the APRs for nontraded goods can be expressed as follows:

$$APR_l = (A_{11}^T \times APR_l) + (A_{21}^T \times APR_2) + (F_{11}^T \times APR_f) \qquad (6)$$

Solving (6) for APR_l gives:

$$APR_1 = [(I - A_{11}^T)^{-1} \times A_{21}^T \times APR_2] + [(I - A_{11}^T)^{-1} \times F_{11}^T \times APR_f] \quad (7)$$

where:

APR_1 = vector of APRs for nontraded goods

APR_2 = vector of APRs for traded goods

A_{11}^T = transposed matrix of direct purchases from nontraded goods per unit of output in nontraded goods

A_{21}^T = transposed matrix of direct purchases from traded goods per unit of output in nontraded goods

F_{11}^T = transposed matrix of factor payments to factor i per unit of output in nontraded goods

APR_f = vector of APRs for factor inputs

APR_f are calculated as conversion factors (CFs) for factor inputs. In the literature, some analysts use the terms "conversion factors" and "accounting price ratios" interchangeably. Conversion factors are aggregate APRs for baskets of goods and services. They are weighted averages of the constituent sectoral APRs, which transform domestic expenditures on a basket of goods and services into their equivalent value in accounting prices. The conversion factors can be calculated as follows:

$$CF_j = \sum_{i=1}^{n} b_i \, APR_i \quad (8)$$

where:

CF_j = expenditure conversion factor for sector j

b_i = weight, that is, proportion of good i in total expenditure by sector j

APR_i = APR of good i

n = number of goods in sector j

Since the APR_1 depends upon the APR_f, which is unknown at this point, analysts need to set APR_f equal to some arbitrary values to derive APR_1.

Step 4. Return to step 2 with the first-round APRs for all nontraded sectors and recalculate the APRs for the traded sectors. Repeat until all APRs for intermediate sectors have converged.

Step 5. Calculate the APRs for factor inputs using Equation (8) with the newly calculated APRs for intermediate sectors. Return to step 3 with the new APRs for factor inputs. Repeat until all APRs for both intermediate sectors and factors of production have converged.

Step 6. Calculate the accounting price for good *i* as follows:

$$AP_i = DP_i \times APR_i \tag{9}$$

where:

AP_i = accounting price for good i
DP_i = domestic price for good i
APR_i = APR for good i

The construction of the APRAM model generally follows this six-step procedure. To simplify the calculation procedure, we assume that the APRs for both traded sectors and factors of production are known and exogenous to the model; consequently, the APRs for nontraded sectors can be calculated in one iteration. In APRAM, steps 4 and 5 are therefore not included.

COMPONENTS AND OPERATION

APRAM is a spreadsheet model that demonstrates a simplified operation to compute APRs. There are two major components in APRAM—the calculation and the noncalculation components. As the location map in Exhibit 12.1 indicates, the calculation portion of APRAM is divided into three sections: the transactions table, the direct-input coefficients table, and the computation section. Each section acts as a work sheet for the calculation of different steps to derive the APRs. The noncalculation component of the model is divided into four sections: (1) macros, which contain all the macro commands; (2) welcome screen and main menu; (3) location map, as shown in Exhibit 12.1; and (4) range description.

Exhibit 12.1

APRAM Location Map

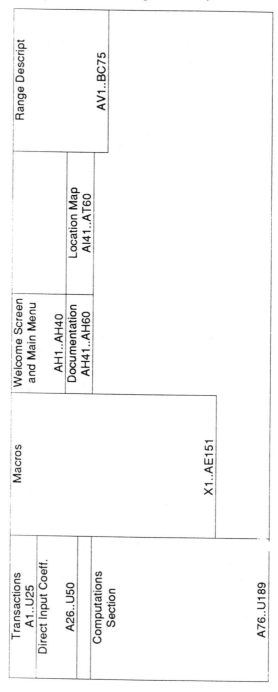

Model Operation

As Table 12.2 indicates, thirteen macros are provided for use in conjunction with APRAM. The Alt-D, Alt-L, Alt-M, Alt-Q, Alt-R, Alt-W, and Alt-Z macros correspond to the standard macros described in Chapter 1. General instructions for using these macros and other spreadsheet macros can be obtained by consulting Chapter 1. The seven specialized macros provided for APRAM are described below:

Table 12.2

APRAM Macros

Alt-C	Compute APRs
Alt-D	Go to Documentation
Alt-E	Erase computations
Alt-I	Input data
Alt-L	Go to Location map
Alt-M	Go to Main menu
Alt-P	Print output
Alt-Q	Quit/save model
Alt-R	Go to Range descriptions
Alt-S	Go to System menu
Alt-V	Save computations
Alt-W	Go to Welcome screen
Alt-Z	Go to macros

Alt-C, Compute APRs. This option is used to compute APRs for nontraded sectors, step-by-step, so that the computing process can be examined and controlled. Four suboptions are provided:

1. Total_inputs computes the column total in the transactions table;
2. Input_coefficients computes the direct-input coefficient table;
3. APRs computes APRs for nontraded sectors and their components; and
4. Return returns to the previous menu.

Because APRAM does the latter computations based upon the results of earlier computations, it is extremely important to execute the Compute commands in the proper order. Always compute Total_inputs first, Input_coefficients second, and APRs last; otherwise, APRAM will give either an error message or the wrong results. The computation of total inputs and input coefficients is straightforward. The Total_input option is used to compute the total input (column total) for each sector in the transactions table. The computed total input is used to calculate the direct-input (technical) coefficients table (or A matrix) with the Input coefficients option.

The APRs command does several things. First, it transposes the A matrix. Second, it calculates the Leontief inverse for the nontraded segment of the transposed A matrix; that is, the $(I-A^T_{11})^{-1}$ matrix. APRAM then computes the contributions of the traded sectors and value added to the APRs for the nontraded sectors. The contribution of the traded sectors to the APRs of nontraded sectors (Traded Share) is defined as $(I-A^T_{11})^{-1}$ x A^T_{21} x APR_2, and the contribution of value added to the APRs of nontraded sectors (VA Share) is defined as $(I-A^T_{11})^{-1}$ x F^T_{11} x APR_f. The sum of the Traded Share and the VA Share yields the APRs for nontraded sectors.

Alt-E, Erase Computations. This option can be used to clean up the model while keeping most of the raw data for the next calculation. This option keeps the sector names, the transactions table, and factor inputs until they are changed at a later time. The APRs for traded intermediate sectors and factor inputs will be deleted, however, as will be the A matrix, the transposed A matrix, the $(I-A^T_{11})^{-1}$ matrix, and the computed APRs for the nontraded sectors. The APRs for traded sectors and factor inputs should be reentered each time after using this option. With this option, the user can insert different APRs for the traded sectors and factor inputs to test the sensitivity of APRs for the nontraded sectors without entering all the initial data.

Alt-I, Input Data. This macro is used to enter the following data: (1) the names of intermediate sectors in a transactions table; (2) the intermediate inputs purchased by all intermediate sectors; (3) the factor inputs (labor and other value added) by each intermediate sector; and (4) the APRs for traded sectors and factor inputs. These data can be entered directly by using the **Alt-I** macro or by retrieving the data from other Lotus 1-2-3® spreadsheets.[4] Users who are unfamiliar with the Lotus 1-2-3® spreadsheet program can use the direct input option (**Alt-I** macro).

After selecting the Input command, the number of sectors in the transactions table should be entered; the maximum number of intermediate sectors APRAM can handle is fifteen. The number of nontraded sectors, say n, should then be entered. The number of APRs for nontraded sectors can range from a minimum of one sector to a maximum equal to the total number of intermediate sectors minus one. APRAM will automatically treat the first n intermediate sectors as nontraded sectors; therefore, it is important to arrange the transactions table so that the first n intermediate sectors are nontraded sectors.

The **Alt-I** macro provides a customized menu at the top of the computer screen, which provides the following data input options:

1. Sectors;
2. Intermediate_inputs;
3. Factor_inputs;
4. APRs; and
5. **Return**

Sectors can be used to label the sectors in the transactions table. Please remember to enter the name of the nontraded intermediate sectors first and limit the sector names to fifteen letters. APRAM classifies value added into two components, "labor" and "other value added," and provides labels for these two components automatically. After entering the sector names, press SPACE and ENTER to return to the input menu.

Intermediate_inputs is used to enter intermediate inputs into the transactions table column by column. Column data for nontraded sectors should be entered first; ENTER should be pressed after each entry; please do not use cursor keys. APRAM will guide the entire data entry process. After the intermediate inputs are entered for the appropriate number of sectors, APRAM will return to the input menu automatically.

The Factor_inputs option is used to enter labor and other value added purchased by all intermediate sectors. Enter the data and press ENTER after each entry; please do not use the cursor key. APRAM will return to the input menu automatically.

APRs is used to enter the ratios for the traded sectors, labor, and other value added. Again, use the ENTER key after each entry. APRAM will then return to the input menu.

If mistakes are made in entering data, complete the rest of the data entry, choose the **Return** option from the customized menu, and then use the **Q**uit option to exit the macro. Move the cursor to where the mistake is made and enter the correct value. After all corrections have been made, use **Alt-M** to return to the main menu to continue.

Alt-P, Print Output. This option can be used to print: (1) the transactions table; (2) the direct-input coefficient table; and (3) the APRs, by using the letters **T**, **C**, and **A**, respectively APRs are printed for nontraded sectors, traded sectors, and factor inputs.

Alt-S, Go to System Menu. This option allows users to activate the customized menu and access the operations provided by standard Alt macros. The following options are provided:

1. Input is used to enter the required data. The available suboptions correspond to the **Alt-I** macro;
2. Compute is used to calculate shadow prices for the nontraded sectors. The available suboptions correspond to the **Alt-C** macro;
3. Print is used to print the tables and results using the options for the **Alt-P** macro;
4. Save is used to save the current computations. The available suboptions correspond to the **Alt-V** macros;
5. Erase is used to erase the current computations;
6. Quit is used to quit the system menu; and
7. Main_menu returns to the main menu.

Alt-V, Save Computations. This command is used to save the transactions table, direct-input coefficient table, and APRs in separate work sheet files. Transactions saves the transactions table into a file named TRANSACT.WK1. Coefficients saves the direct-input coefficient table as COEFFICI.WK1. APRs saves the APRs for nontraded sectors as APRATIO.WK1.

DATA SOURCES

Until recently, most countries did not have up-to-date input-output tables; therefore, analysts could not use the general equilibrium framework for determining accounting prices. Today, many countries have up-to-date input-output tables. The only published Chinese tables at present are the 1981 Chinese 7-sector table used here, a larger 24-sector 1981 national table, a 25-sector 1979 Province of Shaanxi table, and a 41-sector 1983 Machinery and Electronic industry table published in the 1991 book *Chinese Economic Planning and Input-Output Analysis*, edited by Karen

R. Polenske and Chen Xikang. Chinese analysts in state and provincial statistical bureaus, though, have access to the 1987 national 118-sector table and 1987 regional 118-sector or larger tables, which are available for all of the thirty provinces in China except Tibet.

Japan has one of the longest traditions of publishing both national and regional tables. National tables are available from 1955 on a regular five-year basis—the latest one is for 1985 with 84 and 183 sectors (Government of Japan 1990)—and smaller interregional tables, published every five years since 1960 (Abe 1986). Unpublished national data are available on a commodity-by-commodity basis in a 529-by-408 matrix.

Many European countries have time series of input-output tables and publish current tables on a regular basis. A list of many of these and other tables available throughout the world is updated on a regular basis by the United Nations Industrial Development Organization staff (UNIDO 1986). The United States is woefully far behind other countries in terms of officially published national and regional tables. The U.S. Bureau of Economic Analysis published the 500-sector 1982 table in 1991 (U.S. Bureau of Economic Analysis, 1991). At the regional level, about thirty-four states publish input-output tables (Burress, et al. 1988), but most of these are estimations based upon national coefficients through a process known as regionalization (Mourouzi-Sivitanidou and Polenske 1988). The 1963 (Polenske 1980) and 1977 (Faucett Associates 1983) multiregional input-output tables, which are obviously too old for use in U.S. analyses, are the only U.S. input-output data available on a comparable basis for all states.

Thus, sufficient input-output data are currently available in most countries for analysts to use the general equilibrium rather than the partial equilibrium approach for the estimation of accounting prices. Prior to using these tables, analysts should review the major input-output accounting conventions by referring to Miller and Blair (1985) for the United States, to Bulmer-Thomas (1982) for developing countries, and to the latest revision of the United Nations *System of National Accounts* (United Nations 1991) for the general accounting conventions now being employed throughout the world.

SAMPLE APPLICATION

This example uses data for the People's Republic of China, which is assumed to be embarking on a comprehensive coal development project.

We also assume that the first issue that the government officials in China encounter in evaluating the project is estimating the "right price" for coal. The example shows how to use APRAM to calculate the APR for the coal sector in China. From the APR for coal, a "right price" (accounting price) for coal can be derived.

The first step in running APRAM is to enter data. China's data are aggregated into seven intermediate sectors and two value-added components. The seven intermediate sectors are coal, agriculture, light industries, heavy industries, construction, transportation, and commerce. The two value-added components are labor and other value added. Exhibit 12.2 is the transactions table for China. We assume that the coal sector is the only nontraded sector; therefore, column 1 is used to represent the coal sector's inputs and row 1 represents the coal sector's intermediate output in Exhibit 12.2.

Exhibit 12.2

1981 Intermediate Transactions Table for the Chinese Economy
(Rmb [renminbi] millions)

Sector	No.	1	2	3	4	5	6	7
Coal	1	764	103	1,637	9,801	320	427	183
Agriculture	2	140	33,768	67,523	5,155	3,670	10	1,328
Light Industries	3	1,124	5,598	78,968	17,153	8,451	457	12,489
Heavy Industries	4	4,360	19,670	33,285	88,428	36,374	4,512	3,273
Construction	5	0	0	0	0	0	0	0
Transportation	6	256	902	3,237	6,372	2,878	471	625
Commerce	7	215	1,466	4,674	6,201	1,253	832	1,304
Labor	8	4,846	121,060	19,390	24,650	14,994	5,437	11,315
Other Value Added	9	5,047	29,354	74,476	88,422	4,983	11,253	19,939
Total Input		16,752	211,921	283,190	246,182	72,923	23,399	50,456

Source: Center of Economic Forecasting, State Planning Commission of China, 1987, *Input-Ouput Table of China, 1981*. Honolulu: East-West Population Center.

Although the model contains all the required data, users should go through the input stage by just copying the displayed data. To start the input, press **Alt-I**, enter **7**, and press ENTER to enter the number of intermediate sectors. Then type **1** for the number of nontraded intermediate sectors (because China has only one nontraded sector) and press ENTER. APRAM will then display an input menu on the top of your screen. We recommend entering the different input components, that is, sector names, transactions table, factor inputs, and APRs, in the arranged order.

First select Sectors to enter the sector names. The cursor should be positioned on the label for the first intermediate sector, Coal. Type in **Coal** and press ENTER. APRAM will accept your entry and move the cursor down a cell automatically. You can enter the label for the second intermediate sector, Agriculture, and the remaining sectors in the same way. After entering the names for all seven intermediate sectors, press SPACE once and the ENTER key. APRAM will automatically add labels for labor, other value added, and total input to the transactions table.

The next step is entering the intermediate inputs to the transactions table. Select Intermediate_inputs and press ENTER to get into the data entry mode. Remember to enter data in the first column first. APRAM should position the cursor on the cell that will contain the direct input from the Coal sector by the Coal sector, which is the number 764. Type **764** and press ENTER. APRAM will accept the entry and move the cursor down a cell for you. Enter the rest of the intermediate input in the same fashion. Do not enter value-added numbers at this time. After entering all data, APRAM will automatically return to the input menu.

To complete the transactions table, enter the value-added numbers for each sector. Select Factor_inputs and press the ENTER key. An instruction message asking you to divide factor inputs into two components, labor and other value added, will appear. Press ENTER again and APRAM will be ready for input. Enter **4846** for the labor input to Coal sector. Press ENTER and type **5047** for other value added. Press ENTER and APRAM will move the cursor to the Agriculture labor input cell. Finish all other factor inputs in the same fashion. After the last value is entered, APRAM will return to the input menu.

Finally, enter the APRs for traded sectors, labor, and other value added listed in Exhibit 12.3. Select APRs and press ENTER. Type **1.1** and press ENTER for Agriculture sector. Do the same for Light Industries through Other Value Added. APRAM will automatically rearrange the APRs for computation after the APRs are entered. Select Return to go back to the system menu after you complete all inputs. If mistakes are made in data entry, choose **Quit** while in the system menu to exit the macro program. Move the cursor to the mistake(s) and make appropriate corrections. Then press **Alt-M** to get back to the main menu.

Exhibit 12.3

**Hypothetical Accounting Price Ratios (APRs)
for Traded Sectors**

Sectors	APRs
Agriculture	1.1
Light Industries	0.9
Heavy Industries	1.6
Construction	1.1
Transportation	1.2
Commerce	0.9
Labor	1.2
Other Value Added	1.3

You can now compute the APR for Coal by selecting **Alt-C**, APRs from the main menu. The computations must be conducted in the following order:

1. Total_inputs;
2. Input_coefficients; and then
3. Accounting_price ratios.

First press **T** to calculate the total inputs in the transactions table. Then press **I** to compute the direct-input coefficients table. (Refer to Exhibit 12.4.) Finally, press **A** to get the APR for Coal. The calculated APR in this case should be 1.315. Assuming that the price of coal in China is 15 Rmb/ton, the accounting price for coal should be 15 times 1.315 equals 19.725 Rmb/ton (3.7 Rmb [renminbi] equals $1 US).

To print the raw data and the APR for Coal, select **Return** to return to the System menu. Then use **Print** to get into print mode. You can print the transactions table (see Exhibit 12.2) by pressing **T**, all APRs (see Exhibit 12.3) by pressing **A**, and the input coefficients table (see Exhibit 12.4) by pressing **I**. Exit the print mode by pressing **R**.

At this point, you might want to save raw data and the results of your computations by selecting the Save option in the customized menu. Press **T** to save the transactions table under a file named TRANS-ACT.WK1. Press **I** to save the input coefficient table into file CO-EFFICI.WK1. Finally, press **A** to save the calculated APR for the Coal sector into a file called APRATIO1.WK1 and the imputed APRs for other traded sectors into a file called APRATIO2.WK1. **Warning:** APRAM will overwrite the existing files named TRANSACT, COEFF-ICI, APRATIO1, and APRATIO2. To enter your own data, use **Alt-M** to go back to the main menu and **Alt-E**, Erase model, to clean up the spreadsheet.

Exhibit 12.4

1981 Direct Input Coefficients Table
(Direct input per unit of total output)

Sector	No.	1	2	3	4	5	6	7
Coal	1	0.0456	0.0005	0.0058	0.0398	0.0044	0.0182	0.0036
Agriculture	2	0.0084	0.1593	0.2384	0.0209	0.0503	0.0004	0.0263
Light Industries	3	0.0671	0.0264	0.2789	0.0697	0.1159	0.0195	0.2475
Heavy Industries	4	0.2603	0.0928	0.1175	0.3592	0.4988	0.1928	0.0649
Construction	5	0.0000	0.0000	0.0000	0.0000	0.0000	0.0000	0.0000
Transportation	6	0.0153	0.0043	0.0114	0.0259	0.0395	0.0201	0.0124
Commerce	7	0.0128	0.0069	0.0165	0.0252	0.0172	0.0356	0.0258
Labor	8	0.2893	0.5713	0.0685	0.1001	0.2056	0.2324	0.2243
Other Value Added	9	0.3013	0.1385	0.2630	0.3592	0.0683	0.4809	0.3952
Total		1.0000	1.0000	1.0000	1.0000	1.0000	1.0000	1.0000

Source: Calculated from Exhibit 12.2

EVALUATION AND EXTENSIONS

APRAM is developed as an educational model to illustrate the input requirements and direct computational procedure leading to APRs; therefore, three important assumptions are made to simplify the computational process. First, the APRs for both traded sectors and factor inputs are treated as exogenous to the model. Consequently, the APRs for nontraded sectors can be derived in one iteration. In real project appraisals, users may calculate the APRs for the nontraded sectors, traded sectors, and factor inputs simultaneously. This will require an iterative process or other technique to ensure the internal consistency of APRs and conversion factors, as described by Powers (1981).

Second, the Chinese economy is assumed to have only seven intermediate sectors. Users may extend the number of intermediate sectors either for China or other countries to obtain more detailed APRs and accounting prices. Such decisions will depend upon the availability of larger input-output tables and other data and on computer capacities.

Third, import tariffs, taxes, or other types of assessments are not included in the sample calculations. In actual project analyses, users will want to include one or more of the components shown in step 2 above.

APRAM is an input-output model for computing APRs for project appraisal. It provides more accurate estimates of the direct and indirect costs of producing nontraded outputs to an economy than the conventional partial equilibrium approach. Analysts in countries with intensive government interventions will find APRAM useful in helping derive appropriate prices for intermediate inputs, factor inputs, and outputs.

NOTES

1. This section of the paper closely parallels a section of the paper by Polenske (1991).

2. If analysts do not believe that the border price represents an accurate price for a traded good, they can calculate an APR for that good even though it is traded.

3. Note that additional terms could be added to Equations (4) and (5) to represent other types of distortions than taxes and tariffs, including rationing and other administrative controls.

4. In the demonstration example you may use Alt-N to enter the stored transaction table and APRs for traded sectors and factor inputs.

REFERENCES

Abe, K. 1986. Input-output tables in Japan and applications for interregional analysis. Paper presented at the Eighth International Conference on Input-Output Techniques, Sapporo, Japan.

Adler, H. A. 1988. *Economic analysis of transport projects*. Baltimore: Johns Hopkins University Press.

Bell, C., Hazell, P. and Slade, R. 1982. *Project evaluation in a regional perspective*. Baltimore: Johns Hopkins University Press.

Bulmer-Thomas, V. 1982. *Input-output analysis in developing countries: sources, methods, and applications*. New York: John Wiley and Sons.

Burress, D., Eglinski, M. and Oslund, P. 1988. A survey of static and dynamic state-level input-output models. Discussion Paper No. 1988.1. Lawrence: Institute for Public Policy and Business Research, University of Kansas.

Center of Economic Forecasting, State Planning Commission of China. 1987. *Input-output table of China, 1981*. Honolulu: East-West Population Center.

[Jack] Faucett Associates. 1983. *The multiregional input-output accounts, 1977: introduction and summary*. Vol. I, *Final Report*. Prepared for the U.S. Department of Health and Human Services. Washington, DC: Jack Faucett Associates.

Government of Japan, Management and Coordination Agency. 1990. *1985 input-output tables: summary in English*. Tokyo: Government of Japan, Management and Coordination Agency, Statistics Bureau, Statistical Standards Department.

Harberger, A. C. 1972. *Project evaluation*. Chicago: University of Chicago Press.

Jenkins, G. P., and Harberger, A. C., n.d. *Program on investment appraisal and management manual: cost-benefit analysis of investment decisions*. Cambridge, MA: Harvard Institute for International Development.

Lal, D. 1980. *Prices for planning: towards the reform of Indian planning*. London: Heinemann.

Little, I. M. D., and Mirrless, J. A. 1974. *Project appraisal and planning for the developing countries*. London: Heinemann.

Miller, R. E., and Blair, P. D. 1985. *Input-output analysis: foundations and extensions*. Englewood Cliffs, NJ: Prentice-Hall.

Mourouzi-Sivitanidou, R., and Polenske, K. R. 1988. Assessing regional economic impacts with microcomputers. In Klosterman, R. E., ed. *A Planner's Review of PC Software and Technology*. Planning Advisory Service Report No. 414/415. Chicago: American Planning Association.

Polenske, K. R. 1980. *The U.S. multiregional input-output accounts and model*. Lexington, MA: D.C. Heath and Company.

Polenske, K. R. 1991. Interrelationships among energy, environmental, and transportation policies in China. In Tester, J. W., Ferrari, N. A., and Wood, D. O. eds. *Energy and the environment in the 21st century*. Cambridge, MA: MIT Press.

Polenske, K. R., and Xikang, Chen, eds. 1991. *Chinese economic planning and input-output analysis*. Hong Kong: Oxford University Press.

Powers, T. A., ed. 1981. *Estimating accounting prices for project appraisal*. Washington, DC: Inter-American Development Bank.

Ray, A. 1984. *Cost-benefit analysis: Issues and methodologies*. Baltimore: Johns Hopkins University Press.

Roemer, M., and Stern, J. J. 1975. *The appraisal of development projects: a practical guide to project analysis with case studies and solutions*. New York: Praeger.

Schohl, W. W., 1979. Estimating shadow prices for Colombia in an input-output table framework. World Bank Staff Working Paper No. 357. Washington, DC: The World Bank.

Schwartz, H., and Berney, R., eds. 1977. *Social and economic dimensions of project evaluation*. Washington, DC: Inter-American Development Bank.

Squire, L., and van der Tak, H. G. 1975. *Economic analysis of projects*. Baltimore: Johns Hopkins University Press.

United Nations. 1991. *System of national accounts*. New York: United Nations.

United Nations Industrial Development Organization (UNIDO). 1972. *Guidelines for project evaluation*. New York: United Nations.

———. 1986. Inventory lists of input-output tables. Vienna, Austria: UNIDO.

U.S. Department of Commerce, Bureau of Economic Analysis. 1991. *1982 Benchmark input-output accounts of the United States*. Washington DC: U.S. Government Printing Office.

Wood, A. 1984. Economic evaluation of investment projects: possibilities and problems of applying western methods in China. World Bank Staff Working Paper No. 631. Washington, DC: The World Bank.

PART FOUR

Environmental Analysis and Modeling

Chapter 13

SMOKE: Air Pollution Dispersion

Timothy J. Cartwright

One of the more dubious achievements of the twentieth century has been the emergence of air pollution as an almost universal problem. There was a time when belching smokestacks were regarded as symbols of progress and development (Brimblecombe 1987). Not so now, as the effects of air pollution daily become more apparent through acid rain, ozone depletion, and even climate change (Shen 1986). In this century, air pollution has become a problem of truly global proportions (Berlyand 1973; World Commission on Environment and Development 1987).

For urban and regional planners, one of the main difficulties in dealing with air pollution is that its effects are often invisible beyond the immediate vicinity of the source. Furthermore, the effects are almost always widely dispersed in space and can vary substantially from day to day, depending on the ambient wind and weather. This means that even the worst cases of air pollution can take a relatively long time to affect a large number of people to a significant degree—and thus get onto the "political agenda" (Ashby and Anderson 1981; Cook 1988; Crandall 1983; Crenson 1971; Haskell 1982; Jones 1975). For this reason, planners often find it difficult to know what to do about air pollution, short of closing down the source or redesigning cities—neither of which may be realistic or even desirable (Rydell and Stevens 1968).

Several mathematical models can be used to help estimate the impact of airborne pollutants by predicting how a plume of smoke disperses from a point source under different emission, wind, and weather conditions (Grandell 1985; Organization for Economic Cooperation and

Development 1971; Weber 1982). These models can help planners see both where the impact of pollution will occur and how its dispersion might be managed through various control mechanisms (Kneese 1984).

Until now, most of these models have been written in conventional programming languages, such as Fortran and Pascal. Using models like these is far better than doing the required calculations by hand or even with a calculator. However, the linear nature of these models makes it difficult to quickly determine the effect of changing input parameters. The models are also more or less inaccessible to nonprogrammers and often lack convenient graph capabilities.

Fortunately, electronic spreadsheets suffer from none of these weaknesses. As the models in this book demonstrate, spreadsheets can handle even quite complex calculations quickly and easily. Spreadsheets can also do these calculations repeatedly, so that planners can readily see the "what if" implications of changing a model's parameters. In addition, spreadsheets can provide simple and easy-to-understand graphic presentations of the results.

SMOKE is a pollution dispersion model that shows how a plume of smoke from an elevated point source—such as a chimney stack—disperses downwind from the source under different emission, wind, and weather conditions (Jakeman and Simpson 1985). The model also estimates ground-level pollution concentrations at selected distances downwind of the source along the centerline of the plume.[1]

CONCEPTUAL BASIS

Dispersion of air pollution from a point source normally occurs in three dimensions:

- *Longitudinally* along a centerline of maximum concentration running downwind from the source;
- *Laterally* on either side of the centerline as the pollution "spreads out sideways"; and
- *Vertically* above and below a horizontal axis drawn through the source (and, thus, down toward and up away from the surface of the earth).

The most commonly used model for predicting this kind of dispersion is the Gaussian plume model. This model was originally proposed more than fifty years ago by O. G. Sutton and then refined by others in the 1960s (for example, Pasquill 1962). The Gaussian plume model assumes that the emissions from a point source are carried downwind in a continuous plume and that the vertical and lateral pollution concentration (that is, its cross section), at any point in this plume, corresponds to a normal or Gaussian distribution in each dimension.

The Gaussian plume model has been tested in numerous studies (Davison and Leavitt 1979) and has been found to give satisfactory results under normal conditions (Clark et al. 1984). Although the model was originally intended for fairly short time periods (up to several hours, for which the wind and atmospheric conditions could be assumed to remain reasonably constant), it has nevertheless been adapted to seasonal and even annual time frames (Clark et al. 1984). The Gaussian plume model has also been adapted to both multiple point emission sources, for instance, automobile pollution along a highway, and area sources, for example, air pollution in urban areas (Clark et al. 1984). In short, the Gaussian plume model provides a simple, robust, and flexible approach for modeling the dispersion of air pollution under a variety of conditions (Johnson et al. 1976).

Naturally, models like this are designed for idealized airflow and pollution conditions. In particular, this model assumes positive and consistent wind conditions, no overwhelming local airflow disturbances due to nearby buildings or other obstructions, no excessive channeling of airflow due to hilly terrain, moderately dense pollutants, and no significant chemical or physical interaction between pollutants and the ground (Davison et al. 1980; Pasquill 1962).

The fundamental equation of the Gaussian plume model is:

$$C(x,y,z) = \frac{Q}{2 \pi u s_y s_z} + \exp \frac{-y^2}{2 s_y^2} + \exp \frac{-(z-h)^2}{2 s_z^2} + \exp \frac{-(z+h)^2}{2 s_z^2}$$

where:

$C(x,y,z)$ = concentration of emission in micromilligrams per cubic meter at distance x downwind of the source, distance y laterally from the centerline, and distance

		z vertically from the height of the source
Q	=	mass of the emission in grams per second
u	=	wind speed in meters per second
h	=	height of the source above ground level in meters
s_y, s_z	=	standard deviations of a statistically "normal" plume in the lateral and vertical dimensions, respectively.

In this form, the model assumes that a plume is reflected back into the atmosphere whenever it strikes the ground.[2] The critical component of the Gaussian plume model is the two sets of standard deviations (s_y and s_z). Several approaches have been used to define these values. In some cases, they are derived from theoretical calculations of the effect of wind, insolation, nighttime cloud cover, the nature of the terrain, and other factors. In other cases, empirical observation at the site is used to "calibrate" the estimates.[3]

A second critical factor in applying the Gaussian plume model is the fact that stack emissions are rarely just "released" into the atmosphere. Instead, pollution is more likely to "shoot out" of the stack at a relatively high velocity and/or temperature. Because of this momentum and buoyancy, the effective height at which emissions are "released" can be a good deal higher (up to ten times higher) than the physical height of the stack. Clearly, the model should account for this kind of effect.

The third step in the use of the Gaussian plume model is to convert it to a form that yields pollution concentrations at ground level. In this form of the model, maximum ground-level pollution occurs along the centerline of the plume and can be found by setting $y = 0$ and $z = 0$.

COMPONENTS AND OPERATION

As the location map in Exhibit 13.1 illustrates, the computational portion of the SMOKE model consists of sixteen columns and sixty rows. Standard model components, such as the welcome screen, main menu, and model documentation are located to the right of these two sections.

The width of the body of the model is limited to seventy-five characters to facilitate viewing it on the screen and printing it on an eighty-column printer. The top thirty rows are used for entering the model parameters and displaying the results. The lower thirty rows contain labels for the graphic display and otherwise provide a "scratch pad" for some of the more complicated model calculations.

Exhibit 13.1

SMOKE Location Map

		Macros	Range Descript	Location Map
Input Area A1..O10	Welcome Screen Q1..Q20			
Output Area A12..O25	Main Menu Q21..Q40		Z1..AA26	AE1..AS26
Graph Labels A32..A35	Document Q41..Q60			
Calculations A37..O60		R1..V60		

Rows 1 and 2 contain the title of the spreadsheet. Rows 4, 5, and 6 are used to enter the model parameters. Variable names go into columns A and I, and the data go into columns F and N. Rows 8, 9, and 10 describe the atmospheric stability categories. A category is selected by entering the desired value in cell E9. Rows 12, 13, and 14 contain headers for the results table. The distances shown in row 14 are usually treated as constants but may be varied by the user to estimate pollution concentrations at other distances from the source. Similarly, column A in rows 16 to 25 lists ten wind speeds that may also be modified by the user.

The remainder of rows 16 to 25 shows the results of two key calculations: the effective stack height in column C and the ground-level, centerline pollution concentrations in columns E to O at different distances from the source for the wind velocities shown in column A. Details of all the required calculations are provided in this chapter's Appendix.

Rows 30 to 60 constitute the "hidden" part of the model. Rows 32 to 35 provide the labels for the graphs. Rows 39 and 40 convert the input temperatures from degrees Celsius to degrees Kelvin. Rows 41 to 44 contain some interim results in the calculation of effective stack height. Finally, rows 48 to 53 and 55 to 60, respectively, contain the lateral and vertical dispersion coefficients referred to above.

The model produces a simple graph, showing the centerline-ground-level pollution concentration (displayed on the y-axis) as a function of the distance from the source (shown on the x-axis) for a set of curves representing the effect of different wind speeds. Appropriate headings and labels are provided for the graphs.[4]

The entire spreadsheet is protected, with the exception of cells F4, F5, F6, N4, N5, N6, and E9—which are used to enter the seven input parameters. If the user wants to alter the distances in row 14 or the wind speeds in column A, the corresponding blocks can be unprotected and changed.

Model Operation

The SMOKE model has been designed so that the data entry and display components of the model are kept on the same screen—although some up-and-down scrolling is necessary to see results for all wind speeds—so that a user can more easily relate the output of the model to its input parameters. As a result, after viewing the standard welcome screen, the user is automatically moved to the main model screen for running the SMOKE model.

As Table 13.1 illustrates, nine macros are also provided for use with the SMOKE model. This menu can be accessed at any time by pressing **Alt-M**, Go to main menu. The Alt-D, Alt-L, Alt-M, Alt-Q, Alt-R, Alt-W, and Alt-Z macros correspond to the standard macros described in chapter 1. General instructions for using these macros are provided in chapter 1.

Table 13.1

SMOKE Macros

Alt-D	Go to Documentation
Alt-G	Graph dispersion patterns
Alt-I	Go to Input area
Alt-L	Go to Location map
Alt-M	Go to Main menu
Alt-Q	Quit/save model
Alt-R	Go to Range descriptions
Alt-W	Go to Welcome screen
Alt-Z	Go to macros

Only two specialized macros are provided for use with the SMOKE model. The **Alt-G**, Graph dispersion pattern, is used to display the graph showing the air pollution dispersion pattern for the current values of the input data. The graph can also be viewed at any time by pressing **F10**, the Lotus "Graph" key. The **Alt-I**, Go to input area, macro is used to exit the macros model and return to the main data entry screen for running the model.

Data Entry Procedures

As shown in Exhibit 13.2, seven parameters are required to use the SMOKE model. Five parameters pertain to the pollution source: (1) the height of the stack above the ground (in meters); (2) the diameter of the opening of the stack (in meters); (3) the rate at which pollution is emitted from the stack (in grams per second); (4) the velocity of the gas emitted from the stack (in meters per second); and (5) the temperature of the gas as it exits the stack (in degrees Celsius). These parameters should be more or less self-explanatory. The other two parameters are the ambient air temperature (in degrees Celsius) at the source, which is also quite straightforward, and an index of atmospheric stability.

Exhibit 13.2

Sample SMOKE Parameters

DISPERSION OF POINT SOURCE POLLUTION—USING A GAUSSIAN DISPERSION MODEL
   by T. J. Cartwright, York University, Toronto, Canada (c) 1992.

Stack height (m)	30	Gas exit velocity (m/s)	5	|	F10
Stack diameter (m)	2	Gas exit temperature (øC)	200	|	for
Emission rate (g/s)	10	Ambient temperature (øC)	20	|	graph

Atmospheric		1 = Very Unstable	4 = Neutral
Condition	1	2 = Moderately Unstable	5 = Somewhat Stable
Category:		3 = Slightly Unstable	6 = Stable

Atmospheric stability is defined here in terms of the environmental lapse rate; that is, the rate at which the temperature of an air mass varies with altitude (Johnston 1961; Sutton 1960). In "neutral" or adiabatic conditions (that is, conditions in which an air mass neither absorbs heat from nor gives up heat to its environment), the temperature of an air mass cools by about two Celsius degrees per one thousand feet of altitude.[5] If the temperature of an air mass cools at a higher rate, it is said to be superadiabatic; if it cools at a lower rate, it is said to be subadiabatic:

> A rising air parcel, cooling at the adiabatic rate, becomes warmer and less dense than its environment and therefore buoyancy tends to accelerate it upward. . . . In such an environment, the parcel is in unstable equilibrium. Vertical motions upward or downward are reinforced. When the environmental lapse rate is less than adiabatic ("subadiabatic") or negative, a rising air parcel becomes cooler and more dense than its environment and tends to return to its starting point. The parcel is in stable equilibrium (Wanta and Lowry 1976, p. 339–340).

The model therefore requires the user to specify the atmospheric stability in terms of one of the following categories: (1) very unstable (superadiabatic); (2) moderately unstable; (3) slightly unstable; (4) neutral (adiabatic); (5) somewhat stable; and (6) stable (subadiabatic).

These categories represent the tendency of a plume to disperse downward toward the surface of the earth (Pasquill 1962). In unstable conditions, plumes tend to move up and down between the surface and altitude ("looping"). In neutral conditions, plumes tend to spread equally in the vertical and horizontal dimensions ("coning"). In stable conditions, plumes tend to spread more in the horizontal than in the vertical dimension ("fanning").

Using this information, the model estimates the hourly accumulation of pollution at ground level at various points along the centerline of the plume for ten different wind speeds. The model calculates the dispersion for every odd wind speed from one to nineteen meters per second (or from 3.6 to 68.4 kilometers per hour) for distances from the source ranging from five hundred meters to one hundred kilometers.[6]

Computational Procedures

The SMOKE model makes extensive use of three important features of spreadsheets: branching, "lookup" tables, and graphs. Branching is used to choose among various computational formulas (according to the atmospheric stability) and for abandoning calculations when the results become so small as to be insignificant. Lookup tables are used to access the matrix of Gaussian dispersion coefficients for six atmospheric stability conditions located in the lower half of the model. Graphing capabilities are used to graph the dispersion curves described previously.

The model performs four basic actions. It first calculates the "effective stack height," which is the height at which the effluent gas steam begins to "bend over" and disperse downwind. The effective stack height is a function of the ambient temperature and wind speed and the temperature and velocity of the effluent gas. Hot gases emitted at high exit velocities in neutral or unstable atmospheric conditions rise for a considerable distance before beginning to disperse downwind. Under these conditions, the effective stack height will be much higher than the height of the physical stack. On the other hand, the effective stack height in stable conditions may be little higher than its physical height. The effective stack heights for different wind velocities are displayed in cells C16 to C25.

The SMOKE model then calculates the table of Gaussian dispersion coefficients for the lateral and vertical dispersion at specified distances downwind of the source. These results are stored in the lower portion of the spreadsheet (cells E48 to 060).

The model then calculates the ground-level pollution concentration at each point along the plume centerline for the ten different wind conditions. The results are displayed in the top part of the model (cells E16 to 025).

Finally, the SMOKE model graphs the distribution of ground-level pollution along the centerline for each wind speed, subject to the specified atmospheric stability conditions. For example, Exhibit 13.3 illustrates the dispersion of smoke for the conditions specified in Exhibit 13.2.[7]

DATA SOURCES

The data on stack emissions, ambient air conditions, and other parameters required to use the SMOKE model are dependent on the facility being studied. As a result, no general data source is available. However, the data provided with the model are for a real facility and can be used to examine the effects of modifying different model parameters.

SAMPLE APPLICATION

The SMOKE model is distributed with data for a real facility in central Canada. These data can be used to demonstrate that simple simulation models like this can be extremely helpful in allowing planners and private citizens to understand the nature of air pollution better and explore possible solutions and trade-offs more easily.[8]

For example, Exhibits 13.3, 13.4, and 13.5 indicate that atmospheric stability can affect the pollution "footprint" substantially. The unstable conditions shown in Exhibit 13.2 (and graphed in Exhibit 13.3) cause plume "looping" that increases centerline concentrations (at the expense of lateral and vertical diffusion) and substantially increases concentrations close to the source. This graph can be obtained by setting the "Atmospheric Condition Category" value in cell E9 to 1. As atmospheric turbulence become more neutral (see Exhibits 13.4 and 13.5), the plume "cones" out from the source in a more stable fashion, resulting in a smoother distribution in the longitudinal plane. In perfectly stable conditions (see Exhibit 13.5), the plume spreads laterally rather than vertically ("fanning"), reducing centerline concentrations and moving the peak concentrations well downwind of the source. This graph can be obtained by setting the value in cell E9 to **6**. The transition from neutral to stable conditions (that is, from Exhibit 13.4 to Exhibit 13.5) has a particularly dramatic effect on concentrations close to the stack.

Exhibit 13.3

Sample Dispersion Plot for Very Unstable Conditions

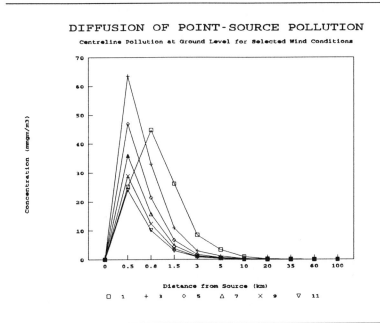

Other weather conditions (for example, wind and temperature) do not fundamentally alter this pattern. Broadly speaking, the effect of wind speed is to skew the profile of the plumes shown in Exhibits 13.3, 13.4, and 13.5 but not to change them fundamentally. Similarly, the changes in ambient temperature raise or lower the profiles slightly but do not alter them dramatically. For example, the effect of lowering and then raising the ambient temperature for the neutral atmospheric conditions shown in Exhibit 13.3 can be shown by setting the value in cell E9 to **4** and setting the ambient air temperature value in cell M6 to **0** (thirty-two degrees Fahrenheit) and then to **30** (eighty-six degrees Fahrenheit).

Pollution concentrations are slightly higher in hot weather and slightly lower in cold weather but there is no fundamental change in the dispersion pattern of footprint of the pollution.

Exhibit 13.4

Sample Dispersion Plot for Neutral Conditions

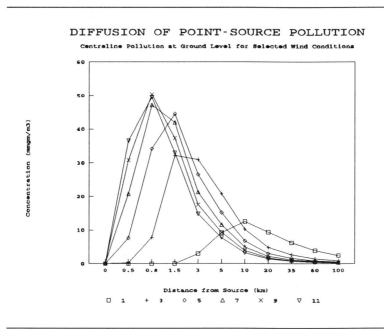

What then can be done to "manage" the air pollution footprint? This model allows planners to simulate the effect of two control strategies: managing the plume discharge and changing the stack design. A comprehensive investigation of these options cannot be conducted here. However, for purposes of illustration, let us examine the effect of some management changes for the sample stack under the neutral atmospheric conditions shown in Exhibit 13.3.

First, consider the effect of varying the temperature and exit velocity of the stack emissions. The effect of lowering and then raising the temperature of the pollution stream as it leaves the stack can be investigated by setting the ambient temperature back to **20** and changing the gas exit temperature (cell M5) to **100** and then to **300**. The effect of decreasing and then increasing its exit velocity can be seen by resetting cell M5 to **200** and setting the gas exit velocity (cell M4) to **3** and then to **10**.[9] In general, it is clear that increasing the temperature or exit velocity significantly reduces local pollution concentrations. These strategies, however, have a less discernible effect further downwind (Harrison and Perry 1986).

Exhibit 13.5

Sample Dispersion Plot for Stable Conditions

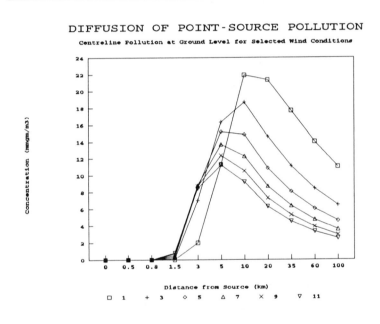

DIFFUSION OF POINT-SOURCE POLLUTION

Centreline Pollution at Ground Level for Selected Wind Conditions

Distance from Source (km)

□ 1   + 3   ◇ 5   △ 7   ✕ 9   ▽ 11

Now consider the effects of changing the stack height and diameter.[10] The effect of lowering and then raising the stack height can be seen by changing the value in cell F4 to **25** (meters) and then to **40**. The effect of reducing and then expanding the stack diameter can be seen by changing the value in cell F5 to **1.5** (meters) and then to **2.5**. Again, there are substantial changes in local pollution concentrations but smaller effects further downwind (Frankenburg 1968; Lee and Stern 1973).

In summary, the model suggests that there is a good deal of potential for managing local air pollution impacts but substantially smaller possibilities for controlling it at long distances. Adequate tools for monitoring meteorological conditions and for controlling stack emissions should therefore allow us to manage the local impact of air pollution quite effectively. On a more global scale, however, management of individual plumes is not going to make air pollution disappear. Moreover, the ability to manage and thus "hide" the more visible (local) impacts of air pollution may create a false sense of security about the larger implications of air pollution—such as acid rain, ozone depletion, and climate change.

EVALUATION AND EXTENSIONS

At best, the SMOKE model provides a rough approximation to real life. As one expert (Pasquill 1962, p. 297) points out, after a lengthy, technical discussion of pollution modeling:

> It is unlikely that the assessment of the distribution of an air pollutant over a region extending up to say 100 km from the point of release can always be confined to the substitution of a single set of parameters in one simple equation. This is so because the growth of a cloud or plume in the vertical will not necessarily follow a simple (e.g., power-law) variation with distance indefinitely. Even when a simple formula is applicable, estimates of the parameters to be used in it will vary according to the quality of the meteorological data available. . . . Moreover, there are aspects of diffusion which have so far been examined only in a very preliminary way, and generalization from the data available is then essentially speculative and should be reappraised frequently.

Air pollution is therefore both more and less complicated than is generally assumed. On the one hand, turbulent flows over smooth surfaces—let alone over the typical features of urban or regional landscapes—are so complex that simulating them with any degree of accuracy for more than a few hundred meters of distance is probably impossible. On the other hand, surprisingly useful things can be done with only a microcomputer and a standard, off-the-shelf software package.

Thus, the real question is not whether models like the one presented here can accurately predict pollution concentrations downwind of a real stack—because the answer is that they probably cannot (Dobbins 1979). The important question is whether and how models like these can help planners do their jobs more effectively.

There are at least three important ways in which simulation models like this can assist planning. First, they help to frame an air pollution problem better. For example, the preceding discussion demonstrates that this model provides a clearer picture of the relationship between centerline and ambient pollution, between peak concentrations and overall footprints, and between local and long-distance pollution.

Second, simulation models like this can help identify the payoffs to be expected from different abatement strategies. For example, the preceding discussion has explored the potential gains to be realized from managing stack emissions as opposed to reconstructing the stack.

Third, this kind of model can be used to conduct sensitivity analysis for determining whether relatively small changes in one or more parameters have a major impact on pollution dispersion. For example, Exhibits 13.4 and 13.5 reveal that the pollution footprint in the example discussed here is particularly sensitive to the transition from neutral to stable atmospheric conditions.

From a planner's point of view, accessible, understandable, and useful models like SMOKE are often much more important than models that are exact, hard to use, and difficult to understand. As a result, the accessibility, flexibility, and transparency of electronic spreadsheets make them an ideal vehicle for creating useful planning models over a broad range of applications—including blowing smoke.

ACKNOWLEDGMENTS

The author is indebted to John McLean of the faculty of Environmental Studies, York University, Toronto, Canada, for his unstinting help with the background research for this chapter.

NOTES

1. A comparable model of the underground transport of pollution in groundwater is included in Timothy J. Cartwright's forthcoming book *Modeling the World in a Spreadsheet: Environmental Simulation on a Microcomputer* (Baltimore: Johns Hopkins University Press).

2. The model can also be modified for cases where a temperature inversion creates a similar "barrier" at altitude (Clark et al. 1984).

3. See Pasquill (1962) or Clark and colleagues (1984).

4. Note that the graphic display does not show explicitly the atmospheric category to which it applies. This could be accomplished by using a set of six nested IF() statements in a label cell. However, spreadsheets typically provide only two lines for the title (heading and subheading), and it was not felt desirable here to sacrifice either for recording the atmospheric category.

5. This is the adiabatic lapse rate for "standard" air. In moist air, the rate is lower (about 1.5 Celsius degrees per one thousand feet); in dry air, it is higher (about three Celsius degrees).

6. Of course, these speeds and distances can all be altered, if desired, by entering new values in the appropriate cells. Indeed, the entire model can readily be converted from metric to imperial units in this way.

7. The x-axes in Exhibit 13.3 are not drawn to a consistent (for example, log) scale, as this feature is not yet available in most spreadsheets. Thus, a bar graph might be more appropriate here (and can readily be produced by a spreadsheet). However, the line graphs shown here are easier to read. Note, too, that the y-axes should be manually scaled to a consistent range in order to facilitate comparisons.

8. The value of rough approximations for helping to "frame" planning problems is one implication of recent research on "chaos" in planning; see Cartwright (1991) and Lee (1973).

9. These effects can be achieved through a variety of means: exhaust gases can be cooled and slowed by means of settling chambers, baffles, or scrubbers (which also help remove larger particulates). Similarly, exhaust gases can be heated and accelerated by the addition of heated air (Stern 1976).

10. Similar effects can be achieved by multiplying the number of stacks instead of increasing the capacity of a single stack. In general, multiple stacks close together tend to create a plume higher than any individual stack but lower than a single combined stack. The effect of a line of multiple stacks is also related to its orientation (parallel or perpendicular) to the wind direction (Strom 1976).

11. I am indebted to Dwayne Plaza and Richard Schwass on the faculty of Environmental Studies, York University, Toronto, Canada for showing me this model.

REFERENCES

Ashby, E., and Anderson, M. 1981. *The politics of clean air*. Oxford: Clarendon Press.

Berlyand, M. E., ed. 1973. *Air pollution and atmospheric diffusion.* Trans. from the Russian by A. Baruch and D. Slutzkin. New York: Wiley.

Brimblecombe, P. 1987. *The big smoke: history of air pollution in London since medieval times.* New York: Methuen.

Cartwright, T. J. 1991. Planning and chaos theory. *Journal of the American Planning Association* 57, 44–56.

Clark, A. I., Lester, J. N., McIntyre, A. E., and R. Perry. 1984. Air quality impact assessment. *Environmental Monitoring and Assessment* 4, 205–232.

Cook, B. J. 1988. Bureaucratic politics and regulatory reform: the EPA and emissions trading. In *Contributions in political science, No. 196.* New York: Greenwood Press.

Crandall, R. W. 1983. *Controlling industrial pollution: the economics and politics of clean air.* Washington, DC: Brookings Institution.

Crenson, M. A. 1971. *The un-politics of air pollution: a study of nondecision-making in the cities.* Baltimore: Johns Hopkins University Press.

Davison, D. S., and Leavitt, E. D. 1979. *Analysis of AOSERP plume sigma data. AOSERP Report No. 63.* Edmonton: Alberta Oil Sands Environmental Research Program.

Davison, D. S., et al. 1980. *Airshed management system for the Alberta oil sands.* 2 vols. Edmonton: Alberta Environment.

Dobbins, R. A. 1979. *Atmospheric motion and air pollution.* New York: Wiley Interscience.

Frankenburg, T. T. 1968. High stacks for diffusion of sulfur dioxide and other gases emitted by electric power plants. *Journal of the American Industrial Hygiene Association* 29, 181–185.

Grandell, J. 1985. Stochastic models of air pollutant concentration. In *Lecture Notes in Statistics 30.* Berlin: Springer-Verlag.

Harrison, R. M., and Perry, R., eds. 1986. *Handbook of air pollution analysis.* 2 ed. London: Chapman and Hall.

Haskell, E. H. 1982. *The politics of clean air: standards for coal-burning power plants.* New York: Praeger.

Jakeman, A. J., and Simpson, R. W. 1985. Assessment of air quality impacts from an elevated point source. *Journal of Environmental Management* 20, 63–72.

Johnson, W. B., Sklarew, R. C., and Turner, D. B. 1976. Urban air quality simulation modeling. Stern, A. C., ed. *Air pollution,* Vol. I. New York: Academic Press.

Johnston, H. 1961. *Weather ways.* Ottawa: Department of Transport, Meteorological Branch.

Jones, C. O. 1975. *Clean air: the policies and politics of pollution control.* Pittsburgh: University of Pittsburgh Press.

Kneese, A. V. 1984. *Measuring the benefits of clean air and water*. Baltimore: Johns Hopkins University Press for Resources for the Future.

Lee, D. B., Jr. 1973. Requiem for large-scale models. *Journal of the American Institute of Planners* 39, 163–178.

Lee, W. L., and Stern, A. C. 1973. Stack height requirements implicit in federal standards of performance for new stationary sources. *Air Pollution Control Association Journal* 23, 503–513.

Organisation for Economic Cooperation and Development (OECD). 1971. *Models for prediction of air pollution*. Mahoney, J. R., ed. Paris: OECD.

Pasquill, F. 1962. *Atmospheric diffusion: the dispersion of windborne material from industrial and other sources*. London: Van Nostrand.

Rydell, C. P., and Stevens, B. H. 1968. Air pollution and the shape of urban areas. *Journal of the American Institute of Planners* 34, 50–51.

Shen, T. T. 1986. Assessment of air pollution impact. *Atmospheric Environment* 20, 2039–2045.

Stern, A. C., ed. 1976. *Air pollution*, Vol. I. New York: Academic Press.

Strom, G. H. 1976. Atmospheric dispersion of stack effluents. In Stern, A. C., ed. *Air pollution*, Vol. I. New York: Academic Press.

Sutton, O. G. 1960. *Understanding the weather*. New York: Penguin.

Wanta, R. C., and Lowry, W. P. 1976. The meteorological setting. In Stern, A. C., ed. *Air pollution*, Vol. I. New York: Academic Press.

Weber, E., ed. 1982. *Air pollution: assessment methodology and modeling*. New York: Plenum Press.

World Commission on Environment and Development. 1987. *Our common future*. New York: Oxford University Press.

APPENDIX

The following calculations are taken from a program written in Pascal (GAUSS.COM, author and date unknown) designed to calculate ground-level concentrations of pollution.[11]

1. Effective Stack Height

Effective stack height (H_{eff}) is given by the formula:

$$H_{eff} = H + \frac{1.6 * \exp[\ln(f_0)/3] * \exp[\ln(3.5*x0)*2/3]}{u}$$

where:

H = physical height of the stack
u = wind speed
f_0 = 3.12 * .785 * v_0 * d^2 * $(t_0-t_1)/t_0$
v_0 = gas exit velocity
d = stack diameter
t_0 = gas exit temperature (in degrees Kelvin)
t_1 = ambient temperature (in degrees Kelvin)

The value of x_0 is determined by f_0 as follows:

if f_0 > 55, then x_0 = 34 * exp[.4 * ln(f_0)]
if f_0 < = 55, then x_0 = 14 * exp[.625 * ln(f_0)]

2. Lateral and Vertical Dispersion Coefficients

For any value of x (the horizontal distance in meters from the source), the standard deviations of y and z under different conditions of atmospheric stability are calculated as follows:

Lateral dispersion (s_y):

A. Very unstable s_y = x * .22 * 1/sqrt(1 + .0001 * x)
B. Moderately unstable s_y = x * .16 * 1/sqrt(1 + .0001 * x)
C. Slightly unstable s_y = x * .11 * 1/sqrt(1 + .0001 * x)
D. Neutral s_y = x * .08 * 1/sqrt(1 + .0001 * x)

E. Somewhat stable $s_y = x * .06 * 1/\text{sqrt}(1 + .0001 * x)$
F. Stable $s_y = x * .04 * 1/\text{sqrt}(1 + .0001 * x)$

Vertical dispersion (s_z):

A. Very unstable $s_z = x * .20$
B. Moderately unstable $s_z = x * .12$
C. Slightly unstable $s_z = x * .08 * 1/\text{sqrt}(1 + .0002 * x)$
D. Neutral $s_z = x * .06 * 1/\text{sqrt}(1 + .00015 * x)$
E. Somewhat stable $s_z = x * .03 * 1/(1 + .0003 * x)$
F. Stable $s_z = x * .016 * 1/(1 + .0003 * x)$

3. Ground-Level Concentrations

Ground-level, centerline concentrations of pollution (C_{max}) are derived from the Gaussian formula, with $y = 0$ and $z = 0$; thus,

$$C_{max} = \frac{1000000 * Q}{A} * [\exp(-(H_{eff}/s_z)2) + \exp(-(H_{eff}/s_z)2)]$$

where:

s_y and s_z are the appropriate standard deviations for the distance from the source and

$$A = 2 * pi * u * s_y * s_z$$

If either of the standard deviations is less than .01, C_{max} is set to zero.

Chapter 14

RISK-EQ: Earthquake Risk Analysis

Steven P. French and Sarah L. Keown

Natural hazards, such as earthquakes, floods, landslides, and hurricanes, pose serious threats to many urban areas due to the loss of life and destruction of property that they can cause. Planners are often called upon to develop strategies to respond to the threats posed by these hazards. While the nature and size of individual hazard events cannot be predicted with a high degree of certainty, probabilistic risk analysis provides a way to estimate the amount of damage that is likely to result from events of various sizes. This type of information can be useful for developing programs designed to decrease the amount of damage (hazard mitigation) or in preparing responses to a hazard event that may occur (emergency preparedness). Jaffe et al. (1984) and Bolton et al. (1986) describe the application of earthquake risk analysis techniques to local land use planning.

This chapter describes RISK-EQ, a risk analysis model that estimates the amount of damage likely to occur from earthquakes of various magnitudes. It has been developed to aid in hazard mitigation and emergency preparedness planning. Damages, estimated in terms of dollar losses, may be calculated for twelve structure types and seven Modified Mercalli Intensity (MMI) earthquake levels (MMI VI through MMI XII). The model can be customized for a particular region or community by entering the number of structures and the average monetary values derived from an inventory of buildings in the study area. While the technique discussed here is developed for earthquake hazards, the general methodology is applicable to the whole range of hazards.

The RISK-EQ model is designed to be interactive. The building inventory and property values can be recalculated to yield new damage estimates. This enables the analyst to revise a mistake, enter updated data, view totals for a new study area, and test different scenarios. The model is driven by a set of macros that make it extremely easy to use. Those more familiar with spreadsheet operation may wish to bypass the macros and use the spreadsheet directly.

RISK-EQ focuses on damage to property, more particularly on structural damage to buildings. The methods for estimating loss of life and injury are much less developed than those for estimating property losses. For this reason, this model characterizes risk as the potential direct dollar damage to structures. It does not provide estimates of loss of life, injury, or economic losses due to interruption of business, which may result from a hazard event. A more thorough analysis of the hazard may need to take these factors into account.

It is useful to distinguish between risk and hazard. A *hazard* is a physical mechanism that can, in some cases, cause damage. A *risk* exists when there is something of value that can be damaged by that hazard mechanism. Earthquakes, like other natural hazards, are only of concern when the natural phenomenon (the hazard) can inflict damage on people or property. An earthquake on a deserted island would be of little more than scientific interest. Both the hazard mechanism and the property of value must be present for a significant risk of damage to exist.

It is important to note that not all areas are subject to the same level of hazard and that the value of property varies considerably from place to place. Since hazard mechanisms and property that can be damaged vary from one area to another, a risk analysis model must provide a way to capture the basic risk relationships in a form that can be customized to reflect the nature of the hazard and property at risk in a particular area. The RISK-EQ model provides such a framework.

CONCEPTUAL BASIS

A number of risk analysis methods have been developed and used over the last two decades. Earthquake risk analysis methods are quite diverse due to the absence of any national program (such as the National Flood Insurance Program) that prescribes a particular method and level of hazard for which to plan.

Numerous special purpose risk analyses have been undertaken, usually to estimate the overall amount of damage to structures that is likely to occur in a given area or to support local or regional emergency planning efforts. Earthquake risk analysis differs from methods developed for other hazards in two important ways. First, the location of the building with respect to the hazard is less important than with other hazards. Second, the structural characteristics of the property at risk tend to be more important in determining resultant damage. Thus, earthquake risk analysis requires significantly more detailed information about the property at risk.

The earthquake hazard is not limited to just those areas along a fault line. Ground motion radiates from the epicenter of the event and generally attenuates with distance. However, ground motion may be intensified by local soil and geological conditions (for example, the 1985 Mexico City earthquake inflicted substantial damage up to 140 miles from its epicenter). In addition, since the epicenter can occur anywhere along a fault (or even in nonfault areas), there is considerable uncertainty as to what the actual ground-motion effects will be at any given site. Thus, most earthquake hazard analyses assume fairly constant ground-motion levels for rather large areas (for instance, an entire city). Therefore, while it is possible to differentiate the level of hazard in space, the scale of spatial differentiation is necessarily coarse.

The structural characteristics of the property at risk are critical in earthquake risk analysis. The performance of a wood-frame building will differ markedly from that of an unreinforced masonry building subjected to the same ground-motion forces. As a result, earthquake risk analysis requires detailed data regarding the structural characteristics of the property at risk in order to apply the risk analysis techniques.

Two reports on earthquake hazards may be of particular interest to the reader: (1) the Building Seismic Safety Council's (1985) recommended provisions for seismic regulations for new buildings; and (2) the Applied Technology Council's (1985) damage estimation method for California. These studies represent some of the most interesting work on identifying the present level of hazard and estimating resultant earthquake damage.

The Building Seismic Safety Council has developed a model ordinance for new construction that incorporates seismic resistant standards. Recognizing that the likely intensity of earthquake ground motion varies considerably across the country, the stringency of regulations for a particular area is determined by the likely intensity of ground motion for that area. To aid local governments in knowing what level of regulations apply to their area, the model ordinance includes a county-level map of effective peak acceleration for all 3,200 counties in the United States. This map can be used as a rough guide for determining the proper scenario earthquake to be evaluated for a particular locality. A more general map that shows the likely MMIs for the United States was prepared by Wiggins (1975) and is reproduced in Petak and Atkisson (1982). By using one of these two sources or more detailed local data on the analysis area, the planner should be able to identify the approximate level of earthquake hazard facing his or her community.

The second report was prepared by the Applied Technology Council (1985). It provides a detailed method for estimating the earthquake damage to urban areas in California. The report describes an inventory procedure to estimate the number and value of facilities in forty classes of buildings and thirty-eight classes of infrastructure components (for example, pipelines, dams, and storage tanks). The study used a panel of experts to develop damage probability matrices that relate earthquake intensity (MMI) to predicted damage as a percentage of property value. The classification of buildings into forty classes and their associated damage matrices along with the suggested inventory procedures provided important background information for developing the RISK-EQ model. While these data were originally developed for California, the damage probability functions can be generalized to other areas.

Risk Analysis Approach

As we have seen, risk depends on the interaction between some causative mechanism (in this case, an earthquake) and something of value (say, a city's building stock). Risk analysis is a procedure through which these two factors are combined to estimate the consequences or potential losses due to a possible hazardous event.

A wide range of risk analysis methods has been developed and implemented over the past twenty years. Many of these are reviewed in National Research Council (1989) and Reitherman (1985). While the scope and sophistication of these methods vary considerably, they generally include three components: (1) information about the hazard itself (for instance, the probability and intensity of likely events); (2) an inventory of the property at risk to the hazard; and (3) estimates of the response of various classes of property to different levels of hazard.

Existing methods range in scale from those using aggregate data at the state level (Petak and Atkisson 1982) to those that focus on the behavior of an individual structure. Detailed methods provide greater accuracy but require substantially greater amounts of input data on the hazard and the characteristics of the property at risk. As a result, for most planning applications, aggregation to the city or county level is generally preferable.

Risk analysis typically involves three distinct steps:

1. Defining the hazard;
2. Inventorying the property at risk; and
3. Applying vulnerability functions to estimate probable damage.[1]

To get a sense of the technical issues involved in conducting a risk analysis, each step will be considered in turn.

Defining the Hazard. The first step is identifying the nature of the hazard. This involves identifying what type of hazard is present and describing the intensity of the hazard that is likely to occur. Generally, events of lesser intensity occur more frequently than those of greater intensity (that is, small earthquakes are more common than extremely large earthquakes).

Many methods of describing the hazard use some type of probability statement to account for the likelihood or frequency of occurrence of the hazard. There are two major ways in which these probabilities can be used: single probabilities for scenario events or the whole probability distribution.

Most simply, an event of a given probability can be chosen and used as the "scenario event." This approach is used in floodplain management. The one hundred-year flood (the flood that has a 1 percent probability of occurring in any given year) is used as the scenario event. Davis and colleagues (1982a, b) provide an excellent example of how this type of analysis can be applied in the earthquake context. They look at the kind of infrastructure damage that would occur using scenario earthquakes in Los Angeles and the San Francisco Bay area.

Alternatively, the probabilities for events over a whole range of severities can be used to characterize the hazard. This frequency distribution provides a more thorough way for characterizing the hazard and its effects. A probability distribution, which describes the likelihood of experiencing different intensity levels, is used to describe the hazard.

These probability distributions are usually based on historical data for relatively frequent events. Extremely rare events for which there are inadequate historical data are estimated using models that simulate the physical mechanism of the hazard.

The RISK-EQ model uses the scenario approach. It can, though, estimate the results of a range of scenario earthquakes. The likely earthquake intensity for a particular community will depend on local seismic conditions and must be determined from exogenous sources. The model can be thought of as a tool for "if-then" testing; if an earthquake of this magnitude occurs, then what will be the resultant damage.

If the probabilities of experiencing each intensity level in a given level are known, then the model can be used to estimate the expected level of damage across the whole range of hazard scenarios. However, in most cases, this level of detailed information about the hazard will not be readily available. In these cases, the analysis can be done only for a single intensity level.

Inventorying Property at Risk. Since risk is determined by the action of a hazard upon some property of value, it is important to know the type, number, and value of the buildings exposed to a hazard. A typical property inventory classifies structures into a finite number of types that are known to experience similar vulnerability to the hazard. Insurance companies use a structure classification scheme for determining earthquake (and fire) premiums (Insurance Services Office 1983). Other classification schemes range from as few as four classes (French and Isaacson 1984) to more elaborate classifications, such as the twelve classes used in the Rapid Visual Screening Method (Applied Technology Council 1988) or the forty building classes used by the Earthquake Engineering Facility Classification (Applied Technology Council 1985). Most of these classification schemes place structures into homogeneous groups based on their construction material, type of framing system, and the age of the structure.

One would assume that the inventory of property at risk would involve little uncertainty since it is basically a problem of counting and classifying the number of structures and components of various types. Indeed, given unlimited resources, this is the case. However, in many cases, adequate inventories do not currently exist, and the cost of developing an inventory based on field inspection can be prohibitive, except for extremely small areas. To use this model, the user must identify the number of structures in each of twelve classes and assign an average value to each structure class. This provides a good characterization of the building stock at a city level.

Applying Vulnerability Functions. Vulnerability models provide the link between the hazard and its resulting damage. These models describe the level of damage as a function of hazard intensity. Damage is generally characterized as a damage ratio, which represents the dollar value of the damage as a proportion of the building's total value. The damage ratio is a function of the hazard intensity at the particular site:

$$DR_i = f(i)$$

where DR_i is a damage ratio at hazard intensity i. Separate vulnerability models are used for different classes of buildings. Many vulnerability models are empirically estimated curves based on past loss experience. The damage curves developed by Algermissen and Associates (1978) are typical of these types of functions and are still frequently used. The Allied Technology Council's (ATC) Report ATC-13 (ATC 1985) provides another set of vulnerability functions.

Table 14.1 shows a typical damage function in which the damage ratio increases with the intensity or severity of the earthquake hazard. This damage function applies to wood-frame structures. It was developed by polling a number of structural engineers with extensive earthquake experience. The probabilities attached to each damage ratio in Table 14.1 (for example, the 68.5 percent chance of 0.5 percent damage to a wood-frame structure from an MMI VI earthquake) represent their collective knowledge based on observations of past earthquakes. Since there is some uncertainty as to the actual level of damage that will result from a given hazard intensity, a distribution of damage ratios is used to describe events of each intensity. These distributions can be thought of as confidence intervals around the actual damage function.

The risk for a given intensity earthquake is best characterized as the expected value of the damage ratios for that hazard intensity. This expected value can be thought of as a weighted average of the damage ratios contributed by weighting each damage ratio by its respective probability. Thus, the most likely damage ratio for a given event is determined by summing the product of each damage ratio by its respective probability. For example, given the data in Table 14.1, the expected damage ratio for wood-frame structures in an MMI VI event would be:

$$DR(i) = (0.037 \times 0.0) + (0.685 \times 0.5) + (0.278 \times 5.0) = 1.7325$$

Table 14.1

Probabilities of Damage to Wood-Frame Structures

Damage	Modified Mercalli Intensity Level						
Ratio	VI	VII	VIII	IX	X	XI	XII
0.00	3.7						
0.50	68.5	26.8	1.6				
5.00	27.8	73.2	94.9	62.4	11.5	1.8	
20.00			3.5	37.6	76.0	75.1	24.8
45.00					12.0	23.1	73.5
80.00							1.7
100.00							

Source: Applied Technology Council 1985, 1988.

This suggests that for an earthquake of this intensity, wood-frame structures would be expected to experience damage equal to approximately 1.7 percent of their value. Generally, this would not be considered a major risk.

The overall expected damage for a specific earthquake intensity i is estimated by multiplying the expected damage ratio by the value of structures in each structure class and summing the damages for all building types. That is,

$$DR(i) = \sum_{j=1}^{n} p(DR_{ij}) \times V_{ij}$$

where:

p = probability of attaining a given damage ratio
DR_{ij} = damage ratio at intensity i for property type j
V_{ij} = value of the property type j that is exposed to intensity i

This expected damage value provides a convenient way to compare the risk for different hazards and locations. The RISK-EQ model allows the user to make these calculations for a range of possible earthquakes and building types.

COMPONENTS AND OPERATION

As shown in the location map in Exhibit 14.1, the RISK-EQ model consists of the following components: (1) welcome screen and documentation instructions; (2) location map; (3) data entry area; (4) weighted damage probabilities; (5) loss calculation; and (6) macros.

As Table 14.2 indicates, eleven macros are provided for use in conjunction with the RISK-EQ model. The Alt-D, Alt-L, Alt-M, Alt-Q, Alt-R, Alt-W and Alt-Z macros correspond to the standard macros described in chapter 1. Instructions for using these and other spreadsheet macros are also provided in chapter 1. The four specialized macros provided for the RISK-EQ model are described below.

Table 14.2

RISK-EQ Macros

Alt-B	Go to Breakdown of losses menu
Alt-C	View Computed total losses
Alt-D	Go to Documentation
Alt-I	Input data
Alt-L	Go to Location map
Alt-M	Go to Main menu
Alt-P	Print output
Alt-Q	Quit/save model
Alt-R	Go to Range descriptions
Alt-W	Go to Welcome screen
Alt-Z	Go to macros

The user must begin by describing the building inventory for the study area. The **Alt-I** macro allows the user to input the number and average value of structures of each type in the study area. Use the arrow keys to move from cell to cell. When data input is complete, return to the main menu by pressing **Alt-M**.

Exhibit 14.1

RISK-EQ Location Map

Welcome Screen A1..A20	Location Map H1..N20	Data Entry O1..T20	Loss Calc U1..AG20	Macros	Range Descript BN3..BS36
Main Menu A21..A40 Documentation		Weighted Damage Probabilities			
A41..A95				AY1..BH94	
		O21..S440			

The **Alt-C** macro is used for a quick overview of total losses. The **Alt-B** macro provides a more detailed breakdown of losses. This macro shows the value of expected losses for each building category. This option can help the user identify which types of buildings present the major risk. The user may choose the MMI earthquake level to be examined from the menu bar and press ENTER to return to the main menu.

Alt-P is used to send a copy of the output to the printer. Again, the user chooses the MMI intensity from the menu bar. This macro assumes that Lotus is properly configured for the printer being used. Experienced users may want to modify the macros to customize the model further.

DATA SOURCES

Two types of building inventory data must be provided by the user: (1) the number of buildings in each structure class; and (2) the average dollar value of buildings in each structure class. The number of buildings can be derived from tax assessors' records, existing land use surveys, or windshield surveys. The average value of each type of structure can be estimated from assessors' records, the local Multiple Listing Service, the Census of Housing, or a sample survey.

This model uses a subset of the building classification system developed by the Applied Technology Council (1988). In this system, buildings are classified into twelve structure types: (1) Wood Frame, (2) Steel Moment-Resisting Frame, (3) Braced Steel Frame, (4) Light Metal, (5) Steel Frame with Concrete Shear Walls, (6) Reinforced Concrete Moment-Resisting Frame, (7) Reinforced Concrete Shear Wall without Moment-Resisting Frame, (8) Unreinforced Masonry Infill, (9) Tilt-Up, (10) Precast Concrete Frame, (11) Reinforced Masonry, and (12) Unreinforced Masonry.

Each of these structure types is associated with a different damage function. Some structure types, such as Unreinforced Masonry, are much more vulnerable to earthquake damage (that is, have much higher damage ratios) than other types of structures. This relatively coarse building classification scheme facilitates data collection and entry by the user. Depending on the classification scheme employed by the jurisdiction under study, some translation may be needed to fit the inventory into these building categories.

Damage Function and Loss Calculations

Weighted Damages. The damage probability matrices developed by the Applied Technology Council (1985) have been adapted for use in the RISK-EQ model. Twelve of the matrices have been selected for this model to correspond to the structure types listed above. Where more than one facility class corresponds to a particular building type, the average values were used. The twelve structure types and corresponding facility classes are shown in Table 14.3.

Table 14.3

Building Types and Engineering Facility Classes

Building Type	Facility Class
Wood Frame	1
Steel-Moment Resisting Frame	73
Braced Steel Frame	13
Light Metal	2
Steel Frame with Concrete Shear Walls	4
Reinforced Concrete Moment-Resisting Frame	88
Reinforced Concrete Shear Wall, no MRF	7
Unreinforced Masonry Infill	79
Tilt-Up	21
Precast Concrete Frame	82
Reinforced Masonry	10
Unreinforced Masonry	75

The expected damage ratio for each structure type and intensity of earthquake is used to characterize the vulnerability of that structure type. As described above, this expected damage ratio is a weighted average derived from the probability distribution of central damage factors included in the ATC damage probability matrix.

Loss Calculations. The total value of the structures in each class is equal to the number of structures multiplied by the average value of structures in that class. This value is multiplied by the expected damage ratio for a given earthquake intensity to estimate the dollar value of losses for each class and intensity. Finally, the total estimated loss for each MMI level is computed by summing the losses for all building types. These operations are handled automatically by the RISK-EQ model.

SAMPLE APPLICATION

A sample application of the model will be presented to illustrate its use and operation. The user begins by entering the building inventory data. The user activates the **Alt-I** data input macro. From the horizontal menu bar at the top of the screen, choose **Building_Type** to enter the inventory for the study area. Let us assume that our case study area includes thirty-five hundred Wood-Frame structures (most single-family homes fall in this category), twenty-four Light Metal structures, thirty Concrete Tilt-Up buildings, and fifty Unreinforced Masonry buildings. Enter each of these numbers in the appropriate cell. Enter a zero in the cells for those building types that have no buildings in the study area. Move between cells by using the arrow keys. Press **Alt-M** when the building inventory data have been entered to return to the main menu.

To estimate the dollar value of losses, the model must have the average cost for each structure type. Press **Alt-I** again, but this time choose **Average_Value** from the menu bar. Enter the average value of the structures as follows: **100000** for Wood Frame; **55000** for Light Metal structures; **200000** for Tilt-Ups; and **57000** for the Unreinforced Masonry. After these data has been entered, press **Alt-M** to return to the main menu. Exhibit 14.2 shows a completed data input screen containing the above data.

We are now ready to see the results of the analysis. The **Alt-C** macro displays the value of the total losses expected to occur from earthquakes of all seven MMI intensities. Choose **Alt-B** for a more detailed breakdown of losses. Again, choose **MMI_X** from the menu bar. As we see in Exhibit 14.3, this macro displays the proportion of losses attributable to each building type. As we might expect, the majority of losses ($74,900,000) is produced by the wood-frame structures since they are the vast majority of the building inventory. We now choose **Alt-P** to print a copy of the analysis.

EVALUATION AND EXTENSIONS

The RISK-EQ model allows planners to estimate the likely earthquake damage for various classes of structures based on a basic inventory of structures and an assumed earthquake. If local data are available on the probability of each level of earthquake, the expected losses across the whole range of potential events can be estimated. Even rough estimates of likely expected damage can be useful to local planners in making strategic choices about the value of various hazard mitigation and emergency response alternatives. The general method presented here is applicable to other hazards, but a different set of vulnerability functions would, of course, be required.

Exhibit 14.2

RISK-EQ Input Data Screen

	[ENTER # BLDG & $ VALUE BELOW:]	
Type	Buildings	Value
WOOD FRAME	3500	$100,000
STEEL MRF	0	0
BRACED STEEL FRAME	0	0
LIGHT METAL	24	$55,000
STEEL FRAME W/CONC SW	0	0
REINF CONC MRF	0	0
REINF CONC SW NO MRF	0	0
URM INFILL	0	0
TILT-UP	30	$200,000
PRECAST CONC FRAME		0
REINF MASONRY	0	0
UNREINF MASONRY	50	$57,000
TOTAL	3,604	

More detailed and sophisticated forms of risk analysis are certainly available. More rigorous approaches will probably provide more accurate damage estimates. However, the value of this improved accuracy must be weighed against increased costs. RISK-EQ is intended to provide planners with a low-cost, easy-to-use tool that can be helpful in designing mitigation and response policies.

Exhibit 14.3

Typical RISK-EQ Output

Type	[ENTER # BLDG $ $ VALUE BELOW:] Buildings	Value	MMI X Losses
WOOD FRAME	3500	$100,000	$74,900,000
STEEL MRF	0	0	0
BRACED STEEL FRAME	0	0	0
LIGHT METAL	24	$55,000	$202,158
STEEL FRAME W/CONC SW	0	0	0
REINF CONC MRF	0	0	0
REINF CONC SW NO MRF	0	0	0
URM INFILL	0	0	0
TILT-UP	30	$200,000	$1,826,400
PRECAST CONC FRAME	0	0	0
REINF MASONRY	0	0	0
UNREINF MASONRY	50	$57,000	$1,899,525
TOTAL	3,604		$78,828,083

NOTES

1. See Bolton et al. 1986; Jaffe et al. 1984; or Scawthorn 1986 for discussions of this general methodology.

REFERENCES

Algermissen, S. T., Lagorio, H. L., 1978 and Steinbrugge, K. V. and H. L. Lagorio. 1978. *Estimation of earthquake losses to buildings (except single family dwellings).* U.S.G.S. Open File Report 78-441. Washington, DC: U.S. Geological Survey.

Applied Technology Council. 1985. *Earthquake damage evaluation data for California.* Report ATC-13. Redwood City, CA: Applied Technology Council.

———. 1988. *Rapid visual screening of buildings for potential seismic hazards.* Report ATC-21. Redwood City, CA: Applied Technology Council.

Bolton, P. A., Greene, M. M., Heikkala, S. G., and May, P. J. 1986. *Land use planning for earthquake hazard mitigation: a handbook for planners.* Boulder, CO: Natural Hazards Research and Applications Information Center, University of Colorado.

Building Seismic Safety Council. 1985. *NEHRP recommended provisions for the development of seismic regulations for new buildings.* Washington, DC: Building Seismic Safety Council.

Davis, J., Bennett, J. H., Bosctardt, G. A., et al. 1982a. *Earthquake planning scenario for a magnitude 8.3 earthquake on the San Andreas Fault in the San Francisco Bay Area.* California Division of Mines and Geology, Special Publication No. 61. Sacramento: California Department of Conservation.

———. 1982b. *Earthquake planning scenario for a magnitude 8.3 earthquake on the San Andreas Fault in Southern California.* California Division of Mines and Geology, Special Publication No. 60. Sacramento: California Deptartment of Conservation.

French, S. P., and Isaacson, M. S. 1984. Applying earthquake risk analysis techniques to land-use planning. *Journal of the American Planning Association* 50, 509-522.

Insurance Services Office. 1983. *Guide for determination of earthquake classifications.* New York: Insurance Services Office.

Jaffe, M., Butler, J., and Thurow, C. 1984. *Reducing earthquake risks: a planners guide.* Planning Advisory Report No. 364. Chicago: American Planning Association.

National Research Council. 1989. *Estimating losses from future earthquakes.* Washington, DC: National Academy Press.

Petak, W. J., and Atkisson, A. A. 1982. *Natural hazard risk assessment and public policy: anticipating the unexpected.* New York: Springer-Verlag.

Reitherman, R. 1985. A review of earthquake damage estimation methods. *Earthquake Spectra* 1, 805-847.

Wiggins, J. H. 1975. *Seismic hazard maps of the United States.* Redondo Beach, CA: J.H. Wiggins Company.

PART FIVE

Management and Decision Making

Chapter 15

MANAGER: Project Management

William J. Siembieda

Project management involves the coordination of a set of tasks in which a manager organizes, directs, and controls resources in order to achieve an objective. Project management is not new. In ancient Mesopotamia, China, and Mesoamerica, rulers and priests used planning, scheduling, and resource control to organize the irrigation systems that united the earliest states (Greenfield and Yamin 1989). Today, planners and administrators use project management methodology in capital works activities, master planning, grant development, budgeting, and program implementation.

Project management techniques can be of great assistance in dealing with tasks that are nonrepetitive or occur infrequently.[1] They are particularly useful because they require planners and managers explicitly to establish project objectives and specifications (Moder et al. 1983).

Archibald and Villoria (1968) and Moder (1988) suggest that network-based management techniques can be useful if:

1. There is an identifiable objective;
2. There is a required completion date;
3. Events and activities are identifiable and interdependent;
4. Time estimates can be made; and
5. Resources can be shifted between activities.

Kasevich (1986) suggests that computerized project management software is useful when a project's time exceeds six weeks, a network diagram is required, there are more than fifteen tasks, costs must be controlled, and there is a need for "what-if" analysis.

The MANAGER model presented in this chapter can be used to construct a project task network, schedule tasks, and identify those tasks that are "critical" for achieving a project's time-related objectives. It also allows new tasks to be added to a project and the impact of these tasks on the project time and schedule to be evaluated.

CONCEPTUAL BASIS

Project management techniques, as we know them today, evolved from general systems theory (Archibald and Villoria 1968; Cleland and King 1968). The extension of the systems control theory of mechanical applications to management environments allowed models of inputs, tasks, resources, outputs, and feedback loops to be constructed. By linking these activities together, networks are formed, providing the basis for what are now called "network-based project management methodologies."[2]

Archibald and Villoria (1968) identify three major phases in using network models: (1) planning, breaking a project into discrete activities and events, and arranging them into a network; (2) scheduling, using the networking system to schedule tasks; and (3) monitoring and control. Moder et al. (1983) divide the network-based project methodology into six steps: (1) project planning; (2) time and resource estimation; (3) basic scheduling; (4) time-cost trade-offs; (5) resource allocation; and (6) project control. In the project planning step, the activities making up the project are defined, and their technological dependencies upon one another are explicitly shown in the form of a network diagram. Moder and associates (1983) see this as the most important step in the procedure and the one in which most of the benefits of systems thinking is derived.

Until the advent of network-based project management methodology, there was no generally accepted formal procedure for assisting project management. Henry Gantt developed project scheduling bar charts (or "Gantt charts") as scheduling devices around 1900 and perfected them for special use in military procurement applications during World War I (Moder 1988).[3] These charts required project tasks to be delineated but did not link the tasks into a network. By the mid-1950s, Lockyer devised a technique called the "longest irreducible sequence of events" for the

British Central Electricity Board (Moder et al. 1983). This established the idea of a critical path for a project and moved away from the Gantt chart approach by adding tabular and arithmetic techniques for project scheduling and network construction.

During the same period, two corresponding developments took place in the United States: the program evaluation and review technique (PERT) and the critical path method (CPM). PERT was developed in 1957 for the U.S. Navy's Polaris Weapons Systems program by a research team from Lockheed Aircraft Corporation, the Navy Special Projects Office, and the consulting firm of Booz, Allan, and Hamilton. The technique is "a tool for setting a schedule for a complex project composed of many interrelated tasks, and for carefully monitoring progress and periodically readjusting the schedule to efficiently deal with difficulties and unforeseen changes in conditions" (Krueckeberg and Silvers 1974, p. 231). It was developed as a method for planning, scheduling, and controlling large and complicated projects where many activities are being conducted simultaneously and the times required to complete projects have considerable variance.

The use of probability theory for managerial decision making was the primary contribution of the PERT method. The PERT system uses three time estimates for each task—optimistic, pessimistic, and most likely—to derive probabilities for project completion dates. Thus, the "definite completion date" procedure of Gantt chart-type scheduling procedures is replaced by a range of times and probabilities for each.

CPM was developed in the 1950s to manage large projects undertaken by the Du Pont Corporation. The technique is distinguished from PERT because it not only helps schedule projects but also determines minimum project costs where the variables are primarily deterministic (Moder 1988). CPM attempts to reduce the time required to perform tasks by identifying the project period, which minimizes the sum of direct and indirect costs, including production costs related to plant downtime. CPM is commonly used in process industries, construction, and single-project industry activities.

PERT treats time in estimated and *probabilistic* terms while CPM treats it in *deterministic* terms. However, both techniques use common tools for identifying tasks that have starts and finishes, determining slack times, and finding minimum project paths. Both techniques also require the development of a project network that, in itself, is a simple but effective method for simulating the project under consideration.

The major value of the PERT and CPM approaches is the process of defining activities (or tasks) and linking these activities with one or more resource units (time being the basic resource). The sequencing of the linkages can then be examined to determine whether improvements can be made in the schedule to conserve resources or to achieve other objectives. PERT is particularly useful for scheduling a large number of interrelated tasks and for adjusting these tasks on a periodic basis. This allows available options for allocating resources among tasks to be evaluated when outside events cause changes in a project's schedule (Page 1989).

The estimated completion time, t_e, for a task can be estimated for the PERT technique as the weighted sum of three completion times. That is,

$$t_e = (a + 4m + b) / 6$$

where: (1) a is the optimistic completion time, that is, the time that could be bettered only one time in twenty if the activity was repeated under similar conditions; (2) b is the pessimistic completion time, that is, the completion time that could be bettered nineteen times out of twenty; and (3) m is the most probable completion time (Krueckeberg and Silvers 1974).[4] The completion time estimates can be obtained by consulting people who have been involved in similar projects or by referring to published studies.

The PERT/CPM procedures require a network to be established. This is done graphically by identifying events (the beginning and ending points of activities), usually with a numbered circle or symbol, and connecting them with arrows. Basic rules for defining the network include:

1. Before an activity can begin, all activities preceding it must be completed;
2. Arrows imply a logical predecessor-successor sequence;
3. Events numbers cannot be duplicated; and
4. Any two events may be directly connected by no more than one activity.

Once a network has been established, a PERT schedule can be built using the MANAGER model. The model is built primarily on the principles of the PERT technique. This approach is particularly applicable because its emphasis on estimating completion times and events is appropriate for many planning and development activities that experience a great deal of variance during the implementation process.

The MANAGER model calculates early and late starts and finishes for a set of tasks and identifies the critical path through the network. The critical path is identified by determining the events that have no "slack" or extra completion time. The model also creates a calendar of dates for completing each event that is useful for making adjustments to local political, cultural, and climatic requirements.[5]

COMPONENTS AND OPERATION

As the location map in Exhibit 15.1 illustrates, the MANAGER model is divided into five tables. The first three require data inputs; the second two display output. The "Early-Start Project Plan Table" computes the earliest possible start and finish day for each task. The "Late-Start Project Plan Table" computes the latest possible start and finish times that will not affect the overall completion date. The "Time Estimation Table" calculates the estimated completion time for each task using the pessimistic, optimistic, and most likely completion times specified by the user. The "Project Date Table" creates a task calendar showing the day, month, and year for each task. The "Critical Task Table" identifies tasks that have no slack time or "float" and thus are critical for the timely completion of the project.

Model Operation
As Table 15.1 indicates, twelve macro commands are provided for use in conjunction with the MANAGER model. The Alt-D, Alt-L, Alt-M, Alt-Q, Alt-R, Alt-W, and Alt-Z macros correspond to the standard macros described in chapter 1. General instructions for using these macros and other spreadsheet macros are provided in chapter 1. The five specialized macros provided for the MANAGER model are described below.

Alt-I, Input Network Data. This brings up a submenu that provides the following choices:

1. Task_des, enter a description of each task;
2. Pre_task, enter preceding task numbers;

Exhibit 15.1

MANAGER Location Map

Welcome Screen A1..A20	Location Map B1..I20	Task Time Calc. L23..P41	Project Date R26..W42
Main Menu A22..A40	Early Start B21..I49		Critical Task R46..U58
Documentation	Late Start B50..J69		Range Descript S70..AB90
A41..A72	Macros		
	B70..I160		

3. Suc_task, enter succeeding task number;
4. Estimate, enter task time estimates;
5. Data_fill, initiate the data fill sequence;
6. Start_day, enter the project starting date; and
7. Main_menu, return to the main menu.

Table 15.1

MANAGER Macros

Alt-D	Go to Documentation
Alt-I	Input network data
Alt-L	Go to Location map
Alt-M	Go to Main menu
Alt-O	Go to Output
Alt-P	Print output
Alt-Q	Quit/save model
Alt-R	Go to Range descriptions
Alt-S	Modify task descriptions
Alt-T	Modify task list
Alt-W	Go to Welcome screen
Alt-Z	Go to macros

Alt-O, Go to Output. This option brings up a submenu with the following options:

1. Dates, go to the project date table;
2. Early_start, go to the early start table;
3. Late_start, go to the late start table;
4. Critical_tasks, go to the critical tasks table; and
5. Main_menu, return to the main menu.

Alt-P, Print Output. This option prints the project date and the critical tasks.
Alt-S, Modify Task Descriptions. This option provides a submenu with the following options:

1. Add_col, insert a column;
2. Del_col, delete a column;

3. **Pre_task3**, add a third preceding task;
4. **Pre_task4**, add more than three preceding tasks;
5. **Suc_task3**, add a third preceding task;
6. **Suc_task4**, add more than three succeeding tasks; and
7. **Main_menu**, return to the Main menu.

Alt-T, Modify Task List. The option provides the following options:

1. **Add_row**, add a row to the task list;
2. **Del_row**, delete a row from the task list;
3. **Copy_task**, copy the late task list to the early task list; and
4. **Main_menu**, return to the main menu.

Data Entry

Entering Task Information. A project is defined in terms of four components: (1) a beginning date; (2) a series of tasks (or events); (3) a sequence of linkages between the tasks; and (4) a completion date. After adjusting for the proper number of project dates and tasks, the user must: (1) identify the tasks; (2) number the tasks; and (3) enter the time period required to complete each task.

The task descriptions are entered in the Early-Start Project Plan Table using the **Alt-I,** Input network data, option. The tasks should be listed in the general sequence in which they will be completed. The first task is always identified as "Dummy Start," an artificial task that is assigned a task number of 0. The model also contains a final "Dummy Finish" task that is assigned a value of 99, that is, a number larger than the highest actual task number. The dummy task is included so that every task in the model will have a preceding and a succeeding task. Since the artificial Dummy Start and Finish tasks do not require any days to complete, "@NA" (for "not available") is automatically entered in the Dummy Start and Dummy Finish cells when the model is loaded.

The MANAGER model is initially set up for a ten-task project with two preceding and succeeding tasks. The number of tasks can be adjusted by using the **Alt-T,** Modify Task List, macro to add rows or delete rows. After the task descriptions are entered, the **Alt-T** Copy_task option can be used to copy this information into the Late-Start Project Plan Table.

Three estimates are required for each task: the optimistic completion time, the pessimistic completion time, and the most probable completion time. These values are entered in the appropriate column. Use the **Alt-I** Est_Time menu option to input the estimates. The user should then press F9 to compute the mean estimates and place them into the correct rows of the Early-Start Project Plan Table.

Preceding tasks, that is, tasks that occur before another can begin, must be identified by task number and entered into the appropriate columns of the Early-Start Plan Project Table. Whenever a task has zero or one preceding tasks, enter the value **0**. For example, in Exhibit 15.2, the "Define Scope" task has no preceding tasks, so a **0** is entered in the preceding task column; @NA is automatically entered as the preceding task for the Dummy Start.

If three Preceding Task columns are needed, place the cursor to the left of the Second Task column and use the **Alt-S**, Add_col, option to add a column. Then use the **Alt-S** Pre-task3 option to adjust the formula in the Early-Start column. Instructions for adding more than three columns are found in the Documentation section of the model.

Succeeding tasks, that is, tasks that immediately follow the completion of a task, must be identified by task number and entered into the appropriate columns of the Late-Start Project Plan Table. Enter a dummy task number of **99** when a task has fewer than two successors. If three succeeding task columns are needed, use the **Alt-S**, Add_col, option to add a column and the **Alt-S** Suc_task3 option to adjust the formula in the Late-Finish column. Adjustment instructions for more than three columns are found in the Documentation section of the model. Once these numbers are entered, press F9. If negative numbers appear in the Late-Start and Late-Finish columns, press F9 repeatedly until no negative numbers appear.

The Project Date Table data requirements are simple; just enter the year, month, and day that the project is to start. Use the **Alt-I,** Start_day, option to move to the @DATE cell for data entry. After entering the start date, press F9 and the table will be created.

Some time estimates are likely to change after a project begins its implementation phase. The new time estimates must then be used to compute new schedules. New time estimates can be entered in the Early-Start Project Plan Table only by using the **Alt-I,** Estimate option. The F9 key must then be pressed to update the entire schedule. New tasks can also be inserted into a project in the Early-Start Project Plan Table and the Late-Start Project Plan Table by using the **Alt-T,** macro.

DATA SOURCES

Data sources for the MANAGER model will vary with the context of the project at hand. For example, if the project is a public sector capital improvements effort (for instance, sewer construction in a deteriorating neighborhood), time estimates may be obtained from the Internal Revenue Service rules governing bond sales, and the engineering companies designing the project. In most capital improvement projects, time lines are established in local ordinances that can be used to determine required project completion dates. If the project involves public planning, many states have statutes that prescribe public meeting requirements. This information, coupled with local and regional work program experience (for example, that it takes two years to complete a local area plan), can provide appropriate data for using the MANAGER model.

SAMPLE APPLICATION

The sample application of the MANAGER model is the preparation of a municipal facilities plan for a city's Parks and Recreation Department (PARD).[6] The model will be used to schedule the activities for completing a park facilities plan using a process that includes strong citizen input.

Preparation of the plan involves the ten tasks identified in the network displayed in Exhibit 15.2. For example, the exhibit indicates that defining the scope (task 1), establishing an advisory committee (task 2), and conducting the inventory (task 3) can begin immediately. After the scope is defined and the members of the advisory committee are appointed (that is, tasks 1 and 2 are completed), the first of two public participation meetings (task 4) can take place. Inventory gathering (task 3) needs to be finished prior to writing the second draft (task 8). The first public participation meeting (task 4) sets the stage for all other activities.

The Parks and Recreation staff wants to complete this Facilities Plan in thirty-six months (that is, in 1,095 days) or less. Exhibit 15.3, the Early-Start Project Plan, and Exhibit 15.4, the Late-Start Project Plan, indicate how many days will be needed to complete the plan.

Exhibit 15.3 identifies the earliest possible start and finish for each task in the last two columns. Exhibit 15.4 identifies the latest possible start and finish days and the slack time for each task in the last three columns. The slack time is equal to either: (1) the late start time minus early start time or (2) the late finish time minus early finish time. For example, the Inventory Existing Conditions task has an early start of day 1 and a late start of day 192; the slack is therefore 191 days. Column 2 in each exhibit lists the estimated time (in days) required to perform each task.

Exhibit 15.2

Sample MANAGER Project Network

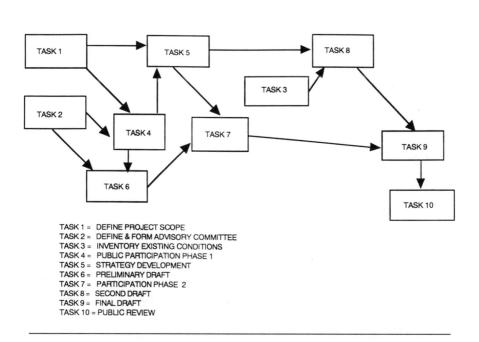

TASK 1 = DEFINE PROJECT SCOPE
TASK 2 = DEFINE & FORM ADVISORY COMMITTEE
TASK 3 = INVENTORY EXISTING CONDITIONS
TASK 4 = PUBLIC PARTICIPATION PHASE 1
TASK 5 = STRATEGY DEVELOPMENT
TASK 6 = PRELIMINARY DRAFT
TASK 7 = PARTICIPATION PHASE 2
TASK 8 = SECOND DRAFT
TASK 9 = FINAL DRAFT
TASK 10 = PUBLIC REVIEW

In Exhibits 15.3 and 15.4, the start day and finish day for each task are shown as the number of days since the start of the project rather than by the corresponding calendar dates. When the planning staff picks a starting date, these day numbers can be converted into actual calendar dates, as shown in the Project Date Table, by using the **Alt-O D**ates option.

The last column in Exhibit 15.4 identifies the tasks that are on the critical path. This column shows the number of days that a task can slip without affecting the overall project completion date. A task that has a zero value in this column, for example, the Define and Form Advisory Committee task, is on the critical path. Any slippage in the completion of this task will delay the overall project completion. Exhibit 15.4 indicates that the facilities plan preparation project has six critical tasks. These critical tasks are also listed separately on the Critical Task Table, which can be printed by using the **Alt-P** macro.

Exhibit 15.3

Early-Start Project Plan

Task Description	Task #	Days	Preceding Tasks First	Second	Early Start	Early Finish
Dummy Start	0	0	0	0	0	0
Define Scope	1	30	0	0	1	30
Define & Form Advs. Comm.	2	121	0	0	1	121
Inventory Existing Cond.	3	400	0	0	1	400
Public Participation	4	60	1	2	122	181
Strategy Development	5	410	1	4	182	591
Preliminary Draft	6	60	2	4	182	241
Public Participation	7	60	5	6	592	651
Second Draft	8	135	3	5	592	726
Final Draft	9	80	7	8	727	806
Public Review	10	90	9	0	807	896
Dummy Finish	99	0	10	0	897	896

EVALUATION AND EXTENSIONS

The MANAGER model presented here is rather simple and will not work on complex projects that have feedback loops. As a result, commercial project scheduling software would be required for complex projects (for instance, building a power generation station).[7]

The model also does not have a built-in variance function. This could be added by including the variance formula $V_T = (b - a) / 3.2$, using the cell address for the mean task time estimates from the Time Estimation Table. The a and b parameters are the fifth and ninety-fifth percentiles of the estimated time distribution and are assumed to be the limits of the distribution (Moder et al. 1983). This formula could be used with the central limit theorem to generate another table showing the variance of an estimated event.

Exhibit 15.4

Late-Start Project Plan

Task Description	Task #	Days	Succeeding Tasks First	Succeeding Tasks Second	Late Start	Late Finish	Slack
Dummy Start	0	0	1	2	0	0	0
Define Scope	1	30	4	5	92	121	91
Define & Form Advs. Comm.	2	121	4	6	1	121	0
Inventory Existing Cond.	3	400	8	99	192	591	191
Public Participation	4	60	5	6	122	181	0
Strategy Development	5	410	7	8	182	591	0
Preliminary Draft	6	60	7	99	607	666	425
Public Participation	7	60	9	99	667	726	75
Second Draft	8	135	9	99	592	726	0
Final Draft	9	80	10	99	727	806	0
Public Review	10	90	99	99	807	896	0
Dummy Finish	99	0	NA	NA	897	896	NA

A problem inherent in most scheduling techniques is the fact that tasks are usually described in terms of a single resource—time. In reality, time is not the only resource involved, and this emphasis may neglect other resource issues, such as human or capital costs. There may also be no true interchangeability of resource units between activities. As a result, a manager may not be able to easily shift resources to an activity that begins to fall behind schedule. However, the MANAGER model does provide an easy-to-use model for managing the types of projects that planners and managers encounter frequently.

NOTES

1. Kasevich (1986) defines a project as a set of related tasks leading to the achievement of a specific goal. When this goal has been reached, a project is considered to be complete.

2. A "network" is a graphical representation of a project plan that links various activities. Networks are also called "arrow diagrams" and, when time estimates and computations are added, may be used as project schedules (Moder et al. 1983).

3. While often used as a scheduling tool, the bar chart is limited when working with complex interrelationships. The advantage of a Gantt chart is that all the information is graphically displayed at once, allowing one to monitor the progress of individual activities. This allows the user to process information faster than would be possible if it were presented in a tabular manner.

4. This formula holds only if the optimistic and pessimistic times are symmetrically placed about the most likely time, that is, only if $b-m = m-a$ (Moder et al. 1983).

5. This model is an adaptation of the version developed by Gardner (1988a, b). It extends his model by adding the Date option, the estimated task calculation tables, and the critical task tables.

6. The activities shown in this model were used by the New Mexico city of Albuquerque's Parks and Recreation Department in its facility planning process. The project sequence and completion dates for each activity approximate the city's estimates.

7. Page (1989) provides a review of project management software appropriate for planning applications.

REFERENCES

Archibald, R. D., and Villoria, R. L. 1986. *Network-based management systems (PERT/CPM)*. New York: John Wiley and Sons.

Cleland, D. I., and King, W. R., eds. 1968. *Project management handbook,* 2nd edition. New York: Van Nostrand Reinhold.

Gardner, E. S., Jr. 1988a. Project manager, part 1. *Lotus Magazine* 4, 1, 82–87.

———. 1988b. Project manager, part 2. *Lotus Magazine* 4, 2, 80–84.

Greenfield, S. S., and Yamin, R. 1989. Project management: a history of its interaction with society. In Kimmons, R. L. and Loweree, J. H., eds. *Project management: a reference for professionals*. New York: Marcel Dekker.

Kasevich, L. S. 1986. *Harvard project manager/total project manager: controlling your resources*. Blue Ridge Summit, PA: TAB Books.

Krueckeberg, D. A., and Silvers, A. L. 1974. *Urban planning analysis: methods and models*. New York: John Wiley and Sons.

Moder, J. J. 1988. Network techniques in project management. In Cleland, D. I., and King, W. R., eds. *Project management handbook*, 2nd edition. New York: Van Nostrand Reinhold Company.

————, Phillips, C. R., and Davis, E. W. 1983. *Project management with CPM, PERT and precedence diagramming*, 3rd edition. New York: Van Nostrand Reinhold Company.

Page, W. G. 1989. Using project management software in planning. *Journal of the American Planning Association* 55, 494–499.

Chapter 16

CROSTIME: Simultaneous Time-Series and Cross-Sectional Analysis

Erik Ferguson and Paul E. Patterson

Many problems in urban and regional analysis have important temporal dimensions. Forecasting changes in employment, population, or travel behavior are just a few examples of areas where temporal processes and interactions may be important for identifying existing conditions, explaining past trends, or forecasting future outcomes of urban and regional policies and planning. Time-series analysis is one method of explicitly incorporating temporal phenomena in regression analysis for forecasting purposes. Time-series analysis is often used as a projection method, based exclusively on the past performance of specific exogenous output variables. Policy input variables, such as spatial or socioeconomic variations in demand, are generally not included in time-series models due to lack of data, lack of analysis software, or both.

Cross-sectional models typically provide more opportunities for testing policy sensitivity. However, parameter estimates and confidence intervals in cross-sectional models may be significantly biased if serial autocorrelation is present. Combined time-series and cross-sectional models offer the possibility of providing policy sensitivity and controlling for temporal estimation biases simultaneously. Unfortunately, few readily available statistical programs allow the estimation or testing of such combined models.

The CROSTIME model provides a tool for estimating and evaluating combined time-series and cross-sectional multiple regression models that may involve first-order, serially autoregressive causal processes. Three types of temporal variability may be considered within CROSTIME: (1) first-order serially autoregressive impacts; (2) first-order seasonally autoregressive impacts; and/or (3) permanent, temporary, and/or lingering impacts of specific events over time. The CROSTIME model can also be adapted to other types of time-series models, such as integrated or moving average models that are theoretically appealing but rarely necessary for accurate parameter estimation.

Transit and aviation passenger travel demand forecasting applications are used to demonstrate how alternate model formulations can be evaluated in terms of descriptive ability (overall goodness of fit), serial autocorrelation (parameter estimation bias), and predictive ability (forecast error).

CONCEPTUAL BASIS

Many types of time-series analysis are available, one of the most common types being autoregressive, integrated, moving average (ARIMA) models. In general, these models do not allow for the inclusion of contemporaneous (cross-sectional) variables, although examples of highly sophisticated regional forecasting models that do so have been identified in the economics literature (Kinal and Ratner 1986).

Cross-Sectional Models

A traditional cross-sectional forecasting model is as follows:

$$Y_t = f(X_{t1}, X_{t2}, ...) + e_t \tag{1}$$

where:

Y_t = dependent variable measured at time t

X_{tn} = n independent variables associated with the dependent variable at time t

e_t = error in prediction at time period t

Serial transformations of the dependent variable that may account for some part of changes in the dependent variable over time do not appear on the right-hand side of such equations. However, the error terms in prediction associated with cross-sectional forecasting models of this type are often correlated with the dependent variable. This serial autocorrelation may result in systematic overestimation of the parameters for the X_t variables, underestimation of parametric error terms, and a resultant misplaced confidence in the reliability of the model and its estimated parameters.

A common test of serial autocorrelation in the distribution of error terms is Durbin-Watson's d statistic (Durbin and Watson 1951):

$$d = \frac{\Sigma(e_t - e_{t-1})^2}{\Sigma(e_t)^2} \qquad (2)$$

where:

e_t =   prediction error for dependent variable in time period t

e_{t-1} =   prediction error for dependent variable in the immediately preceding time period, t-1

In the absence of serial autocorrelation, Durbin-Watson's d has an expected value of 2. Values higher or lower than 2 may indicate serial autocorrelation, depending on the number of observations, independent variables, and degrees of freedom used in estimating the equation.

Time-Series Models

A serial autoregressive time-series model has the following general form:

$$Y_t = f(X_{t1}, X_{t2},... Y_{t-n}...) + e_t \qquad (3)$$

where:

Y_{t-n} =   a serially autoregressive transformation of the dependent variable

Serial transformations of the dependent variable appear in the right-hand side of regression equations to account for the sensitivity of the dependent variable to initial or prior conditions. Durbin-Watson's d generally is not a reliable indicator of serial autocorrelation in these types of models. However, Durbin's h may be used instead (Durbin 1970). That is,

$$h = p\sqrt{\frac{T}{1 - T\,var(b*)}} \qquad (4)$$

where:

p	$=$	$1 - d/2$
T	$=$	total number of observations (*not* degrees of freedom)
b_*	$=$	parameter estimate for the first-order lagged endogenous variable, Y_{t-1}
$var(b_*)$	$=$	variance of b_*, that is, the square of the estimated standard error term for b_*

Durbin's h may be evaluated as a standardized variable, similar in nature to a t-score, with a one-tailed test of significance, because it takes only positive values (Durbin 1970).

In addition to a serial autoregressive term, seasonal variations or incident impacts may also be included in the regression analysis. These temporal variables will not affect the choice of serial autocorrelation evaluation criteria but may influence the value of the estimated test parameter and the test results.

Model Comparison

A comparison of several fundamentally different types of regression equations, all relying on the same data, illustrates the advantages and disadvantages of these different types of models. The first model estimates transit ridership using the following equation:

$$PAS_t = b_0 + b_1 VSM_t + b_2 EMP_t + e_t \qquad (5a)$$

where:

PAS_t	$=$	total transit ridership in time period t
VSM_t	$=$	total transit vehicle service miles provided in time period t
EMP_t	$=$	average service area employment in time period t
b_i	$=$	estimation parameters

Equation (5a) is an example of a standard cross-sectional model. No time-series variables are included, and the model fails to meet Durbin-Watson's d test for serial autocorrelation (Table 16.1). It was used by the

Table 16.1

Alternate Travel Ridership Forecasting Models

	Old OCTD Model	ARIMA Model	New OCTD Model	Incident Model[i]
Dep. Variable	$\ln(PAS_t)$	$PAS_t - PAS_{t-1}$	$\ln(PAS_t)$	$\ln(PAS_t)$
Ind. Variables				
Intercept	-4.708(0.088)	-2.487	-13.116(2.745)	-4.215(0.039)
Mean		123.088(4.908)		
$\ln(VSM_t)$	1.037(0.043)			0.725(0.072)
$\ln(VSM_t/POP_t)$			0.365(0.106)	
$\ln(EMP_t)$	0.740(0.082)		1.743(0.169)	0.707(0.077)
$\ln(FAR_t/GAS_t)$			-0.310(0.091)	
$\ln(PAS_{t-1})$			0.734(0.056)	0.262(0.060)
AR_1		0.385(0.155)		
SAR_4		1.033(0.112)		
MA_1		1.158(0.075)		
SMA_4		0.716(0.204)		
SEA_1				0.040(0.014)
SEA_2			0.032(0.013)	0.101(0.015)
SEA_3			0.047(0.014)	0.039(0.015)
SEA_4			-0.030(0.012)	
$G79_{\bullet}$			0.122(0.037)	0.187(0.041)
$S81_{\bullet}$			-0.252(0.048)	-0.227(0.044)
$S86_{\bullet}$				-0.073(0.042)
$G79_{\bullet+1}$				0.110(0.042)
$S81_{\bullet+1}$				-0.131(0.025)
$S86_{\bullet+1}$				-0.151(0.037)
Number of obs.[2]	63	44	62	62
Deg. of freedom	60	39	52	49
R-squared	0.9808		0.9948	0.9962
Durbin-Watson's d	0.89		2.42	
Durbin's h			1.93	1.56
White noise var.		273,471		
White noise st. err.		522.944		
Prob. (20 resid.AC)		0.660		

1. The "best-fitting" exponential decay parameters in this model were as follows: $G79_{\bullet+1}$ = -infinity; $S81_{\bullet+1}$ = -0.040; and $S86_{\bullet+1}$ = -0.32.

2. Even though identical data were used for all four models, the number of observations may differ depending on temporal variable definitions used and the number of observations removed in order to create such temporal variables.

Note: The standard error for each independent variable is given in parentheses next to each parameter estimate. All parameter estimates listed in this table are significant at the 0.05 level of confidence or higher, using a one-tailed test.

Orange County Transit District (OCTD) in California until 1988 to forecast future transit ridership for their five-year Short-Range Transit Plan. The overall goodness of fit of this model declined after a 1986 work stoppage. This reflected the fact that the model made no provision for temporally related impacts, such as work stoppages.

As a result, the first author developed a time-series model for forecasting future transit ridership in Orange County (Ferguson 1991). This model took the following form:

$$(PAS_t - PAS_{t-1}) = b_0 + b_1 AR_1 + b_2 SAR_n + b_3 MA_1 + b_4 MA_n \qquad (5b)$$

where:

PAS_t	=	total transit ridership in time period, t
PAS_{t-1}	=	total transit ridership in the preceding time period, $t-1$
AR_1	=	serial autoregressive term
SAR_n	=	seasonal autoregressive term
MA_1	=	serial moving average term
MA_n	=	seasonal moving average term
n	=	length of seasonality

Equation (5b) is an ARIMA model that can be estimated using microcomputer-based statistical packages, such as StatGraphics (Cervero 1987). A variant of Equation (5b) using monthly rather than quarterly data was used to project Orange County transit ridership for a two-year period after the 1986 work stoppage occurred. Immediately after the work stoppage ended, the model predicted a permanent downward trend in transit ridership. After data for several more months were available, the model predicted that ridership would recover to prestrike levels within about twelve months after the strike. In fact, Orange County transit ridership performed even better than predicted by the model, setting new all-time-high ridership records less than fifteen months after the strike was over.

This example illustrates the fundamental problem with pure ARIMA models. Although fairly complex temporal processes can be captured within such models, they continue to be little more than highly sophisticated extrapolation techniques. As a result, they cannot account for permanent or temporary changes in future forecast conditions until *after* a new trend line has been established in reality and, more importantly from a modeling perspective, in the input data used to estimate the model.

OCTD did not adopt the ARIMA model for forecasting purposes. Instead, it hired a consultant to develop a new model on their behalf. The Center for Economic Research (1989) developed the following model, which was then used to forecast transit ridership:

$$
\begin{aligned}
\ln(PAS_t) = \ b_0 &+ b_1 \ln(VSM_t/POP_t) + b_2 \ln(EMP_t) \qquad (5c) \\
&+ b_3 \ln(FAR_t/GAS_t) + b_4 \, SEA_2 + b_6 SEA_3 \\
&+ b_7 \, SEA_4 + b_8 \, INC_a + e_t
\end{aligned}
$$

where:

PAS_t = total transit ridership in time period t
PAS_{t-1} = total transit ridership in the preceding time period, $t-1$
POP_t = average service area population in time period t
FAR_t = average transit fare in time period t
GAS_t = average local gasoline price in time period t
SEA_n = 1 if the time period in question occurred during quarterly season n, 0 otherwise
$\ln$ = natural logarithm

Equation (5c) is a combined time-series and cross-sectional model that can be estimated using programs such as MicroTSP (Center for Economic Research 1989). This model includes an autoregressive term (PAS_{t-1}), as well as independent measures of the supply, demand, and relative price of transit services in Orange County. It is clearly superior to the preceding models in terms of its forecasting ability and general policy sensitivity. However, it fails on Durbin's h test, indicating that the estimated parameter values and/or confidence levels may be unreliable predictors (see Table 16.1).

The first author of this chapter developed a revised version of this latter model (Ferguson 1991), which does not exhibit the undesirable serial autocorrelation problems of Equations (5a) and (5c) nor the lack of policy sensitivity of Equation (5b):

$$
\begin{aligned}
\ln(PAS_t) = \ b_0 &+ b_1 \ln(VSM_t) + b_2 \ln(EMP_t) + b_3 \ln(PAS_{t-1}) \qquad (5d) \\
&+ b_4 \, SEA_1 + b_5 \, SEA_2 + b_6 \, SEA_3 + b_7 \, INC_a \\
&+ b_8 \, INC_1 \, \exp^{\delta \, (s-1)} + e_t
\end{aligned}
$$

where:

INC_a = 1 in time period s, 0 in all other periods,

INC_l = 1 in all time periods after s, 0 in time period s and all preceding time periods,

s = the time period during which an incident occurred, and

δ = an empirically derived exponential decay parameter, measuring the rate at which an incident's effect on ridership changes over time.

Equation (5d) is a combined time-series and cross-sectional model that can be estimated using the CROSTIME model. It does not violate Durbin's h test, has the highest R^2 value of any model illustrated, and therefore may be assumed to provide the best linear unbiased parameter estimates and confidence intervals of all four models in Table 16.1. The preferred model includes several more temporal variables than the actual OCTD model to account for both the temporary (abrupt) and more permanent (lingering) effects of incidents such as the 1979 gasoline shortage and 1981 and 1986 work stoppages.

Equation (5d) does not include a pricing variable, as both the price of transit (fares) and the price of alternatives (gasoline) were found to have insignificant effects on transit ridership in this example. Fare policy in Orange County is not determined in the marketplace but rather by the OCTD Board of Directors, most of whom are locally elected officials. In addition, more than 70 percent of Orange County transit users in 1987 were "captive" riders who did not have cars available to them on a daily basis (Ferguson 1991). The price of gasoline may be largely irrelevant to such captive riders, at least on a day-to-day basis. This is not to argue that transit pricing will remain irrelevant. Rather, pricing apparently is not applicable as an important causal factor in the type of aggregate analysis used in this particular example—an interesting and unusual result.

While Equation (5d) provides the "best" overall goodness of fit of any model considered here, it does not allow the user to estimate changes in ridership due to projected future price changes. Whether or not this is important depends on the types and magnitudes of fare or gasoline price changes that are either contemplated or observed (Kyte et al. 1988).

These considerations reinforce the general conclusion that there is no such thing as a "perfect" econometric forecasting model, superior to all others for either forecasting or descriptive purposes in all situations. However, some models are better than others, at least for certain, usually fairly specific, modeling purposes. It is incumbent upon the model developer (and user) to determine which model is "best" for any given purpose, as well as to identify whether or not the model as estimated contains statistical errors or other mechanical flaws that may tend to exaggerate its implied accuracy and precision in prediction.

COMPONENTS AND OPERATION

As the location map in Exhibit 16.1 illustrates, the CROSTIME model is composed of eight basic parts. The welcome screen, main menu screen, and model documentation are located in the upper left hand corner of the spreadsheet, in cells A1 to E120. The program code is separated into two parts, the system macro code in A161 to H1030 and the standard Alt macro code in A1038 to G1093. The location map is located in cells J1 to T20 while range descriptions are found in U1 to Y186. The body of the model, including input data and output forecasts, starts in cell Z1941 and continues down and to the right. The actual size of any given model application will depend on the number of variables and observations specified by the user for the model. Tests for serial autocorrelation are located beneath the body of the model.

Model Operation
As Table 16.2 illustrates, thirteen macros are provided for use in conjunction with the CROSTIME model. The Alt-D, Alt-L, Alt-M, Alt-Q, Alt-R, Alt-W, and Alt-Z macros correspond to the standard macros described in chapter 1. Instructions on using these macros and spreadsheet macros in general are provided in chapter 1. The six specialized macros provided for the CROSTIME model are described below.

All new CROSTIME users should acclimate themselves to the use of the Alt-S system macro before attempting to use any of the standard macros. CROSTIME is *highly* sensitive to the order in which specific macro commands are given. The system menu macro is designed to ensure that proper sequencing of commands is followed throughout CROSTIME operations. Erroneous or misleading results may be obtained if proper sequencing of CROSTIME macro commands is not followed. The entire spreadsheet model may also be corrupted through inappropriate or inconsistent macro- or nonmacro-driven usage. The original

Exhibit 16.1

CROSTIME Location Map

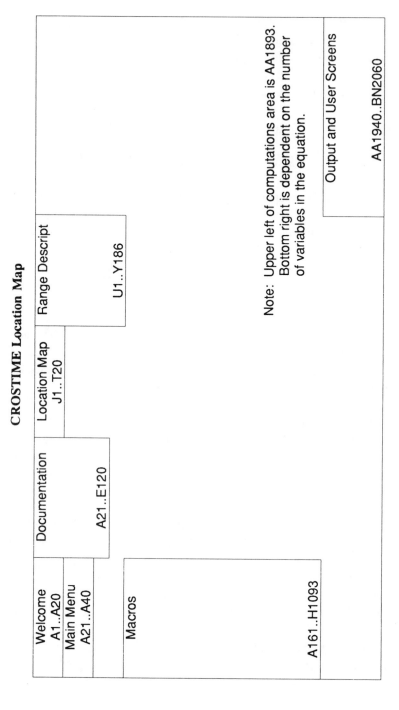

spreadsheet model should be saved in its current form and with its original name. Working files should be given descriptive names associated with the specific application being developed by the user.

Table 16.2

CROSTIME Macros

Alt-B	Modify data Base
Alt-D	Go to Documentation
Alt-E	Estimate regression coefficients
Alt-G	Graph output
Alt-L	Go to Location map
Alt-M	Go to Main menu
Alt-O	View output
Alt-P	Project results
Alt-Q	Quit/save model
Alt-R	Go to Range descriptions
Alt-S	Go to System menu
Alt-V	Save Data base
Alt-W	Go to Welcome screen
Alt-Z	Go to macros

The **Alt-S** system macro provides access to all of the CROSTIME features from a single Lotus-like menu system. The **Alt-S** system menu options include: (1) **D**ata (same as **Alt-B**); (2) **E**stimate (same as **Alt-E**); (3) **P**roject (same as **Alt-P**); (4) **G**raph (same as **Alt-G**); (5) **O**utput (same as **Alt-O**); (6) **S**ave (same as **Alt-V**); and (7) **M**ain_menu (same as **Alt-M**). Each of these system menu options is described under the separate macro headings listed in the "Other Operations" section below. Most of these specialized macros are accessible to the user from one or both of the following: (1) the main menu (**Alt-M**), as separate macro keys; or (2) the system menu (**Alt-S**), as Lotus-like menu options.

The key to understanding and using CROSTIME lies in mastering the data base operations, which must be completed prior to any descriptive or forecasting application. In the operational descriptions that follow, system menu options and suboptions are always preceded by the **Alt-S** macro command for clarity, though the user would typically need to invoke the system menu macro command only once to enter the system. Once in the system, the user is always returned to the system menu or to one of its option submenus after operations are completed, except when the user departs the system to leave Lotus or enter the main menu.

Data Base Operations
Data base creation and modification are critical to running CROSTIME properly. The **Alt-S D**ata option provides the following suboptions:

1. Initialize, clear data base and set it up for a new application;
2. Add, add a single variable to the data base;
3. Delete, delete a single variable from the data base;
4. Edit, edit existing data;
5. Retrieve, import a data base; and
6. Return, return to the previous menu.

The user cannot return to the main menu or exit CROSTIME from the **Alt-S D**ata menu. This restriction is imposed to reinforce the importance of making all data base modifications within the CROSTIME system.

Alt-S, Data Initialize clears the data base and prepares it for a new modeling application. The user is then prompted to provide the number of observations and the number of forecast periods to be used in developing the new modeling application.

Alt-S Data Add provides a submenu with the following options:

1. Independent, add an independent variable;
2. Autoregressive, add a serial autoregressive variable;
3. Seasonal, add a set of seasonal dummy variables;
4. Event, add an event variable; and `
5. Return, return to the previous menu.

Alt-S Data Add Independent creates a new independent variable and allows the user to name the variable and enter data for it, if desired. The user may enter an unlimited number of independent variables, though obviously the number that can be included in regression analysis is limited by the number of degrees of freedom included in the model, n-1, where n is the number of observations included in the data base.

Alt-S Data Add Autoregressive creates a serial autoregressive variable from the dependent variable that is automatically assumed to be included in the model. Only one serial autoregressive variable is allowed.

Alt-S Data Add Seasonal creates a set of seasonal dummy variables. The user is prompted to select the number of time periods, **4** for quarterly data or **12** for monthly data. CROSTIME automatically creates n-1 seasonal dummy variables, depending on the user's selection. Only one set of seasonal dummy variables is allowed in CROSTIME.

Alt-S Data Add Event creates an event variable. The user is prompted to select whether the event variable data will be entered either: (1) Manually by the user or (2) automatically by CROSTIME using time period and decay **F**actor options selected by the user. If the **F**actor option is selected, the user is prompted to identify: (1) the time period in which the event occurred (the nth time period from the beginning of data base); and (2) the decay factor to be used in estimating event variable values in all subsequent time periods. The decay factor is entered as an exponential decay factor, n, ranging from positive infinity (for rapid growth in the impacts over time) through 0 (for constant impacts over time) to negative infinity (for rapid decays in the impact over time). An unlimited number of event variables can be included in the model. Successful estimation of the regression equation may not be possible if too many event variables are included or if those that are included are temporally collinear, that is, spaced together too closely in time (for example, in adjacent time periods).

Alt-S Data Edit allows the user to enter the data base directly, without having to add variables. This option may be useful if the user wishes to change particular values, to correct mistakes in data entry, to change variable labels, or simply to inspect the information currently included in the data base.

Alt-S Data Delete allows the user to delete a variable. Each variable created using **Alt-S** **D**ata Add has *both* a CROSTIME-specified *name* and a user-specified *label*. The user will be prompted to identify the variable to be deleted by its CROSTIME *name*, which may take one and only one of the following forms:

1. DEP (the dependent variable, which cannot be deleted);
2. AR (the first-order serial autoregressive variable);
3. SAR (the set of n-1 seasonal autoregressive dummy variables, all of which will be deleted);
4. INDx (independent variable x, where x represents the order in which the independent variable was incorporated as an independent variable into the model); and/or

5. EVNy (event variable y, where y represents the order in which the event variable was incorporated as an event variable into the model; for example, the third event variable added to the data base is named EVN3 by CROSTIME).

If you are unsure about which CROSTIME *name* is associated with a variable you wish to delete, use **Alt-S** Data **E**dit to identify the appropriate name *before* using **Alt-S** Data **D**elete to delete the variable.

To change the number or types of *variables* employed in the model, the user may use **Alt-S** Data **A**dd, **D**elete, and/or **E**dit, as previously described. To change the number of *observations* employed in the model, the user must perform all of the following procedures in the exact order specified: *first* (1) export the current data base to a separate file using **Alt-S** Save **D**ata base; *then* (2) reinitialize CROSTIME for the new number of observations and forecast time periods using **Alt-S** Data **I**nitialize; *then* (3) identify the correct number and types of variables to be used in the model using **Alt-S** Data **A**dd *VARx*, repeating the command as many times as necessary to enter all of the variables; *then* (4) import the old data base into the modified spreadsheet using **Alt-S** Data **R**etrieve; and *finally* (5) edit the old data base by adding, moving, or otherwise modifying existing values as necessary to update the data base using **Alt-S** Data **E**dit. It should be necessary to change the number of observations for two reasons only: (1) if new time-series data becomes available (for instance, when forecasting models are updated on an annual or semiannual basis); or (2) to test the model's recent performance and forecasting abilities by treating some prior data as forecast period data for backcasting purposes.

It is important to reiterate that all CROSTIME observations and variables must be added or deleted using the **Alt-S** Data menu suboptions. If the user modifies the size of the data base outside of CROSTIME, the model is likely to generate an error message. Even if the model works, the results may be invalid because key elements of the spreadsheet may not be updated properly and the wrong ranges are used in estimating the regression equation.

Do not, under any circumstances, modify the size of the data base, in terms of either (1) the number of observations and/or forecast time periods or (2) the number and/or types of variables, except within the CROSTIME data base management system!

Other Operations

Alt-B, Modify Data Base. This macro is used to initialize, add to, delete from, edit, or import CROSTIME data bases for analysis. It is functionally equivalent to the **Alt-S D**ata system option described previously.

Alt-E, Estimate Regression Coefficients. This macro prepares a regression analysis using the information in the current data base. If no data base exists, the user is prompted to create or import one. This macro is equivalent to **Alt-S E**stimate in the system menu.

Alt-G, Graph Output. This option includes the following suboptions:

1. Event, generate a graph of all event variable impacts identified in the model;
2. Independent, generate a graph of all independent variables used in the model;
3. Model, generate a graph of the dependent variable, including both actual and projected values;
4. Standard_err, generate a graph of the standardized error terms identified in the model; and
5. Return, return to previous menu.

If there is no current data base, the user will be prompted to create or import one. If there is a data base, but no model, a regression analysis will be generated automatically. This macro is functionally equivalent to **Alt-S G**raph in the system menu.

After selecting one of the four standard CROSTIME graphs, the user is prompted to choose whether or not the graph will be displayed in color (**Yes**) or black and white (**No**). After viewing any of these four graphs, pressing ENTER automatically invokes a "Save PIC file (Y/N)?" prompt. A Yes response generates a request for the PIC file name to use and provides a list of all PIC files in the current directory. A No response returns the user directly to the system menu.

Alt-O, View Output. This option provides the following suboptions:

1. Regression, view regression results;
2. Autocorrelation, view measures of serial autocorrelation;
3. Projection, view projected values of the dependent variable and standardized error terms;
4. Variables, view the independent variables;

    5. Documentation, view model documentation; and

    6. X_Return, return to the previous menu.

If there is no current data base, the user will be prompted to create or import one. If there is a data base but no model, a regression analysis will be generated automatically. This macro is functionally equivalent to **Alt-S** Output in the system menu macro.

    For each of the first four **Output** suboptions listed above, the user is prompted to select Display, Print, or Return. **Alt-S** Output Display places the user in the appropriate section of the spreadsheet to view the desired output and allows the user to move around (on top of or beside) the selected area using cursor keys. When finished, pressing ENTER automatically invokes a "Send output to printer (Y/N)?" prompt. A Yes response sends the relevant output range to the default printer. A No response returns the user to the system menu. **Alt-S** Output Print sends the output directly to the printer without displaying the results on screen. **Alt-S** Output Return returns the user to the **Alt-S** Output menu without displaying or printing any of the results selected.

    Alt-P, Project Results. This macro projects the dependent variable into a user-specified number of future time periods, based on the regression estimates prepared by using the **Alt-E** macro. If no data base exists, the user is prompted to create or import one. If a data base exists but no model has been run, regression analysis is conducted automatically, prior to projecting the results into the future. This macro is functionally equivalent to **Alt-S** Project in the system menu.

    Alt-V, Save Model. The **Alt-V** Save macro is identical to the standard **Alt-Q** macro except that it offers two additional features: (1) Data_base, which extracts the current data base from the current model and saves it in a separate data base file; and (2) Return, which returns to the previous menu. **Alt-S** Save Data_base prompts the user to specify a name for the data base file to be saved and provides a list of work sheet files in the current directory. This subcommand allows existing data bases to be updated relatively easily as new time-series data become available or backcasting is desired.

Model Input

The general procedure for using CROSTIME includes the following steps: (1) data entry; (2) model estimation; (3) review of model output; (4) projection of model results into the future; and (5) model evaluation.

These steps may need to be repeated—either individually or in combination—several times, depending on the complexity of the model and the strength of the evaluation criteria used to evaluate the model results.

Data entry begins by clearing the data base using the **Alt-S D**ata command sequence to clear the current data base and initialize it for the appropriate number of new variables and observations to be entered or imported. Endogenous (time-series) variables can be entered, imported, or created within the model. The user should be careful to ensure that the variables are entered in the proper sequence. The dependent variable should always be the first variable entered in any CROSTIME data base. The dependent variable must be followed immediately by the first-order, serially autoregressive term, if one is included in the model. All other independent variables can be entered in any order. CROSTIME places event variables after independent variables by convention. An example of the order in which variables must appear in the data base for correct interpretation by CROSTIME is given in the "Sample Application" section of this chapter.

The estimation of equations and projection of results into the future should be done with the **Alt-S E**stimate and **Alt-S P**roject commands but only *after* the data base has been set up completely and properly. Once a regression equation has been estimated, the user can evaluate the output using **Alt-S O**utput for tabular output and **Alt-S G**raph for graphical output.

The user may need to modify the variable definitions or the variables included in the model several times before identifying a "preferred" model specification. For example, CROSTIME cannot identify the "best-fitting" exponential decay parameter values for event variables, although this could be done, at least theoretically, by applying variants of standard maximum likelihood estimation procedures. The user may input event variable data manually or specify exponential decay parameter values for event variables on an *a priori* basis. Exponential decay parameters could be determined theoretically or iteratively adjusted by the user with repeated reestimation of model equations until "optimality" (that is, the best overall model goodness of fit) was achieved.

Exponential decay parameter values for the three event variables included in the transit ridership forecasting model previously discussed were adjusted iteratively many times. Repeated recalculation of the regression equation in CROSTIME using different assumptions for exponential decay parameters allowed the identification of a unique set of exponential decay parameters providing the best overall model goodness of fit, measured in terms of R^2. This is the previously discussed Equation (5d), the analytical results of which are shown in the fourth column of Table 16.1. Perhaps not entirely coincidentally, the exponential decay parameters finally selected based on empirical estimation corresponded well with *a priori* expectations concerning their relative magnitudes, given the nature and duration of the events they represented.

To summarize, the user must complete each of the following steps in order to estimate a combined cross-sectional and time-series regression equation in CROSTIME: (1) select the length of time-series unit to be used (hourly, daily, weekly, monthly, and so on) and identify all of the dependent and independent variables at a consistent and unbroken series of time periods, keeping in mind that only monthly or quarterly seasonal fluctuations can be considered; (2) enter the dependent variable, exogenous variables, and endogenous variable definitions; (3) run the equation estimation and projection modules; (4) determine whether the model satisfies the desired evaluation criteria; and (5) modify the model, as necessary, to achieve more accurate and/or consistent modeling results. These procedures are illustrated in more detail in the "Sample Application" section below.

Model Output

The CROSTIME model produces four types of output, corresponding to suboptions of the **Alt-S** Output command sequence. For model specification, it provides the estimated parameter coefficients, computed Student's t values, and the following 95 percent confidence interval values: (1) absolute and standardized error terms; (2) Durbin-Watson's d statistic for measuring serial autocorrelation; (3) Durbin's H statistic for measuring serial autocorrelation with autoregression; and (4) computed R^2 values for measuring the overall model goodness of fit. For forecasts, the model provides: (1) the predicted values of the dependent variable; (2) the actual values of the dependent variable used in estimation; and (3) the forecast errors for the predicted and actual values of the dependent variable. In addition, the model produces graphical output through **Alt-S** Graph options.

The principal model output is a forecast of the dependent variable over a user-specified sequence of time periods, which may vary from one application to another, even using the same data base. The basic purpose of the model is to predict stability and/or growth in the dependent variable over time, including the influence of both temporal and extemporaneous effects on the dependent variable over time.

Temporal effects may include autoregressive, seasonal, lingering, and/or temporary impacts. Autoregressive stability may be the result of stability in preferences by the consumers of a particular product or service. Seasonal variations may be due to climatic changes, as well as scheduling of normal work and school activities. Incident impacts are usually due to sudden shocks, which may have permanent, temporary, or lingering effects on the dependent variable.

Greater policy sensitivity may be provided through inclusion of cross-sectional measures of supply, demand, and/or relative price changes over time. Any or all of these types of variables may be incorporated simultaneously with various temporal processes and impacts to estimate the marginal effects of independent variables accurately and precisely while controlling for relevant temporal variations.

There is no universally acceptable format for input or output data presentation. If the standard floating point data format is not desired (for instance, for prices measured in dollars and cents), the user should leave CROSTIME (by pressing CONTROL-BREAK twice in succession). The user might start the reformatting process by using **Alt-S** Output Regression and Autocorrelation, **P**rojection, or **V**ariables to locate specific ranges to reformat. Format changes should only be made after creating or importing a data base. Format changes may be lost after adding or deleting variables. All format changes will be lost after reinitializing the data base. After specifying any desired format changes, the user may return to CROSTIME by using either the **Alt-M** or **Alt-S** macro.

DATA SOURCES

The CROSTIME model requires the following general types of data: (1) time-series identifier(s); (2) dependent variable(s) observations; (3) independent variable(s) observations, including endogenous (time-series) variables and exogenous (cross-sectional) variables; and (4) the number of forecast time periods. The form the model takes is otherwise left completely to the user to determine. Procedures for entering the required data are illustrated in the "Sample Application" section below.

The time-series data used in this model must be continuous in nature. No missing observations are allowed for any of the variables used in the model. Technically, systematically ordered missing observations can be used for accurate model estimation (Lütkepohl 1986; Weiss 1984). However, it is unlikely that planning agencies will have such information available through chance. If a planned model application is to be based on sample data, and the sample plan is temporally based (for example, samples three days out of each week), the sampling procedure theoretically could be systematized to allow for efficient time-series estimation. This would require a rigidly systematic sample, though, rather than a pure random sample for both measurement and analysis.

If the model is to be used for forecasting purposes, projected values for all exogenous variables must be provided external to the model and entered directly into the spreadsheet. All endogenous variables, including autoregressive, seasonal, and incident-related effects, are generated automatically within the model for all forecast time periods defined by the user.

SAMPLE APPLICATION

The sample application uses real data to forecast aviation passenger demand for a hypothetical metropolitan airport. The example will evaluate the following passenger forecasting model for its statistical measurement properties and general forecasting abilities:

$$\ln(APA_t) = b_1 \ln(APA_{t-1}) + b_2 \ln(ACO_t) + b_3 \ln(ATO_t) \qquad (6)$$
$$+ b_4 \ln(ITO_t) + b_5 \, G79_1 \, \exp^{s \, \delta} + e_t$$

where:

APA_t = total aviation passenger demand (embarkations plus debarkations) in year t

ACO_t = total air carrier (commercial airline) aircraft operations (takeoffs and landings) in year t

ATO_t = total air taxi (commuter service) aircraft operations in year t

ITO_t = total itinerant (general aviation) aircraft operations in year t

$G79_1$ = 1 if the time period in question occurs after the 1979 gasoline shortage, 0 otherwise

The raw data required for estimating this equation in CROSTIME are shown in Exhibit 16.2 and illustrated in Exhibit 16.3. The model estimated in CROSTIME is shown in Exhibit 16.4. Future projections based on the estimated model are shown in Exhibit 16.5. Serial auto-correlation diagnostic statistics are shown in Exhibit 16.6. All of these tables and exhibits are based on numerical and graphical outputs that are directly accessible using CROSTIME macro commands and a representative data base included with the spreadsheet.

In order to duplicate these hypothetical metropolitan airport example results, the user should complete the following sequence of steps:

1. Load **CROSTIME.WK1** and press ENTER to access the standard macro menu.
2. Invoke the system menu macro by pressing **Alt-S**.
3. From the system menu, initialize the data base using **Data Initialize**. CROSTIME will automatically erase whatever is currently stored in the data base, leaving space for the required dependent variable. You then will be prompted for the number of observations to be used in the new application. Type **16** and press ENTER. You then will be prompted for the number of forecast time periods for the new application. Type **19** and press ENTER. The data base will now be set up automatically. You will be prompted to name the dependent variable and to enter data for it, if so desired. Press ENTER, name the dependent variable **APAt**, and press ENTER again twice. The dependent variable will be imported in this example, so no data entry is necessary. You will be returned to the system menu.
4. From the system menu, add three independent variables, one at a time, using the **Data Add Independent** sequence of commands. Name the three independent variables **ACOt**, **ATOt**, and **ITOt** in turn, pressing ENTER twice after each variable has been created and named.
5. You may now import the aviation data base, which includes sixteen observations for **APAt**, **ACOt**, **ATOt**, and **ITOt**, as well as nineteen projections for **ACOt**, **ATOt**, and **ITOt**. From the system menu, type **Data Retrieve**. You will be asked whether the spreadsheet has been set up properly in advance to accept the data base to be imported. Answer **Yes** and press ENTER. You will be prompted for a file name and offered a list of work sheet files stored in the current directory. Select **AVIADATA.WK1** and press ENTER. The data base will now be automatically imported into the appropriate section of the work sheet.

Exhibit 16.2

Sample CROSTIME Input Data

	APAT OBSERVATION	AUTO-REGRESSIVE TERM	ACOT	ATOT	ITOT	EVENT VAR DECAY = -2
OBS	DEP	AR	IND1	IND2	IND3	EVN1
1	14.188391178	n/a	10.343289673	7.6088706292	10.209684659	0.0000
2	14.311304368	14.188391178	10.379721732	8.3689251747	10.096089419	0.0000
3	14.400211355	14.311304368	10.464359694	8.7104546882	10.041029642	0.0000
4	14.459077712	14.400211355	10.390256112	8.8265878308	10.120371554	0.0000
5	14.474304878	14.459077712	10.317482842	8.8937099776	10.174239618	0.0000
6	14.5903732	14.474304878	10.423054856	9.2440652414	10.330126896	0.0000
7	14.730901285	14.5903732	10.537601033	9.7029612911	10.526185444	0.0000
8	14.841329907	14.730901285	10.649061135	9.6717446324	10.566536285	0.0000
9	14.880741504	14.841329907	10.621254172	9.6058898153	10.607277893	0.0000
10	14.633796764	14.880741504	10.433880482	10.110501722	10.594507472	1.0000
11	14.636110318	14.633796764	10.363724896	10.173819987	10.502049291	0.1353
12	14.711420608	14.636110318	10.471723225	9.9563645921	10.333710312	0.0183
13	14.766154793	14.711420608	10.547680806	10.025439663	10.308752641	0.0025
14	14.780743442	14.766154793	10.583904041	10.289599932	10.387147508	0.0003
15	14.877460591	14.780743442	10.68948735	10.249839396	10.361133894	0.0000
16	15.059156377	14.877460591	10.880515841	10.427742597	10.420166015	0.0000
-1		15.059156377	10.909103298	10.48412293	10.438987769	0.0000
-2			10.937690755	10.540503263	10.457809523	0.0000
-3			10.966278212	10.596883597	10.476631278	0.0000
-4			10.994865668	10.65326393	10.495453032	0.0000
-5			11.023453125	10.709644264	10.514274786	0.0000
-6			11.052040582	10.766024597	10.53309654	0.0000
-7			11.080628039	10.822404931	10.551918295	0.0000
-8			11.109215496	10.878785264	10.570740049	0.0000
-9			11.137802953	10.935165598	10.589561803	0.0000
-10			11.16639041	10.991545931	10.608383557	0.0000
-11			11.194977866	11.047926264	10.627205312	0.0000
-12			11.223565323	11.104306598	10.646027066	0.0000
-13			11.25215278	11.160686931	10.66484882	0.0000
-14			11.280740237	11.217067265	10.683670574	0.0000
-15			11.309327694	11.273447598	10.702492329	0.0000
-16			11.337915151	11.329827932	10.721314083	0.0000
-17			11.366502608	11.386208265	10.740135837	0.0000
-18			11.395090064	11.442588598	10.758957591	0.0000
-19			11.423677521	11.498968932	10.777779346	0.0000

Exhibit 16.3

Graph of Sample Input Data

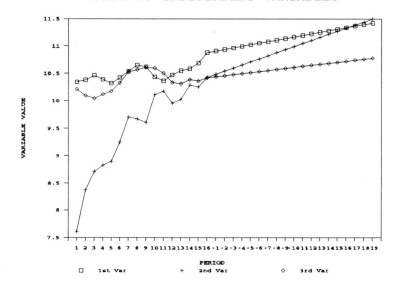

GRAPH OF INDEPENDENT VARIABLES

Exhibit 16.4

Sample CROSTIME Output

Constant			0			
Std Err of Y Est			0.0250002042			
R Squared			0.9893600982			
No. of Observations			15			
Degrees of Freedom			10			
X Coefficient(s)	0.5186607629	0.472977258	0.0322329542	0.1763771231	-0.214199578	
Std Err of Coef.	0.0846156883	0.0774787468	0.0135814175	0.0663408248	0.0345340026	
T-Score	6.1296051988	6.1046064571	2.3733129624	2.6586513453	6.2025702749	
Significant at 95%						
Confidence:	YES	YES	YES	YES	YES	
APAt		AUTO- ACOt	ATOt	ITOt	EVENT VAR	
OBSER-VATION		REGRESSIVE TERM			DECAY= -2	PROJECTED VALUE
OBS	DEP	AR	IND1	IND2	IND3 EVN1	PRED

Exhibit 16.5

Graph of Sample CROSTIME Output

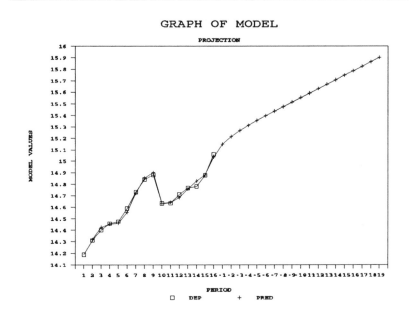

GRAPH OF MODEL

PROJECTION

Exhibit 16.6

Sample CROSTIME Autocorrelation Diagnostic Statistics

DURBIN'S H:
Test for serial autocorrelation in models WITH
autoregressive terms

P :	@abs(1-D/2) =	0.16
T :		15
var(b*):	st.err.(b*)^2 =	0.0072
Durbin's H:	p *	
	(T/(1-T*	
	var(b*)))^0.5 =	0.6571

For 2 Tail Test at 95% Confidence:
NO SERIAL AUTOCORRELATION

6. Type **Data Add Autoregressive** from the system menu to add an autoregressive term. An autoregressive term will be created automatically by the spreadsheet.

7. Type **Data Add Event** from the system menu to add an event variable for the 1979 gasoline shortage. Press **F** and press ENTER to use a decay factor. Then type **10** and press ENTER to specify the time period in which the event occurs. Type **-2** and press ENTER to specify the decay factor to use. A variable will be created automatically for an event occurring in time period 10, with an exponential decay parameter value of -2.

8. Data entry is now complete. Select **Output Variables** from the system menu to view the data. Select **Display** and press ENTER. You may move around on top of the data base by using the cursor keys. Compare the values you imported with those in Exhibit 16.2; they should be identical. When you are finished, press ENTER. You will be prompted to identify whether or not you wish to print the results (Y/N). If you have a printer available, choose Yes and press ENTER when the printer is ready to receive output. If the printed results are not formatted properly, press CONTROL-BREAK twice in succession to leave CROSTIME. Use the standard Lotus **/Print Printer Options** command sequence to access the printer options menu and specify new printer options for your particular hardware configuration. Use **Alt-S** to return to the system menu when you are ready to continue with CROSTIME operations. Type **Output Variable Print** from the system menu to print variable output over again. If the formatting changes have not improved the appearance of CROSTIME output, repeat this procedure as necessary. You will be returned to the system menu automatically after printing has been completed.

9. Select **Estimate** from the system menu to estimate the regression model. Type **Z** and press ENTER to select a zero intercept. All other regression estimation procedures and calculations are automatic.

10. Type **Output Regression Display** from the system menu to review the regression model output on the screen. You can move around on top of the results section for inspection with the cursor keys. The equation you estimated should match the one shown in Exhibit 16.4. Press ENTER after reviewing the regression results and type Yes to send the regression results to the printer. You will be returned automatically to the system menu.

11. Select **Project** from the system menu to project model results into

the future. All other projection procedures and calculations are fully automatic within the model.

12. Select Output Projection Display from the system menu to review the projection output. A graph of the sample data is shown in Exhibit 16.5. Press ENTER after reviewing the projected values and type Yes to send the projection results to the printer. You will be returned automatically to the system menu.

13. Type Output Autocorrelation Display from the system menu to review the serial autocorrelation measures. The values should match those in Exhibit 16-6. Durbin's *H* will be displayed automatically because an autoregressive term was included in the estimated equation. Durbin-Watson's *d* would have been shown if an autoregressive term had not been included. An interpretation of the serial autocorrelation measure's significance at the 95 percent confidence interval is also provided. Press ENTER after you have finished your review and type Yes to send the serial autocorrelation results to the printer. You will be returned automatically to the system menu.

14. Graphics may be viewed by typing Graph Event, Independent, Model, and/or Standard_err from the system menu. Standard error terms are graphed against the dependent variable to illustrate potential heteroskedasticity as well as serial autocorrelation; the time path of the error terms estimated in the model is linearly defined within this context. Graphics may be viewed in color or in black and white, depending on your monitor and printer capabilities. Exhibits 16.3 and 16.5 show the graphic output generated by the CROSTIME model.

The procedure for estimating a model in CROSTIME can be expedited by skipping the estimation and projection steps and proceeding directly from data entry to model graphing. CROSTIME will automatically estimate the model, use the default settings to project the model results, and display the final estimated results.

EVALUATION AND EXTENSIONS

Cross-sectional models are generally evaluated on the basis of their theoretical validity, conformance with theoretical expectations concerning the magnitude and direction of change for the independent variables, as well as overall model goodness of fit. Individual parameter estimation errors and confidence intervals may be significantly biased if serial autocorrelation is present for time-dependent variables.

A variety of techniques is available to prevent temporally related biases from introducing major errors into forecasting models and procedures. Explicit representation of the underlying theoretical temporal processes, specified by transformations of the dependent variable, is generally required to reduce serial autocorrelation. Indirect estimation methods such as those described by Ostrom (1978) can also be used. Time-series methods include the use of serial and/or seasonal autoregressive terms, differenced or integrated equations, moving average models, and so on. If the model's independent variables are influenced by temporal processes, these should be considered, particularly if the "independent" temporal processes are related to endogenous temporal processes that are known or hypothesized to influence the dependent variable.

Estimation and projection models such as CROSTIME may provide more reliable measures of policy sensitivity, as well as more accurate forecasts of future conditions. This can be tested empirically by using *ex ante* or *ex post* comparative evaluation measures. *Ex ante* evaluations require preparing a forecast, waiting for the forecast period to expire, and comparing the forecast results and actual values. *Ex post* evaluation, or "backcasting," is done by excluding some of the most recently available data from the model estimation process and comparing these values with model forecasts based on estimation using less than the full data set currently available. Technically, only information on exogenous variables that was available prior to the backcast period should be used in making *ex post* evaluations.

The CROSTIME model discussed here should become increasingly useful to planners and public policy analysts as time-series analysis techniques and data become more readily available and understood. The use of these techniques in research seems to be increasing. Periodic updating, testing, and evaluation of time-series models and associated predictions by practicing planners will greatly enhance our ability to use these versatile tools as research methods in the future as well. Practical advantages of these types of methods should include more consistent production of more accurate planning forecasts, although verification of this hypothesis must await further testing in the field.

ACKNOWLEDGMENTS

The authors would like to thank the Orange County Transit District and Chapman College in Orange, California, for providing the data on which the original version of this analysis was based. Professor Andrew A. Weiss of the University of Southern California provided useful guidance in developing the time-series equations on which the underlying model and analysis techniques have been based. The authors are responsible for any errors or omissions that remain.

REFERENCES

Center for Economic Research. 1989. *Orange County Transit District econometric forecasting model, final report.* Tustin, CA: Chapman College.

Cervero, R. 1987. Forecasting on the PC: a planner's guide to time-series packages. *Journal of the American Planning Association* 53, 510–520.

Durbin, J. 1970. Testing for serial autocorrelation in least-squares regression when some of the regressors are lagged dependent variables. *Econometrica* 38, 410–421.

Durbin, J., and Watson, G. S. 1951. Testing for serial correlation in least squares regression. *Biometrika* 38, 159–177.

Ferguson, E. 1991. Measuring the temporal effects of incidents on transit ridership in Orange County, California. *Transportation Research Record* 1297, 131–141.

Kinal, T., and Ratner, J. 1986. A VAR forecasting model of a regional economy: its construction and comparative accuracy. *International Regional Science Review* 10, 113–126.

Kyte, M., Cryer, J., and Stoner, J. 1988. A time-series analysis of public transit ridership in Portland, Oregon, 1971-1982. *Transportation Research* 22A, 345–359.

Lütkepohl, H. 1986. Forecasting vector ARIMA processes with systematically missing observations. *Journal of Business and Economic Statistics* 4, 375–390.

Nerlove, M., and Wallis, K. F. 1966. Use of the Durbin-Watson statistic in inappropriate situations. *Econometrica* 34, 235–238.

Ostrom, C. W., Jr. 1978. *Time-series analysis: regression techniques.* Quantitative Applications in the Social Sciences, Vol. 9. Beverly Hills, CA: Sage Publications.

Weiss, A. A. 1984. Systematic sampling and temporal aggregation in time-series models. *Journal of Econometrics* 26, 271–281.

Chapter 17

AHP: Multiple Criteria Evaluation

William M. Bowen

The Analytic Hierarchy Process (AHP) is a flexible, powerful, and simple decision tool for dealing with multiple and conflicting decision criteria or attributes that often make choices between alternatives difficult. AHP is useful because it extends one's ability to deal logically with complex situations by providing a procedure for rigorously prioritizing alternative courses of action, plans, or policies. It functions by combining the decision-maker's value judgment with information about the decision to derive a set of priority measures for evaluating decision alternatives.

The initial and classic work on AHP was written by Thomas L. Saaty in 1980. Numerous articles and books have been written on AHP since then and the process has been used in countless planning and related situations, including electric utility planning, energy policy planning, site selection, and numerous others.[1]

CONCEPTUAL BASIS

The AHP procedure begins by identifying and prioritizing the "decision elements." These elements include the alternative courses of action and the criteria or attributes that will be used to prioritize them. The process of formally recording the elements and their relationships is known as "structuring a hierarchy." The structure is "hierarchical" because decision elements (for example, the decision alternatives and decision criteria) may exist at different levels of abstraction.

AHP can be used to analyze relatively simple situations with "three-level" hierarchies, including one set of decision alternatives, one level of decision criteria, and a single overall goal. Three-level hierarchies are the easiest to understand and are the only type that can be considered with this AHP spreadsheet model. However, more general AHP models can also be used with very complex hierarchies that have one set of decision alternatives and many levels of criteria and subcriteria. The same step-by-step procedure is always employed, regardless of the complexity.[2]

The AHP procedure will be illustrated by considering a situation in which a planner named Michele must recommend a site for locating a hazardous waste repository. The example assumes that Michele must evaluate five alternative waste sites ($j = 1,...,5$) with respect to four decision criteria ($i = 1,...,4$). The decision criteria are: (1) the number of families living within one thousand yards of each site; (2) the environmental degradation resulting from locating the facility in a site; (3) the aesthetic degradation that will be caused in each location; and (4) the cost of locating the facility in a particular site.

The example will proceed by considering the four steps in applying the AHP procedure: weighting the criteria, weighting the alternatives, obtaining the composite weights, and checking for consistency. These steps are used in applying the AHP model to deal with a real multiple criteria evaluation.

Step 1: Weighting the Criteria
Michele must first generate priority weights for each of the four decision criteria. These weights will be labeled w_i, where $i = 1,...,4$. Her goal in this step is generating a pair of weights that correspond to the pair-wise comparisons she makes between each pair of criteria. The judgments are expressed as "pair-wise comparisons" because they reflect her evaluation of the relative importance of each pair of criteria in relation to the overall decision objective. For example, she must decide which of the following two criteria is more important (that is, should receive a higher weight): minimizing the number of families living within one thousand yards of the site (criterion 1) or minimizing the environmental degradation (criterion 2).

All possible pairs of criteria must be compared. Because there are four decision criteria in this example, this means that Michele must make a total of six judgments.[3] The judgments must all be made by applying the 1 to 9 scale found in Table 17.1.[4]

Table 17.1

AHP Measurement Scale

Value	Definition	Explanation
1	Equal importance	Two activities contribute equally to the objective
3	Moderate importance of one over another	Experience and judgment strongly favor one activity over another
5	Essential or strong importance	Experience and judgment strongly favor one activity over another
7	Demonstrated importance	An activity is strongly favored and its dominance is demonstrated in practice
9	Extreme importance	The evidence favoring one activity over another is of the highest possible order of affirmation
2,4,6,8	Intermediate values used when compromise is needed between the two adjacent judgments	

Source: Saaty 1980.

The pair-wise comparisons are recorded in a k x k (in this case, a 4 x 4) paired comparison judgment matrix, $\mathbf{A} = a_{ij}$. Each comparison is assigned one of two types of values. The first type is an integer value between 1 and 9 from Table 17.1. The second type is the inverse of one of these integer values. This will be explained momentarily. In either case, the value in each cell a_{ij} (row i and column j) records the decision maker's judgment concerning the relative importance of criterion i with respect to criterion j.

In this example, the value in cell a_{ij} records Michele's judgment of the relative importance of criterion i (the row) relative to criterion j (the column) for selecting the "best" site. In terms of the two types of values, whenever a_{ij} is greater than one this indicates that the criterion in row i is more important than the criterion in column j. Table 17.1 indicates the degree of such importance. Conversely, values less than one indicate that the criterion in row i is less important than the criterion in column j. Again, Table 17.1 indicates the degree of such importance. This will become clear as the example proceeds.

For instance, assume that Michele's paired comparisons are reported in the matrix of paired comparison judgments shown in Table 17.2. This matrix is constructed as follows.

Table 17.2

Sample AHP Judgments

	Population	Environment	Aesthetics	Economics
Population	1	1/5	6	3
Environment	5	1	9	7
Aesthetics	1/6	1/9	1	1/4
Economics	1/3	1/7	4	1

A $k \times k$ matrix contains k^2 elements. The matrix considers all possible pairs of criteria and there are $k(k-1)/2$ possible pairs of k objects. As a result, Michele must first fill the $k(k-1)/2$ cells above the diagonal. That is, for the four decision criteria in this example, the matrix will contain 4^2 or sixteen elements and she must specify $4(4-1)/2$ or six comparisons.

For example, Table 17.2 reports that Michele assigns a value of 9 for element a_{23} (row 2, column 3), indicating that she views environmental degradation (criterion 2) as "extremely" more important than aesthetic degradation (criterion 3). She assigns a value of 1/5 for element a_{12} (row 1, column 2), indicating that she judges the size of the proximate population (criterion 1) to be "strongly" less important than environmental considerations (criterion 2). If the reader does not agree with these values, after reading this chapter and understanding the process, he or she might as an exercise go back and check the result of adjusting the values to conform to his or her own sensibilities.

After Michele has given all six judgments, there will be $k^2 - k(k-1)/2$ (that is, in this example, 16 - 6 or 10) empty cells in the matrix. Of these empty cells, the k diagonal cells, a_{ii}, are set equal to unity because each criterion is equally as important as itself. The remaining $k(k-1)/2$ empty cells below the diagonal are filled with the reciprocals of the corresponding values above the diagonal. In other words, if the value for cell a_{ij} (row i, column j) is m then the value for cell a_{ji} (row j, column i) is $1/m$. For example, in Table 17.2, cell a_{13} (row 1, column 3) is 6 and cell a_{31} (row 3, column 1) is 1/6.

Criteria weights, w_i ($i = 1,...,4$), must then be computed for each decision criterion.[5] These weights determine at an abstract level which of each pair of criteria is more important in general. Calculating the weights from the **A** matrix is a very simple process. One begins by computing the geometric means for each row by multiplying the k judgments in a row by each other and taking the kth root of the product. The resulting value is called the "geometric row mean." For Michele's judgments shown in Table 17.2, the row means are calculated as follows:

Population: $(1 \times 1/5 \times 6 \times 3)^{.25} = 1.38$
Environment: $(5 \times 1 \times 9 \times 7)^{.25} = 4.21$
Aesthetics: $(1/6 \times 1/9 \times 1 \times 1/4)^{.25} = 0.26$
Economics: $(1/3 \times 1/7 \times 4 \times 1)^{.25} = 0.66$

The geometric row means are then "normalized" by dividing each row mean by the sum of the row means. In this case, the sum of the row means is equal to 1.38 + 4.21 + 0.26 + 0.66, or 6.51, and the normalized values are computed as follows:

Population: 1.38/6.51 = 0.21
Environment: 4.21/6.51 = 0.65
Aesthetics: .26/6.51 = 0.04
Economics: .66/6.51 = 0.10

Thus, in Michele's case $w_1 = 0.21$, $w_2 = 0.65$, $w_3 = 0.04$, and $w_4 = 0.10$; that is, her weight for criterion 1 is 0.21, her weight for criterion

2 is 0.65, and so on. The normalized values always add up to unity. Michele's criteria weights are expressed in terms of a vector, w, made up of the four criteria weights, w_1, w_2, w_3, and w_4.

Step 2: Weighting the Alternatives
After weighting the decision criteria, Michele must then weight the decision alternatives. Weighting the alternatives is a matter of determining how well each of the five sites (decision alternatives) performs with respect to each of the four criteria. To do this, she must first construct a judgment matrix weighting each of the sites with respect to one of the criteria. She then takes a second criterion and constructs a judgment matrix weighting each of the sites with respect to that criterion. Then Michele does the same for the third and the fourth criteria. Once she has determined the weights for all of the alternatives with respect to all of the criteria, she can move on to step 3 and compute a composite priority weight for each of the sites.

The process for weighting the alternatives with respect to the criteria is very similar to the process for weighting the criteria with respect to the overall goal. In both cases, the judgments are expressed in terms of pair-wise comparisons, using the scale given in Table 17.1. In both cases, the judgments are recorded in a matrix and the geometric row means are calculated to determine the weights for the matrix.

One difference in this step is that the comparisons are of different alternatives with respect to one of the criteria instead of comparisons of different criteria with respect to the overall decision goal. That is, instead of asking "How important is criterion i compared to criterion j with respect to the overall decision goal?" the question is "How important is alternative i compared to alternative j with respect to criterion k?" In other words, when weighting the decision *criteria*, the judgment matrix has different criteria in the rows and columns; when weighting the decision *alternatives*, the judgment matrix has different alternatives in the rows and columns.

A second difference is that a three-level hierarchy with k decision criteria has only one k x k matrix of criteria judgments. However, when weighting the alternatives, a judgment matrix is required for each criterion. That is, if there are s alternatives, k alternative judgment matrices are needed, each of size s x s.[6] In this example, there are four decision criteria and five decision alternatives (possible sites); thus, this step requires four judgment matrices, each of which is a 5 x 5 matrix.

Michele's pair-wise comparisons are made by considering the available data concerning the decision alternatives. The profile data for the five alternative sites is shown in Table 17.3. The rows in the table correspond to the five alternative sites; the columns correspond to measurements for each criterion as it relates to the various sites. In this example, the population variable (criterion 1) is the number of families living within one thousand yards of the site; environmental and aesthetic degradation (criteria 2 and 3) are measured on a 1 to 10 scale, with lower values being preferred; and costs (criterion 4) are measured in hundreds of thousands of dollars. As a result, a lower value is preferred for all the criteria.

Table 17.3

Sample Profile Data (p_{ij})

	Criterion (i)	Site (j)				
		1	2	3	4	5
(1)	Population	11	17	19	9	16
(2)	Environment	5	2	7	8	4
(3)	Aesthetics	6	5	1	4	7
(4)	Economics	8.1	8.9	6.5	6.9	7.7

Table 17.3 indicates that site 4 performs best and site 3 performs worst with respect to criterion 1, the proximate population; that is, the value in row 1, column 4, is 9 compared to a value of 19 for row 1, column 3. Similarly, site 2 performs best and site 4 performs worst with respect to criterion 2, environmental degradation; that is, the values for the two sites with respect to criterion 2 are 2 and 8, respectively.

Paired comparisons are used to generate the alternative-by-alternative judgments, just like the paired comparisons for the criterion-by-criterion judgments. Suppose, for example, that Michele provides the judgments in Tables 17.4 to 17.7. These judgments represent her evaluation of the site profile data from Table 17.3, for all of the pairs of sites. The matrices are constructed in a manner similar to the matrices for determining the criteria weights. All of the judgments are stated in terms of the 1 to 9 integer scale in Table 17.1. For the matrix corresponding to each of the four criteria, the $s(s-1)/2$ site-by-site judgments are placed in the appropriate cells above the diagonal, the cells along the diagonal are set equal to unity, and the cells below the diagonal are equal to the reciprocal of the corresponding cells above the diagonal, $1/a_{ji}$.

Table 17.4

Sample Judgments for Population Criterion

	Site 1	Site 2	Site 3	Site 4	Site 5	
Site 1	1	5	6	1/5	4	
Site 2	1/5	1	3	1/7	1/3	
Site 3	1/6	1/3	1	1/8	1/4	
Site 4	5	7	8	1	6	
Site 5	1/4	3	4	1/6	1	
Priorities	Site 1	Site 2	Site 3	Site 4	Site 5	CI/RI - .12
	0.24	0.07	0.04	0.54	0.12	

Table 17.5

Sample Judgments for Environmental Criterion

	Site 1	Site 2	Site 3	Site 4	Site 5	
Site 1	1	1/6	4	5	1/2	
Site 2	6	1	7	8	6	
Site 3	1/4	1/7	1	3	1/4	
Site 4	1/5	1/8	1/3	1	1/5	
Site 5	2	1/6	4	5	1	
Priorities	Site 1	Site 2	Site 3	Site 4	Site 5	CI/RI - .11
	0.15	0.56	0.07	0.04	0.18	

Table 17.6

Sample Judgments for Aesthetic Criterion

	Site 1	Site 2	Site 3	Site 4	Site 5	
Site 1	1	1/2	1/7	1/3	2	
Site 2	2	1	1/5	1/2	2	
Site 3	7	5	1	5	7	
Site 4	3	2	1/5	1	3	
Site 5	1/2	1/2	1/7	1/3	1	
Priorities	Site 1	Site 2	Site 3	Site 4	Site 5	CI/RI - .04
	0.08	0.12	0.57	0.18	0.06	

Table 17.7

Sample Judgments for Economic Criterion

	Site 1	Site 2	Site 3	Site 4	Site 5	
Site 1	1	2	1/7	1/4	1/2	
Site 2	1/2	1	1/9	1/5	1/3	
Site 3	7	9	1	3	6	
Site 4	4	5	1/3	1	3	
Site 5	2	3	1/6	1/3	1	
Priorities	Site 1	Site 2	Site 3	Site 4	Site 5	CI/RI - .03
	0.07	0.04	0.54	0.24	0.11	

For example, consider the values in Table 17.4 that record the decisions Michele made in applying decision criterion 1, the proximate population, to the site profile data reported in Table 17.3. The values in each column of the first row record her evaluations of site 1 (the row) with respect to each of the alternative sites (the columns). The value for row 1, column 1, is 1, indicating that site 1 is equally preferable to itself. The value for row 1, column 2, is 5, indicating that Michele believes that site 1 is "strongly" preferable to site 2 with respect to the population criterion; the corresponding values in Table 17.3 are eleven for site 1 and seventeen for site 2. The value for row 1, column 3, is slightly larger, indicating that site 1 is slightly more preferable to site 3 than it is to site 2. The value for row 1, column 4 is less than one, indicating that site 1 is "strongly" less preferable than site 4. The corresponding population values are nine for site 4 and eleven for site 1.

The site weights for each alternative judgment matrix are calculated by taking the respective geometric row means in Tables 17.4 through 17.7 and normalizing them, exactly as was done for the criteria weights. The priority estimates computed using the normalized geometric row means are given at the bottom of each table. For example, the priority estimate for site 1 with respect to the population criterion is 0.24, as reported in the first column at the bottom of Table 17.4. The "CI/RI ratio" at the bottom of each table is a measure of the consistency of the judgments, as will be pointed out in detail below.[7]

Step 3: Obtaining Composite Weights

Up to this point, the analyst has assigned priority weights for the decision criteria with respect to the overall decision goal and for the alternatives with respect to these criteria. The third step synthesizes the priorities for all of these composite matrices to obtain a single composite priority weight for each site. This step utilizes a set of computations known as Saaty's "Principle of Hierarchic Composition." The procedure yields a single "priority vector" that considers all of the judgments at all levels of the hierarchy.

Given Michele's criteria weights and the site weights from Tables 17.4 to 17.7, the composite priority weight for each site is computed by summing the products of the criteria weights, w_i, computed in step 1, multiplied by the alternative weights for each criterion computed in step 2. That is, if q_{ij} is the priority weight for site j with respect to criterion i, the composite priority for alternative j is computed as follows:

$$\text{Overall priority of site:} \quad j = \sum_{i=1}^{4} w_i(q_{ij})$$

For example, the criteria weights for the four decision criteria computed in step 1 were 0.21, 0.65, 0.04, and 0.10. The site weights for site 1 with respect to the population criterion reported at the bottom of the first column in tables 17.4 through 17.7 are 0.24, 0.14, 0.07, and 0.07, respectively. Therefore, the overall priority for site 1 is equal to (0.21 x 0.24) + (0.65 x 0.14) + (0.04 x 0.07) + (0.10 x 0.07), or 0.16. Similarly:

	Population	Environment	Aesthetics	Economics	
Site 1	(0.21 x 0.24) +	(0.65 x 0.14) +	(0.04 x 0.07) +	(0.10 x 0.07) =	0.16
Site 2	(0.21 x 0.06) +	(0.65 x 0.58) +	(0.04 x 0.11) +	(0.10 x 0.04) =	0.38
Site 3	(0.21 x 0.03) +	(0.65 x 0.06) +	(0.04 x 0.57) +	(0.10 x 0.54) =	0.14
Site 4	(0.21 x 0.56) +	(0.65 x 0.04) +	(0.04 x 0.18) +	(0.10 x 0.24) =	0.17
Site 5	(0.21 x 0.11) +	(0.65 x 0.18) +	(0.04 x 0.06) +	(0.10 x 0.11) =	0.16

These values are the composite priority weights for the five alternative sites. The preferable site is the one with the highest overall priority weight, in this case, site 2. Site 2 has the highest value because, according to Michele's judgments, it is the best site on the environmental criterion, which is her most important criterion.

However, one can also ask whether the judgments used to compute the composite priority weights are consistent. That is, one can ask whether and to what degree Michele's judgments are transitive, that is, whether cases in which she prefers alternative A to alternative B and alternative B to alternative C, she also prefers alternative A to alternative C. The consistency of her choices is evaluated in step 4.

Step 4: Checking for Consistency

The AHP procedure computes a consistency index to evaluate the consistency of the decision-maker's judgments. The smaller the index, the more consistent the decision-maker's judgments are. The general rule of thumb is that if the index is 0.1 or less, the judgments are fine and the weights can be relied upon. If the index is greater than 0.1, the judgments are too inconsistent to be reliable. In this case, the decision-maker must go back and gather the judgments again, attempting to give more consistent judgments. Efficient procedures for helping resolve inconsistencies can be found in Saaty (1980).

The logic of the consistency index is explained below using matrix notation. Readers who are unfamiliar with this notation can proceed to the section titled "The Mechanics of AHP Consistency," which provides a numerical example illustrating the mechanics of calculating the index. These mechanics and the rule of thumb given above are sufficient to use the AHP procedure.

The Logic of AHP Consistency

Given a matrix $\mathbf{A} = (a_{ij})$ of pair-wise comparisons, "perfect consistency" is obtained when, for all elements $i, j, k,$

$$a_{ik} = a_{ij} \times a_{jk}$$

The "ideal" case would occur if $a_{ij} = w_i/w_j$, where w_i and w_j are exact measurements of some physical criteria, for instance, length. This suggests that the matrix $\mathbf{A} = (a_{ij})$ $i,j = 1,2,...,n$ has the form:

$$A = \begin{vmatrix} w_1/w_1 & w_1/w_2 & \cdots & w_1/w_n \\ w_2/w_1 & w_2/w_2 & \cdots & w_2/w_n \\ \cdot & \cdot & & \cdot \\ \cdot & \cdot & & \cdot \\ w_n/w_1 & w_n/w_2 & \cdots & w_n/w_n \end{vmatrix} = w_i/w_j, \quad i,j=1,2,....,n$$

Therefore:

$$A = w(w^{-1})^t = \begin{vmatrix} w_1 \\ \cdot \\ \cdot \\ \cdot \\ w_n \end{vmatrix} [\ 1/w_1, \ ..., \ 1/w_j, \ ..., \ 1/w_n \ ]$$

Using matrix notation, it follows from these conditions that:

$$\mathbf{Aw = nw}$$

In this ideal case, n is equal to the largest eigenvalue (λ_{max}) of $\mathbf{A}$. However, if a_i and a_j are subjective (imperfect) estimates of w_i and w_j, then deviations between the exact and the estimated values will occur, causing changes in the eigenvalues (Saaty 1980). The product for the imperfect estimate is:

$$\mathbf{Aw = \lambda_{max}w}$$

The size of the difference between n and λ_{max} is a measure of the consistency of the judgments, that is, the degree to which the judgments capture the "true" underlying dimensions. Formally stated, this inference is measured by the "index of consistency" (*CI*):

$$CI = [\lambda_{max} - n] / (n-1)$$

CI approaches zero as a_{ij} becomes a better approximation of w_i/w_j. Conversely, increasingly larger values for *CI* imply that a_{ij} deviates increasingly from w_i/w_j. Technically, this is because the dimensionality of the judgment matrix increases.

The Mechanics of AHP Consistency
Michele's judgments almost certainly have some inconsistency. The AHP consistency statistic determines whether the cumulative effect of this inconsistency is severe enough to cause serious difficulties. The following four-step procedure can be used to check for the consistency of the judgments:

1. *Compute Aw.* The first step is to compute the product of the **A** matrix and the criterion weights vector **w**. For this example,

$$Aw = \begin{bmatrix} 1 & 1/5 & 6 & 3 \\ 5 & 1 & 9 & 7 \\ 1/6 & 1/9 & 1 & 1/4 \\ 1/3 & 1/7 & 4 & 1 \end{bmatrix} X \begin{bmatrix} 0.21 \\ 0.65 \\ 0.04 \\ 0.10 \end{bmatrix} = \begin{bmatrix} 0.88 \\ 2.76 \\ 0.17 \\ 0.42 \end{bmatrix}$$

2. *Compute L.* The second step is to compute the *L* value using the following equation:

$$L = 1/n \left[\sum_{i-1}^{n} (Aw_i) / (w_i) \right]$$

In this case,

$$L = 1/4 \ (0.88/.21 + 2.76/.65 + 0.17/.04 + 0.42/.1)$$
$$L = 4.22$$

3. *Compute CI.* The AHP consistency index (*CI*) can then be computed with the following equation:

$$CI = (L - n) / (n - 1)$$

Again using Michele's judgments,

$$CI = (4.22 - 4) / 3 = 0.07$$

4. *Compute CI/RI Ratio.* The ratio of the computed *CI* value to the random index (*RI*) for the appropriate value of *n* in Table 17.8 is then computed. The values in Table 17.8 were generated by the Oak Ridge National Laboratory and the Wharton School using the average *CI* values for randomly generated *n* x *n* matrices filled with values from the 1 to 9 scale given in Table 17.1 (Saaty 1980).

Table 17.8

Values of the Random Index (R_i)

	2	3	4	5	6	7	8	9	10	11	12	13	14	15
R_i	0.0	0.58	0.9	1.12	1.24	1.32	1.41	1.45	1.49	1.51	1.48	1.56	1.57	1.59

The *CI/RI* ratio is equal to zero when the judgments are perfectly consistent. The ratio increases as more and more inconsistency enters into the judgments. For Michele's judgments, the ratio is equal to 0.07/0.9, or 0.08, indicating that the criteria judgments reported in Table 17.2 do not have any serious inconsistencies. The same procedure can be used to evaluate the inconsistency of each matrix in the analysis.

COMPONENTS AND OPERATION

As the location map in Exhibit 17.1 indicates, the data entry portion of the AHP model consists of three sections. The Attribute and Alternative Data Entry section is used to enter the number of and labels for the attributes to be considered in the decision process. Between two and seven decision attributes (or alternatives) can be considered with the AHP model. The Attribute Pair-wise Comparisons Data Entry section is

Exhibit 17.1

AHP Location Map

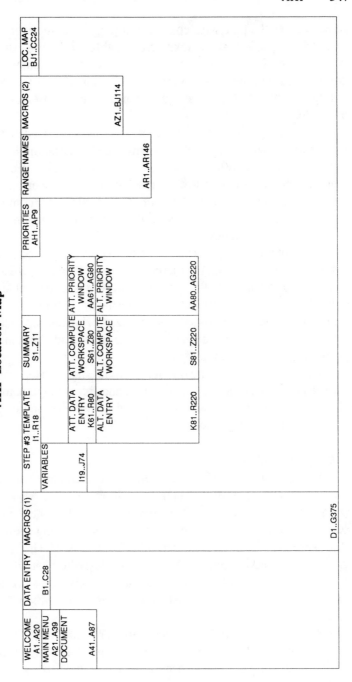

used to enter the pair-wise comparison judgments for every possible pair of attributes, using values taken from Table 17.1. The Alternative Pair-wise Comparisons Data Entry section is used to enter the pair-wise comparison judgments for every possible pair of alternatives based upon a single attribute. A separate judgment matrix must be created for each attribute.

The computational portion of the model includes the Attribute Computation Work Space, the Alternative Computation Work Space, the Attribute Priority Window, the Alternative Priority Window, and the Analysis Summary Window. The computation work space sections display the intermediate steps in the consistency computation. The methods employed were discussed in the previous section, The Mechanics of AHP Consistency.

The attribute and alternative priorities are displayed in the Attribute Priority Window and Alternative Priority Window, respectively. In addition to displaying the priorities, these sections also display the consistencies for the attribute and alternative judgments. The Analysis Summary Window displays the normalized priorities for each alternative. These overall priorities are calculated from the attribute and alternative priorities previously computed.

Other portions of the model include step-by-step instructions, a spreadsheet description, a macro command list, a range name table, a list of variables and their values, and a display of the computed attribute and alternative priority matrices.

Model Operation
As indicated in Table 17.9, thirteen macro commands are available for use in conjunction with the AHP model. The Alt-D, Alt-L, Alt-M, Alt-Q, Alt-R, Alt-W, and Alt-Z macros correspond to the standard macros described in chapter 1. General instructions for using these macros and other spreadsheet macros are provided in chapter 1. The five specialized macros provided for the AHP model are described below.

The **Alt-I** and **Alt-L** macros run the six steps of the program described in step-by-step instructions displayed when the model is loaded.

Alt-I, Input Model Specifications. This command is used to enter data on the number of attributes to be considered in the decision, the names of attributes, the number of available alternatives, and the names of the alternatives. The first step is used to specify the attributes and the alternatives. The second step is used to provide the attribute-by-attribute judgments. The third step is used to provide the alternative-by-alternative judgments. The model automatically adjusts the size of the matrix, depending upon the corresponding number of attributes or alternatives in the analysis.

Table 17.9

AHP Macros

Alt-C	Compute model results
Alt-D	Go to Documentation
Alt-E	Erase data and labels
Alt-I	Input model specifications
Alt-L	Go to Location map
Alt-M	Go to Main menu
Alt-P	Print analysis results
Alt-Q	Quit/save model
Alt-R	Go to Range descriptions
Alt-S	Go to System menu
Alt-V	View data
Alt-W	Go to Welcome screen
Alt-Z	Go to macros

1st_step is used to specify the general characteristics of the analysis problem. This step asks for the number of attributes and alternatives and for the corresponding labels. The number of attributes and alternatives must each be seven or less. The number of attributes and alternatives and the labels for the attributes and alternatives should be entered in column C. Each label should be six characters or less.

2nd_step is used to enter the comparison judgments for each pair of attributes with respect to the overall goal of the decision. Values from the 1 to 9 scale in Table 17.1 should be entered in the cells of the appropriate rows and columns.

3rd_step is used to enter the comparison judgments for each pair of alternatives based on individual attributes. Values from Table 17.1 should be entered in the cells of the appropriate rows and columns. A separate empty matrix will be presented for each attribute listed by the user in the Analysis Specifications. When finished entering the data into a matrix, press PGDN repeatedly to view the next matrix for entering judgments for the next attribute.

When giving judgments, all judgments in the upper right-hand side of each matrix should be either an integer value in the 1 to 9 range from Table 17.1 or the reciprocal of one of these values. All diagonal cells should be filled with values of one, and the lower left-hand cell should always be filled with the reciprocal of the corresponding upper right-hand cell. The model will not work properly unless each judgment matrix is completely filled with the appropriate judgments.

Alt-C, *Compute Model Results*. This macro computes the attribute priorities with respect to the overall goal of the decision by computing the means of the rows of the normalized attribute judgment matrix. In addition, the attribute judgment consistency is measured using the methods described earlier in the "Step 4: Checking for Consistency" section. The results of these computations are displayed in the Attribute Priority Window. It also computes the alternative priorities and judgment consistencies with respect to each attribute by applying the same methods used to compute attribute priorities and consistency. A different set of priorities and consistency measures will be computed for each attribute. Press PGDN repeatedly to see the next set of priorities and consistency measures.

4th_step computes the attribute priorities and consistency measures. In other words, the priorities computed using this step correspond to the attribute-by-attribute judgments. As this spreadsheet analyzes three-level hierarchies only, there will always be only one judgment matrix for this step.

5th_step computes the alternative-by-alternative priorities and the corresponding consistency measures. Each set of priorities coming from this step corresponds to the appropriate alternative-by-alternative judgment matrix. Use PGUP and PGDN to see the priorities and the consistency measures for other such matrices.

If there are x attributes in a particular analysis and the user looks in the spreadsheet at the location for the priorities for attributes $(x + 1)$, $(x + 2)$ and so on, he or she will find error messages. These messages are expected and result from the effort of the model to operate upon blank cells; they do not affect the analysis results.

6th_step computes the overall priorities of the alternatives and displays them in the Analysis Summary Window.

Alt-E, *Erase Data and Labels*. This command clears the model of all previously entered data and calculations so it is ready for a new analysis.

Alt-P, Print Analysis Results.

Alt-S, Go to System Menu. This macro accesses a Lotus-style system menu that provides an alternative procedure for conducting the AHP analysis process. The following options are provided:

1. Input, used to enter on the decision attributes and alternatives. It is equivalent to the **Alt-I** macro;
2. Erase, used to clear the input data and labels. It is equivalent to the **Alt-E** macro;
3. Compute, used to compute the attribute priorities. It is the same as the **Alt-C** macro;
4. View, used to view the data. It is identical to the **Alt-V** macro; and
5. Main_menu, used to return to the main menu.

Alt-V, View data. This macro displays a list of macro commands that can be used to move around the spreadsheet and display various judgments and priorities. The following options are provided:

1. 1-3_Attrib, used to view the priorities and judgments for the first three attributes;
2. **4-6**_Attrib, used to view the priorities and judgments in the second three attributes;
3. **7**_Attrib, used to view the priorities and judgments in the seventh attribute;
4. **Judgments**, used to view attribute judgments and priorities; and
5. **Return**, used to return to the previous menu.

DATA SOURCES

The data for an AHP analysis are pair-wise comparison judgments of the relative importance of two attributes or alternatives in a particular decision situation. As a result, there is no general source for the data needed to use the AHP model.

SAMPLE APPLICATION

The procedures for using this AHP model and the types of information produced by the model will be illustrated using the site selection example discussed earlier in this chapter. The data corresponding to this example have been entered into the distribution version of the model. They will remain in the model as long as the **Alt-E**, Erase data and labels, macro has not been used.

The sample analysis specification contains four attributes: population, environment, aesthetics, and economics. They are labeled POP, ENV, AES, and ECO, respectively. It also contains five decision alternatives (sites). These are labeled S1, S2, S3, S4, and S5, respectively. Once this information is entered, the analyst can use **Alt-I**, 2nd_step to provide the attribute-by-attribute judgments.

2nd_step enters the appropriate values into the judgment matrix field. The diagonal cells should be filled with values of 1 and the other cells are all filled with judgments from Table 17.2. For example, in this case, the value of 1/5 in the first row, second column indicates that the decision-maker considers the ENV attribute to be strongly more important than the POP attribute. The values in the sample matrix are identical to the example discussed in the "Conceptual Basis" section. When the matrix is completely filled in with judgments, the next step is to use **Alt-I**, 3rd_step to provide the alternative-by-alternative judgments.

Alt-I, 3rd_step begins the process of providing alternative-by-alternative judgments. The first set of judgments answers the question, "How important is site *i* (row) compared to site *j* (column) with respect to the attribute POP?" In general, a large proximate population is a negative factor for a site, so the larger the population living within close proximity to a particular site the more important is some other site and the lower the priority for that particular site. This logic is reflected in the values given in the sample matrix for all of the attributes.

There are four attributes in the analysis, so there are four matrices of alternative-by-alternative judgments. The values in each cell are taken from Table 17.1. Generally, there will be the same number of alternative-by-alternative judgment matrices as there are attributes. When all of the matrices have been filled, the next step is to use **Alt-C**, 4th_step to compute the attribute priorities.

In this case, the attribute with the highest priority is ENV, followed by POP, ECO, and AES, respectively. The consistency value of 0.08 indicates that the consistency of the judgments is satisfactory.

Alt-C, 5th_step computes the alternative-by-alternative priorities. The spreadsheet automatically places the priorities for the first attribute on the screen. In this case, site 4 has the highest priority with respect to

POP, followed by sites 1, 5, 2, and 3, respectively. The consistency ratio is also given. The priorities for the sites in relation to ENV, AES, and ECO can be found by paging down the column.

Alt-C, 6th_step computes the overall priorities for the hierarchy. In other words, this step proceeds through the process of hierarchic composition described above. The priorities are the weights for each site, considering both alternative-by-alternative judgments and attribute-by-attribute judgments. These are the values that, according to AHP methodology, follow logically from the set of all judgments given earlier in the analysis. They are the final values toward which all of the earlier work has been aimed. These are the values upon which the final decision recommendation should be based.

EVALUATION AND EXTENSIONS

Though AHP continues to receive and broaden its worldwide acclaim, it is a fairly controversial approach to decision making. Hammond and Adelman (1976) are probably correct when they state that quite a bit of controversy will surround any rational approach to decisions. First, some people question whether the use of any such mathematical model is valuable in decision making. They argue that power and politics are not rational processes and lie at the root of most decisions. Second, assuming that using a mathematical model in this way is valuable, some question exists as to whether or not AHP should be that model.

As for whether or not the use of mathematical decision modeling is of value in a wide range of social decisions, the answer remains largely for the future to reveal. Proponents base their arguments largely on the abundant literature in experimental psychology demonstrating strong cognitive limits to human information storage and processing abilities (Tversky and Kahneman 1974). Moreover, they argue, information storage and processing are precisely the strengths of the computer. Why not then combine our knowledge of how rational decisions should be made with the strength of the computer, augmenting and fortifying the weakness of human cognition in actual decision situations?

The skeptics argue that the human condition does not submit itself readily to such an approach. Humans are political, emotional, spiritual, and occasionally moral beings. To use a mathematical decision model ignores these vital extralogical considerations and therefore cannot reasonably be expected to determine or even substantively inform important, actual decision outcomes.

The controversy largely surrounds the point at which logic and mathematical analysis must and should give way to politics, emotion, and the like. As there is no broad consensus on this point, the question remains largely up to the individual decision-maker to decide.

Assuming that it is decided to use a mathematical model, considerable controversy surrounds the question of whether AHP is a desirable way to proceed (Dyer 1990). Most of the formal controversy centers around a phenomenon known as "rank reversal." Rank reversal can occur when two analyses are conducted with a given set of alternatives. The only difference between the two analyses is that the second one adds an additional alternative in the set. Rank reversal occurs when the decision priorities change when the new alternative is added. The controversy concerns the question of whether this is a tolerable feature of a decision model.

Though the rank reversal issue in the AHP literature has been argued primarily on theoretical grounds, its resolution appears to be largely an empirical question. That is, the important question that needs to be asked experimentally is whether rank reversals are the sort of thing one would expect on psychological grounds.

In summary, the arguments for and against AHP can both be compelling. There seem to be solid grounds for questioning the range of applications over which it is apt to be of value, and the model itself is not fully satisfactory on technical grounds. Nevertheless, the large and growing number of practical applications recorded in the literature indicates that a great number of people find it to be of considerable value for a wide range of situations.

Finally, in terms of user extensions of the model, the author would suggest the use of specially designed software for anyone who finds either the limited number of alternatives and attributes or the three-level hierarchy restriction in this model to be unduly inhibiting. Certainly, AHP can be extended considerably into multilevel hierarchies, thereby allowing much more complex applications. Likewise, there is no reason why many more than seven attributes or alternatives could not be considered. This limit reflects subjective considerations related to the difficulty of preparing the model and the most likely decision situations faced by the potential users. It would be possible to construct an AHP model with a large number of possible alternatives and attributes and in a multilevel hierarchy. However, doing so would require considerable time and very advanced spreadsheet modeling skills. If such applications are desired, it would probably be wiser to purchase specialized AHP analysis software.

ACKNOWLEDGMENTS

The author gratefully acknowledges Norris Hsu's invaluable help with coding the material in this chapter.

NOTES

1. See, for example, Gholamnezhad and Xia (1984), Golden, Wasil, and Harker (1989), Hamalainen and Seppalainen (1986), Rahman and Frair (1984), and Saaty and Gholamnezhad (1982).

2. For an example of a complex hierarchy see Saaty (1977).

3. There are always $k(k-1)/2$ possible pairs in a set of k objects.

4. All AHP judgments, for weighting both the criteria and the alternatives, use this 1 to 9 scale.

5. Any variations between the values in the following example and those in the sample data set provided with the model are due to minor computational differences and rounding error.

6. The situation described here is one known as a "fully connected" situation. In other words, each of the alternatives is compared for each of the criteria. In fact, AHP can be much more flexible than this, allowing for some of the alternatives to be compared for only some of the criteria. For more information about the more complex situation see Saaty (1980).

7. To begin to get a "feel" for the idea of judgment consistency, the reader might compare judgments a_{12} and a_{14} in Table 17.4, which illustrate judgment inconsistency. Judgment a_{12} is 5 (strongly more important), which, according to Table 17.3, corresponds to the difference between eleven and seventeen people. On the other hand, judgment a_{14} is 1/5 (strongly more important), which, according to Table 17.3, corresponds to the difference between eleven and nine people. That is, although a difference of six people is involved in the first judgment and two in the second, the relative "importance" Michele assigned to each of these differences is the same. According to AHP, this is not consistent.

REFERENCES

Dyer, J. S. 1990. Remarks on the analytic hierarchy process. *Management science* 36, 249–258.

Gholamnezhad, A. H., and Xia, S. R. 1984. Formulating energy strategies and policies for China: a systematic approach. *Environment and Planning, B* 11, 213–228.

Golden, B. L., Wasil, E. A., and Harker, P. T. 1989. *The analytic hierarchy process: applications and studies.* Berlin: Springer–Verlag.

Hamalainen, R. P., and Seppalainen, T. O. 1986. The analytic network process in energy policy planning. *Socio–Economic Planning Sciences* 13, 399–405.

Hammond, K. R., and Adelman, L. 1976. Science, values, and human judgment. *Science* 194, 389–396.

Rahman, S., and Frair, L. C. 1984. A hierarchical approach to electric utility planning. *International Journal of Energy Research* 8, 185–196.

Saaty, T. L. 1977. The Sudan transport study. *Interfaces* 8, 37–57.

———. 1980. *The analytic hierarchy process.* New York: McGraw–Hill.

———, and Gholamnezhad, H. 1982. High–level nuclear waste management: analysis of options. *Environment and Planning, B* 9, 181–196.

Tversky, A., and Kahneman, D. 1974. Judgment under uncertainty: heuristics and biases. *Science* 185, 1124–1131.

Chapter 18

CHI-SQR: Chi-Squared Analysis

Chris Banister

Social surveys are one of the basic tools that allow planners and regional analysts to collect information on recommendations or decisions to be taken. The results from a typical survey consist of a large number of completed questionnaires that then need to be coded for computer analysis. The computer can then process, summarize, and analyze these data. The CHI-SQR model described in this chapter can be used for processing, summarizing, and analyzing the responses to certain types of social survey questions.

Many different types of questions can be asked in a survey questionnaire (Gardner 1978), some of which are susceptible to computer analysis. Generally, survey organizations will try to maximize the proportion of questions that can be more easily analyzed by computer. Most questions ask respondents to select an answer from a variety of categories put forward to them. This kind of answer can be analyzed easily by computer and more particularly by the model described in this chapter. The CHI-SQR model also allows the user to investigate the relationship between the answers given to two questions by constructing a cross-tabulation table. This table shows the relationship between the variables by placing one variable in the table's rows and the other in the table's columns. The strength of any interrelationships between the various questions can be tested by using the χ^2 (chi-squared) test (Marsh 1988) provided in this model.

CONCEPTUAL BASIS

Survey questions that can be analyzed in a straightforward fashion by computer either have numerical answers or require the respondent to select an answer from a menu of possible options. Other types of answers do not lend themselves to straightforward computer analysis and will not be considered further in this discussion.

The first and most important part of any analysis is to *code up* the individual responses from each completed survey questionnaire. In essence, this means that a data base needs to be set up. Each completed questionnaire becomes a row in the data base; the fields or columns for the database are the coded responses to each question. This process requires the answers to be put into a consistent form. For numerical answers, this requires that the measurement units be standardized and the number of significant digits specified. For answers selected from a menu of options, categories must be defined uniquely and consistently; otherwise, identical answers may be treated as if they were different.

Once the data have been entered into the data base, the analysis can begin. Numerical answers can be analyzed in a simple summary form by using any spreadsheet program without modification to calculate arithmetic means, standard deviations, and the like. These operations are not included in the CHI-SQR model since they are included in the most basic spreadsheet program. When the data are coded into categories, spreadsheets can also help in the analysis if the numerical codes are used. However, if this approach is taken, the results would require decoding, which increases the possibility of error through misinterpretation.

The model described here allows categorized data to be analyzed and compared with other categorized answers. For example, consider a questionnaire that asked two questions: the respondent's gender and work status. Thus, for each respondent, the completed questionnaire would include two pieces of information. A data base would first have to be created for this information. Gender can be straightforwardly coded as "female" or "male." Work status is more difficult since it does not have an unambiguous meaning. The coding process can be simplified by offering a limited number of answers to respondents. For instance, these could include: full-time employment, part-time employment, retired, at school or college, unemployed, and "other." The "other" category might ask respondents to state their employment status to allow further categories to be added if this were found to be necessary.

The coding process consists of determining the number of questionnaire responses falling in each category. For each answer, the proportion (or percentage) falling into each category can then be calculated.

This simple frequency analysis is the first and most basic analysis that can be carried out on categorized survey responses. This basic analysis may be sufficient, although in many cases it is often desirable to conduct a more thorough analysis examining the relationship between pairs of answers. For example, the gender breakdown of the respondents and their employment status might be useful. However, finding the number of men and women in each employment category may also be useful information. This type of analysis is presented in the form of a cross-tabulation table. Table 18.1 reports the answers to these two questions from a survey of 250 questionnaires.

Table 18.1

Sample Cross-Tabulation

Category	Women	Men	Total
Full-time employment	100	100	200
Not in full-time employment	35	15	50
Total	135	115	250

The χ^2 (chi-squared) test is used as a test of the statistical significance of a hypothesized relationship between two variables. A null hypothesis and an alternative hypothesis are established. The survey results are then used to test the reasonableness of the null hypothesis. Rejecting the null hypothesis implies that the alternative hypothesis can be accepted. Conversely, accepting the null hypothesis implies that the alternative hypothesis can be rejected.

It has to be recognized that, as with all statistical tests, there can be no certainty that a particular conclusion is correct; rather, a certain degree of confidence can be placed on such a conclusion. The analysis is always conducted with a set of sample results. If the survey were to be repeated, a slightly different set of sample results would probably be obtained. Thus, hypothesis testing is used to reduce the risk of drawing spurious conclusions from apparent differences or similarities that may have arisen from the normal variations encountered when taking samples.

Confidence is usually placed on the results of surveys at the 95 and 99 percent levels. At the 95 percent confidence level, rejecting the null hypothesis means that the survey results would be likely to happen on only 5 percent of the occasions, if the hypothesis were true. Rejecting the null hypothesis at the 99 percent level of confidence means that the survey result would be likely to happen on only 1 percent of the occasions, if the hypothesis were in fact true. As we gain more confidence in our results, we reduce the chances of rejecting a true null hypothesis (that is, making "type I" error) but we increase the chances of accepting a null hypothesis that is actually false (a "type II" error). Since we do not know whether the null hypothesis is really true or false, the process of selecting an appropriate confidence level can be decided only after determining which of the two types of errors we are seeking to minimize.

After setting up a cross-tabulation table, the analyst can look for any apparent relationship between the two characteristics detailed in the rows and columns of the table. The χ^2 test can then be applied with a null hypothesis that the two classifying criteria are independent of each other. In other words, if the null hypothesis is rejected, there is a significant statistical relationship between the two classifying criteria, that is, they are dependent on each other in some way. On the other hand, if the null hypothesis is accepted, any observed relationships between the two classifying criteria are not statistically significant.

For example, Table 18.1 shows the results of a questionnaire asking the respondent's gender and whether he or she is employed full-time or not (this assumes that there was an adequate definition of full-time employment). A simple analysis of these results shows that 71 percent of women and 91 percent of men are employed full-time. However, one can ask whether it is safe to conclude that men are more likely to be employed full-time from this evidence.

The null hypothesis in this case is that gender and employment status are independent of each other. On the assumption that the null hypothesis is true, a table of expected results can then be constructed. The table of expected results must reflect the survey results, that is, have the same sample size and the same aggregate answers to both questions. In other words, the table is constrained so that row and column totals are the same as those obtained in the actual survey. To construct such a table, each cell in the table can be calculated using the following formula, where R_i is the row total for the row the cell is in, C_j is the column total for the column the cell is in, and N is the sample size:

$$\frac{R_i C_j}{N} \tag{1}$$

For this example, the expected number of women employed full-time is equal to:

$$\frac{200 \times 135}{250} = 108 \tag{2}$$

The entire expected value table is shown in Table 18.2.

Table 18.2

Expected Frequencies If Null Hypothesis Is True

Expected	Women	Men	Total
Full-time employment	$\frac{200 \times 135}{250} = 108$	$\frac{200 \times 115}{250} = 92$	200
Not full-time employment	$\frac{50 \times 135}{250} = 27$	$\frac{50 \times 115}{250} = 23$	50
Total	135	115	250

The χ^2 value is calculated with the following formula:

$$\chi^2 = \sum_{i=m}^{i+1} \frac{(Observed_i - Expected_i)^2}{Expected_i} \tag{3}$$

where: m is the number of cells and the degrees of freedom (df) is the number of row classifying criteria minus 1 times number of column classifying criteria minus 1.

For this example with two variables and four cells, the χ^2 value has four components. Table 18.3 illustrates these components and shows that the χ^2 value is 6.44. The χ^2 value can then be compared to the critical values in a set of χ^2 tables for the relevant degrees of freedom (d.f.) which in this case is 1, that is, (2-1) × (2-1). The χ^2 value for the 5 percent level of significance for 1 degree of freedom is 3.84; at the 1 percent level of significance, it is 6.63. In this case, we can be 95 percent confident that the null hypothesis should be rejected, that is, that the men and women in the population from which the sample is taken have different employment characteristics. However, we cannot be sure that this is the case at the 99 percent confidence level, and, as a result, this conclusion must be stated with a good deal of circumspection.

Table 18.3

Calculation of Sample χ^2 Value

Four χ^2 components	Women	Men	Total
Full-time employment	$\dfrac{(100-108)^2}{108} = 0.59$	$\dfrac{(100-92)^2}{92} = 0.70$	1.29
Not full-time employment	$\dfrac{(35-27)^2}{27} = 2.37$	$\dfrac{(15-23)^2}{23} = 2.78$	5.15
Total	2.96	3.48	6.44

Degrees of freedom = 1.

Table 18.4 shows another example of larger cross-tabulations with six employment categories. Applying the process discussed earlier produces the expected values shown in Table 18.5. The resulting χ^2 value is 8. There are five degrees of freedom, that is, (6-1) x (2-1), and the critical χ^2 values are 11.07 at the 95 percent confidence or level and 15.09 at the 99 percent level. The example leads to an acceptance of the null hypothesis, that is, that employment status is not influenced by gender.

Table 18.4

Second Cross-Tabulation Example

Category	Men	Women	Total
Full-time employment	150	110	260
Part-time employment	50	50	100
Retired	45	25	70
At school or college	60	55	115
Unemployed	25	10	35
Other	10	10	20
Total	340	260	600

Table 18.5

Expected Frequencies If Null Hypothesis Is True

Category	Men	Women	Total
Full-time employment	147.3	112.7	260
Part-time employment	56.7	43.3	100
Retired	39.7	30.3	70
At school or college	65.2	49.8	115
Unemployed	19.8	15.2	35
Other	11.3	8.7	20
Total	340.0	260.0	600

COMPONENTS AND OPERATION

Exhibit 18.1 shows the location map for the CHI-SQR model. Column A is used for guidance notes and includes areas with documentation, indexes, menu lists, and so on. Adjacent to these information screens are some "setup" screens. These are used to let the user know when the model is calculating and whether he or she will need to wait until these calculations are finished. Error message screens give details on any errors that may occur and how they can be corrected. The Crosstab variable selection screen lists all variables (or questions) and allows the user to change the row and column variable or both components. The

Exhibit 18.1

CHI-SQR Location Map

Home A1..A20	Setup Screens D1..G20	Variable Select H1..S20	Location Map	Range Descript	Input Data	Frequency Output	Crosstabs	Macros
Directory								
A21..A60			T1..V50					
Documentation	Error Messages							
				W10..Y131				
A61..A140	D61..G140							
Welcome A250..A269								
Main Menu A270..A289								
					AA1..BZ???	CA1..DZ???	GA1..HZ???	IA1..IJ399

size of the work sheet will vary according to the number of people surveyed and the number of questions asked. The only practical limit to the number of questionnaires (or cases) is the number of rows in a spreadsheet, 8,192. However, it must be remembered that the processing time will be extensive for such a large number of questionnaires.

Model Operation

As Table 18.6 indicates, twelve macros are available for use in conjunction with the CHI-SQR model. The Alt-D, Alt-L, Alt-M, Alt-Q, Alt-R, Alt-W, and Alt-Z macros correspond to the standard macros described in chapter 1. General instructions for using these macros and the other spreadsheet macros are provided in chapter 1. The five specialized macros provided for use with the CHI-SQR model are described below.

Table 18.6

CHI-SQR Macros

Alt-D	Go to Documentation
Alt-G	Display bar Graph
Alt-I	Data Input and modification
Alt-L	Go to Location map
Alt-M	Main menu
Alt-P	Print output
Alt-Q	Quit/save model
Alt-R	Go to Range descriptions
Alt-S	Go to System menu
Alt-V	View output
Alt-W	Go to Welcome screen
Alt-Z	Go to macros

Alt-G, Display Bar Graph. This macro presents a frequency analysis in bar graph form for a selected variable.

Alt-I, Data Input and Modification. This option is used to enter and modify the input data. Once the data have been assembled, it is not possible to change them since the model has configured itself. To allow for data modification, this option saves the data set in a temporary work sheet to allow the user to modify it and then read it back into CHI-SQR as a default file.

Alt-P, Print Output. This option allows either the frequency data or a cross-tabulation table to be printed.

Alt-S, Go to System Menu. This macro calls up a content-sensitive Lotus-style menu that re-configures itself, depending on what the user can do next. For users who prefer this approach, this is the only macro that they need know about; all other menu choices are available from this macro.

The initial Alt-S menu is available only when starting a completely new analysis with a new set of data. **Alt-I** provides an alternative route into this option. The following options are provided:

1. SetUp allows the user to enter the survey information;
2. Documentation takes the user to a menu that provides three suboptions: (a) **Documentation** that describes the next available actions; (b) **Index** that shows an index of the model's range descriptions; and (c) **Return** that returns the user to the previous menu; and
3. Main_menu returns to the main menu.

The other Alt-S menu options are described in the following section.

Alt-V, View Output. This option allows the user to view either the frequency data or the cross-tabulation table on the screen.

Data Entry

The CHI-SQR model allows the survey results to be entered directly by specifying the number of completed questionnaires (or cases) and the number of questions asked (or variables). The cases are placed in the rows of the data base and the question answers are placed in the columns. Alternately, the survey results can be entered into a separate work sheet file containing just the survey information. Users are encouraged to use this second route, particularly if they have a reasonably large data set because data verification will be simpler.

Each column of the data set should be headed by the variable name. The name can be any label; however, users are encouraged to use as short a description as possible while avoiding confusion or ambiguity. Descriptions must also be given to the values in each field. Each possible value needs to have a unique label that is used consistently. For example, respondents who traveled by car should all be coded as, say, **car**. A description such as **automobile** would be treated as a separate value. Spaces added to **car** at either end of the word would also be treated as unique labels, that is, **car** is different from ␣**car** or **car**␣ (␣ represents a space). Uppercase and lowercase letters are ignored, so **CAR**, **Car** and **car** are all treated identically.

After the data have been classified into frequencies, it is important to check for data entry errors. Once all of the data have been entered and checked, the model automatically computes the frequencies for all of the survey questions. These results are written to the "Frequency Outputs" section of the model. This processing may take some time. For example, the sample application (forty-two cases with nine variables) takes just under ten minutes to process on an 8 MHz 80286 IBM-compatible machine. A 33 MHz 80486 IBM-compatible machine reduces processing time to less than one and a half minutes.

Cross-tabulations can then be produced for any pair of questions. One variable is placed in the row of a cross-tabulation table and the other is placed in the column of the table. These tables are presented in the Cross-tabulations section of the model along with the χ^2 value and the computed degrees of freedom. Any number of cross-tabulations can be produced to allow for as full an exploration of the data as desired. Computing the cross-tabulation may also take some time, for instance, two to two and a half minutes using an 80286-based machine and less than ten seconds using an 80486 machine.

In normal circumstances, SetUp will be selected from the **Alt-S**, Go to System menu. The model then prompts for the number of cases in the survey (such as, how many people were surveyed) and the number of variables (such as, how many questions were asked). A Yes/No choice is then given to allow the data set to be entered directly from the keyboard (**No**) or read from a previously prepared work sheet containing a Lotus data base (**Yes**—preferred for larger data sets). It is also possible to read in a temporary file that had been saved from a previous model run when the **Alt-I** option was used to modify the data.

All of these options insert a data base into the model. This data base has the name of the variables in its top row and survey answers in subsequent rows. Thus, for example, with one hundred questionnaires and ten questions, the data base will have ten columns and one hundred one rows (one hundred one rows because the first row has the variable names in it). If direct keyboard entry is selected, the model prompts for the name of each variable.

If the data are read directly from a file then the model automatically processes them, produces a simple frequency analysis for each variable, and displays the results. When entering the data from the keyboard, the user signifies that the process is complete by pressing the ENTER key. A menu then appears that gives an opportunity to amend or alter the data base. The following options are available:

1. Frequencies constructs a frequency table for each variable and displays the results;
2. Input_area returns the user to the data base;
3. Documentation takes the user to the context-sensitive documentation; and
4. Main_menu return the user to the main menu.

The simple frequency analysis for each variable can then be studied. The data can be viewed graphically, as a bar chart, by selecting the **Alt-G** option. Selecting the **Alt-S** option allows the user to examine the data by selecting the row and column variables to be displayed in a cross-tabulation table. Once this has been done, the table is constructed and displayed.

Pressing **Alt-S** again calls up a menu that allows the data to be explored in more detail. The following options are provided:

1. Swap allows the user to swap the row and/or column variables in the cross-tabulation table;
2. Cross_tab creates a new cross-tabulation table;
3. View allows the user to view or print the frequency analysis or the cross-tabulation analysis; it is the same as the **Alt-V** macro;
4. Graph allows the user to display the frequency analysis in bar graph form; it duplicates the **Alt-G** macro;
5. Documentation takes the user to the context-sensitive documentation; and
6. Main_menu returns the user to the main menu.

DATA SOURCES

Since this model is concerned with analyzing survey data, the only data source that users are likely to employ will be the results of their own survey work. It is important to remember that data collected by a survey need to be assembled into an appropriate framework for analysis with this model. This fact should influence the survey design. Users are thus urged to experiment with the CHI-SQR model before committing themselves to a particular survey scheme.

SAMPLE APPLICATION

Use of the CHI-SQR model will be illustrated with the results of a survey of users of an experimental bus that had been adapted to allow passengers to take their bikes with them. The first nine questions of the survey provide answers that are suitable for analysis using the CHI-SQR model. The tenth question is open ended and must be analyzed independently.

The first stage involves coding the data. Like most surveys, the coding scheme was established when the survey was designed. Thus, question one, for example, allows for five possible answers identifying places where the bus stopped to let passengers and their bikes off. It is appropriate to use exactly the same descriptions given on the survey form for entering these data into the model to make the answers more intelligible.

The first stage of using the model is to enter the data using the **Alt-S** SetUp option. The model first asks for the number of cases (or completed questionnaires). This example has forty-two cases, so type **42** and press ENTER. The model then asks for the number of variables (or question). There are nine in this case, so type **9** and press ENTER. Then select **Yes** to indicate that the data are set up in a Lotus data base. Type **FCTDATA** and press ENTER to specify the spreadsheet data file to be loaded.

Exhibit 18.2 shows a part of this data set. The first row of the data base (row 1) has the names of the variables, or fields, and each subsequent row (from row 2 to 43) has the details from each of the cases or the records. The cursor keys can be used to navigate around the data base and fill in the values.

Once all the data have been entered, the model provides a frequency analysis for each of the questionnaire answers. In our case, this will be performed automatically since the data come directly from a file. Exhibit 18.3 shows this frequency count information for the first two variables. The frequency analysis for the other variables is also displayed on the screen. Scroll horizontally to explore answers for the other variables. Note that the data are presented in percentage form. This stage can also be used for verification of the data input. If a value was mistyped, for example, it would show up as a new category. You should then use the **Alt-I** option save your data to a temporary file named ZCHI!TMP.WK1, exit the CHI-SQR model, and retrieve the temporary file. Use the normal Lotus procedures to edit and save the data. Then reload CHI-SQR again to analyze the corrected data.

Exhibit 18.2

Sample CHI-SQR Data Set

Start trip	End trip	Do again	Learn about	Car	Group	Age	Work status	Bike use
Burbage	Friden	Certainly	Leaflet	No	8	25-44	Paid job	At least once a day
Burbage	Friden	Certainly	Word of mouth	No	6	25-44	Unemployed	At least once a day
Parsley Hay	Ashbourne	Certainly	Newspaper	No	1	45-64	Unemployed	About once a week
Parsley Hay	Ashbourne	Certainly	Newspaper	No	2	45-64	Unemployed	More than once a week
Wirksworth	Wirksworth	Certainly	Newspaper	No	2	25-44	Paid job	At least once a day
.	.	.	.	.	.	.	.	.
.	.	.	.	.	.	.	.	.
.	.	.	.	.	.	.	.	.
Parsley Hay	Wirksworth	Certainly	Leaflet	Yes	4	Under 15	Education	More than once a week
Parsley Hay	Wirksworth	Probably	Leaflet	Yes	4	Under 15	Education	More than once a week
Parsley Hay	Wirksworth	Certainly	Leaflet	Yes	4	25-44	Paid job	More than once a week
Burbage	Burbage	Certainly	Newspaper	No	2	16-24	Education	At least once a day
Burbage	Burbage	Certainly	Word of mouth	Yes	2	16-24	Education	At least once a day

Exhibit 18.3

Frequency Count for First Two Variables

Number of labels	3		5	
Variable name	Start trip	Percent	End trip	Percent
Variable labels	Burbage	31.0	Friden	16.7
	Parsley Hay	57.1	Ashbourne	11.9
	Wirksworth	11.9	Wirksworth	52.4
			Parsley Hay	14.3
			Burbage	4.8
Total count		42		42

The data can also be viewed as a bar chart by selecting **Alt-G** and choosing the variable you want to see displayed in chart form. Exhibit 18.4 shows an example of such a bar chart. Note that the chart is set up and labeled automatically. Pressing any key returns you to the spreadsheet after a graph has been viewed.

Exhibit 18.4

Sample CHI-SQR Graphical Output

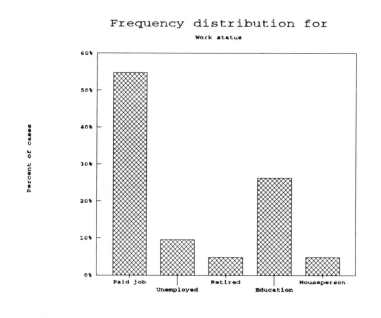

The next stage in using the model is the construction and exploration of relationships between variables using cross-tabulations. Do this by selecting **Alt-S** and specifying the variables for the rows and columns of your table. The model will then construct a cross-tabulation table that you can view. You can then repeat this process by selecting **Alt-S** and swapping variables into and out of the rows or columns. With the nine variables in the example, there are thirty-six unique such cross-tabulations. Exhibit 18.5 gives an example of the cross-tabulations output.

Exhibit 18.5

Sample CHI-SQR Analysis Output

Variable in rows	Car user			Degrees of freedom		8
Variable in cols	Bike use			Chi squared value		14.29

	At least once a day	About once a week	More than once a week	Very infrequently	About once a month	Total
No	13	3	3	1	0	20
Yes	4	7	8	0	2	21
N/A	0	0	1	0	0	1
Total	17	10	12	1	2	42

The results of the χ^2 analysis are shown in the top right-hand corner of the table. The χ^2 result needs to be compared to the critical values for the appropriate degrees of freedom (also shown on the table). Critical values are read from χ^2 tables that are available in most statistics textbooks. The null hypothesis is that the row and column classifying criteria are independent of each other. This hypothesis is supported in the sample output shown in Exhibit 18.5, that is, bike usage does not appear to be related to car ownership.

EVALUATION AND EXTENSIONS

The χ^2 analysis is based upon a number of rather important assumptions (Silk 1979). The observed and expected data *must* be frequencies and not proportions or percentages. This problem is dealt with in this model since the analysis deals only with survey results. The sample size must be larger than twenty and preferably at least forty. Any survey with fewer responses would be suspect. The expected frequencies should not be less than five. More importantly, determining that there is a relationship between two variables does not indicate what the relationship is or why it has arisen. Thus, the results of a χ^2 analysis do not by any means give all the answers one might desire.

The CHI-SQR model might be extended to allow for comparisons between one set of survey results and results collected elsewhere from another survey or from census data. However, it would be difficult to build these extensions into the model. Fortunately, these applications are rarely required.

A further extension would allow the model to present other analytical approaches for examining the numerical data. This is probably not necessary since most spreadsheet users can easily calculate averages, standard deviations, counts, and other statistical analyses using standard spreadsheet functions. Further analysis of numerical data can also be conducted with the standard spreadsheet data functions, for example, sorting the information into numerical order or investigating the distribution of the data.

Cross-tabulations also allow two sets of categorized answers to be compared. Standard analysis of variance techniques allows for comparisons to be made between numerical answers and categorized answers. This could possibly be the most important extension to this model by allowing these types of answers to be summarized and F-ratio testing to be conducted.

REFERENCES

Gardner, G. 1978. *Social surveys for social planners.* Milton Keynes, UK: Open University Press.

Marsh, C. 1988. *Exploring data: an introduction to data analysis for social scientists.* Cambridge, UK: Polity Press.

Silk, J. 1979. *Statistical concepts in geography.* London: Allen and Unwin.

PART SIX

Other Applications

Chapter 19

REIA: Real Estate Investment Analysis

Kirk McClure

The role of planners in the real estate development process has changed rapidly over the last decade. In the past, their role was limited to simple regulatory oversight of a building's height, bulk, and use. Today, planners are called upon to negotiate actively with developers over the detailed aspects of individual development proposals. Fiscal and economic pressures have forced planners to go beyond simple regulatory review and to participate in all phases of the development process. This means that planners must understand and become proficient in the area of real estate investment analysis.

Dowall (1985) offers several examples of how planners may use real estate investment analysis as they negotiate with a developer over a proposal. These include:

1. Establishing the exaction fees that a developer must pay to offset the costs of new public infrastructure required for the development;
2. Requiring a set-aside of housing units at affordable rates in exchange for permission to build more units than would otherwise be allowed;
3. Estimating the impact of urban design requirements upon the ability of developers to make acceptable returns on investment; and
4. Entering into a public/private partnership with each partner making a contribution to the finished development.

These examples illustrate how planners can use development controls in a positive way to achieve public sector objectives. For example, they may use the development process to actively promote development serving many and varied planning goals, such as historic preservation or the provision of affordable housing. However, they also indicate that planners must understand the process of real estate investment analysis in order to achieve these objectives. A failure to properly perform this analysis may lead to problems at either of two extremes. If the planner attempts to exact too much from a proposed development, it may no longer be economically feasible; as a result, the proposal might be withdrawn and the development opportunity lost. Conversely, if the planner fails to exact enough from the new development, the opportunity to utilize the development to help meet planning goals may be lost, and the development may fail to make an appropriate contribution to the community.

CONCEPTUAL BASIS

The process of real estate investment analysis is not exceedingly complex. The process may become highly detailed; the basic procedure, though, is simple and relatively constant for all kinds of development. The analysis employs information on the amount of money invested in a piece of income-producing real estate along with data on the income and expenses for the real estate. This information is used to determine the real estate's cash flow at several points in time, usually at the end of each year of operation. Cash flow is simply the amount of money left over from income after all expenses are paid. This cash flow is then viewed as a return on the amount of money invested. If the return on this investment is competitive with the returns on comparable investments, the real estate investment is considered to be worthwhile. If the return is higher than comparable investments, an opportunity exists to modify the development proposal in order to serve broader community goals. If the return is lower than other returns, the investment is not competitive and the developer may not proceed.

If a planner is to negotiate successfully with a developer, he or she must understand the impact that any public sector constraint or contribution will have upon a real estate investment. The measure of a successful public sector negotiator is not to require so much from the developer that the proposal is withdrawn or to offer more inducements than are necessary to secure the development. Rather, a successful negotiator carefully gauges the costs and benefits of any public sector intervention into the development process so that the developer is willing to incorporate the public sector objectives as a condition for permission to proceed.

A document called a "pro forma" is used to determine how a change in a development proposal will alter the return on investment. A pro forma is an outline of a project's income and expenses along with several measures of its investment performance. Several different pro formas may be prepared covering a range of development alternatives. The differences between the alternatives may relate to the size of the development, the amount of development fees imposed, or any other development characteristic that can be modified. These pro formas can then be compared and categorized. Those that indicate that the developer will enjoy an acceptable return on investment may be considered to be economically feasible alternatives suitable for further analysis and negotiation. Those that indicate that the developer will not receive an acceptable return on investment can be discarded as not being economically feasible.

The preparation of pro formas need not be a tiresome burden. The process can be automated with the assistance of models such as REIA. The analyst needs to obtain financial data on the proposed development or, at least, make reasonable assumptions about its projected income and expenses. These data are entered into the model, and the development's economic feasibility is estimated. The user may then alter the input data to determine the impact that these changes have on the project's return on investment. Many alternatives may be examined quickly and easily to determine the sensitivity of the development's feasibility to changes in its size, cost, or financing.

Guidance on the preparation and evaluation of pro formas can be found in standard real estate investment analysis texts, such as Floyd (1987), Greer and Farrell (1988), and Phyrr and colleagues (1989). Specific instruction in pro forma analysis is provided in Roddewig and Shlaes (1983). Planners are often in the position to evaluate a pro forma submitted for review by a developer; as a result, they need to become familiar with the many techniques used to make a pro forma justify the developer's requests.

It should be remembered that it is often in the developer's interest to structure the pro forma so that any changes made in the development will render it economically infeasible. Examination of the pro forma to determine the assumptions used in its preparation may reveal that these assumptions are exaggerated or unrealistic. Recasting the pro forma with more reasonable assumptions may provide an opportunity to negotiate a better development proposal. However, it is not always easy to spot indefensible assumptions used in the preparation of a pro forma. Martin (1988) discusses several of the most common abuses employed in the preparation of a pro forma and offers suggestions for correcting them.

While analysts may prepare a customized pro forma for each development, a standard spreadsheet model will meet the analyst's needs in many circumstances. The REIA model provides a typical fifteen-year analysis for a development proposal. The model can handle many different situations, providing considerable flexibility in its use. For example, it will handle:

1. Up to three different lease types for residential space plus rental units that qualify for low- or moderate-income housing tax credits;
2. Up to three different lease types for nonresidential space;
3. Up to five different line items for operating expenses;
4. Up to four loans running simultaneously or consecutively;
5. Projects that have a construction period prior to occupancy as well as projects that are acquired for immediate occupancy;
6. Syndication of any low- or moderate-income housing tax credits with the proceeds of the syndication being used to offset development costs; and
7. Variable rates of vacancy, rent increases, and property value appreciation over a period of up to fifteen years.

Once the project data have been entered, the model calculates several schedules, including:

1. A fifteen-year income and expense analysis;
2. Five different measures of investment performance for each of the fifteen years;
3. A schedule of income by unit and unit type along with operating expenses by line item;
4. Amortization schedules for each loan; and
5. Summary schedules of all tax benefits claimed, carried forward, or syndicated.

The REIA model allows the user to enter and edit data, calculate the resulting schedules using those data, view charts illustrating the proposal's investment performance, print various reports, and save the model for later use. All of these functions can be performed from the model's automated system menu. The analyst may also enter the data and perform the calculations directly from the keyboard using the model's macro features.

COMPONENTS AND OPERATION

As the location map in Exhibit 19.1 indicates, the computational portion of the REIA model is organized into four major sections or pages. The Input section contains unprotected cells used to store data. The analyst will be prompted to enter the required information for each part of this section. Once all of the necessary information has been entered, the pro forma and associated schedules are calculated by selecting the Alt-C option. The calculation period may take up to forty-five seconds, depending upon the machine in use. The calculations complete sections two, three, and four of the model.

The Pro Forma section contains a fifteen-year pro forma with before- and after-tax calculations. The calculations cover the cash flow from the operation of the property and from the sale of the property at the end of each year. The investment performance information is displayed at the bottom of the section. The Input and Expense section provides schedules for the property's income, operating expenses, debt service, interest payments, and loan balances. The Tax and Syndication section summarizes the depreciation and interest deductions plus any tax credits that may be claimed for low- and moderate-income housing units.

Model Operation
As Table 19.1 indicates, thirteen macros are provided for use in conjunction with the REIA model. The Alt-D, Alt-L, Alt-M, Alt-Q, Alt-R, Alt-W, and Alt-Z macros correspond to the standard macros described in chapter 1. General instructions for using these macros and other spreadsheet macros are provided in chapter 1. Descriptions of the remaining seven specialized REIA macros follow.

Alt-C, Calculate Pro Forma. This macro calculates the pro forma and other schedules, including schedules for income, expenses, loan

Exhibit 19.1

REIA Location Map

INPUT DATA	WELCOME S1..Y20	MACROS
A1..R56	MAIN MENU S21..Y40	
PRO FORMA	LOCATION MAP S41..Y60	
	HELP	
A57..R112		
INCOME & EXPENSES	S61..Y120	
	ERROR MESSAGES	
A113..R168	S141..Y160	
TAX & SYNDICATION	RANGE NAMES	
A169..R224	T161..Y216	
COMPUTATIONAL TABLES		
A225..T271		AA1..AT276

amortization, and tax liability. The calculations are made for the data currently found in the Input section of the model.

Table 19.1

REIA Macros

Alt-C	Calculate pro forma
Alt-D	Go to Documentation
Alt-G	Graph output
Alt-I	Input and edit data
Alt-L	Go to Location map
Alt-M	Go to Main Menu
Alt-P	Print output
Alt-Q	Quit/save model
Alt-R	Go to Range descriptions
Alt-S	Go to System menu
Alt-V	View output
Alt-W	Go to Welcome screen
Alt-Z	Go to macros

Alt-G, Graph Output. This macro selects graphs showing the project's return on investment. The following options are provided:

1. IRR, graph the project's internal rate of return;
2. ROE, graph the project's return on equity;
3. DCR, graph the project's debt coverage ratio;
4. Cap, graph the project's capitalization ratio;
5. X_Return, return to the previous menu.

Alt-I, Input and Edit Data. This macro can be used to: (1) clear all the data cells, making them ready for new data; (2) edit the project name, or (3) edit the income, expense, financial, taxation, or annual rate of change data. The following options are provided:

1. Clear, clear cells for new data;
2. Name, edit project name;

3. Income, edit income data;
4. Expenses, edit expense data;
5. Finance, edit financing data;
6. Tax, edit taxation data;
7. Yearly, edit yearly data; and
8. Return, return to previous menu.

Alt-P, Print Output. This macro can be used to print a complete report of the project, including the data used, the pro forma, and schedules for income, expenses, loan amortization, and taxation. The following options are provided:

1. Short, print a five-year report;
2. Mid-range, print a ten-year report;
3. Long, print a fifteen-year report; and
4. Return, return to the previous menu.

The reports may be printed for five, ten, or fifteen years of operation of the development in an 8.5-by-11-inch format. The five-year report uses the default printer font. If the user selects either the ten- or fifteen-year report, the template will prompt the user for the printer's setup string, to set the printer to condensed print. The user should enter the string including the preceding backslash.

Alt-S, Go to System Menu. The macro allows the REIA model to be used with an automated Lotus-like command line menu system. This menu provides the following options:

1. Edit, input or edit data; this option is the same as the **Alt-I** macro;
2. Calculate, calculate pro forma and other schedules; this option is the same as the **Alt-C** macro;
3. View, view pro forma and other schedules; this option is the same as the **Alt-V** macro;
4. Graph, graph returns on investment over time; this option is the same as the **Alt-G** macro;
5. Help, view help screens; this option is the same as the **Alt-D** macro;
6. Print, print output reports; this option is the same as the **Alt-P** macro;

7. Quit/Save, go to standard **Alt-Q**, Quit/save menu; and
8. Main_menu, return to main menu.

Alt-V, View Output. This macro can be used to view the pro forma and other schedules calculated by the template. The macro freezes the year of operation along the top of the screen and the line item label along the left side of the screen. The user may then scroll around the template moving up, down, left, right, or back to the "home" position, that is, the first year of the pro forma. The following options are provided:

1. **Down**, go to next screen down;
2. **Up**, go to next screen up;
3. **Right**, go to next screen on the right;
4. **Left**, go to next screen on the left;
5. **Home**, go to home position that is, first year of the pro forma.;
6. **X_Return**, and return to the previous menu.

Procedural Steps

The steps to be employed while using the template are listed below. The specific procedures will vary from application to application and from user to user. Applications will vary in terms of the depth of the analysis that is needed and the style of usage that users prefer. Some will prefer to use the standard Alt macro commands directly while others will prefer to use the model's System menu. The basic steps are the same, however. The user should:

1. Load the model;
2. Clear the data cells making the template ready for the analysis of new data;
3. Enter a name for the new project analysis;
4. Enter the data on the project's income, expenses, financing, depreciation, and taxation as well as its vacancy, inflation, and appreciation rates;
5. Calculate the pro forma and other schedules;
6. View the pro forma and other schedules on the screen and then send them to the printer if the results are acceptable;
7. Save the current data as a work sheet file for later use; and
8. Examine alternative development scenarios; the alternatives may be selectively printed and saved, if desired.

Data Entry

The analyst should enter data into all of the cells of the Input section that are relevant to the analysis being performed. These include:

Income. The income section is divided between residential space and commercial space. The residential space can have up to three different market rent levels. Space is also provided for low- and moderate-income units eligible for the federal income tax credits; these items should not be used unless income tax credits are planned. For each lease type, the analyst must enter the number of apartments of that type and their initial monthly rent. The nonresidential section can accommodate three different lease types. Each type of lease must be specified by entering the square footage of rentable space and its initial annual rent per leasable square foot.

Operating Expenses. The operating expense section allows for five different expense items. The initial annual expenses should be entered for each line item in terms of dollars per year. The inflation rate to be used with each line item must also be entered as a percentage, for example, 5.25, not 0.0525. This rate will be used every year after the first year to account for inflation. The analyst may also enter a label to identify the line item expense.

Financing. The financing section allows four different loans to be entered to cover financing over the property's operating years. For each loan, the analyst should enter: (1) the loan amount; (2) the term of the loan in years; (3) the annual interest rate as a percentage; (4) the year during which the loan will begin; (5) the year during which prepayment is expected; and (6) the type of loan. If no prepayment is expected until the sale of the property, any integer equal to or greater than fifteen must be entered into the prepayment cell. The type of loan can be either: (1) a fully amortized loan (type "0") or (2) an interest-only loan (type "1").

Depreciation and Taxation. This section covers several items relating to taxation. The user should enter the total development costs of the property, including the costs of any new construction or rehabilitation and the purchase price of the property. The investor's marginal tax rate should be entered as a percentage. Conventionally, this will be the highest marginal tax rate for federal income taxation; however, state and local income taxes may also be included. The selling costs should be entered as a percentage of the total selling price of the property.

The depreciable basis of the property should be entered separately for the residential and the nonresidential portions of the property. The depreciable basis of the residential space plus the depreciable basis for the nonresidential space should add up to the total development costs minus all nondepreciable costs. The value of the land is generally used as a good estimate for these nondepreciable costs.

The number of years in the construction period should also be entered. The template will accept only construction periods ranging from zero years (indicating a property acquired with immediate occupancy) to three years; fractional entries are rounded to the nearest whole year. This construction period will adjust the return on investment calculations to control for the number of years that the investor must wait prior to earning any cash flow from operation of the development.

Low- and Moderate-Income Housing Tax Credits. This section should be completed if the development is eligible for low- or moderate-income housing tax credits and will be using syndication to raise funds for the project. The percentage of the project's credits to be sold to investors should be entered; this is usually 95 to 99 percent of the total credits. The yield that the investors expect on these credits should also be entered as a percentage. This yield is generally in the range of 15 to 17 percent but varies with market conditions.

Because different tax credits are given for acquisition, new construction, and rehabilitation, the model provides cells for entering each of these amounts. These costs should be entered for the project as a whole. The user need not calculate the percentage of these costs that is eligible for the credits; the model makes these calculations. However, these amounts must be reduced by the value of any federal grants provided to the project.

The credit percentages must also be entered. Generally, 4 percent credits are allowed against eligible acquisition costs and 9 percent credits are allowed against eligible rehabilitation and new construction costs. The 9 percent credits, though, must be reduced to 4 percent if the project is financed from the proceeds of bonds with interest that is exempt from federal income taxation. For details on these low- and moderate-income housing tax credits see Guggenheim (1987).

Annual Items. The pro forma may have several items that can vary over the operating period of the property. These include the vacancy rates that are expressed as a percentage of gross income and are entered separately for residential and nonresidential property. The user may also enter an assumed rate for rent increases; these are also entered as a percentage, separately for residential and commercial space. The analyst may enter individual annual appreciation rates for the increases in the property's value. These appreciation rates are expressed as a percentage of the total development costs.

Model Output

The pro forma prepared on the second page of the REIA output provides the following information:

1. Income and expenses, before and after taxes, from operation and reversion.
2. The internal rates of return on the investment both before and after taxes, assuming the property is sold at the end of each year. These rates are conventional rates treating equity and cash flows equally. The initial equity amount is equal to the difference between: (a) the total development cost and (b) the sum of the loans taken out during the first year of operation, net any proceeds from syndication.
3. The debt coverage ratio of the property, that is the ratio of net operating income to the total debt service obligation of the development.
4. The before- and after-tax return on equity. These ratios are equal to: (a) the before-tax cash flow, net any additional equity invested during the year divided by (b) the initial equity amount. The after-tax return on equity is similar but uses the after-tax cash flow.
5. The capitalization rate is calculated as the net operating income of the property, expressed as a percentage of the property's value.

The third page of the model output provides a more detailed listing of the income line items, the operating expenses, the costs of financing the property, and the amortization schedules. The fourth page of the model output outlines all of the income tax calculations. Both tax deductions and credits can be carried forward throughout the operation of the property. For credits only, the user may elect to analyze the impact of syndicating those credits not used by the property to reduce its tax liability. If the user enters a nonzero value in the percent syndicated cell of the first page, the credits are assumed to be syndicated.

These schedules can be printed out to cover five, ten, or fifteen years of operation. Often the analyst is interested only in the first few years of operation and assumes that if the development stabilizes during the initial period of operation, later years will follow that initial pattern. As a result, a five-year pro forma may be sufficient. However, trends will often not be obvious during a short time period, requiring longer projections. In order to examine longer investment periods, ten-year pro formas have become customary. Finally, fifteen-year pro formas are used when long-term projections are required. These long-term projections are particularly valuable when low-income housing tax credits are used because the occupancy of the set-aside units must be assured for at least a fifteen-year period.

The model also prepares four different graphs illustrating the development's investment performance over a fifteen-year period. The graphs show: (1) the internal rate of return, before and after taxes; (2) the return on equity, before and after taxes; (3) the debt coverage ratio; and (4) the capitalization rate.

DATA SOURCES

Secondary Data Sources
In many cases, the analyst will find it necessary to develop a pro forma without income and expense data for the project being studied. This will necessitate the use of data from secondary sources. The following data sources may be used:

Income and Expenses. The Institute of Real Estate Management (IREM) publishes several books on an annual basis that provide information on the income and expenses of operating various types of real estate. Of particular interest are *Income/Expense Analysis: Conventional Apartments* (IREM 1990a), *Income/Expense Analysis: Federally Assisted Apartments* (IREM 1990b), and *Income/Expense Analysis: Office Buildings* (IREM 1990c).

Construction and Development Costs. The R. S. Means Company publishes several books on an annual basis that provide information on the cost of building various types of real property. These books include *Means Square Foot Costs* (Means 1990a) and *Building Construction Cost Data* (Means 1990b), covering "hard" construction costs. The Urban Land Institute (ULI) also publishes annual summaries of construction and development costs. The ULI books are particularly useful in that they cover all development costs, including land, construction financing, fees, and other "soft" costs. Their books include *Residential Development Handbook* (O'Mara 1978), *Dollars & Cents of Shopping Centers* (ULI 1990), and *Business and Industrial Park Development Handbook* (Beyard 1988). Many other books on specific types of real estate development are also available through the ULI. The Building Owners and Managers Association (BOMA) publishes the *BOMA Experience Exchange Report* (BOMA 1990), which reports on rents and expenses for office space nationwide.

Financing. Information on financing costs can best be found through many periodicals, including most newspapers. Foremost among these sources is the *Federal Reserve Bulletin* (Federal Reserve Bank 1990), which is published monthly. Several newsletters are also available that monitor interest rates for real estate loans. These include *The Mortgage and Real Estate Executives Report* (Warren et al. 1990c) and *Real Estate Finance Update* (Warren et al. 1990d). Other related newsletters include the *Affordable Housing Bulletin* (Warren et al. 1990a) and *The Housing and Development Reporter* (Warren et al. 1990b).

SAMPLE APPLICATION

The REIA model comes with a complete set of sample data. The user may want to examine these data and the corresponding pro forma as an introduction to the workings of the model. The sample data are described below and reported in Exhibits 19.2 and 19.3. These exhibits give a seven-year report for the sample data. Exhibit 19.2 contains the sample input data; Exhibit 19.3 contains the pro forma.

As shown in Exhibit 19.2, five general types of information are required to use the REIA model. Information is required on: (1) income and expenses; (2) financing; (3) depreciation and taxation; (4) low or moderate income housing tax credits; and (5) annual items. The sample data for each category as reported in Exhibit 19.2 are described below.

Income and Expenses. The sample development is a mixed-use project with one hundred rental apartments and 6,500 square feet of commercial space. The apartments rent from $600 to $700 per month; the commercial space rents for between $12 and $14 per square foot per year. Twenty apartments have been set aside for occupancy by low-income tenants. The rents on these low-income units will begin at $250 per month. The operating expenses for the apartments are initially

Exhibit 19.2

Sample REIA Development Data

Income Data		Number	Monthly					
Residential		Units	Rent/Unit					
Market Rate Units Type 1		20	600					
Market Rate Units Type 2		20	650					
Market Rate Units Type 3		40	700					
Moderate-Income Units		0	0					
Low-Income Units		20	250					
Nonresidential		Sq Ft	Rent/SF					
Lease Type 1		3000	12.00					
Lease Type 2		1500	12.00					
Lease Type 3		2000	14.00					
Annual Operating Expenses		Expense	Percent Increase					
Item 1 Administration		35000	4.00					
Item 2 Maintenance		40000	6.00					
Item 3 Utilities		40000	4.00					
Item 4 Property Taxes		60000	3.00					
Item 5 Insurance & Reserve		25000	4.00					

Financing	Loan Amount	Term in Years	Interest APR	Initial Year	Year Prepay	0 = Amort 1 = Int Only
Loan 1	4800000	2	9.00	1	2	1
Loan 2	2400000	25	10.50	3	30	0
Loan 3	2400000	30	10.00	3	30	1
Loan 4	0	0	0.00	0	0	0

Depreciation and Taxation			
Total Development Costs	6000000	Residential Basis	5000000
Marginal Tax Rate Percent	28.00	Commercial Basis	100000
Selling Cost Percent	6.00	Construc Yrs (0-3)	1

Low- or Moderate-Income Housing Tax Credits			
Percent Syndicated	98.00	Yield on Credits	17.00
Acquisition Costs if Rehab	0	Credit Percent	0.00
Rehabilitation Costs	0	Credit Percent	0.00
New Construction Costs	5000000	Credit Percent	9.00

Annual Items Year	1	2	3	4	5	6	7	8
Vacancy Rate as a Percent								
Residential	10.00	5.00	5.00	5.00	5.00	5.00	5.00	5.00
Nonresidential	33.00	0.00	0.00	0.00	0.00	0.00	0.00	0.00
Percent Increase in Rents								
Residential		4.00	4.00	4.00	4.00	4.00	4.00	4.00
Nonresidential		0.00	0.00	20.00	0.00	0.00	0.00	0.00
Appreciation in Property Value								
Percent Increase	4.00	4.00	4.00	4.00	4.00	4.00	4.00	4.00

estimated to be $2,000 per unit per year. The expenses for the commercial space are assumed to be zero, as the tenants pay all expenses.

Financing. The development's financing reflects a package of loans that the city proposes to arrange in order to encourage the developer to set aside the twenty low-income units. The project will have a loan of $4,800,000 (80 percent of the total development costs) during the first two years. This loan will be at below-market rates, paying only interest (that is, no repayment of the principal) at a rate of 9 percent per year.

After two years, the development should have a stabilized occupancy, making it possible to acquire conventional financing. In this example, the project takes out a loan of $2,400,000 beginning in the third year with an interest rate of 10.5 percent; the loan is a twenty-five-year loan that is fully amortized. The remaining $2,400,000 will continue to be financed with an interest-only loan but with the interest rate going up to 10 percent.

Depreciation and Taxation. The total development costs are $6,000,000; $5,000,000 is for developing the residential space; $100,000 is for the nonresidential space; the remaining $900,000 is the value of the land. The investor is assumed to be in the 28 percent tax bracket. When the project is sold, it is assumed that the broker's fee will be 6 percent of the sale price. The construction period for the project is assumed to be one year.

Low- or Moderate-Income Housing Tax Credits. Because of the set-aside of low-income housing units, the project may claim tax credits against the costs of building these units. These credits will be syndicated, with 98 percent of the credits sold to investor/partners and 2 percent retained by the developer. The investor/partners expect to obtain a 17 percent return on their investment. The total new construction costs are $5,000,000 against which 9 percent credits will be taken on the proportion of the costs attributed to the low-income units.

Annual Items. Vacancy rates are assumed to be 5 percent for the residential space and 0 percent for the commercial space. However, during the first year of operation, the residential vacancy is estimated at 10 percent and the commercial vacancy is estimated to be 33 percent, given the normal problems of leasing space immediately after completion of construction. Residential rents are assumed to increase by 4 percent per year; commercial rents will increase by 20 percent after each five-year lease term. It is assumed that the value of the development will increase at a rate of 4 percent per year.

Exhibit 19.3

Sample REIA Pro Forma

Operations	Year						
	1	2	3	4	5	6	7
Gross Income							
Market Rate Units	636000	661440	687898	715414	744030	773791	804743
Moderate-Income Units	0	0	0	0	0	0	0
Low-Income Units	60000	62400	64896	67492	70192	72999	75919
Nonresidential Space	82000	82000	82000	82000	82000	98400	98400
Total	778000	805840	834794	864905	896222	945190	979062
Vacancy Residential	69600	36192	37640	39145	40711	42340	44033
Vacancy Nonresidential	27060	0	0	0	0	0	0
Effective Income	681340	769648	797154	825760	855510	902851	935029
Operating Expenses	200000	208200	216758	225691	235015	244751	254916
Net Operating Income	481340	561448	580396	600069	620495	658100	680113
Debt Service	432000	432000	511924	511924	511924	511924	511924
Bef-Tax Cash Flow Oper	49340	129448	68472	88145	108571	146176	168189
Interest Claimed	432000	432000	491013	488708	486150	483309	480156
Depreciation Claimed	49340	129448	89383	111361	134345	174791	199958
Taxable Income	0	0	0	0	0	0	0
Credits Claimed	0	0	0	0	0	0	0
Tax on Operations	0	0	0	0	0	0	0
After-Tax Cash Flow Oper	49340	129448	68472	88145	108571	146176	168189
Reversion							
Selling Price	6240000	6489600	6749184	7019151	7299917	7591914	7895591
Selling Costs	374400	389376	404951	421149	437995	455515	473735
Mortgage Balance	4800000	4800000	4779088	4755872	4730097	4701482	4669713
Bef-Tax Cash Flow Rev	1065600	1300224	1565145	1842130	2131825	2434917	2752142
Capital Gain	-85060	279012	612404	977535	1375800	1825068	2310482
Tax on Gain	-23817	78123	171473	273710	385224	511019	646935
After-Tax Cash Flow Rev	1089417	1222101	1393671	1568420	1746601	1923898	2105207
Return on Investment Performance							
Before-Tax ROEquity	5.81%	15.25%	8.07%	10.38%	12.79%	17.22%	19.81%
After-Tax ROEquity	5.81%	15.25%	8.07%	10.38%	12.79%	17.22%	19.81%
Before-Tax IRR	14.61%	20.61%	21.74%	22.02%	21.96%	21.85%	21.66%
After-Tax IRR	15.83%	18.43%	18.70%	18.73%	18.67%	18.65%	18.60%
Debt Coverage Ratio	1.11	1.30	1.13	1.17	1.21	1.29	1.33
Capitalization Rate	7.71%	8.65%	8.60%	8.55%	8.50%	8.67%	8.61%

Model Output

As shown in Exhibit 19.3, the sample pro forma indicates that the project is economically feasible and provides a competitive return on investment. The cash flow is positive in all years, including the first, despite the difficulties of high vacancy rates. These conclusions are drawn from observation of several investment performance trends found in the graphs and at the bottom of the pro forma.

The positive cash flow is the result of the favorable interest rate provided by the below-market-rate loan during the first two years. The analyst may want to consider requiring that the positive cash flows received during the first two years be placed into a reserve fund for future use in the event of cash flow problems in later years.

Exhibit 19.4

Cash Flow as Return on Equity (ROE)

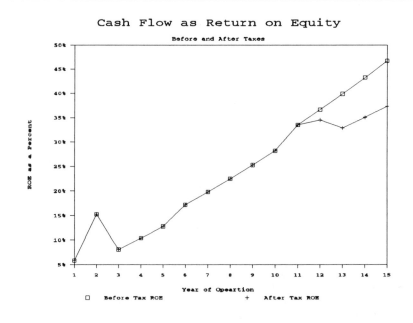

The return on equity is about 6 percent both before and after taxes at the end of the first year. This information is also shown in Exhibit

19.4, which shows the return on equity, or "ROE," graph generated by the REIA model. The returns are the same because the development has sufficient deductions to reduce its taxable income to zero through year eleven. After that year, the development no longer generates enough deductions and credits to shelter all income from federal income taxes. However, the return on equity rises rapidly to more than 12 percent by year five and continues to rise in later years.

The internal rate of return measures the total return on investment if the development is sold at various points in time. The internal rate of return takes into account the returns from operating the development and the profits from selling the development. The internal rate of return stabilizes at about 20 percent before taxes and about 18 percent after taxes. This is shown in Exhibit 19.5, which displays the internal rate of return, or "IRR," graph produced by the model.

Exhibit 19.5

Internal Rate of Return (IRR)

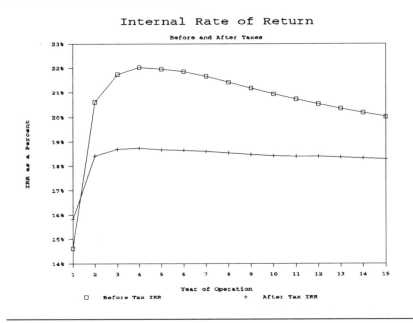

This project has a relatively high rate of return. The return on investment in real estate varies with the degree of risk associated with an individual development. Developments that include units for low-income households generally are expected to generate higher internal rates of return in order to attract investors, and the rates found in this sample development appear to be more than adequate. Because this development contains low-income housing units, it may not be sold prior to year fifteen without suffering high penalties. However, after year fifteen, the ownership may be transferred, provided that assurances are made that the set-aside units will continue in low-income occupancy. In this case, the internal rate of return at that time indicates that the earnings will be good.

Exhibit 19.6

Debt Coverage Ratio (DCR)

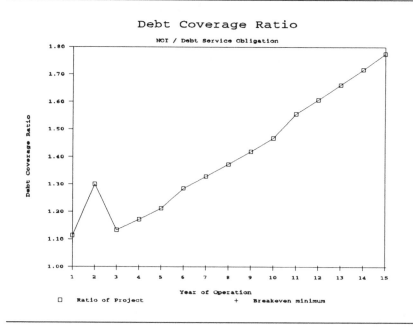

The debt coverage ratio is of particular interest to lenders as it indicates the capacity of the development to pay its debt obligations. The

debt coverage ratio for this sample development is above 1.1 during all
years of operation, which is a generally accepted threshold in order to
attract financing. This is shown in Exhibit 19.6, which contains the debt
coverage ratio, or "DCR," graph generated by the model. The debt
coverage ratio suffers some fluctuations during the early years of
operation due to changes in occupancy as vacancy rates fall and due to
the changes in the financing terms. The overall risk to the lender,
though, appears to be acceptable as the debt coverage ratio never falls
below 1.1.

Exhibit 19.7

Capitalization Rates as a Percentage

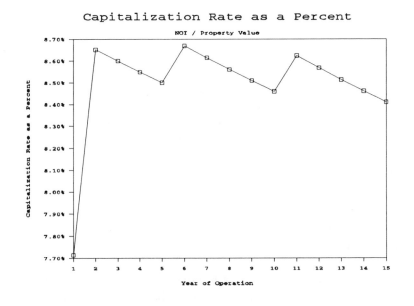

The capitalization rate centers around 8.5 percent, which is typical
of current real estate developments. This indicates that the estimated
property value can be calculated as the net operating income divided by
a figure of approximately 0.085. This is shown in Exhibit 19.7, which
contains the capitalization rate, or "cap," graph produced by the REIA

model. The capitalization rate varies inversely with the value of the property, and these rates vary with market conditions. If the assumptions with regard to income, inflation, and property value appreciation are valid, then the capitalization rate should compare favorably with the capitalization rates of other real estate that presents a similar risk.

This sample development appears to be profitable and should be attractive if offered on the terms used in the analysis. The developer would have to raise about $850,000 in equity, which is a relatively low obligation at 14 percent of total development costs. Syndication proceeds will provide about another $350,000 toward the equity as a result of selling the tax credits to investor/partners. The cash flows to this development are good in that they provide a return well above what would be found in other forms of investment.

EVALUATION AND EXTENSIONS

The REIA model employs commonly accepted techniques for the analysis of investment in real estate. It has sufficient flexibility—in terms of the types of income, the types of expenses, and the forms of financing—to serve as a guide to analysts working with many different situations. The model also allows for the quick testing of alternative development scenarios by editing the data and calculating a revised pro forma and accompanying schedules.

The model does have some limitations, though. It provides annual summaries on the projected income and expenses but does not provide detailed descriptions of a project's cash flow for shorter time periods. Short-term projections may be necessary for some applications, such as tracking a project's monthly income and expenses during its construction and lease-up phase.

The REIA template considers low-income housing tax credits but does not cover historic rehabilitation tax credits. Analysts working with income-earning historic properties will need to adjust the data or develop alternative models.

Finally, the REIA template places absolute limitations upon such entries as the number of operating expense line items, the number of loans, and the number of different lease types. Situations may arise in which a project will call for more detailed projections, which will require the preparation of a different model.

All of these limitations can be overcome through the use of various simplifying assumptions. For example, multiple-income line items can be averaged into a single line item or the proceeds from selling historic rehabilitation tax credits can be entered as an interest-free loan or a reduction of development costs. However, these limitations also suggest areas in which the REIA template can be expanded. Individual analysts will undoubtedly discover more areas for expansion of the template than those mentioned here. To resolve these situations, users can modify the model or create new, customized models that meet their particular needs.

REFERENCES

Beyard, M. D. 1988. *Business and industrial park development handbook.* Washington, DC: Urban Land Institute.

Building Owners and Managers Association. 1990. *BOMA experience exchange report.* Washington, DC: Building Owners and Managers Association International.

Dowall, D. E. 1985. Applying real estate financial analysis to planning and development control. *Journal of the American Planning Association* 51, 84–94.

Federal Reserve Bank. 1990. Federal reserve bulletin. Washington, DC: Federal Reserve Bank.

Floyd, C. F. 1987. *Real estate principles,* 2d ed. rev. Chicago: Longman.

Greer, G. E., and Farrell, M. D. 1988. *Investment analysis for real estate decisions.* 2d ed. Chicago: Longman.

Institute of Real Estate Management (IREM). 1990a. *Income/expense analysis: conventional apartments.* Chicago: IREM.

———. 1990b. *Income/expense analysis: federally assisted apartments.* Chicago: IREM.

———. 1990c. *Income/expense analysis: office buildings.* Chicago: IREM.

Martin, V., III. 1988. Nine abuses common in pro forma cash flow projections. *Real Estate Review* 18, 20–25.

Means, R. S., Company. 1990a. *Means square foot costs.* Plymouth, MA: R. S. Means Company.

———. 1990b. *Building construction cost data.* Plymouth, MA: R. S. Means Company.

O'Mara. W. P. 1978. *Residential development handbook.* Washington, DC: Urban Land Institute.

Phyrr, S. A., et al. 1989. *Real estate investment: strategy, analysis, decision.* New York: John Wiley and Sons.

Roddewig, R. J., and Shlaes, J. 1983. *Analyzing the economic feasibility of a development project: a guide for planners*. Planning Advisory Service, Report No. 380. Chicago: American Planning Association.

Urban Land Institute. 1990. *Dollars & cents of shopping centers*. Washington, DC: Urban Land Institute.

Warren, Gorham, and Lamont. 1990a. *Affordable housing bulletin*. Boston: Warren, Gorham, and Lamont.

———. 1990b. *The housing and development reporter*. Boston: Warren, Gorham, and Lamont.

———. 1990c. *The mortgage and real estate executives report*. Boston: Warren, Gorham, and Lamont.

———. 1990d. *Real estate finance update*. Boston: Warren, Gorham and Lamont.

Chapter 20

TRANSIT: Guideway Systems Cost Estimation

Richard K. Brail

TRANSIT is a cost estimation model for an automated guideway transit (AGT) system in an urban area. AGT is the generic term for any system that operates on an exclusive guideway without the need for an on-board system operator. TRANSIT also can be altered to fit any fixed guideway system, such as a rapid rail or light rail. The model uses linear regression equations that are derived from available data. These equations can be modified by the user for different situations. TRANSIT also contains a scheduling algorithm that includes acceleration, deceleration, and wait times in stations. An earlier version of the model was developed for an AGT study in Atlantic City, New Jersey.

CONCEPTUAL BASIS

AGT systems offer transit planners in urban areas solutions to the problems confronting congested city centers. First, they do not operate on the street and add to already congested roadways. Second, AGT systems can operate without an on-board driver. As a result, additional trains can be added to handle increased volumes without significantly increasing labor costs, the major component of annual operating expenses.

Although lower operating costs and other factors can make an AGT system attractive in an urban environment, the capital costs of these types of systems often make their implementation very difficult. An expensive dedicated guideway must be constructed and advanced computer-based technology must be purchased. AGT systems are new to urban environments, and large capital expenditures are needed at the outset. Some estimates have placed the cost of a single car at between $750,000 and $1 million. Guideway costs range between $25 million and $50 million per mile.

AGT systems have been in commercial passenger carrying service in the United States since 1969, when the Houston Airport system began operations. In 1988, there were twenty-nine AGT systems in operation in the country. They are located predominantly at airports and other activity centers, such as recreational enterprises, universities, and hospitals.

Of the systems currently in operation, only two—Miami and Detroit—exist in urban environments within the United States. The implementation of new technologies in complex urban settings is expensive. Strong financial support from the federal government was central to these two urban systems. Urban areas have a higher population density, a mix of commercial and residential land uses, high levels of vehicular and pedestrian traffic, and diffuse land ownership patterns. As a result, the costs incurred by an AGT system built in an urban environment should be higher than one for an activity center location because of the more complicated forces at work.

Component Costs of an AGT System

The capital costs of an AGT system involve a considerable outlay of money before the operating period begins. These costs include the construction of a permanent dedicated guideway and stations, the acquisition of technologically advanced cars, and the payment of fees for engineering and management. Each component involved in the capital costing of an AGT system will be influenced by variables that are dependent on the particular site chosen for the system, the characteristics of the selected technology, and the specifications that the system must meet.

The analysis of an AGT system's costs can be broken into several components, including:

1. Guideway structures;
2. Stations;

3. Maintenance and support facilities;
4. Power and utilities;
5. Vehicles (cars and trains);
6. Command, control, and communications facilities; and
7. Engineering and management services.

Each component has a range of attached costs that are dependent on the location and scale of the project (Transportation Systems Center 1984).

Guideway Structures. The cost of the dedicated guideway structure necessary for an AGT system includes the footings or pilings necessary for support (or tunnel preparation when the system is to function underground), the material needed for guideway construction, and the labor costs associated with the construction. Each of these factors is influenced by site-specific details and system specifications. Guideway costs ranged from 39 percent of total capital costs at the Miami Zoo to 16 percent for the Disney World/Wedway system.

Stations. Station cost for any transit system can vary widely depending on the design, capacity, and the desired appearance of the system. Station costs ranged from 24 percent of total system cost at the Miami Airport to 3 percent at the Busch Gardens facility.

Maintenance and Support. Maintenance and support costs include the facilities that will be required to keep the system vehicles operating and any special vehicles and equipment that may be necessary to maintain the system. Capital costs for the maintenance facility ranged from 2 percent at the Fairlane demonstration project to 8 percent at the Orlando Airport system.

Power and Utilities. Each type of AGT system has different power requirements for its cars and guideway functioning, resulting in differing costs for the transformers, power rails, and switching mechanisms. Power and utility capital costs ranged from 3 percent at the Houston Airport to 14 percent for the Tampa International Airport system.

Cars and Trains. The capital cost of the cars and trains will vary for different types of systems, the level of technological sophistication, and design options, such as hardware and interior comfort. Capital costs for vehicles ranged from 5 percent of total system costs at Houston Airport to 41 percent at the King's Dominion in Virginia.

Command, Control, and Communications. These costs include wayside and central control and communications equipment, including operational software and voice and video communications systems necessary to maintain system reliability and safety. The capital costs of this portion of an AGT system ranged from 1 percent at the Miami Zoo to 27 percent at the Disney World/Wedway system.

Engineering and Project Management. These costs include the architectural and engineering services required for system design, acceptance testing, and overall project management. The difficulties of constructing an AGT system in an urban environment, such as the need to redesign and move sewer and water lines, can lead to high engineering and project management costs. These costs ranged from 7 percent at the Disney World/Wedway system to 28 percent at the Morgantown, West Virginia, system.

Capital Cost Modeling

The TRANSIT model addresses each of these components by estimating capital costs given certain system specifications, without requiring that a specific type of system be selected. These general costs can then be used as a guide when considering the variations that will occur with routes of differing length and for systems with different carrying capacities and design specifications.

The cost modeling in TRANSIT is based on existing AGT systems. The model assumes that this historical information is reflected in the costs of any generic system proposed in the future. The data are based on AGT systems located primarily at activity centers, such as airports, universities, and recreation parks. Two urban systems, Detroit and Miami, were used for certain cost components.

Guideway Capital Costs. Total guideway costs include the basic cost of the guideway structure, site modifications, guideway additions, and fees and contingencies. The cost per lane mile includes the value of the materials and labor that go directly into constructing the structure itself. These costs were estimated using a linear regression analysis for 1985 data on fifteen AGT systems. Two variables, UNDERGD and WEIGHT, were identified as the best predictors of guideway construction cost per lane mile (GUIDEWAY$). UNDERGD is a dummy variable, coded 1 for an underground system and 0 for an elevated or at-grade system. As one would expect, it costs more to build an elevated system than an underground system. WEIGHT is the gross vehicle weight of the car.

The estimated equation is as follows:

GUIDEWAY$ = 3.87 + 6.021585 UNDERGD + .000014 WEIGHT

where:

$N = 15$
$R^2 = 0.639$
Beta weights: UNDERGD = 0.752
                WEIGHT = 0.099

Other factors involved in the construction of the guideway have been added to the basic lane-mile estimates. These associated costs include site modifications and guideway additions. Site modifications include clearing, street changes, and utility relocation. Guideway additions include power and utilities necessary to run the system, the command, control, and communications necessary to maintain an automated system, and landscaping. The cost estimates were derived from the Atlantic City study discussed in the "Sample Applications" section below. The user may need to alter these estimates to fit the case at hand.

A fees and contingencies component has also been included. An engineering and construction management factor of 18 percent is applied to the total structure and additions cost. This value is based on the experience of existing systems, current bid rates, and discussions with experts. A 10 percent design contingency cost element, applied to structure costs solely, is added to account for unforeseen circumstances that often result in increased costs. A 20 percent construction contingency component, applied to both structure and associated costs, is also used.

Total guideway costs contain all of the components discussed. The grand total, based on 1985 data, is inflated and carried forward to the total cost section.

Station Capital Costs. Two variables, UNDERGD (a dummy variable explained above) and the number of stations (NUMSTATIONS), explained 90 percent of the variation in station capital cost (STATION$). The estimation equation is:

STATION$ = -.32767 + .786958 NUMSTATIONS + 4.285013 UNDERGD
where:

$N = 12$
$R^2 = 0.901$
Beta weights: NUMSTATIONS = 0.976
                UNDERGD   = 0.092

These costs are highly variable and will depend to a large extent on the design features chosen for the stations. The model is based on 1985 dollars, and the total must be inflated to the target year.

Maintenance and Support Capabilities. The maintenance facility costs include the maintenance facility, any special equipment necessary for operations, and room for the administrative staff. The cost of land acquisition for the facility is not considered.

Ninety-two percent of the variation in the costs of these facilities (MAINT$) was explained by the number of vehicles operating on the system (NUMCARS) and WTCLASS, a dummy variable derived from the gross weight of the car. WTCLASS is 1 for a gross car weight of less than 25,000 pounds and 2 for a weight more than 25,000 pounds. The resulting cost estimation equation is:

MAINT$ = -1.3579 + .101476 NUMCARS + 1.468743 WTCLASS

where:

N = 12
R^2 = 0.923
Beta weights: NUMCARS = 0.888
　　　　　　　　WTCLASS = 0.293

This equation estimates the cost of the facility and its equipment. Total costs may be higher if land must be acquired. The model assumes a linear relationship for systems in the region beyond its estimation range, that is, for systems requiring more than seventy-three cars. Economies of scale for larger operations may mean that the costs are overstated.

Car and Train Costs. The model differentiates between systems having cars with a gross weight less than 25,000 pounds, classified as light weight, and systems having cars with a gross weight of more than 25,000 pounds, classified as medium weight. Vehicle costs were averaged across existing systems for both classes. The average cost for a lighter weight car was approximately $326,000 in 1985 dollars while the average cost of a heavier car was $670,000. TRANSIT determines total train and car capital cost using this division between lighter weight cars (class 1) and medium-weight cars (class 2).

The model estimates the number of trains and cars needed for a particular system by calculating the number of trains needed to serve an assumed peak-hour capacity. The train estimation model is run for both weight classes. A particular system configuration is defined by guideway length, the number of stations, the carrying capacity of the trains, and the speed of the trains. The model calculates a round-trip travel time based on a train's operating cycle. The model assumes that the guideway is configured as a loop rather than a point-to-point operation.

Total travel time is comprised of acceleration and deceleration times at stations, dwell time at the station for picking and discharging passengers, layover time at the end of a run, and cruising speed travel time between stations. The calculated travel time is then converted into the number of roundtrips that can be made in one hour. This figure is divided by the vehicle capacity of each class of cars (lighter weight cars are assumed to have more limited capacities) to produce the total number of cars needed for system operation at peak periods. The capital cost of a single car for each class of system is multiplied by the number of required cars to calculate total vehicle capital costs. System headways (the average time between trains arriving at a station) are calculated to determine if the number of cars on the system at peak-hour is feasible.

Total Capital Costs
Different AGT systems can be costed out to determine their viability in an urban setting. Each system is summarized across the four categories: guideway, stations, cars, and maintenance facility. Total costs are calculated using straightforward regression analyses for guideway, station, and maintenance facility costs. The cost of cars necessary to meet the needs of peak hour passenger demand is then added to these estimates. All figures can be adjusted to a future target year through a user-specified inflator variable.

Operating and Maintenance Costs
Operating and maintenance costs include expenses for labor, materials and services, utilities, and general and administrative services. An analysis of operating costs based on fifteen AGT systems (Thompson et al. 1982) shows that labor makes up 55 percent of operating expenses. Other components of operating costs include materials and services (29 percent), utilities (12 percent), and general and administrative costs (4 percent). An examination of various systems indicates that operating costs can be highly variable depending on the cost of labor and utilities in the area.

Nearly 90 percent of the variation in adjusted annual operating costs (OPER$) was explained by the length (LENGTH) of the system. Other variables, for example, the number of stations, the number of cars, and the hours of operation, were examined but could not improve significantly on this single predictor. The resulting equation is:

$$OPER\$ = -.10693 + .927895 \text{ LENGTH}$$

where:
$N = 16$
$R^2 = 0.896$
Beta weight: LENGTH = 1.570420

Large changes in energy costs or wages could cause the annual operating costs of a system to fluctuate greatly. As a result, this simple approach is useful only as a first-stage approximation. Ideally, a more extensive operating cost model should also be developed.

COMPONENTS AND OPERATION

As shown in the location map in Exhibit 20.1, TRANSIT contains many different modules. These include data input, component cost calculations, and summary cost output sections, as well as the standard documentation, range description, and location map areas.

Model Operation

As shown in Table 20.1, eleven macros are provided for use with the TRANSIT model. The Alt-D, Alt-L, Alt-M, Alt-Q, Alt-R, Alt-W, and Alt-Z macros correspond to the standard macros described in chapter 1. General instructions for using these macros are provided in chapter 1. The four specialized macros that represent the core of the TRANSIT model are described below.

Alt-C, Show Component Costs. This macro displays the costs of the different components of the guideway system. The following suboptions show the different cost estimates prepared by the model:

1. Guideway, shows estimated guideway costs;
2. Maintenance, shows estimated maintenance facility cost;
3. Stations, shows estimated cost of stations;

Exhibit 20.1

TRANSIT Location Map

WELCOME	RANGE DESCRIPTION	MACROS	DESIGN COMPONENTS	SYSTEM COSTS	GUIDEWAY COSTS	STATION COSTS	CAR/TRAIN COSTS	MAINT. FAC. COSTS	OPERATING COSTS	REGRESSION EQUATIONS	LOCATION MAP
A1..A20			AB1..AE21 FINANCIAL ASSUMPTIONS	AG1..AJ20	AL1..AP40	AR1..AV20	AX1..BD20	BF1..BL20	BH1..BT20		CE1..DA20
MAIN MENU											
A21..A40 MODEL DESCRIPTION			AB21..AE41								
A41..A60	B1..G60										
		I1..T80								BV1..CC80	

4. Cars, shows estimated cost of cars;
5. Operating/Maintenance, shows estimated operating and maintenance costs;
6. Return, returns to main menu.

Table 20.1

TRANSIT Macros

Alt-C	Show Component costs
Alt-D	Go to Documentation
Alt-I	Input data
Alt-L	Go to Location map
Alt-M	Go to Main menu
Alt-P	Print output
Alt-Q	Quit/save model
Alt-R	Go to Range descriptions
Alt-T	Show Total costs
Alt-W	Go to Welcome screen
Alt-Z	Go to macros

Each component cost estimate is developed for class 1 and class 2
vehicles.

Alt-I, Input Data. This macro is used to enter the system data
needed by the model. The following three suboptions are provided:

1. Design_Components, used to enter the system specifications
required by the model;
2. Financial_Assumptions, used to enter the required bonding
information and cost inflator; and
3. Regression_Equations, displays the regression equations generated by the model; and
4. Main_menu, returns the user to the main menu.

Alt-P, Print Output. This option prints a table showing: (1) the
total capital costs and capital costs per component; (2) the total annual
operating cost and costs for operation and maintenance and debt
repayment; (3) the estimated number of passengers per year; and (4) the
estimated average cost per trip.

Alt-T, Show Total Costs. This macro shows the total costs of the system and generates annualized system costs. This section also contains a cost-per-trip estimate based on the input data and model equations.

Data Input

The input data module drives the model. The user designs a system and enters the necessary information by using the **Design_Components** option of the **Alt-I** macro. The data required include: (1) the length and elevation of the guideway; (2) the number of stations; and (3) the expected passenger loads. The size of the cars, the length of the train, and the cruising speed of the train can be modified from the given values for the two system classes.

The **Alt-I** Financial_Assumptions command sequence is used to enter the required financial information, including an inflator that converts the model output based on historical data into target-year values. The Financial_Assumptions module also contains the interest rate and payment length for any bonding of capital costs. In the United States, the capital costs of public transit systems are often partially supported by the federal government. Bonding is used only occasionally. However, the bonding option is available, if needed. The floating of bonds usually requires a front-end fee and bond insurance. Estimates for these values are included and used in the bonding calculations. If the user enters a zero interest rate, the model ignores the annual payment toward the principal and interest in the calculation of the per-trip price.

The **Alt-I** Regression_Equations command sequence moves the user to the portion of the model containing the equations used in projecting costs. The user should view this section as a work area that can be altered. The cost estimates are generally based on linear extrapolations of data available for existing AGT systems in the mid-1980s. The user may have different data and develop different equations in this section. The user may also use the **Alt-C** command to go to component costs, select a suboption, such as Guideway, and enter actual dollar estimates into the model. The modeler must enter new cost data if a fixed guideway system other than an AGT is under consideration.

The guideway cost module begins with a basic cost-per-lane mile and modifies it with site modification and guideway addition costs. The basic cost-per-lane mile figures are derived from a model found in the Regression Equations section of the model. The site modifications and guideway additions are calculated on a system mile basis. For example, four miles of a double (two-track) guideway is four system miles but eight lane miles. It does not cost twice as much per mile to build double-track guideways as it costs to build single guideways. The system mile site and additions costs are carried to the second page, containing contingencies and fee modifications to guideway costs. The grand total values are shown for the base-year. These base year estimates are modified by the inflator to produce the grand total in the target year.

The Maintenance section uses a regression equation also. Again, the grand total in the target year is the inflated base-year value and is carried to the Output section. The Station module is similar in its use of a regression model to estimate costs. The grand total in the target year is also carried to the Output section. In both the Maintenance and Station modules, the grand totals can be replaced by user-specified data, if desired.

The Car module is different from the others. In this section, the number of cars and trains needed to run the system is determined within the TRANSIT model. The number of cars needed is based on the speed and capacity of the operation. In turn, the average speed of the trains is related to the number of stations, cruising speed of the system, the dwell times at stations, and the layover times at the end of a run.

The Number of Trains Required values are based on the internal model driven by the average-speed calculation. The user may wish to override the internal model and develop the number of trains needed per hour for the two classes. The user should note that the model adds 10 percent to the number of trains needed, as calculated by the model, to allow for repairs and maintenance. Replacing the Number of Trains Required values with user-entered alternatives can be done, overriding the model. However, if this is done, the other information in the Car Cost module *above* the Number of Trains Required line will *not* be accurate. Finally, the operating costs estimates are based on the regression analysis model in the Regression Equations section.

Model Output

The summary output information generated with the **Alt-O** option is found in one screen. The capital cost components are derived from the calculations done in the various sections. The annual operating costs include operating and maintenance as well as debt repayment. The Component Cost section contains the operating and maintenance module.

The Financial Assumptions section has the interest rate and payment years for the debt repayment values. The number of passengers per year is derived from the Design Components module. The number of daily passengers estimated in the Design Components section is multiplied by 261 weekdays and added to 104 weekend days multiplied by one-half (to show reduced weekend loads). This simple conversion can be modified by the user. The average cost per trip is total annual costs divided by annual passengers. The two classes of systems can be compared. Assuming that 100 percent of the annual costs would come out of the fare box, then the cost per trip would represent the average fare that would have to be charged.

DATA SOURCES

Costing out a transit system requires both recent and comprehensive data. The model developed for the TRANSIT spreadsheet uses regression analysis that requires comparable data across systems. One primary source for AGT systems is the *International Transit Compendium*, developed by the N. D. Lea Transportation Research Corporation (Lea and Associates 1983). A second useful source, covering many transportation modes, is the *Characteristics of Urban Transportation Systems* reference volumes put out periodically by the U.S. Department of Transportation. The edited volume by Neumann and Bondada (1985) also provides a wealth of information about AGT systems.

SAMPLE APPLICATION

The sample application uses the TRANSIT model to examine AGT feasibility in Atlantic City, New Jersey. The city is the largest single visitor attraction in the world. More than 30 million visitors come to the city each year, and the numbers continue to increase. The visitors are attracted primarily by casino gambling, legalized in 1977.

Many visitors come for one day, typically arriving by bus between 10:00 A.M. and noon and leaving between 4:00 and 6:00 P.M. Casino workers on shifts leave in the late afternoon. There are several peaks and valleys that only partially correspond to typical urban morning and evening rush hours. Gridlock often occurs on Saturdays in the summer when the combination of visitor and casino worker traffic overwhelms the city's limited street capacity.

A version of the TRANSIT model was used to study alternative AGT system designs for serving the casinos in Atlantic City (Brail et al. 1988). The data provided with the TRANSIT model correspond to a single-lane loop option (Sheakley and Walz 1985) in which all trains travel in the same direction around a single guideway track. This alternative, called the Basic Pacific Loop, runs on both Pacific and Atlantic avenues, which run parallel to the ocean, and serves all boardwalk casinos. The system runs as a double guideway from the terminal to Atlantic Avenue and as a single guideway down Atlantic and Pacific. The terminal facility is located next to the Atlantic City Expressway. At this terminal facility buses unload casino-bound passengers who transfer to the AGT system, much as occurs at Walt Disney World in Florida.

Exhibit 20.2

Sample System Design Components

System Design Characteristics:			
Single-Lane Portion:			4.30
Double-Lane Portion			1.70
Total Length in Lane-Miles			7.70
Number of Stations			15
Elevation (1 = underground,0 = elev'd or at-grade)			0
Car and Train Characteristics:		Class 1	Class 2
Average Vehicle Capacity		25	50
Number of Cars in Train		3	6
Gross Car Weight		18,000	30,000
Cruise Speed (MPH)		16	28
Dwell Time	30	seconds	
Layover Time	120	seconds	
Demand Characteristics:			
Projected Daily Ridership (Average Weekday)			108,000
Peak-Hour Percent of Average Day			10.00%
Projected Peak-Hour Capacity			10,800

To set up the model, the user enters information about the Basic Pacific Loop into the Design Components module evoked with the **Alt-I** menu option. For example, as shown in Exhibit 20.2, the proposed design has fifteen stations (including the terminal) and 7.7 miles of total guideway length. This includes 1.7 miles of double lane and 4.3 miles of single lane. The daily projected ridership is 108,000, which includes both trips to and from the terminal and trips between casinos. This is a very large number of trips, exceeding 39 million trips per year.

The two system classes—class 1 and class 2—have different carrying capacities. Class 1 systems typically carry fifteen to twenty-five passengers per car, while the class 2 cars carry fifty to one hundred passengers. We will assume here that class 1 systems hold twenty-five people on the average while class 2 systems carry fifty passengers. Finally, we will assume that class 1 trains are made up of three cars, while the class 2 trains are made up of six cars.

Exhibit 20.3

Estimated Guideway Cost Components

Guideway Cost Components (Millions of 1985 Dollars)	----- Vehicle Class -----	
	Class 1	Class 2
Basic Cost per Lane Mile (Base Year) Based on regresssion model from existing systems	3.873	3.873
Site Modifications:		
Clear and Grub	0.080	0.080
Street/Highway Modifications	0.760	0.760
Utility Relocation	0.750	0.750
Drainage	0.320	0.320
Guideway Additions:		
Traction Power	1.050	1.409
Landscaping	0.210	0.210
Communications	2.790	2.790
Lane-Mile Site and Additions Costs	5.96	6.319

The **Alt-C** option shows the costs associated with the various pieces of the system. For example, Exhibit 20.3 shows that the basic guideway cost is $3.9 million a lane mile for either class of car. Site modifications and guideway additions are calculated on a system mile basis and added to this basic cost. For the Basic Pacific Loop case, the Total Basic and Additions cost is between $65 million and $68 million for the two classes. Fees and contingencies add to these numbers. The total guideway costs shown in Exhibit 20.4 are between $140 million and $144 million for the two system classes. Station, maintenance facility, and operating costs are also shown in Exhibit 20.4.

Exhibit 20.4

Estimated Transit System Cost

TRANSIT SYSTEM COSTS	-------- Type of System --------	
	Class 1	Class 2
Capital Costs by Component:		
Guideway	$140,233,258	$144,692,038
Stations	$22,379,552	$22,379,552
Vehicles	$140,952,262	$132,898,555
Maintenance Facility	$44,004,154	$18,808,587
Total	$347,569,226	$318,778,732
Annual Operating Costs:		
Operating and Maintenance	$8,445,430	$8,445,430
Debt Repayment	$31,861,640	$29,222,418
Total	$40,307,070	$37,667,848
Passengers per Year:		28,188,000
Average Cost per Trip	$1.43	$1.34

The Cars Cost section is driven by the demand estimates. The needed peak-hour capacity in the Atlantic City case is very high and would not be replicated in most other installations. The large demand figures demonstrate that a class 1 light-weight system would not make sense. The headway for class 1 cars is 0.42 minutes, or only twenty-five seconds between trains. For class 2 systems, the headway is 1.67 minutes, about every one hundred seconds. The assumed dwell time is thirty seconds and the layover time is one hundred-twenty seconds (see Exhibit 20.2). For this case, class 2 trains would arrive every minute and half, a very active system. We might wish to consider an even larger vehicle and longer trains to increase these tight headways.

The cost component information shown in Exhibit 20.4 indicates that the proposed system will cost more than $300 million. We have assumed a target year of 1992, with a 50 percent cost escalation over the 1985 capital costs data inputs and a 20 percent increase over the 1990 operating cost information. The average cost for a trip is modest, about $1.40, assuming all capital costs are paid with bonds that are repaid over a thirty-year period.

EVALUATION AND EXTENSIONS

The TRANSIT model can be improved by using more detailed cost calculations, especially for operating costs. The current model gives generalized results based on average values for existing systems. A particular installation would require more detailed information. However, the model does present a coherent structure for system costing that the user can modify to produce a useful and quite powerful customized cost estimation model.

REFERENCES

Brail, R., Burchell, R., et al. 1988. *A people mover for Atlantic City: issues, impacts, markets, costs, and criteria.* New Brunswick NJ: Center for Urban Policy Research, Rutgers University.

Lea, N. D. and Associates. 1983. International transit compendium—automated guideway transit, Vol. IV, No. 1. Washington, DC: U.S. Department of Transportation.

Neumann, E. S., and Bondada, M. V. A. eds. 1985. *Automated people movers: engineering and management in major activity centers.* New York: American Society of Civil Engineers.

Sheakley, J. T., and Walz, G. 1985. APM system performance and guideway design parameters. *Automated people movers: engineering and management in major activity centers.* In Neumann, E. S., and Bondada, M. V. A. eds. New York: American Society of Civil Engineers.

Thompson, R. R., et al. 1982. *Safety and reliability of automated guideway transit systems.* Columbus, OH: Batelle Columbus Laboratory.

Transportation Systems Center. 1984. *Cost experience of automated guideway transit systems, costs and trends for the period 1976–1982.* Woburn, MA: U.S. Transportation System Center.

Chapter 21

RETAIL: Retail Trade Spatial Interaction

Earl G. Bossard

The gravity spatial interaction model is one of the most popular urban models and has been used for more than fifty years to estimate and predict the interaction over space of various social and economic activities, including trip distributions within metropolitan areas and the distribution of retail sales to residential neighborhoods. The RETAIL model can be used to estimate the proportion of the purchases made by the residents of each neighborhood in a metropolitan region at each shopping center in the region. The market share estimates produced by the model can also be displayed on maps showing the dominant market areas of competing shopping centers using techniques illustrated in Laserna, Landis, and Strategic Mapping (1989).

CONCEPTUAL BASIS

The retail trade spatial interaction model assumes that interaction over space between entities can be simulated by the force of gravity on their masses.[1] The gravitational attraction between two bodies varies directly with their masses and inversely with the square of the distance between them. The spatial interaction gravity model assumes that the attraction between two entities is directly proportional to their sizes; the impedance to interaction is the cost of overcoming the distance between them, raised to an exponential power.

The RETAIL model is a single-constraint gravity spatial interaction model of the form developed by Huff (1963) and explained in many texts (Bracken 1981; Foot 1981; Krueckeberg and Silvers 1974; Oppenheim 1980; Ottensmann 1985). The Huff model can be used to estimate the market share of purchases, $p_{(j/i)}$, by residents from each residential zone i in an urban area made in each shopping center j in the urban area. The original Huff model shown in Equation (1) estimates the attractiveness for spatial interaction, $(A_{(j/i)})$, between each zone i and zone j using an inverse power function in which the attractiveness of each center, (S_j), is raised to the power of a parameter, β, and the impedance to interaction or distance (D) grows by the power of a second parameter, λ.

$$A_{(j/i)} = S_j^\beta D_{ij}^{-\lambda} \tag{1}$$

The market share that center j captures of the purchases by residents of zone i, $p_{(j/i)}$, is found by dividing the attractiveness of shopping zone j to residential zone i, expressed in Equation (1) by the sum of the attractiveness measures for all competing shopping centers in the region. Equation (2) shows this relationship, which also can be viewed as the probability that people from a residential zone i will shop in center j (Foot 1981):

$$p_{(j/i)} = \frac{S_j^\beta D_{ij}^{-\lambda}}{\Sigma_j \ S_j^\beta D_{ij}^{-\lambda}} \tag{2}$$

An alternative expression for the decay of a center's attractions over distance is based on entropy maximization, as pioneered by A. G. Wilson (1970). Under entropy maximization, the spatial interaction attractiveness, $(A_{(j/i)},)$ takes the form of a negative exponential product of the distance and the distance impedance parameter, α, as shown in Equation (3):

$$A_{(j/i)} = S_j^\beta e^{(-\alpha D_{ij})} \tag{3}$$

In practice, the choice between the inverse power and the negative exponential functions is an empirical one in which the preferred choice produces the best fit between the predicted and observed values (Krueckeberg and Silvers 1974; Reif 1973). Figure 21.1, based on Foot (1981), shows that power functions tend to break down for short distances and overpredict short trips; the negative exponential function predicts a finite number of short trips and tends to fall off more gently. Observers have concluded that the exponential function often produces the best fit, as measured by the maximum R^2. The negative exponential function is more likely to reproduce the trip patterns of a mobile automobile-oriented society (Foot 1981).

The power and negative exponential functions can be combined into a composite spatial interaction function that behaves as a traditional inverse power function if α is zero and as an exponential function if λ is zero (Reif 1973). Equation (4) presents the composite travel deterrence function used in the RETAIL model.

$$P_{(j|i)} = S_j^\beta D_{ij}^{-\lambda} e^{(-\alpha\, D_{ij})} \qquad (4)$$

Model Applications

The Huff retail trade gravity model is applied by dividing the study area into basic spatial units (BSUs), that is, neighborhood residential zones for which total expenditure estimates are available. Census tracts are frequently used in the United States to provide information on the number and income levels of households in each analysis zone.

Spatial interaction model performance is affected by the type of BSU used in the analysis (Masser and Brown 1978; Putman and Chung 1989). Factors that can affect the choice of BSU include: (1) the type of expenditures being modeled; (2) transportation modes, costs, and travel times in the analysis region; (3) the capacity of the computer system; and (4) the funds available for the study. Smaller BSUs should be selected for modeling daily convenience shopping, high-cost transport cost conditions, and when large computer capacity and study budgets are available. Larger BSUs are more suitable for modeling comparison shopping goods, low-cost transport conditions, and when computer capacity is low and study budgets are small.

Studies of typical consumer expenditure profiles may be used to estimate the proportion of household incomes spent on the item being

Figure 21.1

Inverse Power and Negative Exponential
Impedance Functions

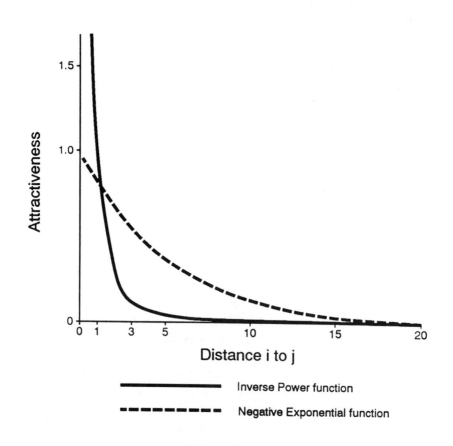

Source: Foot (1981)

modeled. The attractiveness of shopping centers may be estimated in terms of the opportunities they present to satisfy shopping needs. Bigger centers offer more choices and tend to be more attractive. The gross leasable floor area is generally used to measure the attractiveness of shopping centers; other measures can also be used, such as the number of stores, the types of stores, the number of department stores, or the total sales volume.

A centroid is located for each residential zone and the distance from each zone to each shopping center is estimated. Airline distances may be easily estimated from maps. If the study area has many zones and the zone boundaries are available in digitized form (for example, for U.S. Census tracts), then programs such as Atlas*Draw can be used to estimate zone centroids and the airline distance to points representing shopping centers (Laserna, Landis, and Strategic Mapping 1989). Alternative distance measures include the road distance, estimated travel times, and estimated travel costs.

The values of the α, β, and λ parameters depend on local conditions in the study region, particularly transportation costs. These values may be fairly similar for comparable regions but can be sensitive to special conditions.

Calibration is the process of estimating model parameter values for a particular region using the model inputs along with exogenous estimates of the output values the model seeks to predict. The calibration process attempts to find the "best" values of the parameters, that is, the values that reproduce as closely as possible the known results for the base period. Calibration is a mixture of art and science, with calibrated parameters sometimes being the prized trade secret possessions of consulting firms.

The ideal way to calibrate a retail model would be with data from diaries of a representative cross section of area consumers. These diaries should include records of all consumer purchases, indicating the items bought, their cost, and the place, time, and date of their purchase. A less expensive but still costly data source is consumer surveys taken at shopping centers or in residential areas. The survey or diary data could be used to develop estimates of the actual trip probabilities expressed in Equation (2).

Although detailed market share data could be effectively used to calibrate a retail model, the high costs of obtaining these data have favored the use of more easily available, aggregate data. Calibration is often done with total sales data for retail centers, not information on sales by each center to each neighborhood. While this procedure can readily reproduce aggregate sales patterns, it may do so by misestimating the sales to different neighborhoods. In these situations, the model may not accurately predict the results of major changes in the system. Batty (1975) has called this the "bogus calibration problem" and warned of the problems it can cause.

The RETAIL model uses aggregate rather than neighborhood specific sales data and thus may suffer from the problem of "bogus calibration." However, this problem does not necessarily invalidate the calibration procedure. Batty (1975) recommends that mean trip lengths (MTLs) rather than sales data be used for model calibration. The RETAIL model estimates MTLs to centers. Therefore, if the user has access to actual MTL data, the parameters that most closely match the observed MTLs and observed total sales may prove to be useful for making predictions.[2]

COMPONENTS AND OPERATION

The location map in Exhibit 21.1 shows the six functional areas into which the RETAIL model is divided: (1) model introduction and welcome; (2) documentation; (3) data entry; (4) data processing; (5) output; and (6) macros and menu control. The welcome screen is at the upper left "Home" location; the documentation is immediately below. The location map adjoins the welcome screen at the top of the spreadsheet. Every run of the RETAIL model employs the numbered steps described in this chapter's Appendix. The optional calibration step is used to estimate parameters for new settings of the model. The operating areas of the model tend to be clustered around these steps.

The step activities are located in the central area of the work sheet; data are entered in two areas for steps 1 and 2. The data calculations are conducted primarily in steps 3 to 6, arrayed below step 2. Detailed immediate output is included here as part of the data processing steps; a separate section of summary outputs is also provided to the right of the data processing steps. An additional Run Records section is also provided at the bottom of the central work sheet area for storing data from up to six previous runs. These records can either be viewed directly or used as inputs to summary graphs. The macros are placed in the upper right corner of the model, out of the way of any data entry or processing.[3]

Exhibit 21.1

RETAIL Location Map

Welcome A1..A20	Location Map	Ranges Names				Macros	System Tree
Main Menu A21..A38							BZ1..CI31
Document	C1..P59						
	File Record						
	B60..P72	Q1..U153					
	Document (Cont.)						
	B100..L278						
A40..A322							
			Step 1 Neighborhood Data Input X401	Step 2 Shopping Center Data Input AH387	Summary Stats Step 2+ AQ398	BG1..BP381	
			Neigh Descript AE437	Step 3 Attraction Calc AJ443	Step 3 Attraction AQ447		
			Shop Center Descript X475	Step 4 Market Share Calc AJ462	Step 4-2 Dom Centers AQ471		
				Step 5 Pred Sales Calc AI491	Step 5-1 Total Sales AQ501		
				Step 5 -2 Total Sales AK522	Step 5-2 Agg Sales AQ527		
				Step 6 M Trip Length Calc AJ542	Mean Trip Lengths AQ543		
				Calibration Area AG562..BB698	Summary Cal Stats AQ562		
				Step 7 Record Case Outpu AH701	Best GF Cal Stats AN688		

Model Operation

As Table 21.1 indicates, fifteen macros are provided for use in conjunction with the RETAIL model. The Alt-D, Alt-L, Alt-M, Alt-Q, Alt-R, Alt-W, and Alt-Z macros correspond to the standard macros described in chapter 1. General instructions for using these macros and other spreadsheet macros are provided in chapter 1. The eight specialized macros provided for use with the RETAIL model are described below.

Table 21.1

RETAIL Macros

Alt-C	Go to Calculations section menu
Alt-D	Go to Documentation
Alt-G	Graph predicted sales
Alt-H	Go to Housekeeping menu
Alt-I	Input data, headings, or comments
Alt-L	Go to Location map
Alt-M	Go to Main menu
Alt-O	Go to Output data
Alt-P	Print data tables
Alt-Q	Quit/save model
Alt-R	Go to Range descriptions
Alt-S	Go to Systems menu
Alt-V	Go to View menu
Alt-W	Go to Welcome screen
Alt-Z	Go to macros

Alt-C, Go to Calculations Section Menu. This macro is used to go to the various sections of the model corresponding to the calculation steps described in this chapter's Appendix. The following suboptions are provided:

1. 1st_step, go to the step 1 area that stores the neighborhood consumption data;
2. 2nd, go to the step 2 area that stores the shopping center data;
3. 3rd, go to the step 3 area that stores the shopping center attractiveness measures;
4. 4th, go to the step 4 area that stores the market shares estimates;

5. 5th, go to the step 5 area that stores the predicted sales data;
6. 6th, go to the step 6 area that stores the mean trip length values;
7. Cal, go to the calibration work area; and
8. Main_menu, return to main menu.

Alt-G, Graph Predicted Sales. This option is used to produce a series of bar graphs presenting information for the current model run (options ending in _C) as well as for up to six recorded runs (options ending in _R). The following options are provided:

1. **1**_ts_c, graph the total sales for all centers for the current run;
2. **2**_psf_c, graph the total sales per square foot for all centers for the current run;
3. **3**_mtl_r, graph the mean trip length values for up to six recorded runs;
4. **4**_ts_r, graph the total sales for each retail center;
5. **5**_psf_r, graph the sales per square foot for all centers;
6. **6**_mshare_r, graph the market shares for all centers; and
7. Main_menu, return to main menu.

Alt-H, Go to Housekeeping Menu. This option provides direct access to the Housekeeping menu, which can be used to adjust the number of rows and columns, calibrate parameters, erase data, record output, and enter output headings. The following options are provided:

1. Adj_size is used to insert or delete rows and/or columns in the data matrices for changing the number of neighborhoods or centers;
2. Cal provides a submenu offering the eight calibration options described below;
3. Erase provides a submenu for clearing entire data ranges of data for entering new data; the available options are described below;
4. Headings prompts the user for five pieces of information that are used to identify the current model run; up to twenty-nine characters of text can be used for each heading;
5. Rec_output saves the mean trip length, sales, and market share data for the current run; and
6. X_Return, returns the user to the Input menu.

Alt-H Cal options:

1. In_act_sales is used to enter the actual sales data;
2. Param is used to enter the parameter values;
3. GS activates the golden section parameter calibration technique; submenus are provided for selecting the parameter to be optimized and the goodness of fit measure to be used[4];
4. Cal_out views calibration output statistics for selecting the preferred parameter values;
5. Rec saves statistics for the current model run for later display;
6. Adj_con_exp adjusts consumer expenditure data;
7. Un_adj_con_exp, remove consumer expenditure adjustment made with the Adj_con_exp option; and
8. X_Return, return to the Housekeeping menu.[5]

Alt-H Erase options:

1. N_data can be used to erase any or all of six neighborhood data ranges; a submenu identifies the available options;
2. C_data erases one or all of five shopping center data ranges; a submenu identifies the available options;
3. Run_rec provides options for erasing the calibration and goodness of fit record areas, the output run records areas, or the actual sales range;
4. All erases all of the data storage and input areas;
5. X_Return, returns to the Housekeeping menu; and
6. E_Help, displays documentation text on the **Alt-E** macro.

Alt-I, Input Data. This option provides the following data input options:

1. N_data, for entering neighborhood data;
2. C_data, for entering retail center data;
3. Housekeeping, for accessing the Housekeeping options described above;
4. System, for going to the system menu;
5. Main_menu, for going to the main menu; and
6. X_Help, for viewing documentation on the **Alt-I** options.

The suboptions provided for the **N**_data and **C**_data input options are described below.

Alt-I N_data options:

1. **Q**_how_many?, enter the maximum number of neighborhoods to be used in the analysis;
2. Name, enter the name of each neighborhood;
3. **HH**_num, enter the number of households in each neighborhood;
4. Income, enter the mean household income for each neighborhood;
5. CEPI, enter data on consumer expenditures as a percentage of household income;
6. Adj_inflat, go to the inflation adjustment area;
7. Comm, enter comments on the regions (for example, boundary descriptions); and
8. Return, return to the Input menu.

The data should be entered into the cell on which the cursor is placed, press DOWN to proceed to the next entry position, repeating until all data have been entered. The N_data menu should then be called up again and the process repeated until all neighborhood data are entered.

Alt_I C_data options:

1. **Q**_how_many?, enter the maximum number of shopping centers to be included in the analysis;
2. Name, enter the name for each shopping center;
3. Area, enter gross leasable square footage for each shopping center; actual sales can be entered in the row below the area data, if they are known;
4. MTL, enter mean trip length, if known;
5. Dist_NTC, enter the distance between each neighborhood centroid and each shopping center[6];
6. Param, enter the model calibration parameters;
7. Comm, enter comments on each shopping center (for instance, the center address); and
8. Return, return to the Input menu.

Alt-O, Go to Output Menu. This macro provides the following options for viewing the RETAIL model output:

1. Out_sum provides a menu for viewing six sections of the output summary section; the available options are described below;
2. Cal_out is used to view the calibration output statistics;
3. Graph is used to view graphs of the predicted sales; the available options correspond to those provided by the **Alt-G** macro;
4. **M_shares** views the predicted market shares by neighborhood;
5. **T_sales** views the predicted shares by shopping center;
6. Window provides a window for viewing the center size and sales data simultaneously;
7. Xwindow clears the window and returns to a full-screen view; and
8. System, goes to the system menu.

Alt-O Out_sum options:

1. Overall_doc, go to head of column containing output summary statistics[7];
2. **C_sum**, view table of shopping center summary statistics;
3. MTL, view table of mean trip lengths by neighborhood;
4. Dominant, view table of dominant shopping centers;
5. **T_sales**, view table of total sales by neighborhood;
6. Agg_sales, view aggregate sales data for shopping centers;
7. Run_rec, view summary data for past calibration runs; and
8. X_Return, return to the Output menu.

Alt-P, Print Data Tables. This macro provides access to the print menu, which provides the following options:

1. T_sales, print out total sales and sales per square foot data;
2. Sales_n&c, print out matrix of sales by center to neighborhood;
3. N_exp_data, print out neighborhood consumer expenditure data;
4. C_data, print out shopping center input data table;
5. Attraction, print out matrix of neighborhood attraction measures;
6. M_share, print out matrix of market shares;
7. X_main_menu, go to main menu; and
8. R_system, go to the system menu.

Alt-S, Go to Systems Menu. This option directs the user to a Lotus-style menu that provides the following options:

1. View, go to View menu providing the options offered by the **Alt-V** macro;
2. Input, go to Input menu providing the options offered by the **Alt-I** macro;
3. Output, go to Output menu providing the options offered by the **Alt-O** macro;
4. Quit/save, go to standard Quit/save menu;
5. Print, go to Print menu providing the options offered by the **Alt-P** macro;
6. Main_menu, return to the main menu; and
7. Help, view documentation on the **Alt-S** macro.

Alt-V, Go to View Menu. This macro calls up the View menu, which offers the following choices for quickly viewing the RETAIL model:

1. Comp provides a menu of options for going to tables for any of the principal computational steps;
2. Doc produces a menu for viewing eight pages of model documentation/instructions;
3. Files provides a listing of recent file history of this work sheet;
4. Loc_map displays the location of many principal sections of the model;
5. Zmacros is used to view the model macros;
6. Range is used to view the range names table;
7. Tree is used to view the system menu tree; and
8. System is used to active the system menu.

Model Output

The RETAIL model produces several output screens, including tables with neighborhood and center statistics and tables with attractiveness scores (Exhibit 21.2), market shares (Exhibit 21.3), predicted sales to residents of each neighborhood by each shopping center (Exhibit 21.4), and total sales by each center (Exhibit 21.5). Graphs of shopping center total sales, sales per square foot, or any of the four graphs of run records provide other output measures. The graphs of the run records display the mean trip length, total sales, total sales per square foot, or market shares for previous runs of the model.

Exhibit 21.2

Sample Attractiveness Scores

```
#########################################
ATTRACTION OF NEIGHBORHOODS TO CENTERS
#########################################
```

Step 3: Summary Stats

N # Col Cen# Row=	1	2	3	4		N # Col	Total Attraction
1	27	6	1	0	<	1	34
2	4	44	3	0		2	51
3	2	6	18	0		3	26
4						4	0

DATA SOURCES

Three types of data are required to use the RETAIL model: information on neighborhoods, information on shopping centers, and calibration data. Required neighborhood data include the number of households in each neighborhood, their mean incomes, and the estimated proportion of household income spent in the type of centers being considered. Optional neighborhood input data are the name of the neighborhood, comments regarding the neighborhood, and price indices to be used in adjusting for inflation over time.

Required shopping center data include the leasable floor area of each center and the distance from each center to each neighborhood. Optional center data are the centers' names and miscellaneous comments regarding the centers, such as their address and features. Sales and/or mean trip length estimates are required for model calibration.

Household count and income data can be obtained from the decennial census. Household expenditure estimates can be obtained from sources such as the *Estimates of Consumer Expenditures*, published by the U.S. Department of Commerce. Local data sources, such as sales tax receipt records or marketing reports prepared by newspapers or chambers of commerce, can be used to obtain the required shopping center data.

Exhibit 21.3

Sample Market Share Estimates

```
##############################################
TABLE 4—MARKET SHARES
##############################################
```

Subject:	Sample Problem
Region:	Ecotown, California
Analysis Date:	March 9, 1992
Analyst:	A. User
Filename:	Retail.wkl

```
##############################################
DISPLAY SHARES OF EACH CENTER FOR NEIGHBORHOODS
##############################################
```

Cen # =	1	2	3	4
	Center 1	Center 2	Center 3	Proposed
N # Col				New Town
1	0.784	0.184	0.033	0.000
2	0.074	0.877	0.049	0.000
3	0.065	0.243	0.692	0.000
4				

```
= = = = = = = = = = = = = = = = = = = = = = = = = =-
```

Cen # =	1	2	3	4

Total# N = 4

Step 4-2
Identification of dominant center
for each neighborhood

	Dominant	
Market	Center	??????????
Share		# Error ck?

```
= = = = = = = = = = = = = = = = = =??????????
```

78.4%	1
87.7%	2
69.2%	3
	0

```
= = = = = = = = = = = = = = = = = =???????????
```

If market share totals do not add up to 1.000,
an error message appears above in column ..AU480

Ignore dominant center # = 0 displays.

SAMPLE APPLICATION

The procedures for using the RETAIL model will be illustrated by considering Ecotown, California, a fictitious town made up of three neighborhood planning areas, each containing a major shopping center. The analysis will consider the effect on retail sales patterns of constructing a large shopping center in a new town being developed near Ecotown. The example will consider three types of applications that can be conducted with the RETAIL model: (1) estimating the base case conditions; (2) considering alternative scenarios with defined parameters; and (3) calibrating the model with local data.[8]

Estimating Base Case Conditions

The first step, estimating the base case conditions, requires the user to enter the data in the model's Table 7 to estimate the 1990 sales patterns, assuming that no data are available for the sales of the existing shopping centers and acceptable calibration parameters are available.[9]

Exhibit 21.4

Sample Sales to Neighborhoods Estimates

##

DISTRIBUTION OF PREDICTED SALES TO NEIGHBORHOOD RESIDENTS

##

Subject:	Sample Problem
Region:	Ecotown, California
Analysis Date:	March 9, 1992
Analyst:	A. User
Filename:	Retail.wk1

##

STEP 5-1: PREDICTED SALES FROM CENTERS TO NEIGHBORHOODS   Step 5-1

##

(in thousands of $)   Predicted Total Sales

                                                         in Thousands of Dollars

                                                         to Neighborhood Residents

	Cen #=	1	2	3	4		Total	???????????????????
Neighbor		Center 1	Center 2	Center 3	Proposed			
Name	Number				New Town		Sales	Error ck?
Ash	1	$9,404	$2,204	$392	$0		$12,000	OK
Elm	2	$999	$11,836	$666	$0		$13,500	OK
Oak	3	$389	$1,459	$4,151	$0		$6,0200	OK
New Town	4	$0	$0	$0	$0		$0	OK

============   ======================

========== ??????????????????

$31,500 OK

========== ??????????????????

If tot sales to neighbor do not add up to
tot expend by neigh, an error message
appears above in column headed by
AT510

The process begins by using **Alt-I** Housekeeping Headings to enter the data to be included in the model headings. The following data should be entered for each headings item: (1) subject name, **Ecotown Sample Problem**; (2) region name, **Ecotown, CA**; (3) analysis date, the current date; (4) analysis name, name of the person conducting the analysis; and (5) file name, the name of the file to be used in saving the model results.

Exhibit 21.5

Sample Total Sales by Center Estimates

```
#######################################################
Step 5-2:  PREDICTED TOTAL SHOPPING CENTER SALES
#######################################################
```
(Note: Total sales are in thousands of $)

	1	2	3	4	Step 5-2
	Center 1	Center 2	Center 3	Proposed	
				New Town	Aggregate Sales for All Centers
					<-------------------------------????????
Total Sales =	$10,792	$15,499	$5,209	NOT OPEN	= Total Sales $31,500 OK
$Sales/SqFt =	$179.87	$154.99	$130.22	NOT OPEN	= Av Sales PSF $157.50
% Market =	34.26%	49.20%	16.54%	NOT OPEN	OK
					????????
				more ? = = = >	Min Cen Sales $5,209
					Max Cen Sales $15,499
					Min Sales PSF $130.22
					Max Sales PSF $179.87
					=================

The next step is entering the neighborhood consumer expenditures data, using **Alt-I N_data**. In this step, the seven neighborhood data items can be entered, generally in order from left to right. Start with **Q_how_many?** by entering 4 to specify that a maximum of four neighborhood areas will be analyzed.

Alt-O Outsum **C_sum** should then be used to determine whether the specified maximum number of neighborhoods corresponds to the current capacity of the model. Select this option and examine the Max # Neigh cell. An ADJ NEEDED message will appear if the value is not equal to four. The necessary adjustments can be made with the **Alt-H Adj_size** macro; the screen should then report that the Max # Neigh is four and that the number of rows is also four.

The required neighborhood expenditure data are entered next. **Alt-I N_data Hh_num** is used first to enter the number of households in each neighborhood. **Alt-I N_data Income** should then be used to enter the mean household income in each neighborhood in thousands of dollars. The consumer expenditures as a percentage of income should then be entered with **Alt-I N_data CEPI**. **Alt-I N_data Adj_inflat** should then be used to enter **1990** for the year to which the household income data correspond; cell AA444 should be left blank.[10]

Exhibit 21.6

Sample RETAIL Input Data

Neighborhood	# of Households (0'00's)	Mean HH Income ($'000's)	Distance N to C		
			Cen 1	Cen 2	Cen 3
1	3	40	1.5	4	6
2	4.5	30	4	1.5	4
3	3	20	6	4	1.5
Total	10.5				

Center Floor Area					
Area Size ('000's sq. ft.)			60	100	40

Other Base Case Assumptions:

	CEPI	= 0.1
Parameter Values:		
	Beta	= 1.0
	Lambda	= 2.0
	Alpha	= 0.0

The shopping center data are then entered. **Alt-I C_data Q_how_-many?** should be used to enter **4** for the maximum number of shopping centers. **Alt-O Outsum C_sum** should then be used to determine whether this value corresponds to the current capacity of the model. If not, **Alt-H Adj_size** can be used to make the required adjustments.

Alt-I C_data Area should then be used to enter each center's floor area in thousands of square feet. **Alt-I C_data Dist_NTC** is then used to enter the distance from each neighborhood to each shopping center into a four-by-four data matrix. **Alt-I C_data Param** should then be used to enter 1 for the β parameter, 2 for the λ parameter, and 0 for the α parameter.[11] The F9 (Calc) key should then be pressed twice to recalculate the model and prepare the model output.

The model output can then be reviewed. **Alt-C 3rd** can be used to view the attraction measures; **Alt-C 4th** can be used to view market shares data and identify the dominant centers; **Alt-C 5th** is used to view the shopping centers' predicted sales; and **Alt-C 6th** is used to view the estimated mean trip lengths. **Alt-O T_sales** can then be selected to view Table 5-1 (see Exhibit 21.4) showing the predicted sales from centers to neighborhoods, and below that Table 5-2 (see Exhibit 21.5) showing the predicted total shopping center sales and sales per square foot data. **Alt-G 1_ts_c** displays a bar graph showing the estimated total sales for each center; **Alt-G 2_psf_c** shows the estimated sales per square foot of retail space. Press Esc to back out of Lotus graphs.

The final step is erasing the stored data for previous model runs and storing the output from the current run as scenario A; these values can later be compared to the results of other model runs. **Alt-E Run_records Output_run_rec** is used first to erase the values currently stored in the run records storage area. **Alt-H Rec_output** can then be used to save the output for the current run and a brief description identifying the current case.[12]

Considering Alternative Scenarios

The RETAIL model can then be used to consider alternative scenarios using the data shown in Exhibit 21.7. The procedure for all scenario runs will be the same: (1) revise the input data for that run; (2) recalculate the model; (3) observe the output tables and graphs; and (4) record selected output before proceeding to the next run.

The first step is entering the data for the proposed new town (neighborhood 4) and shopping center (center 4). All of the scenarios will assume that one thousand households will reside in the currently vacant New Town area with a mean income of $40,000 (in 1990 dollars). **Alt-I N_data Hh_num** can be used to enter the values **1** and **40** in the neighborhood 4 row. **Alt-I C_data Dist_NTC** can then be used to enter the distances from neighborhood 4 to the four shopping centers and the distance from center 4 to the four neighborhoods. The alternate development scenarios can then be considered in turn.

Exhibit 21.7

Data for Alternative Scenarios

Neighborhood	# of Households ('000's)	Mean HH Income ($'000's)	Distance N to C			
			Cen 1	Cen 2	Cen 3	Cen 4
1	3	40	1.5	4	6	8
2	4.5	30	4	1.5	4	6
3	3	20	6	4	1.5	8
4	1	40	8	6	8	1.5
Total	11.5					

Note: New Town Center will be Cen 4; New Town residential will be Neighborhood 4.

Changeable Factors for Six Ecotown Scenarios

Scenario	Description	Area Cen2	Area Cen4	##HH N4
A	Base Case	100	0	0
	New Town Alternatives			
B	**Regional NTC**	100	250	1
C	**Community NTC**	100	150	1
D	NTC so Cen2 $150 psf	100	93	1
E	Cen2 = 50k & Regional NTC	50	250	1
F	**Super Regional NTC**	100	1000	1

Note: NTC = New Town Center; 50k = 50,000 square feet.

Scenario B. The first alternative to the base case, scenario B, examines the impact of building a regional shopping center with 250,000 square feet in the New Town. This center is far larger than can be supported by the New Town population or the current Ecotown population. Nevertheless, the shopping center developers hope to capture a large share of the rapidly growing regional market. The owners of the existing centers are very worried about the effects that a center of this size will have on their business. Therefore, this scenario and the others will estimate the total sales in the existing and proposed centers in total dollars and dollars per square foot.

Alt-I C_data Area should be used to enter **250** as the area for center 4. After pushing the F9 (CALC) key twice, the output values can be viewed with **Alt-G 1_ts_c**, **Alt-G 2_psf_c**, or **Alt-O T_sales**. The results can be stored with a descriptive label of "B" (or "B: Regional NTC" [New Town Center] for spreadsheet programs with enhanced graphics) using **Alt-H** Record_output.

Scenario C. The second scenario assumes that Ecotown public officials are dismayed to observe that the sales in the downtown (center 2) may drop below the $150 sales per square foot needed to remain economically viable. Therefore, this scenario estimates the sales in all of the existing centers if the new center is constrained to 150,000 square feet.

This option can be explored quickly and easily by using **Alt-I C_data** Area to enter a value of **150** for center 4 in place of the current value of 250. The output results can then be reviewed and stored with a descriptive label of "C" (or "C: Community NTC") using the procedures outlined for scenario B.

Scenario D. The third scenario assumes that Ecotown's public officials want to know how big the proposed shopping center can be without causing sales in center 2 to fall below $150 per square foot. This question can be answered by using an iterative procedure of adjusting the size of center 4 and observing the sales per square foot in center 2. If the sales per square foot for center 2 are below $150, center 4 is too large since it is drawing too many customers away from center 2. This process can take from two to ten or more tries, depending on the modeler's skill (or luck).

Alt-O Window option is designed to assist in this procedure by allowing the screen to be split horizontally with the cursor in the center-size entry location in the upper window and the sales per square foot results visible in the lower window. After the area for center 4 is entered, which produces sales per square foot of exactly $150 for center 2, the windows can be cleared with **Alt-O** Xwindows. The results can then be saved in the Run Records section and the size of center 4 noted, perhaps as a "D: Small NTC."

Other Scenarios. Two other scenarios can be easily considered by following the procedures outlined above. The fourth assumes that center 2, which has been assumed to have 100,000 square feet of floor space, is actually two neighboring centers of 50,000 square feet each. This alternative examines the effect of converting one of these centers into office space (reducing the retail area in center 2 to 50,000 square feet) and providing 250,000 square feet of space at center 4. The final scenario assumes that the new center 4 will have 1,000,000 square feet of retail space and considers the resulting impacts on the other existing centers.

After running the model for all five scenarios, the **Alt-G**, Graph options can be used to examine the pattern of mean trip lengths, total sales, total sales per square feet, and market shares for the existing case and the five scenarios. Note particularly the changes in systemwide mean trip lengths shown in the RETAIL model's graph 3 as center 4 gets bigger, drawing more shoppers away from the existing neighborhood centers. Also observe the sales per square foot bar graph in the RETAIL model's graph 5.

Calibrating the Model

The third major application of the RETAIL model uses the data on the 1990 sales for the existing Ecotown centers and estimated mean travel distance in Exhibit 21.8 to calibrate the β, λ, and α parameters. The calibration procedure attempts to identify the set of parameters that provides the "best fit" between the predicted and observed data for mean trip lengths and total sales in each center.[13] The calibration process begins by using **Alt-H** Cal In_act_sales to enter the actual sales data, in thousands of dollars, for each center. **Alt-I** C_data Dist_NTC can then be used to enter the actual mean trip length data immediately below.

The calibration will be done using only the data for the existing centers and neighborhoods. Therefore, **Alt-I** N_data Hh_num should be used to erase the number of households and mean household income values for neighborhood 4 using the /Range Erase command. Similarly, use **Alt-I** C_data Area to erase the retail center area values associated with center 4. Then press the F9 key twice to run the model with the base data condition and actual data. **Alt-H** Cal Adj_con_exp can then be used to adjust the consumer expenditures so that the total predicted sales equal the actual observed sales.[14]

Exhibit 21.8

Sample Calibration Data

	Cen 1	Cen 2	Cen 3
Center Sales in 1990 ($ '000's)	12000	15200	4000
Mean Trip Length of customers coming to centers (in miles)	1.7	1.87	1.93

The next step is rerunning the model using the golden section method to optimize the β, λ, or α parameters. The goodness of fit measure compares the actual and predicted mean trip lengths on the basis of the percentage error, the total squared error, or the R^2 values.

The initial analysis will use the minimum percentage error criterion to optimize the λ parameter. This can be done by selecting **Alt-H Cal Param** choice and entering **1** for β and **0** for α. At the end of the run, the process will be repeated, solving for β with the λ value that was just identified. The β value that is found will then be used to solve for α, setting λ to zero. Finally, the model will be used to solve for β, using the optimum value of α that was just found.[15]

The calibration process is initiated by selecting **Alt-H Cal GS** to use the golden section technique. λ and **%E_MTL** should then be selected from the menus provided. Next, specify **1** and **3** as the lowest and highest values of λ to consider; a broad range should be used initially since we do not have any experience with these data.[16] Finally, **0.1** should be entered as the difference between successive parameter estimates at which the estimation process should be stopped.[17]

The optimization process ends by displaying a number of output evaluation members, only a few of which will be considered here. For the current model run, the table indicates that β equals 1.0, λ equals 2.605, and α equals 0. This combination produces a 0.13 percent deviation between the predicted and observed mean trip lengths. This is an extremely good fit that reflects the small number of analysis zones and the artificial nature of the data. The calibration results can be stored with **Alt-H Cal Record**.

The model can then be run again by selecting **Alt-H Cal GS B %E_MTL** to keep the λ value at 2.605 and optimize β, using the percentage mean trip length error criterion. However, in this case, **0.5** and **1.5** should be specified as the lowest and highest parameter values to bracket the directly proportional parameter value of 1. The parameter difference at which to stop the search should be specified as **0.1**. The output indicate that for a β equal to 0.97 and λ equal to 2.605, the percentage error in the mean trip lengths is only 0.05 percent. These results can be stored with **Alt-H Cal Record.**

The process can then be repeated with a β value of 0.97 and a λ value of 0 to optimize for α. In this case, 0.2 and 2.0 should be used as the parameter range and 0.1 used as the parameter difference value at which to stop. The output indicate that 1.01 is the optimal α value; this should be recorded.

The process can be repeated a final time, holding the α parameter at 1.01 and solving for β. In this case, the optimum β value is 1.30 and the percentage error is only 0.05 percent. These results should also be recorded.

The results for the four calibration runs can be reviewed by selecting **Alt-O Cal_out** and scrolling to the left edge of the Eval Stats . . . Table and the column heading bracketed by rows of "?????????." Note that the MIN % DEV MTL = = > message points to the row for the fourth run in which the percentage deviation in the mean trip length is only 0.05.

This parameter combination also produces the minimum total squared error and minimum percentage deviation between the predicted and actual sales. However, if our goal were to maximize the R^2 value for sales, the best parameter combination would be a β value of 0.97 and a λ value of 2.605. Whether the α or λ parameters give the best fit is dependent on factors such as the importance of intrazonal trips, the size of the zones, and the goodness of fit criterion employed. Selecting the parameters to be used is ultimately a judgment call.

The preceding analysis has ignored the right side of the output table that examines the differences between the predicted and actual sales values. These data could also be used to calibrate the model if mean trip length data were not available and we were willing to risk the bogus calibration problems discussed by Batty (1975) and Guy (1991).

Running Model with Calibrated Data

The model can now be used to rerun the five Ecotown/New Town scenarios using the calibrated parameters identified in the last section.

Before doing this, the **Alt-E Run** Records macro must be used to erase the run for the first set of runs because only six run records can be stored.

EVALUATION AND EXTENSIONS

The RETAIL model is designed to estimate the changes in the distribution of shopping center sales resulting from changes, such as the construction of a new center or the closing of an existing center. The model can play a key role in three types of applications: (1) determining the feasibility of new retail developments; (2) predicting the shopping patterns for the residents of large new residential developments; and (3) estimating the likely impact that a new development will have on the sales of existing retail centers. With minor modifications, it could also be used to model activities, such as usage patterns for public libraries, hospitals, recreation centers, or professional office centers serving the general public.

The RETAIL model is a large model that strains the capacity of computers with less than one megabyte of memory or operating at less than sixteen megahertz of central processing unit speed. Extensions to the model could be made if it were to be used only on more powerful systems. Separate data entry screens could be added that are less cluttered than the current data entry areas. Larger storage areas could be provided to save more than six records of output. Other graphs could be included, particularly graphs for facilitating comparisons between the output from different calibration runs. Additional matrix space could also be provided to allow for the use of information on the actual trips from each neighborhood to each shopping center, if these data were available.

The β, λ and α parameters currently act as global parameters affecting all centers and neighborhoods. Center-specific parameters would be preferred, especially for different types of centers or for centers with different accessibility characteristics. Different parameters could also be used for different types of purchases.

ACKNOWLEDGMENTS

The following people influenced the development of this work sheet, either directly or through their publications, which are referenced in the text: (1) Michael Batty, for his detailed exposition of calibration issues; (2) Dick

Klosterman, for his assistance in developing the model macros; (3) John Landis, who inspired the interface with Atlas*Draw; (4) Ned Levine, who installed macros in an earlier version of the RETAIL model; (5) Ian Masser, who provided notes on the golden section method; (6) John Ottensmann, for his example of a program with a choice of attraction function; (7) Dave Phillips, for his macro code for the Adjustsize feature; (8) Benjamin Reif, for his attraction equation combining the power and exponential functions; (9) Art Silvers, for his discussion of the Huff-type constrained gravity model; and (10) several San Jose State University students in San Jose, California, for helping debug earlier versions of the model.

NOTES

1. A basic source of several of the constrained gravity model equations used in this work sheet is Krueckeberg and Silvers (1974). Foot's (1981) discussion of retail shopping models is perhaps the best introduction to the topic. Useful details of the gravity model are contained in Oppenheim (1980). Laserna, Landis, and Strategic Mapping (1989) provide useful examples of using a gravity model for trade area analysis and displaying the results in attractive Atlas*Graphics maps. Readers interested in technical details regarding model calibration should see Batty (1975).

2. See Foot (1981), Krueckeberg and Silvers (1974), and especially Batty (1975) for discussions of calibration techniques.

3. The following border symbols are used in the RETAIL model:

- !!! above and below data entry cells
- --- above and below calculated output data areas
- + + + above and below model parameters
- ??? above and below cross-checks for errors or model statistics

4. This macro can take a long time to run if there are a large number of rows or columns and/or a small range of estimates for stopping. The golden section macro was developed using unpublished notes provided by Ian Masser. Batty (1975) provides a detailed discussion of calibration issues, including the golden section technique, explaining why it sometimes reaches different results depending on the starting point and range of values used initially.

5. During calibration runs the user may frequently cycle through the macro choices in the heart of the Cal macro menu, viewing the results of past runs with Cal_out, entering a new parameter value with Param, then estimating its goodness of fit and/or optimized param values with GS or Est, recording the result with Rec, and finally going back to view the results with Cal_out.

6. The distance information can be hand measured from a map and typed in cell by cell. However, if a computerized map is available, the Atlas*Draw desktop mapping program can be used to generate a DIF (Data Interchange Format) file containing the distance data, which then can be imported into the open area below cell A1964.

7. This option provides an excellent way of reviewing all of the output summary information by scrolling downward to view the Center Summary, Dominant Centers, Total Sales, and Aggregate Sales data tables.

8. The principal steps in using the RETAIL model are outlined in this chapter's Appendix.

9. The sample data described below are contained in the distribution copy of the RETAIL model. If desired, the user can leave the data in the model and type over them while following the applications example.

10. This example will not include the option of using price index information to translate the dollar values into constant dollars.

11. Either α or λ should usually be set equal to zero, allowing the other parameter to provide a power or a negative exponential entropy distance decay function. By setting α to zero in this case, the λ parameter is used to provide a gravity-type inverse power decay function.

12. Case identifiers should be five characters long or less (for example, "A") if version 2.01 of Lotus is being used. Descriptions with up to fifteen characters (for instance, "A: Base Case") may be used for programs with enhanced graphics capabilities.

13. The model calibration process is a complex process that relies heavily on experimentation and judgment. As the best-fit set of parameters depends on the nature of the data that may interact in complex ways, the parameter calibration process cannot be reduced to a series of routine steps that would be appropriate for all conditions. Nevertheless, the general calibration procedure outlined below provides a basis for calibrating the RETAIL model using Lotus 1-2-3® 3.1 or comparable updates.

14. The model estimates predicted sales as a share of local incomes spent at the retail centers. These estimates do not consider purchases by sources from outside the study area (which could be handled by including a proxy zone for outside area sources). The consumer expenditures as a percentage of income parameter and the income estimates may also be incorrect.

15. The complex interactions that may occur between model parameters and values require that only one term be changed at a time and the optima from previous runs be used as inputs to later runs. There is no guarantee that this procedure will find the true optimum values; however, it is more likely to do so than a random pattern of guesses. Several optimization attempts, with different search values, should be tried for a particular data set to reduce the chances that the technique will identify a local rather than a global optimum.

16. The optimization procedure may yield a result close to one end of the range if the specified range does not include the optimum value. If this occurs, rerun the technique using a range that puts the initial optimum value in the middle of the range.

17. The smaller the value entered here, the more precise will be the parameter estimate. However, this additional precision will require more iterations of the model and increase the run time necessary to find a solution. If a very small number (for example, 0.01) is specified, ten minutes or more may be required for the model to find a solution.

REFERENCES

Batty, M. 1975. *Urban modeling: algorithms, calibrations, predictions*. Cambridge: Cambridge University Press.

Bracken, I. 1981. *Urban planning methods: research and policy analysis*. New York: Methuen.

Foot, D. 1981. *Operational urban models*. London: Methuen.

Guy, C. M. 1991. Spatial interaction modeling in retail planning practice. *Environment and Planning, B: planning and design* 18, 199–203.

Huff, D. L. 1963. A probabilistic analysis of shopping center trade areas. *Land Economics* 39, 81–90.

Krueckeberg, D. A., and Silvers, A. L. 1974. *Urban planning analysis: methods and models*. New York: John Wiley and Sons.

Laserna, R., Landis, J., and Strategic Mapping. 1989. *Desktop mapping for planning and strategic decision-making*. San Jose, CA: Strategic Mapping.

Masser, I., and Brown, P. J. B., eds. 1978. *Spatial representation and spatial interaction*. Farnborough: Saxon House.

Oppenheim, N. 1980. *Applied models in urban and regional analysis*. Englewood Cliffs, NJ: Prentice Hall.

Reif, B. 1973. *Models in urban and regional planning*. Bucks, UK: Leonard Hill Books.

Wilson, A. G. 1970. *Entropy in urban and regional modeling*. London: Pion Limited.

APPENDIX

Model Operation Steps

Preparation. Erase any input ranges that are to be entirely changed. Menu-selectable macros can clear all input ranges or ranges for particular shopping centers or factors.

Step 1. Enter Neighborhood Consumer Expenditure Data. Enter household data by neighborhood of residence by using the **Alt-I N_data** menu to access the Table 1 input areas. Overwrite unprotected cells to put in new data or use the Erase menu to clear entire ranges for new entries:

1-1. Enter the maximum number of neighborhoods and adjust the matrices, if necessary;
1-2. Optional entry of neighborhood names;
1-3. Enter number of households (in 1,000s);
1-4. Enter mean household income (in $1,000s);
1-5. Enter the values for retail expenditures as a percentage of income;
1-6. Optional entry of inflation adjustors; and
1-7. Optional entry of neighborhood comments.

Step 2. Enter Shopping Center Data. Enter data related to centers by using the **Alt-I C_data** menu to access the Table 2 input areas:

2-1. Enter values for the β, λ, and α parameters;
2-2. Enter the maximum number of centers to be considered and adjust the matrix, if necessary;
2-3. Optional entry of center name;
2-4. Enter center developed floor area in 1,000s square feet;
2-5. Optional entry of actual sales (in $1,000s);
2-6. Enter neighborhood-to-center distances;
2-7. Optional entry of comments on centers; and
2-8. Press F9 (Calc) twice to calculate the mean trip lengths and other model statistics.

Step 3. Attraction Measures. This table shows the quotient of two variables: the center area raised to the β power divided by the center to neighborhood distance raised to the λ power; α can also be used in place of λ if a negative exponential function is preferred.

Step 4. Market Shares Each Center Can Expect from Each Neighborhood. These percentages are obtained by dividing the neighborhood-to-center attraction measures by the total attraction measure to all centers.

Step 5. Predicted Sales of Centers for Each Neighborhood. These dollar measures are the product of the Market Shares (step 4) and Total Consumer Expenditures (step 1).

Step 6. Calculation of Mean Trip Lengths.

Step 7. Record the Output Results.

Calibration Steps.

C-1. Enter actual sales;
C-2. Adjust consumer expenditures so that total predicted sales equals actual total sales;
C-3. Rerun with different parameters using the golden section method;
C-4. Store current parameter statistics values; and
C-5. Select best parameter set.

Chapter 22

LIFE: The Game

Timothy J. Cartwright

"If I were a pattern, I'd be very careful where I fired my gliders!
That game plays a rough game!"
"It does," replied Cal, "as does all nature" (Anthony 1976; quoted
in Gardner 1983, p. 255).

The flexibility of spreadsheets is truly formidable. It is no exaggeration
to say that with a spreadsheet, we can explore the meaning of life and
the nature of the universe. Of course, we pay a price for this flexibility
in terms of speed of execution and elegance of output, but what we gain
with a spreadsheet is accessibility. Spreadsheets, more than almost any
other programming environment, can help demystify computing for the
ordinary user.

The LIFE model provides a spreadsheet version of John H.
Conway's famous "Game of Life" (Life). It will be used first to illustrate
some of the less frequently exploited features of spreadsheets and reveal
some of their limitations. In particular, the model uses: (1) conditional
branching in the work sheet and in the macros; and (2) several index and
statistical functions (notably LOOKUP and COUNT).

Of course, there are other, faster, and better ways of programming
Life using conventional programming languages. For example, Niemiec
(1979) has a one-line program for the game written in the programming
language APL, but the spreadsheet version seems somehow more "open"
and "immediate," even if it is slower and more awkward. Perhaps the
fact that program structure and execution are so closely intertwined in a

spreadsheet model allows the user to feel "closer" to the program than in more traditional programming environments. Moreover, spreadsheets are fundamentally cellular "machines" themselves, so it is entirely appropriate to use them to imitate other such machines, like Life.

This chapter will also use Life to explore the idea of "chaos" and the complex relationship between order and predictability in urban and regional planning. Thus, the implications of this chapter go far beyond computers and spreadsheets to the roots of our assumptions about planning and human behavior. Life illustrates that local order does not necessarily mean global predictability. In Life and similar cellular-automata models, each cell behaves entirely and exclusively in accordance with (usually quite simple) rules. Yet the global result of such behavior can still be unpredictable. If humans—whom John von Neumann (1966) referred to as "natural automata," in contrast to machines, which were only "artificial automata"—are even more complex than Life, then surely human social behavior is even less likely to be predictable.[1]

CONCEPTUAL BASIS

The Game of Life was invented in 1970 by John H. Conway, a mathematician at Cambridge University in England (Berlekamp et al. 1982). Life is "played" on an infinite, two-dimensional space in cyclical time. Each cell in the spatial matrix can have one of only two states—life or death. The state of a cell in any particular cycle is determined by the state of its neighbors in the preceding cycle. The rules of transition are very simple:

1. Birth: an empty cell with three live neighbors becomes alive;
2. Survival: a live cell with two or three live neighbors lives on; and
3. Death: all other cells die from having either too few neighbors ("exposure") or too many neighbors ("overcrowding").

As simple as these local rules may seem, the global behavior of Life is astonishingly rich and complex. Depending entirely on the initial live-or-dead state of its cells, "life" can die out entirely; it can stabilize in a fixed configuration; it can oscillate between two or more fixed states; it can generate various kinds of "travelers" that migrate across space at different speeds; and it can produce "machines" that appear to "create" or "destroy" other Life forms. One of the most famous of the creations of Life is the "glider gun," a kind of "factory" whose products ("gliders") are referred to in the epigraph to this chapter.

In fact, Conway has demonstrated (Berlekamp et al. 1982) that Life can function as a kind of "universal computer" with the usual logical gates (AND, OR, NOT), thus simulating what computer scientists call a "Turing machine." Indeed, interest in cellular automata such as Life was originally inspired by just such motives (Burks 1970; von Neumann 1966). In the last decade, research on cellular automata has been spurred by developments in VLSI (very large-scale integration) technology, parallel computers, systolic (or rhythmically pulsed) algorithms, and RISC (reduced-instruction set computing) architecture (Soulie et al. 1987). For planners, too, Life poses a fundamental question: If social behavior is orderly yet unpredictable, how do we plan?

The Game of Life is run by hypothesizing an initial distribution of "live" automata in the display portion of the spreadsheet. Then the model is set in motion and one cycle or generation succeeds another. Clearly, initial populations of only one or two automata will disappear immediately after the first cycle since any cell requires at least two live neighbors to survive.

Similarly, of the five possible triplet forms, the first three disappear after two cycles, the fourth forms a block of four (which is perfectly stable) on the first cycle, and the last goes into immediate oscillation between a horizontal and vertical triplet. Of the tetrominoes (or rookwise connected sets of four), all either disappear or reach a stable state—which Conway calls "still life"—quite quickly (i.e., within at most nine cycles). The same is true of all but one of the twelve pentominoes (rook-wise connected sets of five).

The exceptional pentomino (which Conway calls the "r-pentomino") does not stabilize until cycle 1,104:

Other "Methuselahs" (the term used by Conway to denote patterns of ten or fewer cells that do not stabilize for at least fifty generations) include the "pi-heptomino" and Charles Corderman's remarkable "acorn," which does not stabilize until cycle 5,206 (Gardner 1983):

In the process of stabilizing, moreover, both the r-pentomino and the acorn throw off all sorts of other formations. One of the most remarkable of these is the five-cell "glider," so-called because it "glides" across the grid, moving down one cell and right two cells every four cycles:

This led Conway to say that the glider travels at "half the speed of light," one cell per cycle being the fastest possible speed of cellular "movement" across the grid.

Conway also discovered three larger "spaceships," which all travel in the same way and at the same speed. As Gardner reports (1983, pp. 222-223):

> As they move, they throw off sparks that vanish immediately as the ships continue on their way. Unescorted spaceships cannot have bodies longer than six [cells] without giving birth to objects that later block their motion . . . [but] longer space-ships . . . can be escorted by two or more smaller ships that prevent the formation of blocking [objects] . . . A spaceship with a body of 100 [cells], Conway finds, can be escorted safely by a flotilla of 33 smaller ships.

Late in 1970, an even more remarkable discovery was made by a group at the Massachusetts Institute of Technology (MIT) led by William Gosper. This was a "gun" that could throw off or "fire" gliders every thirty cycles. Among other things, this discovery seemed to prove that a finite population could beget an infinitely larger one. The MIT group also found a way to position a "pentadecathalon" (a period-15 oscillator)

so that it "catches" and "eats" every glider that comes its way and a way
to position two pentadecathalons so that they can "bounce" a glider back
and forth between them forever. Gardner goes on (1983, p. 233):

> Streams of intersecting gliders produce fantastic results. Strange
> patterns can be created that in turn emit gliders . . . In other
> cases the collision mass destroys one or more guns by shooting
> back. The [MIT] group's latest burst of virtuosity is a way of
> placing eight guns so that the intersecting streams of gliders
> build a factory that reassembles and fires a middleweight
> spaceship about every 300 ticks [cycles].

Still another area of interest in Life is the discovery of what are
called "Garden of Eden" configurations. These are patterns that cannot
occur "naturally" because there is no possible pattern precedent that
could create them. It has been proved that there are such patterns in all
cellular automata (Moore 1962) and some have been found in Life
(Berlekamp et al. 1982; Gardner 1983); but it is not known how many
such patterns there are in Life or, in general, how to find them, except
by "brute force." Moreover, while a "Garden of Eden" has (by
definition) no "father," it may have a "son," and that "son" may itself
have other possible multiple "fathers." The question of whether there
exist patterns with "fathers" but no "grandfathers" is still wide open
(Gardner 1983).

Conway's Game of Life is defined primarily by its three rules of
birth, survival, and death, but there are two other key aspects of cellular
automata that need to be discussed before proceeding to describe this
implementation in a spreadsheet environment.

All cellular automata depend on the concept of a neighborhood, that
is, the number and location of cells surrounding a given cell on which
the state of the latter depends. Originally, von Neumann (1966) worked
with a neighborhood of four cells—those orthogonally adjacent (that is,
directly above, below, left, and right). Subsequently, Edward F. Moore
(1962) proposed an expanded neighborhood, including the four diagonal-
ly adjacent cells as well. Conway's Game of Life illustrates the use of
the larger Moore neighborhood.

Second, cellular automata exist on a grid that is (at least potentially)
infinite in size. The topology of an infinite rectangular surface is
simulated by means of a torus (or doughnut) rather than a sphere. On a

computer, this effect can be achieved by "wrapping around" the opposite edges of the grid and connecting them to each other (that is, the left edge to the right edge and the top edge to the bottom edge). Nevertheless, small toruses differ from larger ones in that "wraparound" (and consequently the possibility of feedback or interference) occurs sooner on small toruses than on large ones. In Life, this feedback can have the effect of either prematurely ending or unduly extending the life of a population.

COMPONENTS AND OPERATION

As Exhibit 22.1 illustrates, the main part of the LIFE model consists of two sections arranged one above the other so that the entire model can be scrolled vertically within the width of a single screen or printed without difficulty on a standard eighty-column printer. Standard model components, such as the welcome screen, main menu, and model documentation, are located to the right of these two sections.

The top part of the model provides the user interface: a square twenty-by-twenty display area in which the user enters the starting population for each run of the model and the computer displays the results for each cycle, a running record of the state of the model, and basic instructions for operating the model. As a result, there is no need to scroll the screen while running the model.[2]

The operational part of the model is in the middle section, which contains a work sheet similar to the display area. The model is cyclical in nature. It works by reading the population displayed in the upper section, calculating and displaying in the middle section the revised population for the next cycle as dictated by the transition rules, and then copying the new population data from the middle section back to the upper one. This process is repeated for the next cycle, and the next, and so on.

The display area shows the current game cycle and the current population. The first cell is incremented by the recalculation process described below; the second uses the COUNT function to determine how many cells in the display area contain numerical characters (that is, a "1"). The display area also records the maximum population reached during the current run and the cycle in which it occurred.

The menu area shows the four basic commands for running the model. The display area is a matrix of blank cells into which the current

Exhibit 22.1

LIFE Location Map

				LOCATION MAP
				AP1..BD20
			RANGE DESCRIPT	
			AI1..AK60	
		MACROS		
		AB1..AE65		
	WELCOME SCREEN			
	AA1..AA20			
	MAIN MENU AA21..AA40			
	DOCUMENT			
	AA41..AA62			
GAME SCREEN				
A1..Z20 WORKSHEET				
AZ27..Z50				

state of the model is copied from the computational portion of the work sheet. The heart of the work sheet itself is a matrix of complicated but symmetrical formulas using conditional branching based on the IF(A, B, C) and COUNT functions. For example, the formula in cell K40 is:

IF(OR(COUNT(J9,J10,J11,K9,K11,L9,L10,L11)=3),
    AND(COUNT(J9,J10,J11,K9,K11,L9,L10,L11)=2,K10=1), 1, " .")

The IF function, IF(A,B,C), means "if A, then B, otherwise C." The COUNT function returns the number of cells within a specified range of cells that have a numerical value. Furthermore, the state of any cell in Life depends on the state of the eight surrounding cells in the previous cycle. In this model, the state of the neighbors for any cell in the computational portion of the model in the previous cycle is recorded in the upper (display) area. Therefore, the current state of cell K40 depends on the state of cells J9, J10, J11, K9, K11, L9, L10, and L11 in the display area.

To simplify the formula, let these eight cells be represented by the expression "...". The formula for cell K40 therefore becomes:

IF(OR(COUNT(...)=3),AND(COUNT(...)=2,K10=1), 1," .")

This expression means: if (1) either (a) cell K10 has three numerical neighbors (that is, cells containing a "1") or (b) cell K10 has two numerical neighbors and cell K10 is numerical, then K40 is set to "1"; otherwise, (2) cell K40 is set to " .". This succinctly states the rules governing the Game of Life.

Model Operation

As Table 22.1 illustrates, ten macros are provided for use with the LIFE model. The Alt-D, Alt-L, Alt-M, Alt-Q, Alt-R, Alt-W, and Alt-Z macros correspond to the standard macros described in chapter 1 where general instructions for using them can be found. The three specialized macros provided for the LIFE model are described below.

Alt-I initializes the LIFE model prior to a new "run" by resetting the counters and clearing the display area. The macro "zeroes" the display area, that is, sets all of the cells to dead cells ("."). The second macro (**Alt-X**) fills the display area with a random distribution of live cells ("1") and dead cells ("."). Users should note that the arrangements for looping in a work sheet (as illustrated in these macros) are fairly primitive: all you can do is "branch" unconditionally to a specific cell.

Table 22.1

LIFE Macros

Alt-D	Go to Documentation
Alt-I	Initialize game
Alt-L	Go to Location map
Alt-M	Go to Main menu
Alt-Q	Quit/save model
Alt-R	Go to Range descriptions
Alt-S	Start game
Alt-W	Go to Welcome screen
Alt-X	Randomize distribution
Alt-Z	Go to macros

The third macro (**Alt-S**) starts and runs the whole model. It begins by removing the cursor from the display area, turning off the dialogue line, and doing a manual recalculation. Then the macro checks to see if the entire population has died off; if so, the macro branches to the last line, where it turns the dialogue line back on and exits. If not, the macro updates the number of cycles the model has run and copies the contents of the lower work sheet area to the upper display area. Then it loops back to do another manual recalculation (to update the lower work sheet area to a new cycle) and continues as before.

SAMPLE APPLICATION

The only "data" the user must input is the initial population configuration. This is done with either **Alt-I** or **Alt-X** (for a random population). When **Alt-I** is used, each of the cells is set to " ." (a space and a dot) to indicate that it is empty or "dead." To reset some cells to a "live" state, the user moves the cursor to the desired cell in the display area and enters the number "1." In fact, cells can be readjusted at any point just by entering (over-writing) the appropriate symbols into the cells: a "1" for a live cell and a space and a dot (" .") for a dead cell.

To get a "feel" for the game, users can start by experimenting with some of the simple examples discussed above. Several books also provide detailed examples of other starting populations (Berlekamp et al. 1982; Gardner 1983; Poundstone 1985). Naturally, the more complicated examples will be difficult to follow on the relatively small (twenty-by-twenty cell) grid allowed by a spreadsheet. Even on a microcomputer, conventional programs for Life (Acero 1989) typically plot single pixels, permitting grids of 320 by 200, for example (at CGA resolution), or 640 by 350 (at EGA/VGA resolution).

Once the game is running, there is nothing for the user to do but sit back and watch Life unfold. The model records the current cycle and current population, as well as the maximum population reached and the cycle in which it occurred. Enthusiasts may want to strive for the initial Life forms that last longest (without either dying out or stabilizing), that produce the highest peak population (two hundred is the theoretical maximum on a four hundred-cell square grid), that result in the highest stabilized population, and so forth.

EVALUATION AND EXTENSIONS

Obviously, we should not read too much into Life. The transition rules are very simple and the grid has only two dimensions. On the other hand, the underlying principle of Life is disturbing. For example, would we be able to dismiss a more general version that had a more complex set of rules and many more dimensions? Some people (for instance, Gardner 1983) have speculated that the entire universe may be some kind of gigantic and highly complex system of cellular automata, just like Life.

Life may be significant for urban and regional planning at two levels. First, the model provides suggestive models for decision making in specific situations, such as residential choice, land use, trip distribution, and so on. Second, if these models prove useful and revealing, they represent a fundamental challenge to the current practice of urban and regional planning (Cartwright 1991).

Planners are generally so conditioned to thinking in terms of "global" trends and "grand designs" that they often overlook the effect of "local" behavior. We explain urban growth in terms of broad social trends, national economic policy, and political choices, all of them exogenous to the processes we want to explain. However, suppose that urban growth is not caused by exogenous factors but rather is the reflection of thousands and even millions of local decisions.

In a particularly perceptive passage of their book on cellular automata, Toffoli and Margolus (1987, p. 142) suggest that:

> Science is concerned with explaining things . . . We say we "understand" a complex system when we can build, out of simple components that we already understand well, a model that behaves in a similar way. The simpler the primitives used to describe a complex system, the greater is the computational burden . . . For this reason, the development of mathematics . . . reflects to a much greater extent than many would suspect the nature of the computational resources available . . . In the past three centuries, enormous emphasis has been given to (1) models that are defined and well-behaved in a continuum, (2) models that are linear, and (3) models entailing a small number of lumped variables. This emphasis does not reflect a preference of nature, but rather the fact that the human brain, aided only by pencil and paper, performs best when it handles a small number of symbolic tokens having substantial conceptual depth. . . .

The advent of digital computers has shifted the region of optimum performance. While much progress can still be made in the more traditional areas, the horizon has dramatically expanded in the complementary areas, namely (1) discrete models, (2) nonlinear models, and (3) models entailing a large number of distributed variables. Such models give more emphasis to the handling of a large number of tokens of a simple nature (for instance, Boolean variables and logic functions)—a task at which computers are particularly efficient.

What is true of mathematics is also true of social sciences and urban and regional planning. Planners may not be able to lay claim to "three centuries" of experience; however, they have certainly emulated the mathematicians in their preference for models that are continuous, linear, and parsimonious. The inevitable effect has been to focus attention on "macro" models and "macro" explanations; planning interventions have merely followed suit. Life and similar examples, though, suggest that it may be time to focus on "microlevel" behavior and intervention.

The conversation quoted in the chapter epigraph takes place between two intelligent and sentient "pattern entities" who have evolved through a process of cellular adaptation in a world of more dimensions than merely human space and time. The dialogue suggests that those who play the Game of Life may be participating in a deeper sense than they realize.

NOTES

1. A related model in which birth, life, and death are influenced in a probabilistic way by the overall state of the "neighborhood" is included in Timothy J. Cartwright's forthcoming book, *Modeling the World in a Spreadsheet: Environment Simulation on a Microcomputer* (Baltimore: Johns Hopkins University Press).

2. Of course, users are free to scroll through the model, if they wish to do so. If they do, it suffices to press the Home key (or run any of the macros described below) to return to the display area.

REFERENCES

Acero, A. A. 1989. AAALIFE. C-language computer program. Ver. 1.0 (May 11, 1989). Email: acero@tank.uchicago.edu.

Anthony, P. 1976. *Ox*. London: Avon.

Banks, E. 1971. *Information processing and transmission in cellular automata*. Project MAC technical report TR-81 (mimeo). Cambridge, MA: Massachusetts Institute of Technology.

Berlekamp, E. R., Conway, J. H., and Guy, R. K. 1982. *Winning ways for your mathematical plays*. Vol. 2. London: Academic Press.

Burks, A. W., ed. 1970. *Essays on cellular automata*. Urbana: University of Illinois Press.

Cartwright, T. J. 1991. Planning and chaos theory. *Journal of the American Planning Association* 57, 44–56.

Dewdney, A. K. 1989. A cellular universe of debris, droplets, defects and demons. *Scientific American* 261, 102–5.

Fogelman S. F., Yves, R., and Tschuente, M., eds. 1987. *Automata networks in computer science: theory and applications*. Manchester: Manchester University Press.

Gardner, M. 1983. *Wheels, life and other mathematical amusements*. New York: Freeman.

Helmers, C. 1975-1976. Lifeline. *BYTE* 1, 2, 72–80; 34–42; 48–55; 32–41.

Macaluso, P. 1981. Life after death. *BYTE* 6, 326–333.

Moore, E. F. 1970. Machine models of self-reproduction. In Burks, A. W., ed. *Essays on cellular automata*. Urbana: University of Illinois Press.

Niemiec, M. D. 1979. Life algorithms. *BYTE* 4, 90–97.

Poundstone, W. 1985. *The recursive universe*. New York: Morrow.

Soderstrom, R. 1979. Life can be easy. *BYTE* 4, 166–9.

Toffoli, T., and Margolus, N. 1987. *Cellular automata machines: a new environment for modeling*. Cambridge: MIT Press.

von Neumann, J. 1970. Theory of self-reproducing automata. In Burks, A. W., ed. *Essays on cellular automata*. Urbana: University of Illinois Press.

Contributors

Chris Banister
Department of Planning and Landscape
University of Manchester
Manchester M13 9PL UK
Phone: 011 44 (061) 275-6883
Fax: 011 44 (061) 275-6893
E-mail: BANISTER@MANCHESTER.AC.UK

Earl G. Bossard
Department of Urban and Regional Planning
San Jose State University
San Jose, CA 95192-0185
Phone: (408) 924-5882
Fax: (408) 924-5828

William M. Bowen
Maxine Goodman Levin College of Urban Affairs
Cleveland State University
Cleveland, OH 44115
Phone: (216) 687-2136
Fax: (216) 687-9239
E-mail: R0340@CSUOHIO

Richard K. Brail
Department of Urban Planning and Policy Development
Rutgers University
P.O. Box 5078
New Brunswick, NJ 08903-5078
Phone: (908) 932-2591
Fax: (908) 932-2253
E-mail: BRAIL@ZODIAC

Timothy J. Cartwright
Faculty of Environmental Studies
York University
North York, Ontario M3J 1P3
Phone: (416) 736-5252
Fax: (416) 736-5679
E-mail: ESTIMCAR@ORION.YORKU.CA

William J. Drummond
City Planning Program
Georgia Institute of Technology
Atlanta, GA   30332-0115
Phone: (404) 843-9840
Fax: (404) 894-3874
E-mail: BILL.DRUMMOND@ARCH.GATECH.EDU

Erik Ferguson
City Planning Program
Georgia Institute of Technology
Atlanta, Georgia 30332-0155
Phone: (404) 853-9843
Fax: (404) 894-3874 FAX
E-mail: ARFACEF@GITVM1.GATECH.EDU

Stephen F. Fournier
Regional Research Institute
West Virginia University
PO Box 6825
Morgantown WV   26506-6825
Phone: (304) 293-2896
Fax: (304) 293-6699
E-mail: sff@wvnvm

Steven P. French
City Planning Program
Georgia Institute of Technology
Atlanta, GA 30332-0115
Phone: (404) 894-2350
Fax: (404) 894-3874
E-mail: SFRENCH@PRISM.GATECH.EDU

Iskandar Gabbour
Institut d'urbanisme
Université de Montréal
P.O. Box 6128, Station A
Montréal, Québec H3C 3J7
Phone: (514) 343-6391
Fax: (514) 343-2338
E-mail: GABBOUR@ERE.UMONTREAL.CA

Jun Han
CIGNA Real Estate Investors
Hartford, CT 06152
Phone: (203) 726-6141
Fax: (203) 726-6110

Yu Hung Hong
Massachussetts Institute of Technology, Room 9-541
77 Massachusetts Ave.
Cambridge, MA 02139
Phone: (617) 253-1878
Fax: (617) 253-2654
E-mail: MITCOMP@ATHENA.MIT.EDU

Richard E. Klosterman
Department of Geography and Planning
University of Akron
Akron, OH 44325-5005
Phone: (216) 972-8037
Fax: (216) 972-6080
E-mail: KLOSTERMAN@UAKRON.EDU

Ned Levine
Graduate School of Architecture and Urban Planning
University of California at Los Angeles
405 Hilgard Avenue
Los Angeles, CA 90024-1467
Phone: (310) 825-7442
Fax: (310) 206-5566
E-mail: IBX3NL1@UCLAVMS

Kirk McClure
Graduate Program in Urban Planning
University of Kansas
317 Marvin Hall
Lawrence, KS 66045
Phone: (913) 864-4184
Fax: (913) 864-5399
E-mail: MCCLURE@UKANVM

Paul E. Patterson
Bowne Management Systems
235 E. Jericho Turnpike
P.O. Box 109
Mineola, New York 11501
Phone: (516) 248-6840
Fax: (516) 747-1396

David L. Phillips
Department of Urban and Environmental Planning
School of Architecture
University of Virginia
Charlottesville, VA 22903
Phone: (804) 924-3122
Fax: (804) 982-2678
E-mail: DLP@VIRGINIA.EDU

Karen R. Polenske
Department of Urban Studies and Planning
Massachussetts Institute of Technology
77 Massachussetts Avenue, Room 9-535
Cambridge, MA 02139
Phone: (617) 253-6881
Fax: (617) 253-2654
E-mail: KRP@ATHENA.MIT.EDU

David S. Sawicki
City Planning Program
Georgia Institute of Technology
Atlanta, GA 30332-0115
Phone: (404) 894-2350
Fax: (404) 894-3874

William J. Siembieda
Community and Regional Planning Program
School of Architecture & Planning
The University of New Mexico
2414 Central Ave., SE, Albuquerque, NM 87131-1226
Phone: (505) 277-5050
Fax: (505) 277-0076
E-mail: LESLIE@BOOTES.UNM.EDU

Yichun Xie
National Center for Geographical Information and Analysis
301F Wileson Quad
State University of New York at Buffalo
Buffalo, NY 14261
Phone: (716) 645-2545
Fax: (716) 645-5957
E-mail: V296W8QH@UBVMS